NEVER PAY RETAIL

NEVER PAY RETAIL

How to Save 20% to 80% on Everything You Buy

Edited by
Sid Kirchheimer

Rodale Press, Inc.
Emmaus, Pennsylvania

Notice

The information in this book has been carefully researched, and all efforts have been made to ensure accuracy. Rodale Press, Inc., assumes no responsibility for damages or losses incurred during or as a result of using this information. Prices quoted and potential savings reported were accurate as of press time, but prices and savings may differ in your area. All information in this book should be carefully studied before taking action based on that information or advice.

Printed in the United States of America on acid-free ∞, recycled paper ♻

Library of Congress Cataloging-in-Publication Data

Never pay retail : how to save 20% to 80% on everything you buy /
edited by Sid Kirchheimer
p. cm.
Includes index.
ISBN 0–87596–302–1 hardcover
ISBN 0–87596–402–8 paperback
1. Shopping—United States. 2. Consumer education—United States.
I. Kirchheimer, Sid.
TX336.N48 1996
380.1'45'000002573—dc20 96–6100

Distributed in the book trade by St. Martin's Press

2 4 6 8 10 9 7 5 3 1 hardcover

2 4 6 8 10 9 7 5 3 1 paperback

OUR MISSION

We publish books that empower people's lives.

RODALE BOOKS

Never Pay Retail Editorial Staff

Editor: Sid Kirchheimer

Contributing Writers: Maureen Connolly, Don Crinklaw, Maryanne M. Dell, Robert Eshman, Dawn Frankfort, Richard Freudenberger, Ed Golden, Sandra Gordon, Brian Paul Kaufman, Diane Kozak, Cece Lentini, Jon Marcus, Kathy Murray, Michelle Nicolosi, Susan Paterno, Ruth Regnis, Elizabeth Seymour, Jennifer Lowe Stanton, Pete Szialgyi, Roger Yepsen

Head Researcher: Jan Eickmeier

Researchers and Fact-Checkers: Susan E. Burdick, Christine Dreisbach, Valerie Edwards-Paulik, Theresa Fogerty, Carol J. Gilmore, Deborah J. Pedron, Kathryn Piff, Sally A. Reith, Sandra Salera-Lloyd, Maureen Sangiorgio, Anita Small, Bernadette Sukley, Carol Svec, Michelle M. Szulborski, John Waldron

Cover and Interior Designer: Lynn N. Gano

Cover Illustrator: Lynn N. Gano

Associate Art Director: Faith Hague

Studio Manager: Joe Golden

Interior Layout: Carl Nielsen / Bookhead Studio

Senior Copy Editor: Jane Sherman

Copy Editor: Linda Mooney

Production Manager: Helen Clogston

Manufacturing Coordinator: Patrick T. Smith

Office Staff: Roberta Mulliner, Julie Kehs, Bernadette Sauerwine, Mary Lou Stephen

Rodale Health and Fitness Books

Vice-President and Editorial Director: Debora T. Yost

Art Director: Jane Colby Knutila

Research Manager: Ann Gossy Yermish

Copy Manager: Lisa D. Andruscavage

Contents

C

D

E

F

G

H

O

P

Q

R

S

T

V

W

Introduction

Let the Buyer Be Aware

Ask some so-called consumer experts for their two cents on the secrets of smart spending, and you'll get advice that's not worth much more than that: "Let the buyer beware."

Sure, we all need to watch our spending, especially in these tough economic times. But that's often more easily said than done. How often have you made a retail purchase—whether a new clock or a new car, a refrigerator or a picture frame—and wondered if you could have gotten it for less than the retail price?

You can. In the year it took us to put together this book, we found there is at least one certainty when it comes to shopping: *You don't have to pay retail for anything.* And that's why we came up with our own adaptation of the tired old cliché: "Let the buyer be *aware.*"

And with this book, you will be aware: Of how to buy nearly 400 retail items for less than retail price. Of the actual retail markups, pricing strategies and marketing gimmicks used by salespeople and manufacturers to make every possible penny on their goods. You'll learn where, when and how to buy virtually everything you want for 20, 40 or even 80 percent less than the sticker price.

Of course, getting this information wasn't easy. Many of the contributors to this book were selected for very specific reasons. Some are in the business or a related field, with a personal history of buying or selling the products they wrote about. Others have personal connections—associates who work as manufacturers, wholesalers, retailers, professional buyers, industry officials and others in the business who know how the retail pricing game is really played. Others are established and well-respected consumer writers. But all are just like you—folks who want to get the best deal on what they're buying.

You may find that some of the buying strategies and savings percentages we found in the course of our research differ in your area. While our writers are scattered across the country and did their best to get universal information, many factors determine the actual retail price of a particular item—everything from store-to-store competition to the location of the manufacturer to the geographic popularity of the particular item.

We conducted thousands of interviews, scoured over 1,000 of the most popular mail-order catalogs in the United States and went on hundreds of shopping trips—and here's the finished product, with over 1,670 specific buying strategies that separate the wheat from the chaff . . . all in order to save you more dough.

—Sid Kirchheimer
Editor

Air Conditioners

Depending on where you live, an air conditioner can be a luxury item or an absolute necessity. And depending on its perceived status, you may balk at the price—which can range from $180 for a basic, no-frills unit at a large discount chain to several thousand dollars for a central unit that's capable of making your entire house comfortable for penguins—or gladly pay it for some much-needed relief.

Whatever you buy, don't wait until you're sweltering through the first heat wave of the summer to start shopping. It will cost up to 30 percent more during "the season" due to low inventory and high demand. That's because there are no manufacturer's suggested retail prices for air conditioners, and prices are usually set by retailers and

What's the Right Size?

The first thing you need to know in order to find the best buy is how much cooling power you need. A general rule of thumb is to buy 20 Btu (British thermal units) for every square foot of living space. But there are several variables that affect the formula, including how many people use the room, whether the air conditioner is placed on the north or south side of the house and what type of insulation your house has, so avoid using simplistic formulas to determine your needs.

A good way to compute all of the variables is to use a Cooling Load Estimate Form, available by sending 35 cents and a self-addressed, stamped envelope to The Association of Home Appliance Manufacturers, 20 North Wacker Drive, Suite 1500, Chicago, IL 60606.

OUTSTANDING OUTLETS

None of the major manufacturers—General Electric, Carrier, Fedders or Whirlpool—have manufacturer's outlets for their air conditioners. Sears, however, which is the leading seller of room air conditioners (window units), operates a national chain of Sears Furniture and Appliance Outlet stores that carry air conditioners—and sell them for up to 60 percent off, depending on inventory and availability.

It takes patience to reap these savings, since some outlets may get a shipment of air conditioners only once every two or three years. Since outlet specials are unadvertised, you will have to check in regularly with store personnel on the status of their stock. To find the nearest Sears outlet, call a local Sears store.

distributors according to what the market will bear. Here are some other ways to help keep your cool without totally freezing your budget.

GO TO A "LUMBERYARD." Because window units are considered a seasonal item and therefore are priced at the whim of retailers, markups for window units range anywhere from 15 percent at discount stores like Kmart to 35 to 40 percent at small appliance dealers. But for the best deals, head to a home center like Home Depot or Builders Square. These large do-it-yourself havens—considered lumberyards by many homeowners—will beat any competitor's price, including those offered by wholesale clubs like Sam's Club or B.J.'s Wholesale Club, by 10 percent. All you need is an advertisement from another store, and you get the discount. Sorry, but central units aren't sold in these stores.

MAKE IT A NEW YEAR'S GIFT. Stores normally order air conditioners in December and begin stocking them in January or February, holding preseason sales in order to get the merchandise moving. Sears, which stocks only its Kenmore brand, usually has a sale every January with savings averaging 25 percent—up to $200 for a high-end unit. Other stores may offer similar savings in the early months of the new year.

The same applies to year-end closeouts. If you can sweat it out or are just looking for a new unit, figure on saving 20 percent if you buy at season's end—usually beginning in mid-September. That's when stores that are overstocked on air conditioners are anxious to move the merchandise. Savings range from about $40 on a $200 basic window unit to up to $200 for larger units. But remember: If it's been an especially hot summer, this tactic might not work, because inventories may be gone.

If you're shopping for a central air-conditioning unit capable of cooling your entire house, try ordering a unit in December from an air-conditioning contractor; you'll get the lowest price of the season, and the contractor will have plenty of time to install it during the slow months of January, February and March. The advantage is twofold: He avoids staff layoffs in slow months, and you get the best labor rate possible.

LOOK FOR A RECONDITIONED UNIT. If someone returns a window unit be-

GREAT MAIL-ORDER BUYS

Air conditioners are a hard-to-find mail-order item. Most catalogs are aimed at distributors, not consumers. But Damark International, based in Minneapolis, specializes in a mixture of up-to-date and closeout merchandise, such as portable air conditioner/dehumidifiers that can be carried from room to room. The brands may be lesser-known imports like Sisco Personal Air Conditioners and Toyotomi, but free shipping is available in the continental United States on some models. For others, shipping costs vary with size, weight and destination.

The best deals on air conditioners are available in catalogs published from early spring through late summer. Consumers can save an additional 10 percent by joining Damark's Preferred Buyers' Club. For a free catalog, call 1-800-729-9000.

INSTALLATION: LEAVE IT TO THE PROS

Although any self-respecting do-it-yourselfer can install a window unit—the easiest have a slide-in chassis—you should leave central units for the pros. Recent federal laws to protect the ozone layer impose fines of up to $30,000 for the release of ozone-depleting refrigerants into the air. And this is very likely to happen if you don't have the proper tools and certifications, which are now required by the Environmental Protection Agency. Besides, improper installation will make the unit more costly to run.

cause it's not working properly, some stores, such as Sears, will repair it and then resell it as a reconditioned unit. These units work fine—and often go for as much as 25 to 35 percent less than a similar new unit. The tradeoff is that they usually have a repair-only warranty, although the repair work is guaranteed and the unit is fully operational.

DISPLAY YOUR NEED FOR A DISPLAY MODEL. Another way to cut as much as half off the cost of a window unit is to ask for a display model that's been used to show customers its operation and features. Ask for it, and you'll be getting a good unit (stores rarely display their dogs) for 35 to 50 percent off. Discontinued models can also yield savings of 20 to 50 percent; these are last year's models that the store is trying to unload to make room for new inventory. And figure on cutting at least 10 percent if you buy a window or central unit with scratches, dents or other minor glitches that don't affect its operation.

AVOID THE FRILLS. Some models include a 24-hour timer, which can be used to turn on the unit prior to your arriving home. This feature, considered unnecessary by most experts, typically adds $30 to the cost. Salesmen will also likely try to sell you a unit with an energy-saver switch that turns off the fan when the compressor is not running, adding another $50 or so to the price. But very little energy is saved by turning off the fan, and leaving it on helps make the house feel cooler by circulating the air.

Airline Tickets

Those skies may be friendly, but they sure ain't cheap. What's worse, they're not even equitable. At any given moment, there are as many as 13 million different air fares available on the world's 750 airlines.

That's why you may feel anything but sky-high when you discover that the schmoe in the next seat paid $100 less for his ticket than you did for yours. The reason: Airlines will get as much from you as they can. But the more you know about their pricing strategies, the more you can save. So here's how to increase the odds in your favor and pay less than others for air travel.

Think small. You can buy tickets for 30 percent less by booking your flights to and from a smaller airport rather than a giant "hub" airport. That means Oakland or San Jose instead of San Francisco, Milwaukee instead of Chicago, Newburgh instead of New York City, Baltimore instead of Washington or Orange County instead of Los Angeles.

The savings result because these smaller airports—and there's at least one near most major hubs in the United States—have lower overhead and smaller fleets and use price wars to compete with the bigger airports. Besides, they tend to be less congested (for both planes and commuting vehicle traffic), and parking and other expenses tend to be lower.

Book at night. Many experts say you can usually get a better deal by calling the airline directly instead of going through a travel agent. (The savings once offered by agents are becoming less obvious, especially since many full-service agencies now charge processing fees that eat into whatever discount you would have gotten.)

But your timing is crucial for getting the lowest fares. The best time to call is after 8:00 P.M. or on weekend mornings, when usually harried reservations agents have more time to scour the computer for a bargain.

BE A JOHNNY-GO-EARLY. Fares to summer destinations generally start to increase in mid-June, and those to winter destinations go up in early December, so if you can adjust your vacation plans accordingly, you can save 25 percent or more.

No matter what the season, international flights are generally cheaper when they depart and arrive on weekdays, while domestic flights tend to cost less on weekends.

OR WAIT UNTIL THE LAST MINUTE. Sometimes it can pay to procrastinate. Encore Short Notice (1-800-222-6235) specializes in selling unsold airline seats at "the last minute," which can be as long as four weeks before the departure date. But the savings of 20 to 50 percent may make it worth the wait. Travel agencies can also find cheap last-minute tickets, but don't expect this from the airlines—they usually raise prices as the departure date approaches, since that's when free-spending business flyers on expense accounts tend to make their reservations.

LOOK FOR OFFERS IN "UNLIKELY" PLACES. A supermarket bulletin board may be the last place you'd expect to find coupons good for a 15 percent discount on airline tickets. But look there anyway—many airlines offer such deals as part of joint promotions with supermarkets and other national chains. If you can't find the bulletin board, ask the customer service representative.

Here are some other "unlikely" places to get a discount.

- Those entertainment coupon books sold by charities occasionally have discount offers or a buy-one-get-one-free arrangement with a particular airline.
- Credit unions frequently have an arrangement that offers members up to 20 percent off regular fares, especially in the summer.
- And don't forget that some people who buy nonrefundable tickets will sell them through the classified ads if their plans change. Just remember that if you buy one, you have to fly under the name on the ticket and even change your baggage tags. (But never buy an international ticket this way, since it obviously won't jibe with the name on your passport.)

CASH IN ON YOUR AGE. If you're 62 or older, you can get senior citizen discounts of 10 to 30 percent on most American and virtually all foreign airlines. (Similar discounts are available for military personnel and their dependents, medical students, clergy, Red Cross workers

CASH FOR CARRY

More than 35,000 people each year fly overseas for less than half the regular price—simply because they're willing to carry documents, spare parts or other small items.

Acting as a courier is one of the best ways to get international airline tickets for a song, and apparently there's plenty of need. The International Association of Air Travel Couriers of Lake Worth, Florida (407-582-8320) updates its list of opportunities for registered couriers twice daily. It tracks 70,000 courier flights a year worldwide. The cost of becoming a registered courier is $45.

Other courier agencies include Now Voyager in New York City (212-431-1616) and Way to Go Travel in Los Angeles (213-466-1126), which does courier travel to Sydney, Australia.

and government employees.) Older travelers also can buy flat-fee coupons from most airlines for multiple tickets for domestic travel that cost half the price of regular coach tickets.

BUMP YOURSELF. If you don't absolutely, positively have to be there, volunteer at the departure gate to stay behind in case of overbooking. Ever since the old Allegheny Airlines had the inconceivably bad judgment to bump consumer advocate Ralph Nader off a flight, federal law has entitled bumped passengers to refunds of up to $200 off the ticket price if a substitute flight arrives more than an hour after the original flight. As an alternative, passengers get coupons for future free travel, with almost no restrictions.

If you're *trying* to get bumped from a domestic flight, travel on a Monday morning, when the airlines are the busiest.

ASK ABOUT "FAMILY EMERGENCY" DISCOUNTS. If you need to travel because of a serious illness or a death in the family, ask the airline for a bereavement fare. Airlines don't usually publicize this service—and some don't have it—but when you get a "compassion discount," your fare can be up to 50 percent less than regular fares. You're in the best position to get a compassion discount if you make a personal appeal directly to the airline rather than going through a travel agent. And be prepared to show some proof of your needs, such as a

SEEK OUT OTHER "TRAVEL AGENTS"

For the convenience of a travel agent at bargain prices, check out these alternatives.

No-frills agencies. These work like other travel agents, except that they stress savings over service. Instead of plush offices with glossy posters and brochures, you'll get airline tickets for at least 10 percent less than from full-service travel agencies. These agencies tend to charge a small flat fee for booking your flight and then pass to you the commission they get from the airline as a rebate. Some no-frills agencies include Travel Avenue in Chicago (312-876-1116), Travel World in Los Angeles (310-479-6093), Smart Traveler in Miami (305-448-3338) and All-American Traveler in Naples, Florida (941-261-6269).

Consolidators. These middlemen purchase unsold seats in bulk at cut-rate prices directly from airlines and then sell the tickets to you for about 30 percent off regular coach rates. Expect the best deals on international routes—savings of up to 75 percent can be had for tickets to Europe and Asia—but keep in mind that consolidator tickets generally don't earn frequent-

death certificate or the name, address and phone number of the funeral parlor.

LOOK INTO CHARTERS. You don't necessarily have to rent an entire plane and crew to save up to 40 percent off airline tickets. Some charter companies now book some flights like other airlines—they run a regular route (especially to popular vacation destinations), and reservations are taken on a first-come, first-served basis.

So don't overlook charter services when you're shopping around for prices. They're usually listed in the yellow pages under "Aircraft Charter, Rental and Leasing Services."

ASK HOW YOU CAN WHITTLE DOWN THE PRICE. No matter where you book, after you're quoted their "best" price, ask how you can further reduce it—by flying during off-peak hours, for example, or on a different day or a holiday. Some reservation-takers readily suggest these savings programs, but others play a "wait-and-see" game with customers to determine who's travel-savvy. Besides, when reservation-

flyer mileage and don't allow free stopovers. One company, Interworld in Miami (305-443-4929), deals exclusively with travel to Europe and South Africa and is hooked into the vast computer network shared by international consolidators. To find other consolidators near you, check the travel section of your Sunday newspaper.

Although most consolidators are on the up-and-up, experts advise that you always double-check your reservation with the airline and pay with your credit card for added protection.

Barter services. Airlines get some goods and services by trading tickets, which end up on the barter market—often at barter clubs that sell them to the public for up to 75 percent off.

Two such barter companies include IMS Travel of Austin, Texas (1-800-788-8169), which specializes in travel to Mexico and the Caribbean, and Travel World Leisure Club in New York City (1-800-444-8952), which barters domestic tickets on about a dozen airlines. To find other barter clubs, look in the yellow pages under "Barter and Trade Exchanges."

takers see that you're willing to compromise by making changes in your plans to save money, they're more likely to reveal these special "hidden" deals.

CHECK OUT A CLUB. There are "travel clubs" that offer across-the-board discounts to members, who pay yearly dues of about $50. Check your Sunday newspaper supplement for clubs in your area, but two of the better-known national clubs are Travelers Advantage (1-800-548-1116) in Stamford, Connecticut, and Travel World Leisure Club in New York City (1-800-444-8952).

ANTIQUES

Stepping into an antique dealer's shop provides a welcome change from a hectic 1990s lifestyle. The setting is warm, the atmosphere is relaxed, and the merchandise is filled with history—the antithesis of a department store, where the beat is fast-paced and the inventory new and shiny.

But an antique shop isn't necessarily as genteel as its nature. On average, dealers mark up their inventory about 150 percent, and some charge three times their cost. To get an edge before you shop, it's smart to study antique and reproduction guides like *Warman's Antiques Price Guide* or *Kovels' Antiques and Collectibles Price List*, which are available at bookstores. And once you hit the stores, try these strategies to save.

GET CLUED INTO CODES. Most antique dealers have their own unique system for pricing an item, and by knowing this code you're in a better position to save money—or at least not be taken. Some dealers do it numerically, others use letters, and still others might use a combination. Look for price stickers in the lower left-hand corner of the antique, where many dealers place their price tags.

Dealers reveal that some code systems work something like this: The price tag lists a price of $30. Just below the price the dealer lists "Ax" or "Ay," meaning that the dealer paid $10 for the item; "Bx" means $20 paid, "Cx" is $30 and so on. Knowing what the dealer paid gives you a platform for bargaining. Other dealers might use letters to represent a certain reduction in 5 percent increments—with the letter *A* equaling 5 percent off, *B* 10 percent off, *C* 15 percent off and so forth. So if you see a *C* on the sticker, try asking for 15 percent off. Be aware that there are no set code standards in the antique business, so it is always best to use your best judgment and trust your instincts.

LOOK FOR A HANGER-ON. A price tag on an antique can also tell you how long that item has been at a dealer's shop—and the longer it's

THE BEST FOR LESS: PAIRPOINT AND WILKINSON

When it comes to antique lamps, Tiffany Original is the most prestigious and sought-after name. But a Tiffany Original lamp with a bronze base and a Favrile glass shade in a poppy pattern can cost over $40,000—which certainly dims the hopes of most would-be owners.

But insiders say that you don't need to spend a good-size fortune to own Tiffany Original quality. A Pairpoint or Wilkinson leaded glass lamp is of similar craftsmanship and beauty but costs a lot less: Either can be purchased for between $900 and $15,000 at better-stocked antique shops.

been sitting around, the more likely that you can negotiate a lower price. Some dealers code each piece of inventory with an individual number as it hits the showroom, so lower numbers represent items that have been around longer.

If you see one item that has the number 150 on it and another with 370, the one with the lower number has been in stock longer—and the dealer may be more willing to lower the price for a quick sale. Also look for old or weathered-looking stickers, which also indicate the item has been sitting around.

PAY CASH. Credit card companies charge dealers each time a customer makes a purchase with plastic, usually 3 percent of the item's cost. Some dealers are willing to cut the cost by that amount or slightly less in order to make a cash sale.

But don't mention your method of payment until you've negotiated your best deal. Then say you want to charge the purchase, unless there's a discount for paying with cash.

BE A LATE BUYER. Just as car dealers need to sell inventory at the end of the month, antique dealers also want to make the sale before the 30th or 31st. Depending on the price, some dealers discount items anywhere from 10 to 25 percent in order to move them out before the new month. If the item you want is not marked

Where to Go

If you're into antiques and reproductions, then no trip to New York City is complete without a visit to one of the most interesting antique shows in the nation: the Chelsea Antiques Building at 25th Street and Sixth Avenue. With wares from over 200 dealers on 12 floors, it's open from 10:00 A.M. to 6:00 P.M. daily. Call (212) 929-0909 for more information.

For information on other shows and auctions nationwide, *Antique Week* magazine has two editions—one for residents of central and midwestern states and one for those on the East Coast. Subscriptions are $27.45 and $23.45 respectively. For a sample copy or to place an order, call 1-800-876-5133. *Antique Review*, which also lists hot shows and "worth-seeing" dealers, costs $20 per year. Call 1-800-992-9757 for more information.

down, simply offer that much less than the asking price.

And when shopping at estate sales, try to wait until the end of the day to make a purchase. Doing so can save you as much as 50 percent off the asking price. At that point, the items will likely be picked over and the pickings may be slim, but sellers will be highly motivated to sell to avoid having to haul them back or give them away.

Be willing to haggle. Contrary to its uppercrust reputation, the antique business not only accepts haggling from customers—it expects it. But dealers also expect reasonable offers—no more than 25 percent below the sticker price. In fact, many encourage customers to ask "What is the best price you can give me?" Some dealers tell us that they raise their asking prices by about 20 percent in anticipation of haggling. So don't be shy about asking for a better price.

Be a clubber. If you're into a specific type of antique, such as Chippendale furniture or Lionel trains, there are clubs for virtually every type of specialized collector. Besides being an excellent way to buy antiques from fellow collectors, being part of a club is also an opportunity to share your passion with others of a similar ilk. To locate clubs in your area or individual collectors with a similar collecting interest, consider purchasing *Maloney's Antiques and Collectibles Resource Directory*, available in most bookstores.

Athletic Shoes

There's a reason that those celebrity jocks are always smiling in TV ads for athletic shoes: More than $700 million a year is spent for them to hawk the latest and greatest in sports footwear.

Those one-time "sneakers" have become a $12-billion-a-year business whose impact goes far beyond the basketball court. Each year, the equivalent of 1½ pairs is sold to every man, woman and child

Outstanding Outlets

Athletic shoe outlets are now a dime a dozen, but New Balance is one of the few companies that manufacture most of their shoes in the United States, and its factory stores have the unique distinction of actually being attached to factories.

The company sells off closeouts, discontinued models and slightly blemished top-of-the-line stuff at its manufacturing facilities in Skowhegan, Maine, Lawrence, Massachusetts, and Boston's Brighton section. Discounts range from 20 percent on new merchandise to 75 percent on discontinued styles. There are special promotions once a month, which reduce the price by an additional 20 percent in exchange for a trade-in of your old athletic shoes.

The mother of all sales is in April in conjunction with the Boston Marathon, when the stores sell current-model, first-quality athletic shoes for a tough-to-match 10 percent off the list price.

(including those that can't even walk yet) in the United States. And with an average retail markup of over 50 percent and some pairs costing more than $150, you may feel financially stomped trying to "outfoot" the brood. But here are some ways to get a toehold on the high cost of athletic shoes.

KNOW WHEN TO BUY. Most major manufacturers keep their inventory costs down by forcing retailers to place their orders six to eight months in advance. If the store is too conservative and has to order more shoes later, it pays an extra 10 percent for the order—an increase that's passed on to you. So to keep their costs down, retailers

FOR THE BEST DEALS, GO TO ORLANDO

Orlando, Florida, is the runaway best place to get a deal on athletic footwear: Adidas, Converse, Nike and Reebok all have outlets there, offering deals ranging from 20 to 50 percent off retail prices. Barstow, California, where Asics has a company store and Reebok also has an outlet, is a runner-up.

Adidas has a total of 11 outlet stores. Besides Orlando, they're in burgs such as Draper, Utah, Boise, Idaho, and Spartanburg, South Carolina. Asics has another store in Camarillo, California, near Santa Barbara. There are 14 Avia stores across the country, most of them in Florida, Illinois, Washington, Missouri and Wisconsin, with average markdowns of 30 percent. Saucony has five outlets in New England, known as Saucony Spot-bilt or, near Boston, Hyde Factory Outlet Stores. Converse has 27 stores throughout New England, Florida, California, Kansas and Hawaii. Nike has 32 outlets from coast to coast, and Reebok has retail outlets throughout the country, but neither really needs to discount their hot products too much, and they don't.

Bigger athletic footwear retailers also now have outlet stores that offer 10 to 25 percent discounts on current, discontinued and closeout first-quality shoes: The Athlete's Foot has six outlets located in strip malls. It also has many more outlets in manufacturer's outlet malls, where you can find more modest savings on current and some discontinued styles.

GREAT MAIL-ORDER BUYS

Road Runner Sports is the biggest mail-order house for running shoes and also has a wide selection of specialty footwear for a variety of other sports, including hiking, basketball, volleyball and tennis.

While it's tough to get the best fit from a photo in a catalog, mail-order companies charge less than retail price, and their knowledgeable staff tells you up-front about discrepancies in sizing, as well as helping you select the best model shoe for your running style. You can figure on paying around $4 in shipping and handling charges per pair, but the company often holds clearance sales that knock 30 percent off the typical retail price—making shipping costs a drop in the bucket. Order your catalog by calling 1-800-551-5558. (Road Runner also runs an outlet center from its San Diego headquarters; you can get more information by calling the number above.)

tend to order on the high side—and then get stuck with extra shoes they have to dump at clearance prices.

When can you find these bargains? The best times are from early January to mid-February and then again in late July and early August. The reason: Athletic footwear manufacturers introduce new models almost every month, but most enter the market during these times. Since athletic shoe buyers are a fickle lot, wanting the latest styles and colors, retailers unload their current inventories then—giving you closeout prices on the previous season's perfectly good, first-quality athletic shoes.

KNOW WHERE TO BUY. Ever wonder what happens to the old inventory that isn't sold when the new styles come to market? Often it winds up at off-price clothing stores like T.J. Maxx and Marshalls. Although most manufacturers insist they don't sell shoes directly to the discount places, industry insiders say that enough do to keep off-price stores well-stocked. Low-overhead middlemen called diverters, who move shoes from wholesalers to retailers, are another source of inventory for these stores—and that means great savings for you, especially after February and August: One industry report reveals that the same pair of athletic shoes that costs $47 in sporting goods stores and $57 in athletic shoe stores will run only $17 at off-price stores.

AND ESPECIALLY HOW TO BUY. One possible reason that we spend $12 billion a year on athletic shoes? We can't seem to get the right fit. Most athletic shoes generally run a half-size smaller than they did just a few years ago, while your feet tend to grow bigger with age. That one-two punch—or rather, pinch—is why most Americans wear shoes too small for their feet, according to the American Orthopaedic Foot and Ankle Society.

What this means is that some people assume they know their size and don't even try on new shoes. And even when they do try them on, they may assume that the "tightness" they feel is the result of the shoes needing to be "broken in." Wrong! If the shoes don't feel right the first time you lace them, they won't—and whatever you spend is wasted cash. Experts say you should always measure your feet before you buy; feet tend to swell toward the end of the day. And be sure to try on both shoes—the right and left shoe of the same pair are often made on two separate assembly lines, possibly even in different countries. The dye lots and shoes are then matched up later.

This is especially important if you buy by mail order, which is where some of the best deals on top-quality shoes are. Before choosing from the catalog, go to a specialty store and try shoes on. When you find the right fit, order the same model through mail order. Even from the same manufacturer, some styles are sized "true to size," some a half-size small and some a half-size large.

DON'T BE TEMPTED BY THOSE BELLS AND WHISTLES. Athletic shoes with more expensive "special features" like gel, "air" and pumps are hot—especially with teens and preteens. Are they necessary? Probably not. Fashion statements aside, nearly half of all consumers purchase their athletic shoes only for casual use. That's twice as many who buy shoes specifically for exercise or competition. (The remainder purchase the shoes for work or school.)

But if you decide that the extra cushioning and other frills are worth the extra dough, make sure you're getting what you pay for. Polyurethane cushioning provides the best value for your money because it holds its compression properties the longest, which in turn makes the shoes last longer.

Nike's encapsulated gas technology is also extremely durable, but take a look at the heel and sole: You'll know you're not getting the real McCoy if you see tiny air bubbles (a sign of inferior blown foam). Another hint: Nike tightly controls distribution of its high-quality "Air" brands, so you won't find them in mail-order catalogs or discount chains. If you do, they're probably fakes.

GO THE EXTRA MILE. Fans of Saucony running shoes might take note of that company's Extra Mile Club. After trading in shoes purchased from a Saucony Extra Mile retailer, you can get a membership kit and a $5 coupon on your next pair of shoes (valued at $55 or more). After buying your seventh pair, you get a coupon worth $10 off your eighth pair. (Keep in mind that serious runners go through three or four pairs of running shoes per year.) The deal gets better after 12 purchases, when Saucony rewards patrons with a free pair. Call 1-800-365-4933 for more details.

Athletic Wear

Despite our best intentions, only one in every four Americans exercises the recommended three times weekly for at least 20 continuous minutes. But a heck of a lot more folks dress as if they do.

Americans spend more than $8 billion each year on athletic wear like leotards, jogging suits, tank tops, shorts and other "nonsneaker" apparel. Most of it has a retail markup of about 50 percent. But you don't have to go the distance when it comes to the price of suiting up for sports. Here are some ways to trim your fitness clothing bill.

Shop off-season. When buying retail, you're in the best position to run up savings if you shop in January or July. That's when prices on athletic wear are discounted as much as 40 percent as retailers try to make room for new inventory.

Hit the outlets. Of course, the best deals aren't usually in retail stores. Reebok, New Balance, Patagonia and nearly every other big-name athletic apparel manufacturer has factory outlets located in outlet malls, as well as a factory store adjacent to their corporate headquarters, that offer great savings. These stores usually stock merchandise that's one season old or has minor imperfections, such as improper stitching or slight stains. But the savings are substantial: anywhere from 25 to 90 percent below regular retail prices.

Don't expect these company stores to always be named after the company, however. Patagonia's company store, located down the street from its corporate headquarters in Ventura, California, is called Real Cheap Sports. Patagonia has outlet stores under its own name in Dillon, Montana, Freeport, Maine, and Salt Lake City.

To find a factory outlet or company store near you, call the corporate headquarters of your favorite fitness apparel manufacturer. (You can get the number by calling 800 directory assistance at 1-800-555-1212.) Or look for a copy of "The Factory Outlet Guide," which includes hundreds of athletic wear factory outlets across the country, in your local library or bookstore.

GREAT MAIL-ORDER BUYS

Road Runner Sports Factory Outlet is catalog heaven for runners and other athletes, featuring a great selection of shoes and brand-name athletic wear by New Balance, Reebok, InSport and Champion at up to 65 percent off retail. Although some items are one season behind, other merchandise is current-season overstock. You can order a catalog by calling 1-800-662-8896. (Road Runner also runs an outlet center from its San Diego headquarters; you can get more information by calling the number above.)

In addition, California Best in Chula Vista offers a decent selection of athletic shorts, socks, tank tops, T-shirts and swimwear at up to 40 percent less than retail. Join the California Best SportClub for a one-time fee of $25 and you'll save an additional 5 percent on every order—plus every dollar you spend earns bonus points that can be redeemed for free merchandise. For a catalog and more information, call 1-800-225-2378.

The catalog from Jazzertogs in San Diego features women's leotards, bike shorts, tank tops and tights—many with gold metallic embroidery and colorful patterns and stripes. But stick with the "basics" line in solid colors and you'll cut 30 percent off the price of these quality goods. For a Jazzertogs catalog, call 1-800-348-4748.

BUY THE "BASICS." Many fitness catalogs and some retailers carry a no-frills line of fitness wear known in the business as the basics line, or house brand. The clothing may lack special features like racing stripes and "motivational" prints, but most basics are made of the same high-performance materials as the flashier items—and sell for anywhere from 20 to 30 percent less. Look for basic products in the middle of your favorite athletic wear catalog or in company-run outlet stores.

JOIN THE CLUB. Many athletic apparel companies—especially those that sell their merchandise by mail order—feature frequent-buyer clubs that typically offer members a discount on all orders, usually between 5 and 10 percent. Other benefits include priority and free shipping on larger orders, subscriptions to newsletters, advance notice of future sales and even travel and rental car discounts. Some also offer a bonus point system that allows you to earn merchandise credit for every dollar you spend.

Such clubs usually require a one-time joining fee of about $30. For more information, check your catalog or ask your favorite athletic apparel dealer for details.

START IN THE MIDDLE. If you're shopping by mail order, first check the order form that's usually in the middle of the catalog. That's where clearance items tend to be posted, and they're typically discounted up to 60 percent off regular prices. If sale items aren't featured on the back of the order form, however, they're probably close by. The middle of the catalog tends to be a hot spot for savings.

ASK FOR THE DEALS. When phoning in your order, ask if there are any telephone specials. Some athletic wear companies feature five to six items at a time from past catalogs that have been reduced by 35 to 50 percent—but they aren't listed in the catalog.

COLLECT CREDIT FROM YOUR CARD. If you're a credit card user, those coupons that come with your monthly statement can help you save on athletic wear. MasterCard, for example, frequently features MasterValues Coupons that can be redeemed for discounts on athletic apparel. Recently, customers who spent at least $65 on merchandise offered through the Road Runner Sports fitness apparel catalog could receive a free pair of running shorts (a $23 value) if they paid with their MasterCard.

AUDIO EQUIPMENT

Competition in the $9-billion-a-year audio electronics market is so stiff that it's driven some retailers to extremes—from strategically placing speakers in listening rooms so that the most expensive models sound the best to—get this—selling some items for just a few dollars over their wholesale costs.

Well, before running out to the local stereo store for those great deals, you should realize that most equipment still sells for 50 to 70 percent more than what the retailer pays. That's certainly not the highest retail markup, especially when you consider the high costs of advertising and other overhead that some audio equipment retailers have. So while you can't expect huge discounts, here's how you can save when buying stereos, radios and other audio gear.

TIME YOUR PURCHASE. From about April on, don't expect much in the way of discounts on audio items, since demand is high when some new products are introduced. But there's a window of opportunity between the Christmas holidays and early spring, when demand drops off and retailers need to clear out the old models.

Start checking the Sunday newspaper for ads from stereo stores trying to unload merchandise in early January, and keep your eyes peeled until mid-March, when prices tend to dip as much as 20 percent. Also check in early September, when some retailers run back-to-school sales offering similar markdowns on some items.

SHOP FOR PRICE, NOT NAME. It's not uncommon for audio manufacturers to make audio equipment under several names—or even hire other companies to manufacture their components. Yamaha, for instance, hires Pioneer to make some of its higher-end equipment, while Matsushita, a Japanese conglomerate, makes equipment for Panasonic, Technics and several other brands. Advent speakers are made by International Jensen. In fact, a handful of companies produce audio equipment bearing over a dozen different names—including some off-brands you've probably never heard of.

OUTSTANDING OUTLETS

While Sony, Bang & Olufsen and other manufacturers have opened "galleries" in trendy neighborhoods of major cities, they tend to sell their wares at full list price. Only one major audio maker sells direct to the public at a discount: Cambridge SoundWorks, which has a national catalog and more than a dozen factory stores in northern California and New England.

The brains behind this company belong to Henry Kloss, who founded Acoustic Research, Advent and other top-rated manufacturers. Cambridge SoundWorks designs, manufactures and sells most of the products in its catalog and outlets, cutting out the middleman. It also offers a growing selection of components from Pioneer, Sony, Koss and others at about 40 percent off list price and has generous additional discount coupons tucked away on the order form. But the best deal is the company's "Happy Returns" policy—its 30-day money-back guarantee. It even pays the postage on returns, which is great if you have problems with a product. It's even better if you're looking for a bargain, since these returns are checked for damage, repackaged and sold at deeper discounts in the Walnut Creek, California, and Newton, Massachusetts, stores. For more information, call 1-800-367-4434.

In addition, Famous Brand Electronics, a division of Radio Shack, carries factory-refurbished audio equipment from virtually every major manufacturer. The equipment is as good as new—at prices anywhere from 10 to 80 percent less than retail. There are more than 20 Famous Brand stores, most in major outlet centers. Call Radio Shack at 1-800-843-7422 for a Famous Brand location near you.

While there are some differences between brands, the main reason that people buy at higher prices is often only customer loyalty—especially when it comes to compact disc players. In fact, all CD players use the very same technology and the same lasers (which are all made by one company), no matter what their price. So save your money and buy the cheapest brand you can find.

LOOK FOR A COMMISSIONED SALESPERSON. When all is said and done, getting the best price on stereo equipment often requires some not-so-fancy footwork. You simply have to trudge to a store and get a price, then go to another to see if they'll beat it. But where you go can make a big difference—as much as 25 percent. A sales staff that's on commission probably has a greater motivation to be flexible on price because they have a financial interest in seeing you buy. Their rivals who are paid only an hourly wage may not.

UPGRADE WHAT YOU HAVE. If you hear a wobble in your tunes, pick up a $1 stabilizer ring for your CD player before shopping for a new one. If your machine sounds tinny, install a set of soft rubber feet—priced at $30 for a set of four—to help reduce vibration. Or try replacing the connector cables for about $10 or applying spray chemicals for about $15 to help cut laser refractions.

While these minor repairs may not be the answer, they certainly are a cheap way to explore problems before going out and buying new components.

FORGET THE BOX, KEEP THE CASH. You can find discounts of as much as 50 percent below retail on display models and returns—items that usually have no box. These items may have some scratches or dents, but they are fully covered by the same warranty as "in-the-box" items. Some retailers may even have specific open stock and scratch-and-dent sales.

Don't be afraid to try the demonstration model on the shelf or ask to take it home for a trial. And remember that last year's model almost certainly sounds precisely the same as this year's, perhaps minus any new bells or whistles. There also are occasional deals on closeouts, overstocks and discontinued models, although these discounts are not as great—usually in the range of 20 to 35 percent off.

BUY BY MAIL ORDER. You can usually cut at least 15 percent by buying audio equipment through mail-order houses rather than in retail stores. For the best prices, contact several dealers—you'll find them listed in advertisements in magazines like *Stereo Review*. These magazines also do product comparisons.

But when buying by mail order, be sure to use the manufacturer's toll-free number to make sure the mail-order house is an authorized distributor. And insist on factory-sealed cartons; tell the dealer you will not accept boxes that have been resealed. Also ask for a 30-day

THE BEST FOR LESS: SONY

Sony co-invented CD technology, perfected the portable stereo and continues to get the highest marks from consumer magazines and critics alike in virtually every category of components it produces—and it produces more than anybody else.

The trouble is, buying a top-of-the-line Sony system—compact disc player, surround-sound speaker and receiver set and dual-cassette tape deck—will run you more than $4,700.

The solution? First, get the components as a package in a mini-system, commonly called a shelf system. And second, buy it from the Aiwa Company, a Japanese company half-owned by Sony that incorporates the same high quality into its shelf systems. Instead of forking over thousands, you can get a model with a three-disc CD changer, a 100-watt-per-channel amplifier with Dolby sound and extra bass, a dual-cassette tape deck with auto reverse, surround-sound speakers and even a built-in karaoke system for about $500. For information on where to buy it, call 1-800-424-2492.

return period that allows you to return merchandise for a full refund. (Some dealers will not allow returns on equipment that has been opened.)

GO BACK TO SCHOOL. Used equipment might seem like a disaster waiting to happen, but a stereo receiver that's kept in good condition can last 20 to 30 years. If something's been dropped, you'll be able to tell immediately from the outside. And if beer was spilled through the vent, it won't play.

So buying used can be a way to get a good stereo at a great price—especially if you hit the local colleges. Students who are leaving school or going off to study abroad frequently sell their stereos for a fraction of what you'd pay retail, so check the bulletin boards on campus or put up a notice of your own. If there is no local university, check the classified ads in a local alternative weekly.

DO IT YOURSELF—WITH HELP. Installing your own car stereo can save you between $45 and $100. But doing it yourself doesn't mean you have to go it alone. Crutchfield Corporation (1-800-955-3000), a mail-order company based in Charlottesville, Virginia, will walk you through the car stereo installation process and send you a custom installation kit, free wiring harnesses and detailed instructions tailored to your car. They'll tell you if the stereo you like fits into any of 4,124 vehicles dating back to 1964. And for $6.95, they'll throw in videotaped installation directions.

Crutchfield also sells a huge selection of car stereos (as well as home audio equipment, TVs, VCRs and camcorders) through its catalog at 40 percent off list price—about the same as what you'll find at a discount retailer or electronics superstore. The company occasionally offers deeper discounts; you can find out what's on sale by calling Crutchfield's Price Information Hotline at 1-800-555-9407 for a recorded announcement.

BYPASS THOSE EXTENDED WARRANTIES. Only 4 to 15 cents of every dollar paid for those pricey service contracts is ever actually spent on service, according to the Financial Standards Accounting Board. The rest just lines the pockets of the retailer. The odds are that you'll never need service within the first two years of buying new equipment, so an extended warranty is not usually worth the cost, which ranges from $30 to $100 or more, depending on the plan.

AUTOMOTIVE PARTS AND SUPPLIES

Slapping a fabric name badge on a pair of overalls and trying to pass yourself off as a mechanic *may* get you a discount on your next auto parts purchase. But with a little knowledge, you can learn to navigate the rows of gadgets and gizmos in auto parts departments—without flattening your wallet. Here's how.

GET THE BASICS AT A MART SALE. Although their automotive departments are somewhat limited, discount chains like Kmart, Wal-Mart and Target Stores tend to run frequent sales on basic auto supplies: motor oil, filters, wiper blades, windshield washer fluid, spark plugs and similar items.

Every week there are sales on select items, often at prices up to 25 percent less than those at traditional auto parts retailers. The best deals tend to be on cases of motor oil, which usually goes on sale for as little as $1 to $1.25 per quart. Head to a gas station and you could pay $3 for the same product. In fact, you'll generally pay full price for most products at a gas station.

MAKE FRIENDS WITH THE COUNTER GUY. For other parts, it's best to go to a large auto parts retailer such as National Auto Stores. These multi-store chains have the buying power to get volume discounts from parts manufacturers, so depending on the item, you can pay as much as 40 percent less than you would at a car dealership's service department.

And if you get to know the store clerk, you can save even more. Insiders reveal that there's a two- to three-tier pricing structure at auto parts retailers. Casual walk-ins (the folks who don't know anybody) pay the most—top retail. Mechanics from the garage down the street pay the trade price, a discount commonly known as wholesale. The true wholesale, of course, is what the supplier—the jobber—pays, but

THE BEST FOR LESS: OEMS

The best parts for your car are those specifically made for it by the original equipment manufacturer; they're known as OEMs in the trade. For Ford cars, they're Motorcraft; for General Motors, they're Delco; and for Chrysler products, look for Mopar. Other car companies also have their OEMs, but whatever you drive, you'll save at least 10 percent if you buy them at an auto parts retailer like National Auto Stores instead of a car dealership.

he's paying the manufacturer; you won't get that price. But you might get the trade price—if you give the impression that you'll be a steady customer.

REQUEST "REMANUFACTURED." Perhaps the best bargain in auto repair, remanufactured parts can save you between 40 and 60 percent off a new part price. After they're taken apart and cleaned and worn components are replaced, remanufactured parts are reassembled to strict specifications of the manufacturer. A new alternator for a 1992 Ford Explorer costs $332 at a dealership, for example, while a remanufactured alternator for the same vehicle, with a one-year warranty, costs $195 at an auto parts store.

In addition to auto parts stores, remanufactured parts are available at the newest trend—retailers that deal strictly in used and remanufactured parts. They are listed in the yellow pages under "Automobile Parts and Supplies—Used and Rebuilt." You can also get remanufactured parts at repair facilities and dealerships, but you'll probably have to ask for them.

When shopping, though, be sure to demand remanufactured parts, not rebuilt parts, which have just been removed from vehicles, repaired when needed and cleaned. (The exception to this is carburetors, which are usually better after being rebuilt.)

FILL YOUR TRUNK WITH JUNK. For talented—if untested—home mechanics, junkyards offer car parts by the acre at substantial savings. In fact, instead of paying hundreds, you might find what you need on a junked car for a few dollars. The problem: You may not know until you get home whether the part still works. Some recycling yards are now linked by computer to one or more networks of yards; it's often no longer a matter of picking through the grunge. Also called recyclers, junkyards are positively the best source for auto body parts—sheet metal such as fenders or expensive items like headlamp assemblies for some of the new foreign cars.

BABY FURNITURE

Anyone who suggests that new parents immediately start putting aside some money for their infant's college education obviously hasn't been shopping for baby furniture. As if the prices of cribs, bassinets and changing tables at better baby stores aren't enough to make the proud parents start thinking seriously about vo-tech schools instead (those three items alone can cost over $1,000 at some shops), there are also bureaus, lamps and other accessories that you need to take Junior well past the first couple of years.

Retail markups on baby furniture tend to be very low—usually 10 to 35 percent—and discounts are common because of stiff competition. So with careful shopping, you should be able to furnish a nursery for a song and still put aside something for higher education.

One key: Shop before the arrival. Although most expectant parents hit the stores several months before the baby is due, those who wait until the baby is born tend to pay a premium price because they have little time to comparison-shop—or to schmooze their way to a bigger discount, which can typically net an additional 10 percent off the price. Besides negotiating a better deal, here are some other ways to save when buying baby furniture.

REMEMBER DECEMBER. While birthing babies isn't exactly a seasonal business, insiders admit that selling furniture is—and December is the slowest month. Because of this, you may find prices cut 10 to 20 percent below what you'd pay the rest of the year. But hurry, because the low prices are short-lived, spiking again in January through March as manufacturers announce price increases.

BE SAVVY ABOUT SAMPLES. While baby furniture sales are unpredictable, sample sales occur every day. Cruise the showroom of most large baby furniture shops with an eye for floor samples—and focus your attention on buying those items.

They may have some dents and dings from being displayed, but a floor model typically sells for up to 30 percent less than the same

THE BEST FOR LESS: SIMMONS

Both baby and parents can sleep easy with nursery items from Simmons. This well-respected furniture maker puts out over 50 models of cribs, as well as bureaus and other items for baby's bedroom.

Crib prices start at $200—about twice what you'd pay for a basic crib at a major discounter—but industry insiders say the product is well worth it. Simmons isn't available at big discount chains like Kmart and Toys "R" Us, so you'll have to buy at a specialty store. To get a price break, shop around: You'll see price variances of up to 30 percent, depending on sales, close-outs, overstocks and other special promotions.

You're also in a better position to negotiate a deal—usually 10 percent off or so—by shopping at these specialty stores, where the salespeople are more likely to be on commission.

item in a box. If you don't see any floor samples for sale, ask.

SHOP A SPECIALIST. While major retailers like Toys "R" Us, T.J. Maxx and Target Stores offer rock-bottom prices on some baby furniture, you're still better off buying from a smaller specialty shop.

That's because cribs, changing tables and other baby furniture items that are available at discount stores are sometimes made with cheaper materials—soft or pressed woods, fewer support rods and wood or plastic "hardware"—than those found at baby furniture specialty stores. So while you'll save a few bucks at purchase time, you may need to replace it before the baby has outgrown it. Plus, the difference in price is usually not that great: A Jenny Lind crib from a reputable dealer will cost upwards of $150, while a discounter will sell the "same" model for $89. The style is the same, but the cheaper model uses plastic hardware that can wear out prematurely.

Also, since salespeople at large discounters aren't on commission, they're usually not as eager to make a sale as those who work at (or own) smaller specialty stores—or as willing to drop the price.

DISCOVER CLASSIFIED DEALS. The "Used Furniture" section of the classified ads in your local newspaper is a treasure chest of nursery values. We found a top-of-the-line Bellini crib that sells in stores for $750 offered for $300, and a Simmons Napoli crib that retails for $349 listed at $75. And these prices are as soft as the proverbial baby's bottom.

Some experts advise that you should halve the asking price and take it from there: Most people who place classified ads are more interested in making a sale than a profit. Of course, you'll have to give every item a careful inspection—and take along a handy friend if you are a mechanical novice.

HAUL IT YOURSELF. Retailers typically charge up to $50 to deliver your purchases—whether you buy a single crib or an entire bedroom. Some baby items, like elaborate crib centers and plastic outdoor toy sets, are huge even when unassembled. So borrow a vehicle that's big enough to cart your purchases home—and have some helping hands to assist with unloading them when you get there.

Baby Goods

Kids may be priceless, but the cost of raising them has definitely been calculated: The typical parent shells out nearly a quarter of a million dollars to raise each child from birth to college age—and that doesn't include tuition.

The typical family with two kids spends an estimated $15,000 each year on children's expenses alone—everything from Nikes to Nintendo but not including the mortgage, mini-van and other expenses that you might not have without children. And the biggest shock seems to be in the first two years, when Junior needs diapers, formula, baby food and other necessities. Here's how to put a lid on these items.

Save green by being green. Although 85 percent of households use disposable diapers, using cloth diapers for your baby's bottom is better for your bottom line. Compare the costs and you'll see that the cost of hiring a diaper service to wash and deliver cloth diapers is between 30 and 50 percent less than buying the same number of plastic disposables.

What's more, the cost of these services decreases as your child gets older and needs fewer diapers. And you can save even more, since many diaper services throw in complimentary diaper pails to store the soiled diapers; with plastic diapers, you pay for trash bags. You'll find these companies listed in the yellow pages under "Diaper Services."

Sure, you could buy cloth diapers and do your own washing and save even more, but it's usually better to spend the $15 to $20 a week on a diaper service, since most household washers can't clean cloth diapers as well as the machines used by professional services.

Or go with store-brand disposables. If you opt for plastic, you can save up to 40 percent by reaching for the store brands—sold under the name of the drugstore, supermarket or toy store chain. These diapers cost about 10 cents less than top brands like Huggies and Luvs,

GREAT MAIL-ORDER BUYS

Although rare is the person who buys diapers through mail order, you can get them—as well as blankets, waterproof sheets and similar products for about 25 percent less than the suggested retail price—from Chock, a mail-order company that sells underclothing and sleepwear for all members of the family. The company sells cloth diapers and other goods in its 66-page catalog, which can be yours by sending a $2 check to Chock, 74 Orchard Street, New York, NY 10002. Your $2 is refundable on your first order.

saving you about $30 to $40 per month. Although you won't get the coupons the big-name brands offer, many stores run promotions in which you get a free box of diapers after buying ten at full price.

BLEND YOUR LEFTOVERS. Bite for bite, commercial baby food is among the most expensive food items you'll find in the supermarket. And for what? The same vegetables and fruits that you eat, only blended and perhaps mixed with sugar and other flavorings. So do both your child and your wallet a favor—make your own baby food by blending a mixture of leftovers and putting it in jars. It costs nothing and can provide a more nutritious meal than commercially prepared baby food, since you're less likely to add extra ingredients for taste.

GET A "FREE" CAR SEAT. In most states, it's mandatory that children under the age of four be secured in an approved children's car seat whenever riding in an automobile; in some states even older children must use one. Because of this, many hospitals, health bureaus, police agencies and even some businesses offer free use of a children's car seat to motorists; call for information in your area.

You may have to leave a deposit, but you'll get it back when you return the seat—and you save the $50 to $120 it costs to buy a new car seat. Some businesses, such as Midas Muffler and Brake Shops, have jumped on this bandwagon. When you buy a car seat from Midas, you get a certificate for automotive services equal in value to the cost of the car seat. After your child outgrows the car seat, you return it and redeem your certificate for free car care.

THINK BIG. No matter what you need, you'll probably save by going to the biggest retailer you can find. Megastores like Toys "R" Us have the volume buying power, display space and niche marketing to purchase baby goods like diapers, formula and baby food for less than supermarket or drugstore chains.

For most items, you'll typically pay about 10 to 15 percent less at these massive retailers than you would at the supermarket or drugstore. Savings can be up to an additional 20 percent on a per-item basis when you opt for the "big" package: the 72-count diaper box over the 36-count box, for instance.

BAKED GOODS

Baking homemade cookies, breads, cakes and pies may be a lost art for many Americans. But for most of us, eating them isn't a problem. With each American consuming a total of about 90 pounds of commercially prepared baked goods each year, this industry has become a $20 billion annual business.

At the supermarket or bakery, the average retail markup on bread, rolls, cakes and pies ranges from 10 to 50 percent. At gourmet retail stores and mail-order companies, it can easily top 75 percent. Given these statistics, it's hard not to think of these delectables as luxury items. But here's how to get a taste of the sweet life without going through a lot of dough.

SHOP AT NIGHT. With bakery products, a premium is placed on freshness. But good things—namely savings of as much as 50 percent—come to those who wait. Many local and supermarket bakeries offer price reductions on unsold baked goods after 5:00 P.M. Look for sim-

GREAT MAIL-ORDER BUYS

There are occasional opportunities to buy baked goods through the mail—often at wholesale prices. Among the best is Baldwin Hill Bakery in Phillipston, Massachusetts, hailed as one of the country's foremost bakeries by "bread heads" across the country. It turns out 10,000 loaves of hearth-baked organic sourdough bread in 13 varieties. Buy 6 loaves and you get them at wholesale (with a $1.50 surcharge). To order a catalog, call (508) 249-4691.

OUTSTANDING OUTLETS

With stores located in scores of factory outlet malls across the country, Sara Lee sells its famous layer cakes, pies and cheesecakes, as well as many other top brands of baked goods and food service items such as lasagna, bagels and pizza, at 30 to 40 percent off retail prices. To find a Sara Lee outlet store near you, call 1-800-323-7117.

ilar savings on leftover holiday-oriented novelty items such as hot cross buns, Irish soda bread and heart-shaped cakes the day after the holiday.

VISIT THE COMPANY STORE. Many local bakeries have an on-site company store that offers everyday discounts of 10 to 50 percent off their regular retail prices.

These stores also tend to hold seasonal warehouse sales—usually between January and August—featuring discounts of up to 60 percent on overstocks and seasonal merchandise.

BE THRIFTY. If you buy bread at a supermarket—especially on weekends—don't assume it's necessarily fresh from the oven. Why not save 20 to 75 percent and actively seek out "day-old bread" at a bakery thrift or outlet store? Bakery products that aren't sold on the first day of sale at the supermarket (they have a seven-day shelf life) often don't stay on the shelves too long. After two or three days, many commercial bakeries will pick up their remaining products and take them to a namesake "day-old" bakery, where they are discounted for quick sale.

Two nationwide bakery thrift stores to seek out in your area are Wonder/Hostess and Dolly Madison/Butternut. Interstate Brands Corporation of Kansas City, Missouri, has acquired these stores. Wonder/Hostess has 600 thrift stores across the country, and Dolly Madison/Butternut has 800 stores. To get information on one in your area, call (816) 502-4000.

BUY IN BULK FOR WHOLESALE SAVINGS. For bakeries that supply to both retail and wholesale markets, the only factor that separates the two types of customers is quantity. At Bread Alone, for example, a bakery located in Boiceville, New York, that makes breads with organically grown grains and bakes them in wood-fired brick ovens, a minimum order of $25 (about ten loaves of bread) will qualify you for wholesale prices—an 11 percent savings. Other specialty and commercial bakeries offer similar discounts, but the amount you'll need to spend to qualify for the wholesale price varies per vendor.

For the best list of bakeries across the country that are willing to strike up a wholesale bargain with you, check the AT&T Toll-Free 800 Directory under "Bakeries." The directory is available at most local libraries.

SEEK OUT SPECIALS. Another way to take advantage of discount opportunities on baked goods during peak times like holidays—when savings are hard to find—is to ask the company or local bakery that you'd like to buy from if they have any specials.

Wolferman's English Muffins in Lenexa, Kansas, for example, makers of Deluxe English Muffins that "tower over ordinary brands" with a 2-inch height and a 3½-inch width, typically holds three phone specials each week that offer some products at significant markdowns. To learn about these specials, call Wolferman's customer service at 1-800-999-1910.

Local bakeries also tend to offer specials on items they want to sell quickly or on novelty items they want customers to try and buy again. When you shop, ask for the day's special.

Baskets

They used to appear only once each year, to hold candy on Easter Sunday, and then fade as mysteriously as Peter Cottontail. Now baskets are everywhere and in every shape, size and material. Haute caterers use them to hold crudités, and kitchen designers go rustic with pull-out baskets doubling as drawers. Decoraters use them to adorn walls and hang from ceilings.

This new-found interest in baskets has been good for retailers, who still compete for sales with constant markdowns and low markups—a mere 5 to 7 percent on lower-end baskets. But here's how you can store up great savings the next time you're shopping for baskets.

The Best for Less: Nantucket Baskets

Maybe you'd balk at paying $18,000 for a set of eight nesting baskets inlaid with whalebone and ivory. But others don't, knowing the care that goes into virtually every Nantucket basket.

Handmade from oak, cane, rattan and other materials in a rustic basement shop (sawdust on the floor, nails hammered into beams to hang displays), Nantucket baskets are known for their detail and tightness of weave. Retail prices at finer department stores start at $125 for a small basket and run well into five figures for more elaborate creations. But you can save on these world-renowned baskets by calling (508) 228-2518 and buying directly from the company, based in Nantucket, Massachusetts.

GREAT MAIL-ORDER BUYS

Save up to 50 percent on a wide variety of shapes, sizes and colors from the New England Basket Company in West Wareham, Massachusetts. You'll find sturdy country potato baskets, picnic hampers and pastel-tinted baskets perfect for holding or giving baked goods. There are even baskets made especially for the holidays. New England Basket Company also sells bows, ribbons, enclosure cards and even shrink wrap. Call 1-800-524-4484 for a catalog.

HEAD FOR WHOLESALERS. Most cities have a wholesale flower mart, where retail florists and caterers buy the freshest blooms in the wee hours of the morning. Basket dealers usually set up shop in or near these flower marts, selling their wares at up to 40 percent below retail. And many will sell to the public, provided you pay sales tax.

GO TO A SPECIALIST. From supermarkets to the corner five-and-dime store, you can find baskets just about everywhere. But you'll get the best deals at larger retailers that specialize in selling them—arts and crafts shops or basket retailers, for instance. Look for these stores in the yellow pages under "Arts and Crafts" or "Baskets"; you'll pay up to 20 percent less for the same item you'll find at grocery stores and other places. Plus, you'll get better-quality goods.

OR SHOP AT A "CASUAL" FURNITURE STORE. Another great place to find baskets for below retail is a store like Ikea or Pier 1 Imports that sells ready-to-assemble and other casual furniture. These chains have significant buying power and are able to buy baskets in sufficient volume to pass on savings in the 20 to 25 percent range.

BUY IN THE OFF-SEASON. Wherever you shop, it pays—or rather, saves—to go at the right time of year. You know you're going to need baskets for holiday centerpieces and decorations, and so does everyone else. So why wait to buy them? Prices increase up to 50 percent as Christmas and Easter approach. So buy in the off-season—from early May to early November and then again between January and March, when prices are at their lowest. The worst time to buy is between mid-November and late April.

MAKE SECONDHAND STORES A FIRST STOP. Of all the places to find rock-bottom deals on baskets, nothing beats a secondhand store or garage sale. Florists and caterers haunt them for deals—and often find gold in that straw. So before you pass up those tattered finds, consider a little repair work. If the basket has handles and one of them is loose or broken, just remove both of them. No one will ever know it wasn't made that way.

And with a can of spray paint, a hot-glue gun and decorations like pine cones, ribbon and bells, you can turn even the homeliest basket into a work of art. You can find decorating ideas in books sold at arts and crafts stores.

B.Y.O.B. If you're more interested in what's *inside* the basket than in the basket itself, take your own to a gourmet shop. They'll provide the goodies, and you can knock between $6 and $25 off the total bill.

BEDDING

Considering that you'll probably be spending three of the next ten years in bed, it pays to invest in a quality mattress and box spring. And as you may have noticed, it also costs.

On average, each piece (and there are two) of twin bedding costs in the range of $100 to $200, while full-size bedding is about $149 to $249 per piece. Both queen- and king-size beds are usually sold in sets—the mattress and box spring together generally cost between $500 and $900. The retail markup ranges from 45 to 200 percent, depending on where the bedding is sold. While bedding is often a matter of individual taste, here's how to get it for less money.

AVOID DEPARTMENT STORE SALES. Probably the worst place to buy bedding is at a department store, where prices are often inflated just to be reduced for a "sale." Industry insiders say that department stores tend to have the highest retail markup for bedding, charging up to 200 percent more than its wholesale cost. Then they put it on sale, but you're still paying twice what you would at furniture stores, bedding shops and warehouse clubs, which tend to have retail markups between 45 and 55 percent for their "everyday" prices.

CUSHION YOUR SAVINGS, NOT THE MATTRESS. Most mattresses have a couple of layers of 1.8-density foam, which is sufficient. But you can pay 40 percent more for additional layers of foam with a higher density. The mattress will feel softer, but experts advise buying a firmer mattress for better sleep and longer mattress life.

Also, some manufacturers stuff their beds with exotic cushioning like wool, cashmere, silk and other natural fibers. Not only do these fabrics cost more, but some, like cashmere, may bunch up and compact uncomfortably. Again, you're better off with the standard synthetics like Dacron and polyfills, which are comfortable and longer-lasting; they'll also cost at least 15 to 20 percent less than natural fabric fills. And the tufted, woven damask fabric on the outside of a mattress looks attractive, but it doesn't serve any real function

OUTSTANDING OUTLETS

Dial-a-Mattress is a unique telemarketer of bedding nationwide. With locations in many major cities, the phone retailer receives 5,000 calls a day for bedding that it sells at up to 60 percent less than department store prices.

The major bedding brands it sells are the Big Four: Sealy, Serta, Simmons and Spring-Air. (These four brands account for six out of ten beds sold in the United States.) Spring-Air is private-labeled as the telemarketer's house brand Dial-a-Pedic. That brand can save you an additional 15 to 20 percent.

When you call, a company bedding consultant will ask about size, needs and price range. The bedding is sent out within hours, depending on location, and you test it in your home then and there. If it's satisfactory, you pay on the spot. If not, it will be immediately removed, with no obligation.

Dial-a-Mattress charges $19 to $39 for delivery but will remove old bedding for free. The company sometimes runs promotional campaigns and provides free gifts with purchases, such as frequent flyer miles, jewelry and movie tickets. For ordering and other information, call Dial-a-Mattress at 1-800-MATTRES.

and can cost at least 20 percent more than a simple polyester chintz fabric.

BYPASS THE HANDLES. On mattresses, handles are sewn on the side more for looks than actual function: You can align the mattress just fine without them. The problem is that handles can tear off easily, and they add an average of 10 percent to the cost of a mattress compared to the same model without handles.

BUY IN SETS. No matter what the size, you're better off buying new bedding in sets—getting the mattress and box spring at the same time. Besides saving up to 20 percent compared to buying the pieces individually, experts say it helps your bedding last longer. Some people simply replace the mattress, but an older box spring may not adequately support a new mattress, causing it to sag prematurely.

CHOOSE A WOODEN FRAME. The highly touted steel frames marketed by some manufacturers typically add 20 percent to the cost of the bedding, but they don't add much proven benefit. Stick with the traditional wooden frame and you can pocket the difference—and you probably won't notice any difference in sleep quality.

NEGOTIATE FOR THE LONG HAUL. While there is no longer a "white sale" season, when you'll be likely to find better deals on bedding (those department store sales usually don't offer great bargains), many retailers are willing to cut prices—especially for those who make it easy for them. Offer 10 percent less than the retail price, and *insist* on it if you own a van or truck and can haul away your purchase.

Many retailers grudgingly offer delivery and removal of old bedding to bring people into their stores. But customers who haul their own bedding—and give their old mattress and box spring to charity—usually walk away with a better deal.

DON'T FAWN OVER WARRANTIES. A big marketing tool of bedding makers is the warranty, but some industry veterans say they're much ado about nothing. A 15-year warranty sounds impressive, but read the

THE BEST FOR LESS: KINGSDOWNS

Kingsdowns, a small manufacturer in Mebane, North Carolina, has been making the best-kept secret in bedding since 1904. While its bedding costs about the same as finer models by the Big Four (Sealy, Serta, Simmons and Spring-Air), Kingsdowns puts its money into materials and other manufacturing costs rather than advertising and promotion: a better grade of foam, "smarter" coils that adapt to your body; and other features.

The Kingsdowns Sleeping Beauty queen-size set retails for about $800—about the same as other top-of-the-line beds. Unfortunately, Kingsdowns sells its 50 different mattresses and box springs only at specialty bedding stores east of the Mississippi, mostly from New York to Florida. For more information on a dealer near you, call Kingsdowns at 1-800-354-5464.

fine print and you'll probably find that the guarantee is pro-rated on a sliding yearly scale, and the so-called guarantee is not very guaranteed. Also, some manufacturers require you to mail the defective bedding back to them, requiring you to foot the postage. Actually, if there's a problem with bedding, it will generally make itself known within the first six months after purchase—soon enough that you can call the store directly for a replacement.

Belts, Hats, Gloves and Scarves

Accessories like belts, hats, gloves and scarves may seem like frivolous wardrobe items. But judging by how much retailers charge for them, they're anything but. With a standard retail markup of 60 to 75 percent, some designer silk scarves, sculpted felt hats and Italian leather gloves and belts, for example, can easily cost more individually in department stores than an entire outfit.

But we pay it because these accessories can add an important component to a wardrobe—or make up for shortages in it. Depending on the styles you choose, these accents can help you look more

Great Mail-Order Buys

Get your name on the mailing list for Tweeds, based in Roanoke, Virginia, and you'll get a catalog featuring the latest in seasonal women's hats, scarves, classic leather belts and gloves (in addition to other classic and trend-setting fashions). Each Tweeds catalog features a clearance section offering a great selection of items at 20 to 25 percent less than regular prices (which tend to be slightly cheaper than retail). Tweeds usually publishes an end-of-season sale catalog twice a year offering similar savings on *all* items. To order your catalog, call 1-800-999-7997. (If you don't place an order within three months, the company will stop sending catalogs; if that happens, call to order another.)

mysterious, sophisticated, elegant, dapper, professional, funky or carefree. And here's how they can make you feel a little less poor.

SHOP SECONDHAND. Thrift stores, flea markets and consignment shops generally offer the best savings—as much as 90 percent below retail. Plus, they offer the best opportunity to get one-of-a-kind styles.

While most of their wares are preowned, more thrift stores, like the Cancer Care Retail Thrift Store in New York City, now sell donated merchandise. Because of this, some is brand new but sold at secondhand prices. If you buy used goods, examine them to make sure the stitching is even and there are no loose edges or tears. Leather items shouldn't be pitted, and gloves should have some give.

FOLLOW THE SEASONS. As with other apparel, accessories tend to be priced lowest by most retailers toward the end of a particular season. Beginning in July, for example, summer accessories such as straw hats and chiffon scarves are generally at least 50 percent less than regular retail prices. In August, prices fall even more. Likewise, December and January are good times to begin stocking up for the following year on discounted winter accessories like wool scarves, felt hats and leather belts and gloves. Watch for newspaper inserts advertising these deals, or browse through the store frequently, since some of these end-of-season sales are unadvertised.

Of course, you'll get the biggest savings at off-price stores like T.J. Maxx and Marshalls, which typically sell accessories for up to 60 percent less than full-price stores. Their end-of-season sales may offer the same savings percentages as department stores, but because of their lower prices, you'll save even more in real dollars.

BE AN EARLY BIRD. Another way to save on accessories is to buy them just as they hit the stores, although markdowns for preseason sales aren't as great as those in the postseason—usually in the 25 to 30 percent range. Preseason sales on fall accessories such as lined leather gloves and winter hats, for example, usually begin in August. And warm-weather styles usually go on sale in January.

BUY AT A BOUTIQUE. You can save at least 30 percent on belts, hats, gloves and scarves at specialty accessory shops, simply because they run frequent sales to build customer excitement about new merchandise and keep store traffic moving. An added bonus: Besides frequent sales, many accessory boutiques offer additional discounts to loyal customers with frequent-buyer programs that chop an additional 10 to 20 percent off prices.

Accessory boutiques usually offer a wide selection of classic-style

OUTSTANDING OUTLETS

Although it's technically a regular retail chain, The Icing is an 86-store operation that sells a wide array of fashionable hats, belts and scarves at 30 percent below regular retail prices throughout the year. Regular customers are then tracked by database so that they receive additional discount opportunities—namely coupons for 25 percent off and other discounts for the busy holiday shopping season.

Liz Claiborne hats, belts, scarves and gloves, which are traditionally fashionable, understated and classic, can be found at the 55 Liz Claiborne outlet stores across the country. Firmly rooted in savings, the outlets offer Claiborne merchandise for 40 percent less than their retail prices. Call (201) 662-6000 for the location of an outlet near you.

items, which can help you steer clear of trendy, one-season-only styles. A hint: When shopping, take the clothing items you intend to accessorize to the store with you to guarantee a good partnership.

STICK WITH THE BASICS. Wherever you shop, you'll get the most for your money by choosing accessories in conservative colors, styles and patterns. Your best bets for long-wearing colors include the core neutrals—black, brown, beige, navy, off-white, gray and burgundy. Avoid extreme hues like russet, most shades of green, pinks, purples and plaids. Style-wise, anything that's in style right now will likely last only one season, so stick with classics, such as a black straw hat instead of one that features a large flower or a brown or black leather belt rather than one in a leopard print or hot pink.

TREAT 'EM RIGHT. To make your savings last, treat your purchases with care. Always store gloves flat. Belts should be hung or rolled, not bent. Stuff tissue paper in the crowns of hats to help gather hair spray and dirt that may remain from your hair and place the hats in individual boxes to keep them from gathering dust. Scarves should be folded and stored flat. If they become wrinkled, iron them with a warm iron, using a pillow case as a protective go-between.

Bicycles

In the retail bicycle business, less is more. The lighter the bike, the more you'll pay. But technological advances also mean you can ultimately get more bike for less money.

About 13 million bicycles are sold in America each year, a number that hasn't changed much in the last few decades. What has changed is the type of bikes being sold: The once-trendy ten-speed, narrow-wheeled road bikes have been falling out of style, replaced by fat-tire, off-road mountain or hybrid bikes, which now account for two of every three bicycles sold in the United States.

Actually, there are over 1,000 different types of bicycles manufactured by over 100 companies for the U.S. market. The lowest-cost bicycles tend to be made of steel. As the price goes up, the materials "lighten up" to more costly aluminum, titanium and chromium. But no matter what you buy, here's how to get it for less.

Buy in the fall. Nearly one-quarter of all bicycles are sold in October and November—and with good reason. Most dealers order their new inventory after two big trade shows in September. The new stock starts arriving in October, meaning that dealers need to clear their showrooms and usually offer the best deals of the year in those two months. Look for discounts at bike shops in the 15 to 25 percent range on most inventory, but for even greater savings, ask the dealer if there are any leftover unassembled bicycles in the basement.

If there's no marked price reduction, ask for one: You're in the best position of the year to negotiate a discount of up to 25 percent.

Go to a discount store. Mass merchandisers like Wal-Mart, Kmart and Toys "R" Us handle 83 percent of all the bicycles sold in the United States, and there's a good reason that these stores sell so many bikes: Their average price is about $110, compared to $250 for a comparable model in a specialty bike shop.

Don't think you're getting a bargain on a lousy bike. While the choice of brands is smaller and product knowledge more limited

THE BEST FOR LESS: SPECIALIZED ROCKHOPPER COMP A1

There are definitely more expensive mountain bikes—serious riders often shell out several thousand dollars for a top brand. But there are few that are better than the Specialized RockHopper Comp A1—despite its relatively low cost of about $700.

Named the beginner's choice for 1995 by *Mountain Bike* magazine, this bike, built in the United States, is stylish and durable. But experts say that, unlike most other beginners' bikes, you won't outgrow the RockHopper, even if your casual interest in mountain biking turns into an off-road compulsion.

You're most likely to wheel and deal a discount on this bike in early fall, as retailers try to clear their inventory for the new stock that arrives in October. For more information on where to buy a RockHopper, call (408) 779-6229.

than what you'll find at a bike shop, many marts have begun to carry quality entry-level models with brand-name components from the same manufacturers that have traditionally supplied bike shops.

OR HEAD TO A WAREHOUSE CLUB. You'll notice that there aren't a lot of bicycles sold at warehouse clubs like Sam's Club and B.J.'s Wholesale Club. But occasionally you will see a great deal on some models—up to 60 percent below bike shop prices. There's nothing wrong with these bicycles: They are usually diverted to warehouse clubs by middlemen who buy the inventories of bankrupt bike shops.

KEEP IT SIMPLE. Wherever you buy, avoid the biggest novice rider's no-no: Buying more bike than you need. Most casual bicyclists will have a hard time distinguishing between a $500 mountain bike and a $1,300 model. And technological advances—especially in shifting—mean you'll pay a basic price for a solid product that to most riders is virtually indistinguishable from the more expensive styles.

In fact, you should beware of a low-cost bike with lots of options. If you get suspension on an entry-level mountain bike, for instance, as-

GREAT MAIL-ORDER BUYS

Two mail-order houses dominate the industry—and according to some experts, the dominance is well-deserved. Performance, based in Chapel Hill, North Carolina, and Bike Nashbar, in Youngstown, Ohio, offer similar savings, with frequent sales that slash the costs of bikes and accessories anywhere from 10 to 50 percent off regular prices. They will refund the difference if the product you buy goes on sale within 15 days (Bike Nashbar) or 30 days (Performance) after delivery.

Bike Nashbar also operates a discount outlet next to its headquarters in Ohio. To order catalogs, call Performance at 1-800-727-2453 and Bike Nashbar at 1-800-NASHBAR.

sume the manufacturer has cut corners elsewhere. Most bike components are interchangeable, making it easy enough to upgrade, so instead of making a huge initial investment, buy basic and see if you enjoy the sport. If you do, it's cheaper to upgrade later.

BUY USED. Serious cyclists are constantly trading up, which means there are a lot of great used bikes for sale—usually selling for 30 to 50 percent less than a similar new bike. Check the classified ad section of the local newspaper or call Cycle $eller, a national used-bicycle exchange based in Chicago, at (312) 292-9292. But before buying any used bike from the classified ads—especially sight unseen—ask the seller to take it to a dealer for an experienced opinion.

DICKER OVER THE EXTRAS. Because inventory is so controlled by manufacturers and there's not much in the way of closeouts, surplus or damaged goods, don't expect to do a lot of negotiating when buying a new bike. In fact, many bike shops make their money from repairs, spare parts and accessories—not the bikes themselves.

But you can dicker over the cost of accessories like helmets, gloves and other equipment—especially when you're buying a new bike. Generally you can get a flat 10 to 15 percent off accessories, or the bike shop may be willing to either upgrade the components on a bicycle you want without adding to the price or downgrade to a generic brand and pass the savings on to you.

Binoculars and Telescopes

Bird-watching and staring at the stars are inexpensive ways to gain appreciation for God's creation. But if you want to take a closer look, it's going to cost you.

Binoculars and telescopes are a $60-million-a-year business, with choices ranging from $20 models at the local toy store to $16,000 computerized units. The funny thing is, margins are so thin on these more expensive models—only 10 to 15 percent—that retailers actually make more profit selling the junky department store versions.

But whatever your price range or needs, here's how to avoid spending astronomical amounts in your quest to scan the heavens—or whatever else holds your interest.

Binoculars

Know the unwritten rule of "performance" pricing. Insiders have a rule of thumb when pricing binoculars: Every time the price doubles between $50 and $250, performance improves by 20 percent. But when the price doubles after $250, performance improves by only about 10 percent. So while hefty price tags and pushy salesclerks may try to make you think more expensive binoculars are better, your eye—and wallet—should be the final arbiter.

Focus on the slow selling seasons. Weather helps dictate price breaks, so the extreme temperature months of January, February, June, July and August are slow periods for binocular sales. You may find retailers ready to knock 10 to 20 percent off retail at these times. If you don't see advertised sales, ask for a discount.

Make a mail-order purchase. It's common to find binoculars discounted 10 to 40 percent by mail-order companies. An example: Although Bushnell Nature View binoculars cost about $160 retail, most mail-order houses trim that price to around $120. With a lifetime warranty, a fine focus and easier use and less eyestrain for glasses

THE BEST FOR LESS: MEADE 12-INCH LX-200 (TELESCOPE) AND CELESTRON 12 × 80 (BINOCULARS)

Weighing in at 313 pounds and featuring state-of-the-art optics, the 16-inch Meade LX-200 telescope certainly will make you feel like you got your money's worth—all $15,000 plus shipping and handling. But for a quarter of the price, you can have three-quarters of the performance with a Meade 12-inch LX-200. It weighs just 120 pounds, and it's considered the best "portable" telescope available. Call Meade at (714) 556-2291 for a dealer near you.

And when the experts compare notes on the best binoculars, one model heads the list: Fujinon's FMTSX Polaris series. Featuring a flat field—which prevents distortion of images at the edge of the view—this model lists for $880. But you can get Fujinon quality for about $250 less by opting for the Celestron 12 × 80. It's available at binocular dealers or through mail-order companies.

wearers, experts say the Nature View is probably the only pair of binoculars you'll ever need. You'll find a good selection of binoculars in some photography equipment catalogs, which are advertised in photo magazines like *Shutterbug*.

TELESCOPES

HANG OUT WITH STARGAZERS. Before you spend a dime on a telescope, experts recommend that you spend some time with a local astronomy club. Numbering over two million nationally, members of these clubs are often willing to share their telescopes and knowledge to help you find the best model for your money. Some clubs even get discounts for buying telescopes at a group rate.

Astronomy magazine publishes a yearly Observer's Guide that contains a list of North American astronomy clubs. If your library doesn't have a copy, call the magazine at (414) 796-8776.

REMEMBER YOUR JS. You could save between 10 and 30 percent by buying your telescope at the right time—namely the middle of the summer or just after Christmas. Sales are brisk during spring and fall—the peak viewing seasons—but as with binoculars, extreme hot and cold weather puts a chill on sales, with only the hard-core observers buying at that time. This results in retailers lowering prices. Start looking for savings in early July and January; each sale season will last about two months.

KEEP IT SIMPLE. Telescopes that feature computers capable of finding, tracking and photographing stars are popular and cost several thousand dollars. But you shouldn't spend more than $300 to $500 on a quality entry-level reflector telescope made by a reputable manufacturer like Meade. Although short on gizmos, experts say these telescopes have six- to eight-inch apertures—the unit that captures light and makes viewing possible. For best viewing, you shouldn't have an aperture of less than four inches.

If you're convinced stargazing is your next full-fledged hobby, you might consider a $900 model. Although most telescopes in this price range are still without a lot of extras, experts say you'll literally be able to see the edges of our solar system.

PUT A USED TELESCOPE UNDER THE MICROSCOPE. Where once you were lucky to a find a single used telescope at a garage sale, the used-optics market is now a business—even supporting its own publications like *The Starry Messenger*, a monthly newsletter that bills itself as the "Astronomy Classified Shopper." In one recent issue, a used Schmidt-Cassegrain telescope that retails for $1,300 new was offered for $800. You'll also get good deals on used telescopes from astronomy club members looking to upgrade. And if you cruise the information superhighway, check out ads on America Online and Internet newsgroups from people who are selling and swapping optical equipment.

The Starry Messenger is $3 an issue, or $23 a year, and contains 24 pages of classified ads per issue, offering deals on telescopes for less than half their retail price. For information, write P.O. Box 6552-J, Ithaca, NY 14851. *Astronomy* and *Sky and Telescope* magazines also carry classified ads for used equipment and are available at better-stocked libraries and newsstands.

UPGRADE THAT OLD PURCHASE. Before you step up to a higher-priced

GREAT MAIL-ORDER BUYS

You can get some of the best prices on binoculars and telescopes by ordering through the mail. One company, Astronomics in Norman, Oklahoma, sells quality optics for as much as 40 percent off suggested retail. For a free catalog featuring telescopes and binoculars, call 1-800-422-7876.

model, try upgrading your present telescope; you could save several hundred dollars. Spending $50 on a new eyepiece, for example, could provide a wider field of view and richer colors. A new finder scope—also $50—grabs more light and makes viewing easier, while a new mount helps ensure sharper focus and prevents the telescope from jiggling. These small outlays can help more serious stargazers avoid the expense of a new telescope, but don't bother upgrading if your aperture is smaller than four inches. If so, it's time to buy another telescope.

TRAP ONE IN BIG BEAR. Held each Memorial Day, the Riverside Telescope Makers Conference in Big Bear, California, is geared toward binocular and telescope hobbyists. The major manufacturers are there with seconds and discontinued lines, which are sold for as much as 80 percent below retail.

The fee for attending the conference ranges from $15 to $75, depending upon accommodations. Contact Robert Stephens, Riverside Telescope Makers Conference, 9045 Haven Avenue, Suite 109, Rancho Cucamonga, CA 91730.

Boats

You could fill a barge with all the things a potential boat owner needs to consider before making a purchase.

There's size: Experts say it's best to buy the longest boat you can tow, handle and store. That's because longer boats generally ride and sail better and are more forgiving, roomier and safer.

There's engine type—inboard or outboard? Number of sails (the more, the better)? Hand-laid or sprayed-on fiberglass? Even the number of seats in a canoe needs to be considered.

But perhaps the biggest question is price. Boat dealers normally work on a 25 percent profit margin but are usually willing to sell their wares for 10 to 15 percent below the sticker price. So whether you're buying a dinghy or a yacht, here's how to keep from sinking in an ocean of debt when you buy.

Add your own options and save. Since large profit margins on options are standard in the boating industry, you can save as much as 50 percent on the cost of each option when you install it yourself. And that can translate into savings of literally thousands of dollars when you consider the laundry list of potential items—everything from bottom paint to microwave ovens. Install a 30-amp battery charger on your own, for instance, and you'll save almost $300, or add a remote spotlight after purchase and save $200; having these options dealer-installed just about doubles their cost.

The one caveat with do-it-yourself installation is that it requires ordering a boat without the options you plan to install. Since many boats are already outfitted with certain options, this cuts into your savings strategy.

Buy an unfinished boat and build it. Few pleasure boat builders offer their products in partially completed form, but many builders of work boats do. These don't have the cosmetic glitter you may have come to expect, but they are well-built and offered at various stages of completion—saving you at least 25 percent off the cost of a ready-

THE BEST FOR LESS: MASTERCRAFT

Those who know ski boats and other runabouts know there are basically two names that leave the others in the dust . . . or rather, the docks: MasterCraft and Correct Craft Ski Nautique. Choosing the best is a toss-up, since experts agree that both are superb vessels.

But the MasterCraft might have a slight edge, since it's the boat most used in water-ski tournaments. And while a new MasterCraft might cost you between $25,000 and $36,000, depending on the model, you could get it for 20 to 30 percent less by buying a promo MasterCraft that's been used in ski tournaments. These promo boats are expertly maintained and usually used for one season of tournaments, then sold—usually with a full warranty. And unlike other boats, these promos tend to have all the bells and whistles.

You may have to be patient to get this kind of deal because promo boats are often promised to buyers a year ahead of time. You'll also need to track down a promo boat. Your best bet: Start attending water-ski tournaments. To find out about schedules for state and pro tours, look in magazines such as *Water Ski* magazine or contact the American Water Ski Association at 1-800-533-2972.

made boat. On the East Coast these boats are called kit boats; on the West Coast they're called partials. To find one, check *National Fisherman* magazine.

If you're an energetic boat lover, you can buy plans and build your own wooden boat. Wooden boat-building courses are offered at various locations, particularly in Seattle and Maine. For more information, see a copy of *Wooden Boat* magazine.

SHOP THE BOAT SHOWS. Attending a boat show is perhaps one of the best ways to do comparison shopping. But boat shows are also great places to save up to 25 percent off retail prices, because shows typically occur during the off-season, when dealers have more incentive to negotiate. During shows, dealers can also offer volume discounts not available at other times of the year. Take your time, and be prepared to make more than one trip to the show. But be wary of glitzy showroom features that you won't use after you buy the boat, such as a full galley under the port seat of ski boats.

BUY LAST YEAR'S MODEL. Many dealers will sell leftover boats at only a few hundred dollars above their cost in an effort to move them out—and normally, you'll still get the full warranty. You'll save at least 10 percent by buying last year's inventory, but the downside is that you usually can't get the selection or the freedom to pick and choose op-

GREAT MAIL-ORDER BUYS

There are many discount marine supply catalogs that sell everything from boating supplies to the actual vessels. But insiders say that the two best—offering substantial discounts over retail—are West Marine and M&E Marine Supply Company.

Both companies offer comparable discount pricing, although the West Marine catalog, with its 864 pages and full-color format, is more comprehensive and easier to read. The catalog, available by calling 1-800-538-0775, also includes the "West Advisor," an in-depth buyers' guide with information on several categories. Within the section on navigation equipment, for instance, is a one-page guide complete with color graphics on what to look for when buying night vision scopes, what they do and how they work. Based in California, West Marine also operates 62 discount marine stores nationwide, which are listed in the catalog.

M&E Marine Supply Company operates four discount stores—three in its headquarters state of New Jersey and one in Delaware. Its catalog offers similar savings but is printed in a no-frills black-and-white format with a few color pages. Call 1-800-541-6501 to order yours for $2.

tions that you do when you buy the current model year.

TRIM THE TRAILER. A boat trailer typically costs $1,200 to $1,500. But if you boat in just one area in the summer and use the trailer only to pull the boat in and out of the water, you may be better off paying someone to store and launch your boat; that usually runs about $200 a year. Since the average person keeps a boat for only three years, you'll end up saving money in the long run.

SHOP IN MIAMI. The best place to buy a boat outside of a boat show is Florida, where over $352 million is spent on boats each year—far more than in any other state. You can also save on used boats in Florida because there are so many boat dealers and competition is stiff. There are two drawbacks, however. First, the cost of transporting the boat back to your home port may outweigh the savings, so keep that in mind before signing on the dotted line. And second, Florida waters are notoriously hard on boats, so beware when purchasing a boat that has cruised those beautiful subtropical waters. Overall, if you're in the market for a used boat, try to find one that's been used mainly on fresh water.

GO FOR A REPO. Repossessed boats often cost 35 percent less than new models, and since they've been seized from their owners—usually without warning—they're usually already equipped with life jackets, water sports equipment and other accessories. You can find repo boats at boat dealers and auctions and through newspaper classified ads. But be warned: Some repos may not be well-maintained.

As with other used boats, you should never buy a repo without having it inspected by a certified marine surveyor, who is able to determine the soundness of the vessel. And with any boat, never make a purchase without first taking it on a trial run in the same type of waters you'll be sailing.

Books

Who says nobody reads anymore? Americans buy over two billion books annually—about 40 million more *each year* since last decade. That translates to over $23 billion a year for the latest and greatest hardcovers and paperbacks. But the quest to feed your mind doesn't have to empty your wallet if you follow these tips.

Buy books where you buy underwear. Book for book, you'll get the best deals at a discount department store chain like Kmart or a warehouse club like Sam's Club. Large supermarket and drugstore chains also have substantial discounts off retail prices. In fact, these nontraditional book-selling venues now account for 40 percent of all book sales; independent bookstores handle only one-third of the market.

Outstanding Outlets

Started in the home of an MIT-trained chemist in 1957, the New England Mobile Book Fair is now run by his sons out of a sprawling warehouse in Newton, Massachusetts, on the outskirts of Boston. What it lacks in charm, it makes up for in economy. There isn't much overhead, and the family is renowned among publishers for negotiating the lowest conceivable wholesale price. Almost all the books are 20 percent off—specials are even cheaper—and the inventory is fabulous. Ask any employee about almost any book, and chances are he's read it and can find it among the millions of volumes. The Book Fair also sells by mail order. For more information, call (617) 527-5817.

The reason: A warehouse store can buy thousands of copies of a single title from publishers and wholesalers; the owner of a corner bookstore can stock maybe a dozen. Because these chains buy such large quantities, they get great deals from the publishers and can sell the books to you minus the typical 40 percent retail markup. Of course, selection is more limited than at a bookstore, but these chains usually stock the hottest best-sellers and other sought-after titles.

GET SUPER DEALS AT A SUPERSTORE. If you like the ambience and inventory of a traditional bookstore, head for the *right* bookstore—a big one. Tiny mall bookstores pay high rent and can't buy in sufficient quantities to pass substantial savings on to you. But because of their size, "superstores" run by companies like Barnes and Noble have buying power similar to that of chain stores and get much of their inventory directly from the publishers. That translates to discounts of 10 to 20 percent for most books, and best-sellers are often 30 percent below retail. Encore Books and Borders Books and Music offer similar savings as well as a knowledgeable staff and a large inventory.

BUY IT HOT OFF THE PRESSES. Publishers sometimes lower the price on a first printing to help boost sales, then raise it for new editions. So a new book—especially one by a "hot" author—can be anywhere from 10 to 25 percent less than future printings. This is especially true of books that are expected to become movies.

LOOK FOR THE MARK OF A REMAINDER. You can also save by looking for remainders in mid-August and during the last fiscal quarter (between October and December), as publishers try to unload their warehouse inventory to make room for new titles or because the book's sales are fatiguing. You can tell you're getting a remainder because it has a small notch or a thick line running across the pages at the top or bottom of the book. Different stores offer different discounts, but discounts on some books can be as much as 90 percent off regular retail prices.

ASK TO BROWSE THROUGH THE "DAMAGED" BOXES. When the roof leaks at the print shop or a crate of books falls off a truck, publishers pile the damaged goods on factory skids and sell them to retailers in sealed boxes for next to nothing. There are best-sellers along with throwaways, great books and lousy ones. Retailers wind up tossing about one-third of these, and many others end up in those $1.99 racks set up at the front of the store to lure you in. But there are many diamonds in the rough, and with a little digging around, you can find some great books for next to nothing. Incidentally, these sealed

GREAT MAIL-ORDER BUYS

Daedalus Books, in Hyattsville, Maryland, sells books and remainders through a free catalog filled with long reviews by members of its staff. Current titles sell for 25 percent below retail and recent hardcover books for as little as $4.98. Get your catalog by calling 1-800-395-2665. Shipping charges nibble at your savings, but you don't have to pay sales tax unless your books are delivered to a Maryland address.

Upper Access Books specializes in hard-to-find books from smaller publishers; many are remainders or have minor damage, such as a dented cover (the pages are fine). Discounts are in the 20 percent range. A free catalog from the Hinesburg, Vermont, company is available by calling 1-800-356-9315.

boxes are the main supply source for the books-for-a-buck joints down at the hard-luck mall or factory outlet center.

BUY THROUGH THE MAIL. If you read a lot, consider joining a book club. While you'll pay about $3.40 in shipping and handling costs for the first book, you can still save if you buy several books. That's because book clubs offer current titles at 10 to 30 percent below retail prices, and the more you buy, the lower your shipping costs per book. An added bonus: When you buy three or more books, some clubs offer incentives that can cut individual prices in half.

There are more than 120 book clubs in the United States, many specializing in hard-to-find categories. Together, they sell $800 million worth of books per year. Some, like the Quality Paperback Book Club, offer otherwise unavailable paperback editions of current titles at up to 75 percent off the hardcover cost.

PLAY THE WAITING GAME. Generally it takes between six months and a year for a hardcover book to come out in paperback, which tends to be less than half the price of the hardcover. A paperback is the same book, except for the cover and a smaller size. So if you don't mind waiting, you can get your books for a lot less just by holding out for the paperback.

Briefcases and Portfolios

A business case is equal parts carrying case and fashion statement, a fact that helps retailers sell seven million of them each year at an average price of $60. But since many cost hundreds or even thousands of dollars—$5,800 for ostrich skin and $7,800 for American alligator attachés from Charles Underwood of Dallas, for example—that's a good indication that there are plenty of bargains at the low end.

There are three types of business cases: the old-fashioned box-shaped, hard-sided attaché, whose sales have fallen from nearly all of the market to barely a third; the flat, zippered envelope, carried under the arm; and the briefcase, which opens at the top and whose name originated from the fact that it once was used exclusively by lawyers to carry legal briefs. These days, the name *briefcase* is commonly used to describe all three types of business bags. But whatever your taste, here's how to get it for less.

Buy in July—or January. Is it really necessary to have one briefcase for the winter and another for the spring? Manufacturers think so.

Great Mail-Order Buys

With low overhead, many mail-order companies are able to sell brand-name business cases for as little as half the regular retail price. Two of the best include Ace Luggage and Gifts in Brooklyn (1-800-DIAL-ACE, or 718-891-9713 for New York residents) and Al's Luggage in Denver (303-295-9009), which sells mostly Samsonite and Travel Pro.

OUTSTANDING OUTLETS

A division of the classy El Portal luggage company, California Luggage Outlets sell high-end briefcases at 20 to 50 percent off retail prices. The merchandise consists of closeout, discontinued, irregular and shopworn merchandise from Hartmann, Tumi, Samsonite and Zero Halliburton, whose molded aluminum models come with a lifetime guarantee and aren't available anywhere else at a discount. California Luggage Outlets have stores in three states—California, Nevada and Hawaii—but there are plans to expand soon to Arizona and Colorado and ultimately nationwide. Call (707) 447-7720 for locations.

They introduce new designs twice a year, and that's when the past season's products go on sale. Briefcases sold in fall and winter use heavier-grained materials and deeper tones in keeping with the season. In spring and summer you'll see more design elements, such as side panels and a fabric lining.

What does this mean to you? End-of-season clearance sales in July and January with savings of 25 to 50 percent below regular retail prices. Many briefcase manufacturers also encourage sales in the spring, when Father's Day and graduation season converge, although savings might be slightly lower.

SAVE WITH SCRAPS. Most quality briefcases sold are made of leather, and the grade affects both quality and cost. Top- and full-grain leathers come from surface layers of the hide; they're the most durable but also the most expensive. Split leather is from the underside; while it's not quite as durable, it is cheaper. But you'll save the most—about 30 percent or more—by buying reconstituted leather, which is made from scraps that are glued together and finished so the seams don't show.

OR GO WITH MAN-MADE MATERIALS. Of course, vinyl is the cheapest alternative to leather, starting around $20, but it doesn't look as good or last as long. If you're looking for a quality briefcase, check out molded plastic or aluminum cases. They're virtually indestructible, have a slick, "high-tech" look and start at about $40.

Another alternative: Canvas and nylon totes with shoulder straps. These are not only cheaper than leather but also newly fashionable, practical, durable and generally waterproof. Many are expandable and can double as carry-on bags. To buy the best, look at popular mail-order catalogs—or better yet, check out manufacturer's outlet stores. Several models are available for $20 to $50 at Eddie Bauer's 40 outlet stores; call 1-800-645-7467 for locations.

LOOK FOR A LOOK-ALIKE. Top-grade manufacturers are selling you their name, and it costs a bundle. But you can get nearly identical briefcases with no-name brands at half the cost. For example, Jack Georges makes bags that look and feel like Coach bags, but without the prestigious name and at about half the price.

BE OUTLET BOUND. About 1 in 13 briefcases is sold at outlets—and

THE BEST FOR LESS: HARTMANN

In an age of vinyl knockoffs from Asia, Hartmann business cases are made in America with generous full-grain leather, nickel-plated hardware, padded handles, brass locks and other fine materials. Hard-sided attachés use only wood frames, and the seams are hand-sewn. But this quality costs, and Hartmanns go for $195 to $1,365, depending on the styling and materials, at department stores and luggage shops.

But you can pick one up for as little as half that price at the factory store in Lebanon, Tennessee. If Tennessee isn't in your travel plans, don't worry. You'll find irregular and discontinued Hartmann business cases at clearance prices in five national outlet stores that are cleverly disguised under the name of Hartmann's parent company, Lenox, which makes pricey dinnerware and fine china. For the Lenox shop near you, call 1-800-331-0613; there's one each in Maine, New York, Georgia, Texas and Pennsylvania.

with good reason. Manufacturers are often left with discontinued overstock that hasn't even left the warehouse when the season ends. So this inventory increasingly is shipped to company outlet stores, which sell the merchandise at 20 to 60 percent off the retail price, no matter what the season.

Even the premium names now have outlet stores and clearance centers. Some, such as American Tourister, sell first-quality, in-season business cases at 25 to 50 percent off their regular prices; call 1-800-547-2247 for locations of the company's 120 outlet stores. Bally (1-800-332-2559) has 10 outlets in the United States and 1 in Canada, with discounts of from 25 to 50 percent, while Coach (1-800-444-3611) sells its high-quality classic leather goods at 20 to 25 percent below regular prices in its Coach Factory Store outlets. You'll also find bags there from the Coach "sister" company, Mark Cross, for the same discounts. And Samsonite (1-800-262-8282) has 12 outlets across the country.

There are two national chains that sell a variety of brands at outlet prices: Leather Loft (603-778-0374) and Bag and Baggage (1-800-360-0829).

OR HEAD TO AN OFFICE SUPPLY STORE. Since a briefcase is basically a traveling office, it makes sense—and saves dollars—to buy one at an office supply store. Stores such as Office Depot, OfficeMax and Staples sell one of every five briefcases in America. And while selection is more limited, you'll save up to 40 percent.

BUILDING SUPPLIES

It's hard to imagine that a little more than just a century ago, houses were constructed from materials gathered right at the building site. The skill of the woodwright turned cut timber into a finished structure, and only a few things—perhaps nails and glass—had to be sent from elsewhere. Today manufacturing plants do the preparation and millwork, and a large percentage of building materials are manmade from minerals and synthetics.

So now it's the skill of the shopper that plays the key role when it comes to building supplies. Americans buy over $105 billion worth of building supplies each year—and the supply network is multilayered and complex. But among all this structure there's still room for a bargain. Here's how to get it.

BUY WITH YOUR BUDDIES. As with other merchandise, building supplies are cheaper by the dozen—or in orders large enough to warrant a volume discount. A minor repair job might make it difficult to buy in quantity, but if you can coordinate projects with friends or neighbors, you can save up to 15 percent.

You're most likely to get the best break at an independent lumberyard rather than one of the large home centers, but keep in mind that those independents tend to be more expensive to start with. To sweeten the deal, be ready to pay in cash or by check rather than charging your purchase to plastic or putting it on account.

SALVAGE THOSE SAVINGS. The word *salvage* can imply used or damaged goods, but not in this case. Lumber and other related building supplies are a commodity, traded on a market rather than priced through a calculated series of psychological marketing strategies. Supply and demand dictate the cost, and the buying and selling climate can change quickly and without warning.

Salvage supply warehouses deal in all sorts of building supplies—lumber, plywood, doors, windows, drywall, paneling and roofing. If you're looking for the best price, you needn't worry about where the

HEAD FOR THE HILLS

Lumber is only one of the commodities of the building trade, but it's one you can get for 40 percent less than retail if you happen to live in or near a rural community.

That's because they're outside the big cities, in locations where the independent sawmills thrive, and they're the source for sound, full-dimension lumber in a range of species beyond the lumberyard woods harvested for the commercial market. Wood bought directly from a sawmill can be custom-cut or picked from yard stock already cut to standard dimensions. Local sawmills can usually plane and surface the lumber at their site for a minimal charge, and they will usually deliver, too.

Finding an independent sawmill near you may not be easy. It's not the kind of operation that's likely to be listed in the yellow pages, so you may have to ask local woodworkers or carpenters or contact millwork shops to get some leads.

merchandise came from; sources include speculative buyers, unclaimed rail shipments and bankrupt developers. Depending on the market, you can save up to 25 percent compared to buying retail. You'll find these salvage supply warehouses mostly through word of mouth, but also check the yellow pages.

DICKER FOR DAMAGED GOODS. A large building supply retailer moves tons of merchandise every week, and a portion of it is bound to get damaged in handling. But by taking the time to ask to see these damaged goods—which are usually set aside for insurance adjustment, return or salvage—you can get incredible deals: A $42 screen door with a take-it-away price of $10 because the screen is ripped, or a stack of drywall worth $290 being sold for one-third the cost. Be prepared to do some repairs, but the overall savings are there.

The best way to get in on it is to circumvent the inside counterman completely and go directly to the customer loading dock at the back of the store. Locate the shipping supervisor and ask to see what's been damaged. Sometimes the store will put a "sold as is" price on the goods; in other cases, you may have to make an offer. In either case, be ready to take it away on the spot.

HIT THE MASS MARKETS. Since building supplies don't lend themselves to mail-order sales, the only other way for companies to amass the needed clout to buy in the staggering volumes they do is to operate the huge warehouse-style sales outlets we've become familiar with: Home Depot, Lowe's and other prominent national chains.

By and large, outfits such as these can offer the best "general" discount pricing compared to local lumberyards or independent building supply dealers—as much as 30 percent on some items. They also carry a wide selection and keep a large stock on hand. Keep in mind, though, that in comparing item for item, the large merchandisers may not be able to beat the prices of salvage-warehouse dealers or the occasional closeout specials of local lumberyards.

Camcorders

Once the size of a suitcase, camcorders now fit in your palm—their weight has fallen from more than 13 pounds to less than 2. The only problem is, with an average starting price of $500, you may feel you have to grease the palm of the camcorder salesman.

Not necessarily. Because camcorders are such a high-ticket item, only about three million are sold in America each year—about half in the 8mm format, 30 percent in the compact-VHS version (which uses smaller VHS tapes that are transferred to a regular cassette) and 20 percent that use standard VHS cassettes. But no matter what you're shopping for, here's how to get it for less.

Head to an electronics store. The best deals on camcorders aren't in camera shops—they're at huge electronics discounters like Circuit City. These megachains buy in huge quantities, so they're able to sell their wares for less. But even more significant, their sales staff tends to work on commission, and since camcorders are owned by only 4 percent of Americans, they know that camcorders aren't a fast-moving item.

The result: In order to make the sale—and their commission—they know they often have to negotiate a lower price. So even if you see a camcorder on sale, shoot for a price break of 15 to 20 percent—especially if you're shopping at the end of the month, when sales quotas are being tallied.

Read all about it. The back pages of magazines like *Video* feature ads from companies offering prices below even those you'll find at electronics stores. *Video* refuses to accept ads from businesses accused of unfair trading practices, so if you see ads from a company appearing consistently in that magazine, you'll know the seller is on the up-and-up.

These magazines also have regular buyers' guides with brand evaluations. But when buying by mail order, beware of excessive shipping charges and the common 5 to 10 percent "restocking" fees for

WHAT DO YOU NEED?

There are 125 different models of camcorders on the market, and it pays to know exactly what you need before you shop.

First, choose a format: The less frequently advertised models that take 8mm tapes record up to two hours, versus 30 minutes for most VHS models, and tend to have better sound. But realize that the tapes won't work in your VCR, and you may have to view them by connecting your camcorder directly into your TV set, in the same outlets where you plug in your VCR.

High-band versions of both formats (Hi-8 and Super-VHS-C) will practically double your cost, but the quality is noticeably better. You can also get special effects features to create titles, closeups, dissolves, freeze-frames, zooms and wide angles. But those features aren't necessary for most people.

What you do want, feature-wise, is a power zoom that allows closeups and far shots to remain in focus with the push of a button so you don't have to focus the lens by hand. You'll also want a color viewfinder, built-in light and an image stabilizer, which all but eliminates shaking.

returns. These two items can be negotiated by the savvy customer.

MAKE SURE YOU'RE GETTING THE ENTIRE PACKAGE. No matter where you buy, be sure that your purchase includes *all* the extras: a recharger, a rechargeable battery, cables, a shoulder strap and an adapter. Some companies advertise low prices for the camcorder itself and then sock you with the price of the accessories. But manufacturers are selling the whole package.

In fact, it doesn't hurt to ask about getting an extra battery, shoulder mount, camera bag or tripod. Stores that are trying to move their inventory will often throw in one of these extras (but don't expect all four).

BUY BIG. You may notice that even in the standard VHS format—the largest and heaviest camcorders—models tend to get smaller and smaller each year for easier handling. By seeking out a bigger model, or any "older" type, you can save 30 percent or more. The cameras

THE NAME GAME

What's in a name? Apparently, very little when it comes to camcorders. There may be a wide range of prices from brand to brand, but consider this: Ricoh and Nikon camcorders are actually made by Sony. And Quasar, Panasonic, JVC and some Minolta camcorders are all manufactured by Matsushita in Japan. So when you're shopping, keep features in mind instead of brand loyalty.

work just as well, except they may lack some of the newer features that many home moviemakers really don't need.

So when you're shopping, ask the sales staff for last year's model or anything in the back room from previous years. As with other items, prices tend to increase slightly with each year because of "new and improved" features. But if you want a good, basic, new camcorder at a good price, seek an older version.

SHOP FOR A RENTAL. If you only need a camcorder for a special occasion or two, you're better off renting one at the local video store or camera shop—for about $10 a day. But if you think you'll be using a camcorder more than 50 times over the course of the next few years, you may want to buy one of these rentals—for anywhere from 35 to 60 percent less than a new one. You'll be buying used, but the stock tends to be very well-maintained for its frequent use.

Camping and Hiking Equipment

Nearly 74 million campers and hikers pack up their outdoor gear at least once a year to commune with Mother Nature. However, even an occasional few days of roughing it in the Great Outdoors can be a great strain on your finances, requiring several hundred dollars' worth of tents, sleeping bags and backpacks to stow equipment like lanterns, stoves, cookware, coolers and clothing.

All told, camping and hiking equipment has become a $1 billion-plus industry, with retailers ranging from discount chains like Wal-Mart and Kmart to specialty shops selling high-as-Everest gear capable of withstanding all that nature can dish out. Hard goods like tents, sleeping bags and backpacks are usually marked up 40 percent by retailers, while smaller accessories like tent pegs may be double the wholesale price (since consumers usually don't comparison-shop for those items). But no matter what you buy or where you're shopping, here's how to get your equipment for less.

Quality Check

Look for tents made of nylon, including the floor; cheaper models have polyethylene flooring, which doesn't hold up. Also look for models with American-made fiberglass poles, which are a better grade than their foreign-made cousins and are less likely to splinter.

And look for sleeping bags with a double layer of insulation so that you won't have cold spots on the seams. Make sure you can pull the two layers apart.

GREAT MAIL-ORDER BUYS

There are over 40 mail-order catalogs specializing in camping and hiking equipment; for a complete list, consult the *Catalog of Catalogs IV* by Edward L. Palder in the reference section of your local library.

Some of the best offerings, however, are from Campmor in Paramus, New Jersey. Its catalog offers 30 percent off retail prices on many standard and hard-to-find items. Established nearly two decades ago, this no-frills newsprint catalog is published six times a year, and each issue offers special sale items at additional savings. Call 1-800-CAMPMOR for a free copy.

For a one-time $15 fee, you can net 10 percent savings through Recreational Equipment, a Seattle-based company that is the largest camping and hiking co-op in the country. It offers a comprehensive assortment of quality outdoor gear and clothing through its mail-order service and retail locations. Savings over retail cost are paid with a yearly dividend check or merchandise credit. Call 1-800-426-4840 for a free catalog and the location of a retail store near you.

GET INTO THE OLD. Sleeping bags don't change much from year to year, but tents, backpacks and boots do. In fact, these items are often discontinued simply because of a color change. But this practice can translate to you keeping more green.

That's because new-hued items mean closeouts for the current inventory. Closeout sales are usually held in late January through February, since retailers start getting their new merchandise in early March. Look for discounts in the 30 to 50 percent range—especially at smaller camping specialty shops—but occasionally you can even find some items selling at below wholesale cost.

SEEK THE FLOOR MODELS. After months of showcasing display models on the floor, retailers usually sell them at substantial savings. Buying a floor model tent, for instance, can cost you about half the price of the same boxed item; the same goes for sleeping bags, air mattresses and other items. But don't expect similar savings on display model cook stoves and the like—they will generally be marked down only 15 to 25 percent.

Your best bet is to simply ask for the floor model, especially if it's just beginning to look worn—showing fringed edges or other signs of wear and tear. But seasoned campers know the savings are worth a little sacrifice in newness: After just one trek to the woods, your gear will probably look just as worn.

DON'T OVERLOOK THE SCOUTS. Although most Boy Scouts provide their own sleeping bags and other incidentals, the troop itself usually provides the tents, cooking equipment and lanterns. When that gear gets

OUTSTANDING OUTLETS

Eureka Camping Center is an outlet center in Binghamton, New York, adjacent to the factory where Eureka and Camp Trail camping gear is made. This outlet sells factory seconds of Eureka tents and Camp Trail backpacks at 40 to 50 percent below retail prices. Besides the factory seconds, the center also sells first-quality camping gear such as canoes, kayaks and sleeping bags at significant savings.

Its line of two-man Timberline tents, which are popular with scout troops, normally sell for about $165 retail; you can buy one for about $90 at the outlet. All merchandise comes with a one-year warranty and a 30-day return policy. For additional savings, shop during the annual four-day high inventory sale that starts the first Thursday in March. For directions and information, call (607) 779-2265.

In addition, the Coleman Company operates an outlet store next to its Wichita, Kansas, factory, offering 25 to 30 percent savings on sleeping bags, coolers, camp stoves, lanterns and canoes. The items in the store are factory seconds with cosmetic defects such as small scratches and dents. Lanterns and stoves that typically retail for $49 sell for $37 at the outlet. The store also features a bin of $15 sleeping bags that normally sell for $50. Call (316) 264-0836.

CAMP FOR LESS

For the best deals in campsites, head for state parks. Generally, entrance and site fees are 15 percent less than at campsites run by the federal government. Besides, state parks tend to be less crowded. You can probably get a complete list by contacting the Bureau of State Parks (or related office) in your state capital.

For a list of national parks, send for a free "National Park System Map and Guide," available from the Office of Public Inquiries, National Park Service, Department of the Interior, P.O. Box 37127, Washington, DC 20013-7127, or call (202) 208-4747.

The U.S. Army Corps of Engineers has developed 4,300 recreational areas. For a set of regional maps showing the corps' projects, contact the U.S. Army Corps of Engineers, Corps Publications Depot, 2803 52nd Avenue, Hyattsville, MD 20781-1102.

old or a troop disbands because of dwindling participation, the troop sells its equipment at bargain-basement prices—often 80 percent or more below retail prices.

While some of the gear is sold because it's in lousy shape, a lot of it still has years of use—especially for an occasional camper. So if you want to camp without a huge investment, contact your local Boy Scout troop or call your area's local scout council, listed in the yellow pages under "Youth Organizations and Centers." Even if the troop isn't selling its old gear, the troop leader often knows of neighborhood people who are selling used camping equipment.

BUY FOR YOUR NEEDS. Retailers say that most overspending by recreational campers comes from buying equipment well beyond their needs. The most overbought products are sleeping bags. Consumers often invest in a sleeping bag rated for subfreezing temperatures when they plan to use the bag only during the spring and summer—adding up to $100 to their purchase. Many people also tend to buy top-quality tents and cooking gear for their maiden voyage instead of getting middle-of-the-road quality "to test the waters" and then moving up if they become serious campers.

JUST ASK FOR A DISCOUNT. Don't be afraid to ask for a discount—especially if you're shopping at a camping and hiking specialty store. These smaller shops are dying for loyal customers and often sell their older "back room" inventory for up to 75 percent off in hopes of getting return shoppers. But don't expect the same savings at larger sporting goods stores, which usually sell their wares for less anyway.

GET A DEAL FROM YOUR UNCLE SAM. It's no surprise that you can find no-frills but well-constructed camping and hiking gear at Army-Navy stores for anywhere from 15 to 60 percent below retail prices. But if you happen to live near a military base, your savings can be even greater.

Each branch of the military, as well as the Department of Defense, holds periodic sales where tents, sleeping bags and other items are sold for a fraction of retail prices. Sure, the stuff is old, but if it can withstand the rigors of Uncle Sam's fighting forces, it can usually take anything your family can dish out. Contact the public information office at the nearest base or your local Army reserve unit for information on when these sales are held.

For a copy of *How to Buy Surplus Personal Property*, a pamphlet describing how to get on the national bidders list and how to find out about local sales, write to the International Sales Office, Defense Reutilization and Marketing Service, 2163 Airways Boulevard, Building 210, Memphis, TN 38114-5211.

Carpet

Selecting carpet is an important decision when you're decorating your home because the carpet pulls various elements like furniture, walls and even windows together. Yet shopping can be a confusing and frustrating experience, since you're faced with hundreds of choices concerning color, style, quality and price.

There are over 25 carpet manufacturers in the United States, and they produce more than 90 percent of the nearly $14 billion worth of carpet sold in this country each year—most of it with a retail markup of up to 60 percent. That translates to a cost to you of from $10 to $50 per square yard, with another $2 to $5 per yard for padding and about $3.50 per yard for installation. To figure the per-yard price you can afford, divide the total amount you can spend by the number of

Beware of Padded Claims

Don't let retailers pull the wool over your eyes with promises of free padding and installation for your carpet. Usually, the free padding is very lightweight and of poor quality, and you'll have to pay extra to upgrade. And industry insiders say that stores that use this practice tend to jack up the price of their carpet or another service connected to your purchase—like delivery. Better: Shop around for the best deal on the carpet itself, then negotiate padding and installation separately.

And those "three rooms for $399" claims are no bargain, either. What you'll probably find is that the carpet offered in the ad is of inferior quality or that the quoted price applies only to rooms of dollhouse proportions.

square yards you need for the room you plan to carpet. But to get it for less, try these strategies.

GO TO A SPECIALIST. There are many retail stores that sell carpet, but your best bet is to go to a specialist—a store that sells only carpet and other floor coverings. Department stores also sell carpet, but with their overhead and limited buying power, their markup tends to be at least 50 percent (and usually 60 percent). At carpet stores, however, the markup from the mill is only about 40 percent—saving you as much as 20 percent over department stores.

ROLL UP SAVINGS WITH ROLLS. You can cut an additional 15 percent or so at a carpet store by buying carpet from an in-store roll rather than ordering the merchandise from display swatches. That's because retailers tend to get a price break from the mill for buying the larger volumes that come in rolls rather than placing "special orders"—even though the rolls may be the same item as the swatches (in-store stock is ordered on the basis of those swatch samples).

You can save even more on installation on larger rooms—between $50 and $200, depending on the room—by opting for a 15-foot roll rather than the traditional 12-footer. That's because, if your room is wider than 12 feet, fewer seams are needed for installation. Besides, the carpet will last longer, since the seam areas tend to wear out more quickly.

PIECE TOGETHER REMNANTS. It's even cheaper to piece together several remnants than to buy one large piece of carpet—even from a roll. Remnants are leftover pieces from previous "roll" jobs, usually available in 6-by-9-foot to 10-by-12-foot pieces. By getting two of the same remnant—usually packaged and rolled in the back room—you can save up to 25 percent compared to buying a single piece that's cut from the roll.

ASK ABOUT AN OVERSTOCK. Carpet retailers get a deal on mill overstocks—carpet that's been "overproduced" and is left over in a manufacturer's inventory. Asking for overstocks can save you between 20 and 50 percent compared to other goods, and you usually get the same quality. This carpet is usually in rolls and may be what's already advertised as "clearance-priced."

FALL INTO FALL AND SPRING BUYING. While there's no official "sale" season in the carpet biz, and retailers tend to mark down their goods as needed, industry insiders say that sales tend to occur during the spring and fall.

BUY DIRECTLY FROM THE MILL. Probably the least expensive way to buy

GREAT MAIL-ORDER BUYS

S&S Mills, a carpet mill based in Dalton, Georgia, sells carpeting directly to the consumer at wholesale prices—meaning you can save up to 50 percent off regular retail prices. Call 1-800-241-4013 to have carpet samples and pricing information sent to your home. The samples usually arrive in less than a week and include several grades and colors of carpeting; prices range from $6.59 to $26.99 per square yard.

carpet is to bypass the retailer totally: You can save up to 60 percent off retail price by buying directly from the carpet mill.

The wholesale shop-by-phone carpet business has grown rapidly in the last few years, with mills sending carpet samples directly to your home. You not only save on the cost of the carpet, you may also avoid paying sales tax if you purchase carpet from out of state. Most carpet mills are located in Georgia.

But there are some drawbacks: You have to pay the freight costs to have the carpet shipped to your home. And once the carpet arrives, you (not the truck driver) have the responsibility of getting a several-hundred-pound roll of carpet into the house. You must also find an installer to properly measure for your carpet.

Padding from these mills is also less than retail, but it's sold only by the roll. And if there's a problem with the carpet that shows up after installation, your contact will be a voice on the telephone, not a local firm. To find shop-at-home carpet mills that deal directly with the public, check out the advertisements in the back of home improvement magazines. Most have toll-free numbers.

CAR PHONES AND CELLULAR PHONES

If you think car and cellular phones are only used by Hollywood bigwigs, think again: About eight million people join the ranks of mobile communication each year—about 28,000 a day, or roughly twice the number of babies born daily in the United States.

Why? That's a good question. True, the typical rate for wireless service has dropped to about $1.85 a day—about one-third the price of just a few years ago. But even so, this talk certainly ain't cheap: Depending on how and where you use your car or cell phone, you could be paying as much as 50 times more than you do for residential phone service. But here's how to save on the purchase and service of these portable telephones.

GET THE PHONE FOR FREE. There's absolutely no reason to buy these phone units, since they're usually given away by retailers or sold for ridiculous amounts ranging from one cent to under $20 in exchange for signing up with a service carrier or buying accessories like chargers and adapters. (Keep in mind that the wholesale price of a stripped-down "flip" model cellular telephone is more than $100, and some of these freebies retail for over $200.)

Advertisements for these freebie offerings can be found year-round in the business section of your local newspaper, but they seem especially widespread during the spring. Also check the Sunday supplements for ads from electronics chains like Circuit City.

GANG UP. The real money that's spent on car and cellular phones isn't for the actual equipment but for the monthly service. Basic rates are about $20 a month (your cheapest option), but they can go as high as ten times that amount, depending on the amount of "air time" you want. Figure that it generally costs $1 per minute to use a car or cell phone, so if you want it only for emergencies, avoid paying $50 a month for 20 "free" minutes. You'll make unnecessary calls in order to use your time—and they're anything but free.

Whatever service plan you choose, keep in mind that these monthly rates are set by the service carrier and are usually not negotiable. In most areas, there are usually two service carriers—a Baby Bell and an independent carrier—and their rates tend to be identical. But in some cases, these carriers will cut you a break on the monthly service—usually if you provide volume business.

Industry insiders recommend collaborating with friends, relatives

THE BEST FOR LESS: MOTOROLA STARTAC

The Motorola name became a cellular standout for its MicroTAC line—a series of those "flip" phones that resemble the communicators seen on the original *Star Trek*. While other companies make flip phones, industry insiders say those made by Motorola are the best. And none is better than the StarTAC model.

Unlike less expensive pocket-size flip (and other styles) cellular phones, the StarTAC is small and light—slightly larger than a pager and complete with its own "holster" (to free your pockets, no doubt). Yet this mighty mite has excellent sound quality and plenty of features.

While pricing is set by individual cellular phone services like Cellular One, the suggested retail price of the StarTAC is about $900, although you're sure to get it for less when you sign up for cell service. Of course, if you're looking for a free phone, don't expect a StarTAC. If you're given a choice, opt for a more basic model in the Motorola MicroTAC line over models from other companies.

Chargers, car adapters, built-in answering features and other accessories, including long-lasting batteries good for up to 60 minutes of talk time, are also available. To find out where you can get a StarTAC, call 1-800-331-6456.

or co-workers for a group rate, usually 10 to 30 percent less. The more fellow customers you gather, the lower the charges each of you will have to pay.

SEEK AN "OFF-PEAK" OFFER. Another way to negotiate service is to insist on getting an "off-peak" rate. Check the definition of *off-peak* before you sign—it varies, depending on the carrier—but figure you can save up to 60 percent off the normal per-minute charge by having this option in your service contract. And don't expect the seller to offer it; this is a benefit usually gotten only by savvy consumers.

SAY NO TO TACKED-ON FEES. Retailers often drive up the cost by making you pay what's called an activation fee—a one-time fee of about $40 for starting your service. Industry insiders say this added cost is common but unnecessary. Retailers will often waive this cost for those who insist on not paying it (don't believe the line that it's "standard procedure").

Another extra cost is a "roaming" fee, a charge of about $3 a day for being able to use your phone outside your normal calling area—such as when you're taking a trip. You must pay this roaming fee whether you use the phone or not, so think twice before agreeing to this charge.

GET THE EXTRAS FROM A "SPECIALIST." Car and cell phones are available everywhere these days—from department stores like Sears and JCPenney to warehouse clubs like B.J.'s Wholesale Club and Sam's Club. But for accessories needed for these phones, like adapters and battery chargers, you're better off going directly to a retailer who deals exclusively in cellular and car phones.

True, you can pay up to 25 percent more for the phones at a specialty retailer than at a warehouse club (and about the same as at a department store like Sears), but since these phones can be gotten for free, that point is moot. But nearly $900 million is spent each year on accessories like battery chargers and adapters. Even with a free phone, many retailers make a bundle from selling these "extras," but by signing up for a service contract with these specialists, you may be able to get them for up to 80 percent less by negotiating a discount. You'll get no discounts, meanwhile, at electronics stores or warehouse clubs.

GO WITH CELLULAR. If you have your heart set on a car phone, reconsider. A portable cellular phone may be a better choice, especially now that transmission signals are stronger. Car adapters are available for most cellular phones, and taking them with you not only gives you the convenience of a phone at your fingertips at all times, it also means you haven't left an expensive piece of equipment on display in your car to invite a break-in.

While some car phones are cheaper than cellular phones, cellulars can be a better buy in the long run. Besides being more reliable, a cellular phone is covered automatically by your homeowner's insurance, while car phones require a special endorsement that could increase your car insurance premium.

RENT, DON'T BUY. If you plan to use a car or cellular phone only rarely or while traveling, consider renting one. This lets you avoid getting locked into a multiyear commitment and a monthly fee for services you seldom really need. Shared Technologies Cellular in Wethersfield, Connecticut (1-800-933-3836) is the nation's biggest cellular phone rental company and rents phones on a daily, weekly or monthly basis. Each phone comes with a carrying case, two batteries, a charger and an adapter for your car. The per-minute rate is $1.95, with a three-minute minimum per day, and there are no roaming charges. For other companies, check the yellow pages under "Cellular Phone Rentals."

Cars and Trucks

If shopping for a new car has given you a serious case of sticker shock, consider this: While the prices of new cars and trucks seem like they've shot up faster than the space shuttle (the average price of a new vehicle is now close to $20,000), dealer margins have not.

Retailers of other goods often enjoy markups of 100 percent or more. But car dealers make a mere 6 to 8 percent on small cars and 10 to 12 percent on more expensive vehicles—about 40 percent less than just a few years ago.

Don't break out the violins for car salesmen just yet, however, because they still try to squeeze out every dollar of gross profit they can. But if you do your homework and are willing to negotiate, lower margins can mean more metal for your money. Here's how to drive a real bargain when buying vehicles.

Hit the Library Before the Auto Mile. Your first stop on the road to a new vehicle should be your local library or newsstand. There you'll find various price guides like *Edmunds* and *Pace* that detail invoice prices on cars—literally what the dealer pays the manufacturer for them. The guides also list the manufacturer's suggested retail price (called the MSRP) and the loan value—what the bank will lend you for the vehicle. These books range in price from $5 to $10 each.

Knowing the invoice price and the MSRP is important, since conventional wisdom dictates that the dealer must get at least $500 above invoice to make money on the deal.

Cash incentives to dealers for selling a particular model are detailed in the back pages of *Automotive News*, the trade weekly of the auto business, also available at your library or dealer. The magazine lists the manufacturer and model and the expiration dates of the incentives, information that may help you knock several hundred dollars off the price of your car.

Read the Small Print. While you should be wary of car dealers that run ads offering the sale of the century, scanning the newspaper will help you discover the true going rate for the car you want and where to find it—without any sales pressure. And while you're at it, be sure to check the smaller print that's free of exaggerated claims—the classified ads for cars being sold by individuals, another great place to hunt for a deal.

BUY LOCALLY. You may be able to buy a car for less elsewhere, but some experts recommend purchasing from a dealer close to work or home. If you do buy elsewhere, the theory goes, your neighborhood dealer is less likely to welcome your car problems or fight your warranty battles. The best test of a prospective dealership: Walk into the

THE BEST FOR LESS: MERCEDES BENZ

Since few items generate the passion and customer loyalty of autos, the "best" is a matter of interpretation. There's resale value, dependability, drivability, cost of ownership, engineering and comfort. When it comes to these values, few argue that Mercedes rates at or near the top of the list.

Unfortunately, it also ranks high in sticker price. The "S" Class Mercedes—its Cadillac-size and most prestigious car—ranges in price from $62,000 to $130,000. One way to get a Mercedes for less—at least for the short term—is to lease it, since the monthly payments can be hundreds less. But industry insiders caution that this is not a real money-saver, since there's no equity in the car, and you're basically only renting it.

Instead, you can get Mercedes quality for half the price by opting for its "C" class—smaller cars that compare with the Lexus and BMW 5 series. These cars start at about $29,900 and have many of the same luxury features as the "S"-class vehicles. Another option: Ask your Mercedes dealer about the Encore Program, in which you can buy a previously owned late-model Mercedes—reconditioned, fully inspected and with up to a three-year warranty—for thousands below the retail price of a new model.

customer service waiting area and grab a seat. A few minutes of listening to and talking to customers will speak volumes about how the dealership handles customer concerns.

WAIT UNTIL THE END OF THE MONTH. Have you ever noticed that the antics around your neighborhood car dealer are even a little more frantic at the end of the month? That's because dealerships have monthly sales goals and contests that often conclude at the end of the month. By shopping then, you're more likely to find a hungry sales rep who needs just one more sale to clinch salesguy-of-the-month honors, and you may get your car for at least 10 percent less than someone who shopped earlier in the month.

The single best day to shop? December 26. Not only are you likely to be the only person on the lot, but both monthly and annual sales quotas should help make the sales rep even more eager to deal. Besides, many dealers need to unload inventory before year's end, so they're more willing to negotiate. If it's been a particularly hard winter, you're in the best position of all: Bad weather tends to keep people from shopping for cars.

LOOK FOR "LIKE NEW." Because a new car is worth 20 to 25 percent less the minute it leaves the lot, you may be better off buying late-model used cars, especially "program vehicles." Turned in at the end of a lease, returned from a rental fleet, used as a demonstrator or even briefly loaned to a celebrity for a special event, these vehicles usually have low mileage and are in great condition. And they tend to sell for about 20 percent less than a comparable new model.

OR CHECK OUT RENTAL CARS. Concerned about buying a rental? Don't be. Although rentals tend to have more mileage, it's usually "easy" highway mileage, and the cars are often better-maintained than leased cars because down-time costs the rental company money. Many rental companies sell their fleets in auctions once or twice a year, so savings of up to 30 percent below new retail prices are not uncommon. Check your local newspaper for these sales or call local rental companies.

STEER CLEAR OF THE SUPPLEMENTAL STICKER. One gimmick used to jack up car prices is something called the supplemental sticker. Nearly indistinguishable from the blue-and-white sticker that's displayed by law on the side window of sale vehicles (the real McCoy is called a Monroney label), supplemental stickers list such absurdities as a "simulated convertible roof" or an "availability charge." These extras can add $200 or more to your purchase; their very presence should

IS LEASING FOR YOU?

All the rage, leasing is keeping the luxury car market alive—nearly half of all luxury cars are leased. But how good is it for your financial health?

Simply put, a lease is a rental. For a fixed monthly sum, usually plus some money up front, you have the use of a car for a specific time and usually for a minimum number of miles—about 15,000 a year. And you can't walk away. You sign a two-year lease, you owe for two years.

Unless otherwise stated in your contract, maintenance isn't free. Nor will the car be replaced if it is stolen or you have an accident—unless it's in your contract. Gap insurance is often sold to cover the difference between what you owe on the lease and the value of the car you just might total.

The good news: Lease prices are negotiable—and negotiating can bring the monthly cost down considerably. When cutting the deal, consider these tips.

- A closed-end lease allows you to walk away without having to buy the vehicle. If you don't get a closed-end lease, you may be required to buy the car at the end of the lease.
- Residual value—the predicted value of the car at the end of the lease—can be a benefit if the value at termination is more than the prediction. Just make sure the predicted value is consistent with real expectations.
- Beware of "wear and tear" or "damage" clauses. You could wind up facing a big lease-end repair bill. When negotiating your lease agreement, be sure it does not include these clauses, as well as security deposits, end-of-lease charges, document charges and excess mileage assessments—all of which can cost you hundreds more a year.

be at least a warning to exercise caution—and probably a signal to exit. If you find these stickers on a car you like, tell the dealer you're wise to the "extras" and insist on *not* paying for them. You probably won't have to.

SAVE BY THINKING SAFETY. If you don't think safety has cash value, price it out with your insurance company—you can save hundreds each year. Many companies quote lower rates for cars with airbags and an anti-lock brake system (ABS)—although some experts say the industry is attempting to discredit the value of ABS to avoid those discounts.

Different models command different rates, too. Volvo owners pay less than Camaro fanciers, for example, because crash statistics justify the difference. The bottom line: A reliable though seemingly dull sedan is much cheaper to insure than a high-powered sports coupe.

LET LOOSE WITH A LOW-BALL. When you've found a car you like, make your offer purposely low—closer to the wholesale price than to the retail. If it's rejected, ask the sales rep what it would take to buy the car today. He'll be more interested in learning what you want to pay (so he can steer you to a car he won't have to haggle over), but stick to your guns. When increasing your offer, do so only in small increments—$50 on a lower-priced car, $100 on a higher-priced set of wheels. Most dealers try to raise prices in higher increments, usually by several hundred dollars at a shot.

WATCH OUT FOR "YES." If your first offer is accepted, it was probably too high. It's not uncommon, however, for a salesperson to say yes to a low-ball offer and have you commit to a purchase and make a deposit, only to tell you solemnly a few minutes later that his sales manager has balked at your offer. What comes next is that you're ushered into the sales manager's office for a hard sell. At this point, a lot of people lose their nerve and end up spending more.

Instead of caving in, politely but firmly ask for your money back, shake hands and walk out. Chances are you won't even make it through the door before the sales manager changes his mind and accepts your offer. If not, expect a call the following morning.

POO-POO THE PACK. A pack is a collection of dealer-added extras, such as rustproofing, vinyl roof trim, that phony convertible top, waxes, paint treatments and the like, aimed at making you pay more than you should. This is the kind of stuff you might find on a supplemental sticker (another reason to know the MSRP). Most of these so-called extras are window-dressing that can add up to $500 to your purchase. But a car is designed (and sold to the dealer) with these features provided at the factory, and they're included in the dealer's price.

WAIVE THE EXTENDED WARRANTY. Here's another way that dealerships add bucks to your hard-won bottom line. After you've signed the

SELL YOUR OLD CAR YOURSELF

Many people trade in their old car for a new one without much thought of selling it on their own because they don't want the hassle. That may be a big mistake: Dealers typically offer only half of what a used car is really worth, especially on later-model vehicles.

By selling the car on your own, you're in a better position to reap its full value. To determine that, check the classified ads for the retail price range of the model you plan to trade and also visit used-car dealerships. Wholesale and retail values of used cars, trucks and sport utility vehicles are also listed in used-car price guides published by the same companies that put out new-car price guides. Some guides, like *Pace*, combine new and used prices in one volume.

On the downside, when you are selling a car yourself, you need to figure in the expense of advertising your vehicle. And when you don't trade in your old car at a dealer, you wind up paying tax on the full value of the new car—which can increase your costs by several hundred dollars.

If you plan to finance a new car, you can save the cost of the price guide by asking the bank to quote you the value of the car you plan to sell. The table of values for used vehicles is based on cars in good condition and average mileage, around 12,000 to 15,000 a year. Unusually high mileage can reduce your asking price, but a two- or three-year-old high-mileage car is worth more than a six- or seven-year-old car with extremely low mileage. And a rust-free body with no dents and good paint adds hundreds or even thousands in extra value, even if the mileage is unusually high.

If you decide to sell to the dealer, negotiate your new purchase before mentioning any possible trade-in: Some dealers are inclined to try to sway you to pay more for a new car in exchange for a better trade-in. But keep in mind that they are not inclined to be overly generous with allowances for hard-working trucks.

purchase-and-sale agreement, usually the same people who are arranging your financing will give you a speech about the value of extended service plans, warranties and even insurance designed to pay off your loan if you die. All of these can add $500 or so to the final tab. Most newer cars are fully covered for three to seven years, and the extended warranty often doesn't cover all that the sales pitch says it will cover. Instead, industry insiders say you should use these warranties as a negotiating tool: Buyers can demand that they be included at half price or for no charge as a condition of the sale.

CONSIDER KEEPING YOUR CASH. Thanks to rebates and low-interest financing, it may be a better idea to keep your cash in the bank than to bankroll your new car purchase. The key: comparing your financing rate with how much your money can earn for you. Let's say you're planning to purchase a $20,000 car with a trade-in worth $5,000 and $15,000 in cash. If passbook savings interest hovers around 2 percent, U.S. Treasury bills earn around 6 percent, and certificates of deposit earn just over 5 percent, paying cash could potentially cost you between $300 and $900 extra.

But if the dealer is offering you 2.9 percent financing for two years, whatever money you don't use for the car could still be earning 5 percent. The difference: 2.1 percent, about what a savings bank pays. It doesn't sound like much money, but it's better than the alternative: being out of cash, earning no interest and watching the car depreciate.

Caskets and Memorials

It used to be that when a loved one died, you were at the financial mercy of the local funeral home because no one would dare quibble at such a tragic time. But lately consumers have been increasingly rejecting the costly pomp of traditional funerals, prompting the burial business—one of the last remaining family-dominated industries—to practice the same price-cutting and marketing techniques as other retailers.

Cremation, the least expensive option, is being done twice as often this decade as during the 1980s. Discount caskets have entered the market—and not a moment too soon, since the retail markup can be as much as 900 percent. And the fact that people are living longer has also hit the bottom line of funeral directors. Arranging a memorial service never comes without an emotional cost, but here's how to make it less expensive.

Great Mail-Order Buys

If you want the beauty of an ornate wooden casket carved from mahogany, cherry or walnut but your budget says otherwise, there may be a way to cut the cost in half: Order from Family Heritage Casket Gallery in Memphis.

A solid cherry casket that sells for more than $4,000 at a funeral home can be purchased for less than $2,000. Although primarily a local business, Family Heritage will ship anywhere in the country. Air freight costs can range between $250 and $350, which still adds up to a savings of more than 40 percent. Call (901) 685-0723 for more information.

PREPARE AHEAD—WITH CAUTION

The funeral service industry's answer to cost concerns is to prearrange and prepay for a funeral. This concept isn't new, and theoretically, it works this way: You select the type of funeral service, casket and burial arrangements you want, then pay for them at current prices. So whether you die tomorrow or 40 years from now, the price will be the same—and you'll also save several hundred dollars because of built-in discounts. A cremation that costs $995 when prearranged and prepaid, for instance, is about $1,295 when arranged after a death occurs.

While a prearranged funeral is cheaper, to minimize risks, make sure you discuss the following information before you sign on the dotted line, suggests the Funeral Service Consumer Assistance Program (FSCAP), a nonprofit organization that resolves consumer problems concerning funeral services and products.

- The manner in which the preneed funeral is funded—

CASKETS

SUPPLY YOUR OWN. Tradition once dictated that you buy the casket from the funeral director conducting the services—in fact, traditional funeral homes once refused to handle caskets from outside vendors or charged a substantial fee for doing so. But a 1994 Federal Trade Commission ruling required funeral homes to handle coffins from third-party vendors free of charge.

Since you can usually get a casket cheaper elsewhere, check the yellow pages to see if a discount casket dealer is located in your area; they're listed under "Caskets and Memorials." You can buy a casket for half the cost charged by the local funeral director. If none are listed, you can still save by purchasing the casket you want from a dealer outside your area and paying the freight charges to have it shipped. Two dealers that offer to ship caskets at substantial savings over funeral home costs are Family Heritage Casket Gallery, based in

through life insurance, a bank trust, an annuity, a savings account or other source.
- The relationship between the entity providing the funding and the funeral home. How are payments to be made?
- Any tax considerations.
- The existence of any guarantees. Are you guaranteed a funeral without further cost to you or your estate, for example?
- Can you change your mind about the type of service or burial?
- Is there a penalty if you fail to make any required payment or cancel the contract?
- If there is insufficient money at the time of need to pay for the funeral you arranged, will your family or estate have to pay more?
- If you relocate, will your funding arrangement change?

To contact FSCAP with any additional questions, call 1-800-662-7666.

Memphis (901-685-0723), and Lloyd Mandel Funeral Store in Skokie, Illinois (847-679-3939).

RENT IT ONLY FOR THE SERVICE. If you are planning a cremation or want a nicer casket just for the service, consider renting. You can get a casket only for the visitation or memorial service and purchase a cardboard casket for the cremation process or a less expensive "pine box" for the actual burial.

A casket typically rents for less than half its sale price. For example, you could rent a steel casket with a velvet interior, which typically sells for $2,100, for only $600. Both funeral directors and casket retailers rent caskets.

BUY USED. It sounds a bit macabre, but you can purchase a used casket and save up to half the cost of buying one. In this situation, the casket you buy is one that was previously rented for the service for someone who was cremated. The interior, however, must be new, because laws governing human waste disposal don't allow the reuse of casket interiors. The selection of used caskets may be limited, but most funeral directors who handle cremations offer this option.

MEMORIALS

PLAY THE WAITING GAME. There's no need to rush the process of purchasing a memorial. During the weeks immediately following the death of a loved one, a roller coaster of emotions can cloud your judgment and influence your decisions—raising the cost of a memorial in two ways: Not only are you more likely to buy a more extravagant memorial, but some companies will charge extra for a "rush" preparation job.

The design of the memorial symbolizes your family, so take your time deciding on the size and type of marker and the inscription and lettering that you want. The average single memorial costs between $1,200 and $1,500, but prices can start as low as $275 for the cheapest grade of granite, usually used for flat memorials.

Granite is priced based on its brilliancy and color, with the cheapest grade coming from the upper shelves of the quarry. Gray is the cheapest color; others cost up to 40 percent more.

SKIP THE SALES PITCH. Monument dealers who employ a sales staff generally have prices that are 20 to 40 percent higher than dealers who sell directly to the consumer. These commissioned salespeople usually work from catalogs, and you're more likely to be disappointed with the finished product.

Better: Find a dealer who stocks monuments so that you can view color and brilliancy of the stone firsthand. The prices will generally be cheaper, and you are also likely to find stones that are discounted.

Ceiling Fans

The gentle breezes from a ceiling fan are among the most economical ways to cool a room. A well-placed ceiling fan can make an 82° room feel like a more tolerable 75° while using only the scant amount of energy it takes to light a 100-watt light bulb.

Because of this, it was during the energy crunch of the 1970s that sales of ceiling fans soared—even though they've been in use for about a century. That trend continues today, with 14 million ceiling fans being sold each year in the United States.

Prices vary widely, from under $30 for a cheaply made no-name import (that's likely to hum and wobble within a year) to nearly $1,000 for a top-of-the-line unit. But there's no need to spend that much for a good fan: Many quality units sell for between $80 and $200 and have a retail markup of between 35 and 50 percent, depending on where you shop.

Fan blades range from 28 to 62 inches; the bigger the blades, the more air the fan moves—and the more it costs. A fan with 36-inch blades is fine for a 10-by-10 room, but larger rooms are better handled with a 42-inch or larger model. Whatever size you buy, try to a get a "reversible" unit that allows you to change blade direction with the flick of a switch. This way, you can also cut your winter heating bills, since the fan pulls heated air up more efficiently and spreads it around the room. Here's how to also cut your spending.

Hone in on a home center. You can get ceiling fans from virtually any type of retailer—from large stores like Sears and JCPenney to smaller lighting specialty shops. But you'll usually get the best deals at home centers like Home Depot and Builder's Square. Since they buy in such large volume and have a wide assortment of fans, they're able to offer the lowest retail markup—generally 35 percent or even less. So even when there is no sale, you'll usually save at least 15 percent compared to what you would pay at other retailers, which generally sell fans for 50 percent more than their wholesale costs.

THE BEST FOR LESS: REGENCY MARQUIS

While Casablanca and Hunter have long been regarded as the Cadillacs of the fan industry, the lesser-known Regency Marquis ceiling fan is receiving high accolades—from consumer publications and fan experts alike—as the up-and-coming quality buy.

The Regency Marquis offers the same high-tech features as some of the top models offered by Casablanca and Hunter but without the added cost. While comparable in features and function to the Casablanca Delta, which retails for almost $400, the Marquis retails for about $270 and can be found at some discount dealers for as little as $175—especially after Labor Day. And unlike many other fans, it can be adapted to four- or five-blade styles and has four mounting options so it's adaptable to sloped or vaulted ceilings or long or regular downrods, and it can be mounted flush—and it's ideal for low ceilings without needing special brackets or other equipment. It also has a limited lifetime warranty.

To find a Regency dealer near you, call the company at (314) 349-3000 or write to 1760 Gilsinn Lane, Fenton, MO 63026.

But the savings don't stop there, since home centers tend to have frequent sales on ceiling fans—especially in the early spring and again in the fall and winter. That's when you're likely to find prices on some units discounted an additional 10 to 20 percent.

CLOSE IN ON CLOSEOUTS. Another advantage of shopping after Labor Day: You're in the best position of the year to find year-end closeouts—leftover styles that will not be manufactured next season. Although the actual fan mechanism changes very little, features in many ceiling fans tend to be revised from year to year—a new style of light fixture or a different type of hardware, for instance. And from September to December, many manufacturers offer retailers special discounts on the "old" models.

In turn, retailers sell these closeouts for up to 40 percent less than similar units. While these closeouts may be limited to only a model or two, ask the sales staff if they have any. You're in the best position to find closeouts at smaller specialty shops, since home centers and larger discount chains tend to order their inventory only once a year.

ASK FOR THE DISPLAY UNIT. Another way to save is to try to buy a display model—one of the fans hung overhead for customers to see. When displays change or new inventory comes in, the displays are often replaced. Some stores sell these units—already built and fully operational—for up to 50 percent less than new boxed units. Don't expect to find these displays marked for sale, though: You'll have to ask the sales staff if they have any available. And even though the fan has been used, the warranty is usually still new. An added benefit: You get a better idea of how durable the fan is. If it still runs like new after hanging in the store for a couple of years, it's probably a good product.

CHEESE

Interesting fact: Since becoming aware of the importance of eating less fat and cholesterol, our consumption of cheese (a significant source of both) has never been higher: As a nation, we consume 20 billion pounds a year—or about 34 pounds per person. That's twice as much cheese as we ate during the nutritionally unenlightened days of the 1960s.

Our arteries may suffer, but you won't hear cheese sellers complaining. Their markup ranges from 30 to 75 percent for domestic cheeses and even more for imports. But no matter what your tastes in cheese, here's how to buy it for less.

ORDER DIRECTLY FROM THE DAIRY. If you don't mind driving out to the country, you may be able to get your cheese directly from the farmer—and save up to 70 percent off retail prices. Many farmers sell

OUTSTANDING OUTLETS

Most mail-order cheese catalogs can't offer significant savings over retail because of packaging expenses. But you can buy cheese at near-wholesale prices from several mail-order companies by shopping at their warehouses.

One of the best is The Wisconsin Cheeseman, located in Sun Prairie, Wisconsin. Each year this company holds a warehouse sale the week before Christmas and occasionally at the end of January. Here you can get savings on gift packs, blocks of cheese and other products. The more perishable the product, the greater your savings.

FREEZING YOUR ASSETS

Most commonly purchased cheeses can be frozen for up to three months—good news to those of you who buy in bulk. But due to changes in texture that occur, keep in mind that once thawed, previously frozen cheese is best used crumbled, shredded or in cooked dishes.

For best results, freeze pieces of a half-pound or less in airtight and moisture-proof wrapping. The cheese should be thawed in the refrigerator and used immediately after thawing. Cheeses that retain the most freshness while frozen include Swiss, Cheddar, Colby, provolone, Parmesan and Romano.

All cheeses should be refrigerated at temperatures of 35° to 40°F in the original wrapping or container or in wax paper, transparent wrap, foil, plastic bags or a tightly covered container. For best flavor and aroma, serve cheese at room temperature. When cooking with cheese, think low and slow—cook at a low temperature just long enough for the cheese to melt, so that it doesn't become tough and stringy.

to the public, usually for slightly more than wholesale prices. In fact, some farms offer tours for the city-dwelling curious in hopes of selling their wares.

Although dairy farms are scattered across the country, most are located in Wisconsin, California, Minnesota, New York and Pennsylvania—usually close enough to urban centers to make daily deliveries to supermarkets and retail stores. To locate one near you, visit a gourmet retailer's cheese department or the gourmet cheese department at your local supermarket, since many stock cheeses from local dairies. Check the label of your favorite brand for the name and location of the dairy farm near you and give it a call.

SEEK OUT SPECIALTY SHOPS. Slice for slice, at a cheese specialty shop you can save 25 to 30 percent compared to retail supermarkets—especially on unadvertised specials. These shops are usually listed in the yellow pages under "Cheeses."

Cheese shops offer savings for two reasons: Because cheese is a perishable product, wholesalers are constantly under pressure to move their cheese supplies quickly. To encourage this outcome, they'll sell their stock to retailers at a reduced price, with the savings often passed on to you. Besides, specialty cheese shops tend to perceive themselves as cheese educators. As a result, they will frequently offer promotions as an incentive to try an unusual cheese that you otherwise might not buy.

BUY THE BIG BLOCKS. Warehouse clubs like Sam's Club and B.J.'s Wholesale Club typically sell five-pound slabs of sliced cheese and other large packages for about 40 percent less than supermarket prices on a pound-by-pound basis. That may sound like a lot, but considering that the average American eats almost three pounds a month, a family of four can polish off a five-pound block in a couple of weeks.

JOIN A FOOD CO-OP. You can save up to 50 percent off your cheese bill by becoming a member of a neighborhood food cooperative (also called a buying club). These community-based operations work like retail supermarkets, except that their members are the employees who run the store. Food co-ops usually have extensive cheese departments because they buy their inventory from cooperative distributors, who have alliances with local dairies. Besides the savings, it's a great way to get to know the members of your community.

Every food co-op operates differently. Most require a one-time joining fee or an annual fee and a commitment to help out at the co-op as a cashier or shelf stocker or on the administrative staff for one hour per month.

To locate a retail food co-op store or to obtain information on buying-club referrals in your state, send a self-addressed, stamped, business-size envelope to Co-op Directory Services, 919 21st Avenue S, Minneapolis, MN 55404. Or order the National Green Pages, a yearly directory that lists hundreds of socially and environmentally responsible businesses, including dozens of food co-ops nationwide, by sending $6.95 (which includes shipping) to Co-op America, 1612 K Street NW, Suite 600, Washington, DC 20006. Co-op America also publishes the *Co-op America Quarterly*, which includes information on how to start a food co-op in your neighborhood; to order a copy, send $4 to the above address.

Children's Clothing

Children's clothing is a lot cuter now than when we were kids—and it costs a lot more money. It's not unusual to see little clothing with big prices, sometimes what you'd expect to pay for items in your own wardrobe.

Americans spend more than $22 billion a year on everything from designer babywear to familiar-label toddler outfits to clothing for boys and girls that looks just like what adults wear. Depending on where you shop, markups range from around 40 percent to 100 percent. And designer names, fancy additions such as appliques and more expensive fabrics can boost the cost even more. But here's how to avoid paying full price when buying clothes for your half-pints.

Hit the suburban thrifts. It's no secret that secondhand stores can be a gold mine for children's clothing. After all, kids outgrow some items before they're even well-worn, and thrift stores and consign-

Outstanding Outlets

The Hanna Andersson catalog offers some beautiful clothing—at a hefty price. But the company operates three outlet stores on opposite ends of the nation that sell these same great top-quality duds at prices at least 20 percent off those of catalog offerings. Some irregular and off-season clothing is sold at huge markdowns. The stores are in Lake Oswego, Oregon, Portsmouth, New Hampshire, and Chicago. For a catalog or other information about the outlets, call 1-800-222-0544.

GREAT MAIL-ORDER BUYS

Playclothes, based in Memphis, sells sturdy children's clothes at prices that won't weaken your wallet. Top-quality shorts and tops can be had for less than $10 each, with outfits around $30 or less. And popular styles of sneakers range from $9 to $16—up to 50 percent below retail.

A new catalog comes out every two months or so, and residents of some states pay no sales tax. Playclothes occasionally offers deferred-payment credit plans. What's more, you can hand your children the catalog to make choices rather than dragging them unwillingly to the mall. Call 1-800-362-7529 to order your catalog.

ment shops offer great deals—up to 90 percent off the retail price of new duds.

But for the best selection—designer labels and other top-quality clothing—head to the suburbs. A growing number of thrift stores, like those run by Goodwill Industries and the Salvation Army, have joined consignment shops in better-heeled areas. Local residents tend to unload clothing their children have outgrown at the nearest places, so look for these stores in newer strip malls in suburbia. You'll find them listed in the yellow pages under "Thrift Stores" and "Consignment Shops."

Of course, neighborhood garage sales and flea markets are also great places to pick up secondhand threads for next to nothing. The best time to cruise these sales is before 10:00 A.M., so you'll get first crack at the offerings (kids' clothing tends to sell very quickly). These sales tend to be most common throughout the country in early spring and the fall.

SHOP IN AUGUST. If you want to go the retail route, the best time to shop for new children's clothing is in August, just before the school year begins. That's when department stores pull out all the stops in an effort to move goods quickly during their busy back-to-school buying season. You'll be likely to find basics such as jeans, T-shirts, casual shirts, sweats and shorts marked at least 25 percent off. And in communities with many stores, retailers get especially competitive for customers, so prices can drop even lower.

ASK ABOUT A FREQUENT-BUYER CLUB. More retailers that specialize in children's clothing—like the Kids Mart chain, which is based in California and carries apparel, toys and stuffed animals—now have programs offering across-the-board savings for customers who become "preferred members." The annual fee is about $6 (but may vary, depending on where you shop) and generally entitles you to 10 percent off all regular purchases. Additional savings are passed on to the preferred member through dual-price ticketing: the price tags have two prices, and members pay the lower one. You're also added to a mailing list for advance notification of special sales, where you'll typically save 25 percent off regular prices. So ask your retailer about these programs.

CHECK OUT OFF-PRICE STORES. Dollar for dollar, you'll get the most for

THE BEST FOR LESS: OSHKOSH B'GOSH

There are various manufacturers of top-quality children's apparel, but few make clothing that holds up as well as OshKosh B'Gosh. Best known for its colorful overalls and other tough-as-nails clothing for toddlers and elementary-school-age tykes, this line is as fashionable as it is durable.

In retail stores, you'll pay dearly for OshKosh duds, but the company runs 80 outlets in 27 states that offer tremendous savings.

Perfect items are generally 30 percent less than regular retail, while irregulars are 40 percent off. For example, a pair of those world-famous overalls that cost $18.00 to $20.00 in retail stores are just $14.95, and a large-size children's sweatshirt that normally sells for $18.00 might be $13.99. Seasonal sales that drive prices down further are also common.

your money on new clothing at off-price stores like T.J. Maxx and Marshalls, where children's apparel typically sells for 30 percent below retail prices and some items are marked down as much as 60 percent. There's no problem with selection, either, since these stores tend to offer a huge inventory of name brands. From late August to mid-November is the time to find the best deals, since these stores often get leftover inventory from department stores.

GIVE CARDS SOME CREDIT. If you're shopping for an entire wardrobe for your kids, take advantage of opening a store charge account. At many department stores, you can get a one-time discount of 10 to 25 percent off all purchases for one day—even if those items are on sale.

Already have a credit card at that store? Open one in your spouse's name. Some stores overlook dual card ownership in an effort to get you to buy on credit. Just be sure to pay off the credit card promptly, so you won't be walloped with interest charges, which can be over 20 percent.

SHOP CLEARANCE RACKS AFTER CHRISTMAS. If you like to cruise the clearance racks but have found slim pickings, maybe your timing is off. These 50 percent and more sales are usually best for most children's clothing just after Christmas, while baby goods tend to be clearance-priced in late October through late November.

CHINA

They may be biased, but chinaware experts agree: You should use china every day. Most people use stoneware or earthenware dishes for daily use and reserve fine china for those few-and-far-between formal occasions.

But the fact is, china is fired at much higher temperatures and is less susceptible to chipping and crazing, the spidery lines that can develop on a dish's surface. While the finest bone china needs very delicate handling, the newer "everyday" types of china made by Mikasa and other manufacturers are now frequently microwave- and dishwasher-safe, making them even more suitable for the work week.

The trick, say the experts, is to choose a pattern that is versatile enough to use for every occasion and to buy it for a great price. Most recommend a plain pattern, such as a lightly embossed off-white or simple banded design. And for savings, here's what they suggest.

CHECK OUT A RESTAURANT SUPPLIER. Those who need china for their daily existence—restaurant owners, caterers and even dining room operators for cruise lines—know that restaurant supply houses sell large supplies of everyday china, and to a lesser extent, fine bone china, at rock-bottom prices—often pennies on the dollar of what you'd pay retail.

There are a few catches: Unless you're prepared to beg, you usually must buy in quantity—a dozen seems to be the minimum for most chinaware items. Also, stock is eclectic, if vast. Much of the merchandise arrives from bankrupt businesses, so it's not uncommon to find china plates with the logo of a defunct country club or cruise ship line alongside porcelain rice bowls from a belly-up Chinese joint. But basic dishes are always in plentiful supply. Check the yellow pages under "Restaurant Equipment and Supplies" and call ahead to get an idea of what stock is on hand.

THINK CHRISTMAS IN JULY. Tableware is seasonally driven, and sum-

OUTSTANDING OUTLETS

Major china manufacturers are plugging into the factory outlet craze by opening shops that can slash prices anywhere from 30 to 50 percent—or more. The catch: Most sell seconds—china with slight imperfections, such as minute bubbles in the glaze or a nick in a gold band. Few of these are perceptible to the casual buyer—or dinner guest. To find the locations of the factory outlets near you, call your favorite manufacturer. A yearly consumer magazine, *The Joy of Outlet Shopping*, lists up-to-date news on factory outlet and discount chain openings, trends and bargains. Copies are $6.95; for information, call Value Retail News Publishing at 1-800-669-1020.

But according to some in the china business, Mikasa is fast gaining a reputation for having the best outlets. With over 110 outlet stores nationwide, Mikasa offers its wares, both top-quality and factory seconds, at prices 10 to 50 percent or more below retail—and the imperfections on seconds are usually barely noticeable. For more information on a location near you, call Mikasa at 1-800-489-2200.

mer is the best time to find discounts of up to 40 percent on Christmas dinnerware and other china—at both department stores and specialty china shops. Other good times to shop include September and October, as retailers try to unload the leftover wedding-season inventory, and also after the Christmas shopping season.

BUY MORE NOW, SAVE LATER. Unless you live in a rubber room, chances are you'll break some of your precious china sooner or later. Replacing those items on a per-piece basis can be time-consuming and expensive: Production lines and patterns change frequently, and replacement settings purchased individually typically cost twice as much as the same items in a set. To avoid this, try to buy extra pieces of your pattern while it's still in production. Instead of 8 place settings, try to buy 10 or 12.

MIX AND MATCH. Want to save hundreds off department store prices and simultaneously score a table full of conversation pieces? If you're the daring sort, compile a china service from scratch—with an eclectic assortment rather than the more traditional matching set. Individual pieces are available at estate sales, garage sales and secondhand stores and from relatives. And mixing and matching china is a growing trend.

Coordinate colors and styles as you would clothes—saucers and cups can match without being identical. When in doubt, fill in with plain, off-white pieces to form a neutral background for more outlandish choices. All told, you'll save hundreds.

PHONE IT IN. Over a dozen mail-order discount houses offer china for up to 65 percent off store prices, with average discounts of 30 to 40 percent. This is new merchandise, delivered to your door within two weeks (longer if an item is out of stock). If you don't know what you want, most companies offer catalogs and will even open up a bridal registry over the phone.

Of course, you won't have to pay tax if the order is shipped is out of state. But beware: Most mail-order houses charge hefty shipping

THE BEST FOR LESS: LENOX

If you have the cash—and we're talking about *lots* of it—then Herend, the hand-painted import from Hungary, is the china to buy. Its quality is legendary—but at about $200 to $500 or higher per setting, so is its price.

While there are several American manufacturers offering comparable value and quality, which makes choosing the best china usually a matter of individual taste, industry insiders mention one name most frequently: Lenox. Not only is it superior china, it can also offer tremendous investment potential, say those in the know. Lenox sells for between $75 and $300 per setting retail, but it's available at many china outlets and during sales for as much as 40 percent less.

fees. In some cases, these raise prices to normal retail levels.

Among the best mail-order discount houses that carry merchandise from most leading manufacturers such as Mikasa, Noritake, Wedgwood, Villeroy & Boch, Spode, Royal Doulton and others are Barrons in Novi, Michigan (1-800-538-6340), the China Cabinet in Tenafly, New Jersey (1-800-545-5353), Corson's Glasshouse in Hingham, Massachusetts (1-800-533-0084), Michael C. Fina in New York City (1-800-288-3462), Geary's in Beverly Hills (1-800-243-2797), Midas China & Silver in Chantilly, Virginia (1-800-368-3153), Ross-Simons in Cranston, Rhode Island (1-800-556-7376), Michael Round Fine China & Crystal in Lorton, Virginia (1-800-752-6622), Nat Schwartz & Company in Bayonne, New Jersey (1-800-526-1440), Albert S. Smyth Company in Timonium, Maryland (1-800-638-3333) and Thurber's in Richmond, Virginia (1-800-848-7237).

Chocolate

Ever since the country's first chocolate factory was established in 1765, we've had a love affair with chocolate—and continue to prove it with our wallets. According to the Chocolate Manufacturers Association of the United States of America, Americans spend an average of nearly $13 billion each year on chocolate and cocoa products, consuming almost 11 pounds per person.

Just visit a candy counter and you'll see that retail chocolate prices run the gamut. At better department stores, for example, it's not uncommon to pay from $9.00 per pound for high-quality American brands such as Ghirardelli to $36.00 per pound—or $1.80 per piece—for imports like Neuhaus, Godiva and other top brands. With an average retail markup for all types of chocolate running at about 50 percent, that comes to a pretty sweet deal for sellers. But here's how to satisfy your cravings for less.

Great Mail-Order Buys

You'll get the best prices on smaller quantities of the finest chocolate by ordering through the mail. In the heart of their 83-page cake- and candy-making catalog, Sweet Celebrations in Minneapolis offers a dozen kinds of chocolate for prices we found to be roughly 30 percent below department store prices. You can get a catalog by calling 1-800-328-6722. But keep in mind that due to high heat, which can cause chocolate to melt, the company doesn't ship during the summer months.

QUALITY CHECK

There are basically three kinds of chocolate: dark (bitter or semisweet), milk and white. For the highest-quality dark varieties—considered the connoisseur's choice—look for brands that have a strong chocolate scent and are shiny, with a rich, dark color to indicate that they are made with a higher percentage of cocoa beans. Avoid those that look soft, grainy or dull. Cocoa butter should be the only kind of fat mentioned on the ingredients list.

Quality milk and white chocolate also contain cocoa butter as their primary fat source, but they have milk solids added to yield a smooth, velvety texture. Cocoa butter should still be among the top three ingredients (milk solids should be lower on the list). But no matter what you buy, avoid chocolates that contain vegetable oil or artificial flavorings—that's an indication that you're not buying quality.

HONE IN ON THE HOLIDAYS. To save 20 percent off the retail price of high-quality chocolates, watch for price reductions several weeks before traditional chocolate gift–giving occasions such as Christmas, Easter and Valentine's Day. Around the time of these three holidays, you'll find specially wrapped merchandise, such as heart-shaped candies, Easter eggs or chocolate-covered Santas, that has been discounted. But as the holiday approaches and last-minute gift-shopping panic sets in, the price reductions vanish. President's Day and other holidays not normally associated with chocolate gifts are also good times to buy, since they give retailers a good excuse to mark down their wares in the 25 percent range.

The day after a major holiday, however, is the best time to buy. Usually specially wrapped merchandise will be marked at least 50 percent off in an effort to move it. So while your sweetie probably won't want chocolates the day after Valentine's, you can save big by buying them on December 26 to give later.

THINK NO-FRILLS. You can save 10 to 40 percent off retail prices by shopping at confectionery specialty stores like Mr. Bulky, warehouse clubs like Sam's Club or bag-it-yourself warehouse supermarkets. The only catch is that you'll have to buy in quantity—a case instead of a few pieces or chocolate bars at 18 per box instead of the more typical 8 to 10.

GO DIRECTLY TO THE FACTORY. Small regional chocolate factories—and there are scores of them across the country—typically have adjacent stores that sell their brands at 50 percent off retail prices. But don't expect the same great deals at factory stores of larger manufacturers like Hershey's or Ghirardelli; they tend to not mark down their items, or they offer only slight discounts.

SHOP LIKE A PRO. If you live in or frequently visit a metropolitan area, shop at specialty baking stores and enjoy near-wholesale prices. New York Cake and Baking Distributors in New York City, for example, sells 50-pound blocks of top-notch chocolate at wholesale prices. If this is too much chocolate for your needs, you can go in with a few friends. To find the nearest store to you, look in the yellow pages under "Chocolate" or "Baking Supplies."

You might be able to save at least 25 percent off retail prices by purchasing chocolate directly from a local cooking school. Culinary institutions often buy chocolate in large quantities and may have extra supplies on hand. Some but not all sell ingredients and equipment to the public. Buying chocolate in the summer, for example, when the enrollment for baking classes is down and the demand for chocolate is less, may increase your odds of cutting the best deal. Check the yellow pages under "Cooking Schools."

Christmas Decorations

Your idea of Christmas decorations may be the understated elegance of bow-tied boughs of evergreen. Or maybe a cool Yule means a lawn full of plastic reindeer. But whatever your tastes, most people agree that the holiday season just isn't complete without a Christmas tree covered with ornaments.

The first ornaments actually were better-suited to the kitchen table than to a tree: Apples, nuts and cookies were first hung as decorations in mid-1500s Germany. By the 1800s, blown-glass ornaments were adorning trees, a tradition that remains strong today. What's also blown, it seems, are the retail markups, which can be as high as 100 percent on some items. But here's how to save when buying Christmas decorations.

Join the club. There are hundreds of local chapters of clubs for collectors of Christmas ornaments whose members get special discounts and advance notice of special sales in their area. These price breaks are usually in the 10 to 25 percent range.

Two of the biggest decoration clubs are sponsored by Hallmark and Enesco. To find out about a local Hallmark Keepsake Ornament Collectors' Club, call (816) 274-4000. For Enesco collectors' club information, call (708) 875-5404 and ask for the Treasury of Christmas Ornaments manager.

Be a New Year's bargain hunter. It's no surprise that the best deals on decorations occur after Christmas, but that doesn't necessarily mean you should rush out on December 26. While greeting cards, gift wrap and ribbons tend to go fast—usually at half-off prices—there's not as great a rush on ornaments, tinsel and other decorations. Figure you'll save at least 75 percent off regular prices immediately after Christmas, with even bigger savings a week or two later.

Or be an early bird. Some stores that carry collectible figurines will offer preseason sales during the summer months, selling better ones

OUTSTANDING OUTLETS

If you want to shop the world's largest inventory of Christmas decorations, head for Bronner's Christmas Wonderland in Frankenmuth, Michigan. This store carries over 50,000 items and attracts two million visitors a year. Bronner's also publishes a 40-page catalog featuring unique ornaments, as well as its own line manufactured in Europe. But the best deals are at the store rather than through the catalog, which has numerous sales coordinated with holidays like Valentine's Day and St. Patrick's Day. To get information about the catalog or store, call Bronner's at (517) 652-9931.

And Lenox, the china company, runs 20 factory outlets across the United States that sell porcelain ornaments for up to 75 percent below retail prices. Most are slightly flawed and priced from about $5 to $50. The outlets also carry pewter ornaments by Gorham for about 50 percent below retail. To find the location of the Lenox outlet nearest you, call 1-800-423-8946.

for about 50 percent less than regular prices. Since many of these figurines cost upwards of $25 at regular retail prices, this is a good time of year to get a deal. Check the yellow pages under "Christmas Lights and Decorations."

CLEANING SUPPLIES

Perhaps the most surprising thing about cleaning products is who they really clean out: retailers. While you may balk at $15 boxes of laundry detergent and $5 containers of bathroom cleaner, those who sell these items certainly aren't getting rich from them.

Most cleaning products have a retail markup of only 15 to 20 percent. And with manufacturers' rebates and coupons and good old-fashioned competition, retailers must cut their prices even more. That means finding a real steal isn't going to be easy. But here are some money-saving tricks for buying cleaning items, from those in the trade.

LINK INTO CHAIN SALES. Common sense suggests that you'll find the lowest prices where the pros shop—at janitorial and restaurant supply houses. And true, those jumbo jugs are cheaper on an ounce-by-ounce basis than what you'll find elsewhere.

But when you consider that cleaning products are popular "loss leaders" at supermarkets, home centers and discount chains—priced below retailers' cost to lure people in—and are popular coupon items, you'll actually pay less if you play the sales at these more traditional retailers. Most janitorial supply houses and warehouse clubs catering to quantity cleaner buyers don't accept coupons and rarely offer the type of sales you'll find at places like Kmart, Home Depot and many supermarkets.

BULK UP. Wherever you buy, you'll usually save by going with the biggest container or package available. Buy a gallon container of liquid soap and you'll pay up to 70 percent less than you would for those smaller containers. And an eight-bar pack of bath soap is about 30 percent cheaper than a two-bar pack. For cleaners, the biggest containers tend to be about 50 percent cheaper on an ounce-by-ounce basis than smaller bottles.

GO FOR "ALL-PURPOSE." On a per-use basis, products marketed specifically as "bathroom cleaners" can cost twice as much as all-pur-

GREAT MAIL-ORDER BUYS

Edge Distributors near Chicago sells discounted case lots of Easy-Off and Lysol cleaning products. Orders are shipped via UPS and must be prepaid by check or money order. Call 1-800-373-3726 for ordering information.

And Staples, the office supply chain, also sells discounted soap via mail order. A gallon bottle of Palmolive dishwashing liquid, for example, costs more than 40 percent less than four individual quart bottles. If your order tops $50, Staples pays for shipping. Call 1-800-333-3330 for a catalog.

pose formulas, yet they may not be any better at cleaning. And stick with the old-fashioned screw-on cap: Those trigger-spray pumps, flip-top containers and other packaging gizmos can add up to 15 percent to the price of the same or a similar product.

MAKE YOUR OWN BREW. The best way to save is to avoid buying retail altogether. To mix your own window cleaner, combine one pint of ordinary rubbing alcohol, a half-cup of sudsy ammonia and one teaspoon of dishwashing liquid in a bucket. Then add enough water to bring the level up to a gallon. Fill a spray bottle with this mixture for immediate use and store the remainder in a sealed container.

TAKE A POWDER. Although dishwasher gels and laundry liquids may be more convenient, powders can be about 50 percent cheaper on a per-use basis.

CLOCKS

The clock business is big-time, with nearly 50 million of them being purchased each year. But even in an expanding market, time is on the customers' side, since extreme competition keeps clock prices down—or at least steady.

Most clocks have a retail markup of about 40 percent, whether it's an heirloom-quality Grandfather clock or a $10 bedside model whose main purpose is to wake you. But whatever your taste in keeping time, here's how to satisfy it for less.

BE A HOLIDAY SHOPPER. Gift-giving is the main incentive for retailers to discount clocks, since one of every four clocks in the United States is purchased as a gift. Instead of raising prices during peak buying periods, clock retailers actually lower them to move 'em out. Besides, models change so little from year to year that there's no hurry to mark down prices on the old inventory when a new shipment comes in.

Christmas is the best time to buy a clock, since retailers sell nearly 40 percent of their inventory during the four-week shopping season. Expect discounts of up to 40 percent—near-wholesale prices—on many models. The month between Mother's Day and Father's Day is another good shopping period. Besides those holidays, clocks are discounted in June, a popular time for weddings, anniversaries and graduation.

SHOP NO-FRILLS, BUY NO-FRILLS. You can spend $50 or more on a wall clock or a bedside alarm clock at a department store, but it probably won't keep time any better than a $10 model purchased at Kmart. In fact, you should buy it at a discount chain, since fierce competition among these marts results in little retail markup on clocks, little difference in quality between manufacturers and the acknowledgment that few people shop long and hard for a bedside alarm clock. Prices at these discount marts tend to be at least 15 percent lower than for similar clocks at department stores.

If you want a fancy clock—those costing $200 or more—always

THE BEST FOR LESS: SLIGH

Eighty percent of the clocks sold in the United States cost less than $25, and industry insiders say there is so little difference between them that one manufacturer is barely distinguishable from another. But among high-end clocks, one name seems to stand out: Sligh.

Besides superior mechanisms that result in better time-keeping accuracy and a longer life, Sligh clocks are known for having the best-built cases and finishes in the business. The suggested retail price for Sligh clocks ranges from $250 to $12,500, but they can be purchased at fine clock and furniture dealers nationwide for prices up to 30 percent lower than suggested retail. The discounts vary widely, depending on where you live and also from dealer to dealer. So do your homework and compare prices at fine clock stores in your area. Your best bet for finding a clock dealer who sells Sligh products is to check the yellow pages under "Clocks."

go to a bona fide clock store. The cabinets need care, the machinery of windup and cuckoo clocks needs maintenance (even if it's only winding), and setting the clock up—on a shelf or counter, carpet or linoleum—may require an expert. That's why appliance stores and many furniture stores got out of the high-end clock business: They are too hard to retail.

CHOOSE DIGITAL. If you don't have a preference in clocks, look for a digital unit. With an illuminated computer readout that's easier to see, digital clocks are actually more accurate than dial clocks. And what's more, they're marginally cheaper—between 5 and 15 percent, depending on the model and features. The only bad point is that they can't be repaired, but because of their low replacement cost, few people actually repair bedside alarm clocks.

COATS AND JACKETS

Good news! You can actually find coats and jackets cheaper now than you could five years ago—mostly because retailers realize that the best way to keep their inventory moving is to offer frequent and substantial price markdowns.

And lower prices don't necessarily mean below-grade workmanship. Dollar for dollar, coats and jackets can represent the best value in your wardrobe. That's because manufacturers use more fabric and man-hours in making a coat than they do for most other garments. And a quality garment should last at least three years.

QUALITY CHECK

Here's how to tell for sure that you're getting quality goods when buying coats and jackets.

Feel the fabric. It should be smooth to the touch, without bumps in the cloth (unless it's tweed or another rough fabric). The shine should be consistent throughout the garment, not more faded in certain areas.

Check the label. For a dress coat, an 80/20 blend will cost between 10 and 20 percent less than pure wool, yet both wear the same. Also, a foreign-made coat will cost about 35 percent less than one manufactured in the United States, and it's usually just as good.

Examine the lining. A wide band of outside fabric inside the coat denotes quality; a narrow one indicates a lesser-caliber garment.

THE BEST FOR LESS: LONDON FOG

A good raincoat is essential to any wardrobe, and when it comes to cloudy skies, there's one brand of rainwear that outshines the rest: Burberry.

Unfortunately, even outlet prices are enough to rain on your financial parade. So unless you're prepared to pay $300 or more for a Burberry at an outlet—retail prices can be twice that amount—industry insiders recommend spending far less on a raincoat that, dollar for dollar, may provide the best value.

London Fog was the first manufacturer to offer a raincoat with style, high-quality materials, strong construction and superior water repellency. (Prior to 1954, when London Fog introduced the raincoat for which it's famous today at Saks Fifth Avenue in New York City, water repellency was more a concept than a reality.)

You can buy London Fog rainwear and outerwear starting at 25 percent off regular prices at the company's 100 factory outlet stores in 39 states—at prices from about $40 and up. To find the outlet nearest you, call (410) 795-5900. And when buying a raincoat, get one with a zip-out lining. It provides added warmth on colder days and can be removed during warmer weather.

Still, the retail markup can be as much as three times a retailer's cost, which may explain why many stores offer such significant discounts and frequent sales. Americans spend about $15 billion each year on coats and jackets—and the average person owns at least two. But here's how to spend less the next time you go shopping.

WAIT UNTIL MIDSEASON. When it comes to buying coats and jackets, the later in the season, the lower the price. Reductions on winter coats in department stores and other retail shops are usually 25 to 33 percent during September and October, while they jump to 50 percent after Thanksgiving. But after Christmas, the savings soar to as much as 70 percent off—leaving you plenty of time to get good use from the garment.

The same goes for lighter "spring" jackets. Look for moderate sales when they first get in the stores—around February or early March—with additional markdowns in the 20 percent range every four to six weeks thereafter.

DON'T LOOK FOR THE DESIGNER LABEL. The exception to these hefty discounts is designer coats. Because they cost more—for retailers and consumers—designer coats and jackets tend to never get discounted more than 33 percent, no matter when you buy. By buying nondesigner coats, your savings will be more significant.

GO FOR A MAN-MADE FILLING. You can save about 25 percent on parkas, ski jackets and other coats with a man-made filling like Thinsulate, Thermoloft or other polyfills compared to similar coats with

OUTSTANDING OUTLETS

The nation's largest seller of coats and jackets, with 230 stores in 41 states, Burlington Coat Factory Warehouses offer thousands of first-quality, better-name coats and jackets for about one-third off most department store sale prices. They also offer similar savings on designer names like Evan-Picone, Misty Harbor, Jones New York, Oscar de la Renta and Christian Dior.

Burlington will also order a coat you've seen in a department store and knock at least 25 percent off that price—and you'll likely have it within two weeks of your order. Just provide the manufacturer's name, style number, color and style.

For leather coats and jackets, head for the nearest G-III Outerwear Company Store. At its seven outlet stores, you'll find the manufacturer's own brands for men and women—such as G-III, Colebrook, Siena and Siena Studio. Because you are buying directly from the manufacturer, you can save 20 to 70 percent off suggested retail prices. To find a store near you, call (201) 867-6454.

natural goose or duck down—and they keep you just as warm. Another bonus: These man-made fillings are machine-washable, while natural fillings must be laundered by a professional.

SHOP AT AN OFF-PRICE STORE. Stores like T.J. Maxx, Ross Dress for Less and Marshalls buy huge inventories and have streamlined distribution systems—giving you savings of up to 30 percent below even sale prices at department stores. The selection varies—sometimes you'll find more, sometimes less. But from October on, off-price stores tend to be well-stocked with winter coats, and from mid-March on, you'll probably find a good selection of lighter jackets.

CHECK OUT A WAREHOUSE CLUB. What they lack in selection, they make up for in savings. Warehouse clubs like Sam's Club and B.J.'s Wholesale Club tend to offer the biggest discounts on coats and jackets, even beating out off-price stores. You may find coats discounted 40 percent or more—especially on designer labels—but inventories tend to be limited to only a few styles.

Coffee and Tea

If you think that morning cup of coffee or tea is all it takes to give you a jolt, you haven't been shopping lately. With the popularity of special flavors that are available both in the local supermarket and in coffee and tea "bars," some types now cost more on a per-pound basis than the very finest cuts of meat.

But we don't seem to mind paying, because consumption of both beverages is ever perking. Sales of coffee are expected to double in

The Best for Less: Yuban

Much of the coffee available in supermarkets and specialty stores is a combination of the cheaper robusta and more expensive arabica beans. Price is often determined by the way the beans are combined—more expensive brands contain more arabica beans, while cheaper ones are overwhelmingly robusta.

The brand with a difference? Yuban, which is *all* arabica beans. Insiders say that it tastes far better than most other brands, even though it's about the same price or only a few pennies more per can. But it's not just the beans that make Yuban stand out. It is only lightly roasted for a milder flavor, while other brands tend to overdo the roasting process.

Most supermarkets sell Yuban, but you'll get it for less at discount or warehouse supermarkets where you bag your own groceries.

the 1990s compared to the previous decade, and tea consumption is growing at a rate of about 15 percent a year. What's also growing is the markup: Specialty coffees and teas average a retail markup of 45 percent, while the by-the-cup brews you'll find at the coffee bars are twice that amount. But no matter what your taste—and that can range from basic morning fuel to decaf hazelnut and vanilla creme—here's how to get your coffee and tea for less.

COFFEE

LOAD UP ON BRICKS. Coffee is packaged in several ways: in bags (either prepacked or self-serve), cans or foil-wrapped bricks. Generally, the bricks are the cheapest way to go. You'll pay an average of 10 percent less on an ounce-for-ounce basis when you buy bricks compared to cans, which is the way most people buy their coffee. Don't let size fool you: Even though they appear bigger than bricks, most cans contain 11 to 15 ounces, while bricks typically contain 13 to 16 ounces.

AVOID SELF-SERVE. More supermarkets are taking a hint from coffee specialty stores and selling whole beans that you grind and bag yourself. But usually you'll pay a premium for this self-serve coffee—generally, twice as much on a per-pound basis as regular prepackaged coffee in cans and foil bricks.

And don't assume you're getting better quality, either. Those "specialty" coffees featured in the self-serve bins usually contain the same beans as the prepackaged stuff like Folgers and Maxwell House—a combination of cheaper robusta and more expensive arabica beans. While the actual combination of these beans may vary from brand to brand, the main difference in taste between these self-serve specialty coffees and prepackaged brands has more to do with the addition of flavorings like vanilla and other ingredients. The beans are usually identical.

BYPASS THE BIG CAN. Coffee is one of the few items that doesn't cost less in the bigger size. In fact, you may even pay a slightly higher per-ounce price—as much as 10 percent—for the biggest can compared to the more typical 11- to 15-ounce cans. That's because supermarkets rarely put these larger cans on sale. While discount chains like Kmart do, the savings tend to be insignificant.

The exception: Buying in large quantities can save you when you shop at warehouse clubs like Sam's Club. Prices tend to be about 20 percent less on a per-ounce basis than you'll find in supermarkets.

GREAT MAIL-ORDER BUYS

The Supreme Bean Coffee Company is a small mail-order house in Redwood City, California, that consistently beats the competition for a wide variety of flavored and specialty coffees made with beans hailing from Guatemala, Colombia and Costa Rica. Figure you'll spend about 30 percent less than at Starbucks and other companies; shipping costs are also much less than those charged by other places. To get a catalog and ordering information, call 1-800-974-5282.

Tea drinkers should contact the San Francisco Herb Company or its sister company on the East Coast, the Atlantic Spice Company, for mail-order savings of up to 85 percent off retail. And while most other companies charge big prices for small amounts—usually selling only in ⅛- and ¼-pound quantities—these companies sell by the pound, for huge savings. The only hitch: A minimum order of $30 is required, so you may have to have a tea party with your friends to reap the savings. Call 1-800-227-4530 for a free San Francisco Herb catalog or 1-800-316-7965 for a free catalog from Atlantic Spice.

WATCH THE WEATHER CHANNEL. Those sudden drastic hikes in coffee prices—which can be 30 percent or more—tend to result from freezes or other weather conditions that affect the bean crop. So keeping your eye on weather conditions in Colombia and Brazil can give you an idea of expected price hikes.

Keep in mind that the hikes don't occur immediately after a freeze but usually two to six weeks afterward. So if you hear about a freeze (which would occur during our summer, since most coffee is grown south of the equator, where seasons are reversed), stock up before the price hikes hit.

TEA

BUY IN SEPTEMBER. Most tea leaves grow between May and August, and the new crop is sold to buyers in September. This is the time when leftover inventories are sold at drastically reduced prices, and wholesalers and retailers frequently pass their savings on to buyers. Besides taking advantage of price reductions of up to 15 percent at supermarkets and tea shops, it's also the best time to buy by mail order, since many catalogs run specials in the early fall.

GO WITH THE HOUSE BRAND. Most supermarkets sell generic brands of tea—usually in a large box containing 100 tea bags instead of the more traditional 15 to 30 bags. But you'll usually pay 60 percent less for these generic brands, even though many are produced by big-name companies.

MAKE YOUR OWN FLAVORED TEAS. Bag for bag, flavored teas are four times as much as regular tea—yet all are made from the same black tea leaves. The difference is in flavorings, not the actual leaves. So if you like the more expensive flavored teas, make your own by squeezing a few drops of orange or lemon juice into your cup or adding sweet cinnamon or peppermint leaves to get that flavor.

BAG THE BAGS. The cost of bags, box liners and staples doubles the cost of tea, so cut your spending by buying "loose" tea in cans or other containers. You just spoon out the desired amount and strain it.

COMPACT DISCS AND CASSETTES

It costs about $1.35 to manufacture a compact disc—and a lot less for a cassette. Add another $3.60 in royalties and copyright fees for the recording artist and other expenses and you've got a bottom-line manufacturer's cost of less than $5. So why are you paying an average of $17.99 for CDs and $10.99 for cassettes?

The recording industry says it's because the 10 percent of recordings that are chart-toppers have to subsidize the 90 percent that aren't. The manufacturers also claim they're still paying patent license fees and development rights on CD recording technology, introduced in 1982. While prices on CD and cassette players have fallen drastically since that time, prices on the music itself have hardly budged. Since a few distribution companies virtually monopolize the $12-billion-a-year recording industry—and also control the biggest mail-order music clubs—don't expect them to suddenly

OUTSTANDING OUTLETS

Wherehouse Entertainment, based in Torrance, California, claimed a major victory for the music-buying consumer when it stood up to the major labels for the right to offer used CDs, despite the threatened loss of millions in joint advertising. Wherehouse has 346 stores in 11 western states, and the majority sell both new and used CDs. On the East Coast, Strawberries Music and Video Stores also sell a large selection of used CDs. Besides a great selection, you'll get prices of anywhere from 10 to 40 percent below retail.

THE BEST FOR LESS: NAXOS

If you like classical music, look for the Naxos label. Launched by Hong Kong Philharmonic founder and international business mogul Klaus Heymann, Naxos charges about one-third the cost of bigger labels—for the same compositions. They do this by getting talented yet unknown musicians to do the recordings and paying them a low flat fee instead of royalties. The artists get recognition and you get classical CDs for under $6. The concept has been so successful that Naxos, based in Hong Kong, has cornered nearly 10 percent of the classical music market and now has its own racks in many music superstores.

Bigger-label competitors are trying to muscle in on Naxos's customer base, mostly by slapping discount prices on reissues that are not digital recordings. Exceptions are Sony Classical's Infinity Digital CDs, quality-recorded new music that can generally be found in music stores for under $5.

change their tune and offer great discounts. But here's how you can get better deals on your favorite recordings.

BUY USED. In one sense, compact discs are victims of their own success—they virtually never wear out. Although the recording industry has put pressure on retail stores that sell used CDs—only 1 percent of all CDs sold are used—more stores are now doing it, for anywhere from 40 to 60 percent less than new CDs. Cassettes, however, do tend to wear with age, so you won't usually find used cassettes for sale in music stores.

Some retail stores have a used CD display; others might sell used CDs but not advertise it. But your best bet is to go to an independent store that specializes in used CDs (you'll find them listed in the yellow pages or in advertisements in your local newspaper). Most used CDs run between $5 and $9. Just be sure to examine the CD before buying it, looking for scratches and other indications of inferior playing quality.

LOOK FOR AN OFF-BRAND LABEL. The biggest recording companies—RCA, PolyGram, Arista, Columbia and others—are the last places willing to offer you consistently great deals. True, they sometimes discount their inventory, but usually it's for the work of artists they have trouble selling or those that they want to be chart-toppers. Smaller recording labels tend to pay their artists a fixed fee—always—so the more recordings they sell, the bigger profit they make. Often they'll discount their music in an effort to sell at high volume.

And often the music is the same. One review of Gershwin's *Rhapsody in Blue* found that prices in the same store ranged from $5 for the no-name CD product to $17 for the major-label version. In fact, sometimes the more expensive version is the exact same recording as the cheaper version; only the packaging is different. Advice: Rifle through the bargain bin, where prices are low because the material tends to be old and the music is in the public domain, meaning the producer pays no royalties. While some of these discs are cheaply manufactured, keep in mind that even "cheap" CDs and cassettes have decent sound quality. If you have your heart set on a current title by a particular artist, though, you'll probably pay full price.

SHOP WHERE YOU BUY DISHWASHERS. The big record labels have prevented many record stores and even some discount chains from taking too much off the cost of first-quality releases by threatening to withhold their products from retailers that sell CDs at or below wholesale price (about $10.65 for a CD that lists for $16.98, and about the same difference for cassettes). But at least one company, Circuit City, has somehow gotten past this, probably because their main bread-and-butter isn't CDs but electronics and home appliances. Its stores offer many CDs and cassettes for just pennies above wholesale cost—all the time.

BECOME A CRITIC. If you buy some CDs or cassettes and review them for your local newspaper, you may be able to get free recordings from the manufacturer. Just send the clipping of your review to the recording company with a request to add your name to the review list. Music critics at major daily papers get from 15 to 40 recordings per week. Since many smaller papers don't have a bona fide music critic, often they use other staff members or even readers to do their reviews. You may not get paid for your efforts, but there's a very good chance you'll get your music for free. The giveaway: A notch in the plastic casing indicates that a CD was a free reviewer's copy, and you'll see hundreds of them at a used CD store.

USE MUSIC CLUBS TO YOUR ADVANTAGE. Music clubs can provide you with some great deals on CDs and cassettes—as long as you know how to play them. The clubs usually offer a set number of free recordings—sometimes as many as 12 tapes or CDs—as long as you agree to buy a minimum number of recordings per year (usually 4 to 6). You'll pay shipping and handling, which can add several dollars to the full price of these recordings. The lure of the deal is that the clubs gamble that you will like the convenience of having the recordings delivered to your door or you'll fall for the follow-up specials and keep ordering after you've fulfilled your membership requirements.

But after you buy the minimum, it's time to quit. It's more than likely that within a few months, the club will want to woo you back with another offer of freebies for a minimum purchase. There are two major mail-order houses, Columbia House and BMG Music Service; BMG offers better incentives and Columbia offers a wider selection. Both are worth joining—your free selections alone translate to substantial savings—but selection for selection, BMG tends to offer more savings. It has lower up-front costs, with only one required purchase, and better follow-up incentives.

COMPUTER SOFTWARE

There aren't any hard-and-fast rules in the computer software selling game, since the business is still in its infancy. Still, that won't stop you from crying like a baby when you see the sticker prices on computer games, spreadsheets and other programs. And prices aren't likely to get any better: Unlike just about every other product, software frequently costs *more* at the wholesale level than from a retail seller, so retailers have little incentive to offer great deals. Plus, markups tend to be low, ranging from 5 to 30 percent.

Software sales are about $7 billion a year, and you can expect that figure to increase. One of four homes now has a personal computer, and the fastest-growing software categories are "home" products such as educational and entertainment programs, including games. But no matter what software you buy, here's how you can keep more of your cold, hard cash.

CHOOSE YOUR SOFTWARE WHEN YOU BUY HARDWARE. It's no surprise that most new computers come with predesignated, preinstalled software—especially when you buy a unit with CD-ROM. What you may not know, however, is that you don't necessarily have to take what's offered. Competition is fierce for your computer-spending dollar, and savvy retailers aren't willing to lose a sale over a software package that's thrown in free by the manufacturer.

So if you don't need what's offered, or you simply want to get something extra, ask for it. Stores will often throw in what they have in the stockroom; the software collecting dust in the back room is often worth less than the commission they'll get for a computer sale. Mail-order computer companies are particularly flexible about packaging your choice of software with the hardware they sell you, and they'll usually install it before they ship your computer.

AVOID THE TRENDS. Having the latest software may be trendy, but it seldom makes much difference in the long run. Some software is periodically updated, but most of these "improvements" are just bells

GREAT MAIL-ORDER BUYS

PC Connection/MacConnection in Marlow, New Hampshire, isn't the biggest mail-order source for software, but it offers great prices along with toll-free technical support—as well as 30-day money-back guarantees on many products (something most companies don't do) and overnight delivery at no extra charge. It has IBM-compatible and Macintosh products in the same 180-page catalog, available by calling 1-800-800-1111.

and whistles for the serious technophile. You can save as much as 50 percent when ordering through mail-order houses by sticking with an earlier version. (You generally can't get earlier versions at computer stores, though the bigger ones may be willing to match mail-order prices on the new stuff.)

Advice: Read software reviews in computer magazines or the business pages of your newspaper to find out when the newest version of the software you want hits the shelves. Then buy the previous version from a mail-order company.

DO YOUR HOMEWORK BEFORE YOU BUY. Most people spend too much on software simply because they don't do their homework; they walk into a computer store without having first decided on the type of software they need. The result: They "overbuy" and get a more expensive package that offers too much for their needs. All brands of software in a particular category have the same ultimate function, but the way you operate them differs drastically.

So try out a friend's software or skim the reviews in popular computer magazines to find out exactly what you need before you start shopping. Some programs have more features than you'll ever use, which only raises the price and also eats up your computer's memory. But remember: No matter where you buy your software, register it with the manufacturer. That way you'll get on their mailing list and be able to upgrade later at a fraction of the cost.

LEARN TO SHARE. Some of the newest software can be yours for free or at rock-bottom prices in the form of "shareware." All you need is a modem (standard on many newer computers) and a telephone.

Thousands of programs are available on home-grown electronic bulletin boards and on-line networks for anyone who wants to dial in and download them. Shareware scared off most computer users in its early days, when it occasionally turned out to be a conduit for destructive electronic viruses. But the format has regained respectability with stricter safeguards and the formation of an oversight group called the Association of Shareware Publishers.

Today most shareware sells for about 30 to 50 percent less than comparable mainstream software. Payment is on the honor system, but it's best to send the money. Beyond the issue of honesty, it's required by law and allows you to call in for technical support and ask questions about how the software works, plus get manuals, upgrades and bonus utilities.

The biggest advantage of shareware is that you get to try it out before you pay; by comparison, it's virtually impossible to take most store-bought software for a test drive. Shareware can be found on mainstream networks such as America Online, Prodigy and CompuServe (you can get around their monthly fees by signing up for a free trial period) as well as on the Internet and home-grown electronic bulletin boards that advertise their telephone numbers in the back pages of computer magazines. Each of the mainstream networks mentioned has various introductory offers and provides a wide selection of shareware products for downloading by their users. So be sure to ask your on-line service about their shareware offerings.

Cookware

You don't have to be Betty Crocker to want good cookware. While Americans are spending less time in the kitchen than ever before, opting for heat-and-serve meals and other quick fare, we're spending record amounts on pots, pans and other cooking equipment—more than $2 billion a year.

One reason: Cookware today is for more than just cooking. Experts say that beautiful (and costly) copper-bottom pans are bought as much for decorating purposes as for cooking. And while Mom's old reliables—cast-iron and stainless steel—are still popular, more expensive, space-age materials like anodized aluminum are becoming more popular. Whatever you buy, here's how to get it for less.

Shop where the pros do. A restaurant supply house is probably your best bet for buying cookware at below-retail prices. These stores, which sell everything from salt and pepper shakers to upright freezers for those in the food preparation business, often sell professional-

Great Mail-Order Buys

Besides the catalogs offering great deals on "unique" items, like Crate & Barrel and the Chef's Catalog, it's worth a call to order a catalog from Kitchen, Etc. in Northampton, New Hampshire. You'll find first-quality cookware such as All-Clad Ltd., Calphalon, Cuisinart, Le Creuset, Revere and T-Fal for up to 40 percent off suggested list prices. The company also sells dinnerware, flatware, crystal and cutlery at similar savings. For more information, call 1-800-232-4070.

OUTSTANDING OUTLETS

Because most manufacturers of premier cookware want to keep tight control over the discounting of their products, few operate outlet stores. But several manufacturers of more moderately priced cookware do. Corning Revere has more than a dozen outlet stores throughout the country (call 1-800-999-3436 to find one near you) where you can get 25 percent off retail prices on items like Corning Ware and stainless steel Revere Ware. But those prices are similar to what you can find at a good sale at Wal-Mart.

For the best deals, you should go to the Corning Revere clearance store in Depew, New York. This clearance center sells closeouts and other hard-to-move items for as much as 50 percent off.

grade cookware for 30 to 60 percent below retail prices—sometimes less than you'd pay for mediocre department store brands.

Most larger cities have numerous restaurant suppliers, often on the same block; check the yellow pages under "Restaurant Equipment and Supplies." Still, that probably won't get you an additional discount, since the competition between them tends to be friendly and prices are very competitive. But you may be able to snag additional discounts of 5 to 10 percent if you're buying numerous pieces of cookware.

MAKE A SOLID INVESTMENT IN LIQUIDATIONS. For even better deals on cookware, you can capitalize on the misfortune of others—specifically, the owners of failed restaurants. About half of all new restaurants go out of business within the first few years of operation, resulting in numerous liquidation sales, where top-quality cookware can go for a song.

These sales are usually advertised under "Public Notices" in local newspapers. Sometimes they're held like an auction, with open bidding, and sometimes the items are prepriced and you pay that amount. Just make sure you inspect the offerings beforehand, because items may be *too* well-used. And some restaurant cookware sized for commercial stoves may be too big for yours, so before you buy, make sure you know the right sizes for your needs.

SET YOURSELF UP—OR MIX AND MATCH. You'll usually pay 20 to 35 percent less to buy a set of cookware than to purchase the same number of pieces separately. But a set isn't a bargain if you end up buying more pieces than you need. Most preboxed cookware sets contain eight or ten pieces, although some manufacturers sell sets with as few as three or four items.

If you can't find a small set, there's no rule that says you have to buy *matching* cookware. In fact, most professional cooks prefer mixing up an ensemble. For instance, copper-bottom pans are better for sautéeing, while cast-iron skillets are the choice for blackening food. Most retailers are interested in moving their merchandise, so even if you want to mix rather than match, you can probably negotiate a 10 to 30 percent discount on your total purchase, depending on the number of items you get.

SHOP IN SPRING. Cookware goes on sale frequently, so if you're not seeing discount signs, hold on to your wallet until the next markdown. Most stores have sales every few months, with especially

THE BEST FOR LESS: CALPHALON

Those in the know almost universally cast their cookware vote for Calphalon. Made of anodized aluminum and treated so it won't pit, discolor or otherwise react with food, this cookware looks good and works like the stuff professionals use.

Unfortunately, because of its reputation, its manufacturer wants to keep its hot product blazing, which means it's not carried in discount stores or outlets. But three times a year—usually in March, September and November—the Chef's Catalog in Northbrook, Illinois (one of Calphalon's largest distributors), has a warehouse sale offering a complete range of products at 30 to 50 percent off regular prices. Call the folks at the Chef's Catalog at 1-800-338-3232 for more information.

good price reductions during the Christmas shopping season. But the best time to buy is probably in the spring, just before manufacturers phase in new product lines (and prices) for the June wedding season. Closeouts abound in April and May, offering discounts of up to 50 percent off.

LOOK AT THOSE UNIQUE OFFERINGS. Some housewares catalogs best known for the uniqueness of their inventory are great sources of cookware. Crate & Barrel in Northbrook, Illinois, for example, sells its exclusive kitchen wares at quite reasonable prices, and you can get extra savings during their seasonal sales. To get a Crate & Barrel catalog, call 1-800-451-8217.

The Chef's Catalog, also in Northbrook, is another source of loads of hard-to-find items, including gourmet cookware at up to 40 percent off retail prices. It's available by calling 1-800-338-3232.

And A Cook's Wares in Beaver Falls, Pennsylvania, offers savings of 20 to 40 percent on French copper pans and other unique quality items. Call (412) 846-9490 to order a catalog.

BUY THE RIGHT STUFF. To make the most of your money, buy cookware that suits your needs. If you frequently use both a microwave and a conventional oven, you're better off with more versatile products like Visions by Corning Ware. You can get a 14-piece set for around $99, and it's fairly easy to clean, won't rust or react with food and conducts heat adequately. Another bonus: It costs substantially less than metal cookware.

If you choose metal cookware, stick with pots and pans with flat bottoms—concave surfaces may be better-looking, but they don't conduct heat as well. And look for handles that are held in place by rivets, which are more secure than those that are welded or screwed into place. Finally, stay away from metal handles unless you're the kind of cook who automatically reaches for a hotpad; plastic or wooden handles are better.

Cosmetics

Beauty may be in the eye of the beholder, but the price of that beauty is sometimes beastly. No other industry is built on such promises, such hype, such shiny packaging and straight-to-our-vanity pitches as the cosmetics industry.

Industry statistics show that we spend more than $16 billion a year trying to wipe out wrinkles, lengthen our lashes and silken our skin. It's easy to see why: Some people spend as much as $700 just for the basics at the trendy La Prairie counter at department stores. But here's how to look like a million bucks without spending the moola.

Head for Kmart, not the department store. You can spend $5 for Revlon or Cover Girl lipstick at your local Kmart or drugstore, or, depending on where you shop, shell out up to four times as much at your favorite department store for a high-end version of the same item.

Great Mail-Order Buys

For discounts on name-brand cosmetics up to 90 percent below retail prices, send for the Beauty Boutique catalog, which offers fragrances, cosmetics and skin-care products. You can get it by calling (216) 826-1712. If you want discount cosmetics that use only natural ingredients, environment-friendly packaging and no animal testing, catalogs from two companies—The Body Shop by Mail in Wake Forest, North Carolina (1-800-541-2535) and the Self-Care Catalog in Emeryville, California (1-800-345-3371)—are worth having. Discounts in both these catalogs are about 30 percent off retail prices.

OUTSTANDING OUTLETS

You can find brand-name fragrances and cosmetics at between 20 and 75 percent off retail at a chain of outlet mall stores called Prestige Cosmetics, which operates in 38 states. The huge discounts stem from the fact that Prestige (like other outlets) often stocks discontinued lines or merchandise that was left over from a department store purchase. There's nothing wrong with the products themselves; usually they're just part of the previous year's inventory. East Coast residents can learn of the nearest Prestige store by calling (407) 345-0101; those in the West can call (213) 887-1135.

The difference is mainly the price: Insiders say that the actual ingredients are the same or very similar for most products. For every dollar spent on cosmetics, no matter what or where you buy, less than 10 cents goes to the product itself. Instead, the added cost of department store cosmetics helps pay for that fancy glass-encased counter and the white lab coat worn by the salesclerk, who may wear the "uniform" but isn't necessarily a cosmetician (someone trained in the use of cosmetics) or a cosmetologist (someone trained to give beauty treatments).

GO GREEN TO SAVE GREEN. More cosmetics counters, including green-minded The Body Shop, are selling their wares in returnable containers—you simply take back the empty and save on your next purchase of the same brand. While the savings may seem minimal—usually between 25 cents and $1—this no-effort policy can save you 10 percent or more on each purchase.

ASK FOR SAMPLES—LOTS OF THEM. No matter where you shop, you can try any brand of lipstick, rouge or other cosmetics free of charge. Simply ask for several days' worth of samples; they're usually tucked away under the counter. The key is to ask for several: Most clerks gladly hand out one sample—usually because no one asks for more.

BUY DURING GIFT-WITH-PURCHASE PERIODS. Besides flat-out sales, which are nonseasonal and can be held anytime the store needs to move its merchandise (you need to keep your eyes peeled for them), most cosmetics companies offer two types of money-stretching promotions: A "purchase-with-purchase" program and a "gift-with-purchase" sale. The first is there to lure you to spend more than you need to; you'll pay a so-called discounted price for a wide array of goods, yet you'll actually wind up spending more because you're buying some products you don't really need. The gift-with-purchase program, however, usually offers a lower price for the actual cosmetics as well as a freebie like a watch or umbrella. Look for these sales at most places where you buy cosmetics around Christmas.

LENGTHEN THE LIFE OF YOUR COSMETICS (AS WELL AS YOUR LASHES). The longer cosmetics last, the less often you'll have to buy them. And there are several things you can do to keep them from drying out. For example, if you use a lip brush when applying lipstick, you'll get at least 20 more applications per tube. You can also use the brush to pull lipstick from the bottom of the tube. And while it's unwise to use mascara that's more than six months old, you can prevent premature crustiness by *not* pumping the tube, which causes it to dry out faster. Also, run the mascara tube under hot water before each application and it will last several weeks longer. Knowledgeable salesclerks know other tips to extend the life of cosmetics, so ask them.

Costume Jewelry

You may think of it as "cheap," but costume jewelry sure isn't priced that way. In general, it has one of the highest markups of any retail item—generally selling for four times its wholesale or manufacturer's cost. That means that a ring that sells for $8 was purchased by the retailer for about $2.

It also means there's a lot of room for markdowns. With the costume jewelry business experiencing a downturn, prices are falling, and you can get some terrific buys. In fact, costume jewelry may be one of today's truly great accessory bargains. While it won't be made of gold, it is durable, and some of the gold electroplating and precious faux stones or crystals look like the real thing for only a fraction of the price. Here's how to get a deal.

Follow the seasons. As with other accessories, you can save by buying jewelry in the off-season—usually several months after it's in fashion. Costume pearl jewelry and pastel-colored jewelry are popular in spring and summer, so buy them in the fall and winter months to save 30 percent. And since it's popular in the winter, jewelry with dark-colored stones—including imitation rubies, sapphires and emeralds—generally costs about one-third less when purchased during the spring or summer.

Buy a boxed set. Look for costume jewelry in boxed sets and save big—at least 30 percent compared to buying the same items individually. The reason: Packaging costs. A box costs a manufacturer at least 50 cents, and he usually charges the retailer twice that amount. But with boxed sets, extra packaging is eliminated, so the set can be sold for less.

Or look for novelty cards. Another way to eliminate the expense of boxes is to package multiple sets of earrings on cardboard and sell them at greatly reduced prices—up to 60 percent off regular per-item costs. Usually they are packaged in two ways, as a "calendar" card containing 30 pairs of earrings (one for each day of the month) or as a 12-inch "ruler" card with a pair of earrings located at each inch of the ruler. The per-pair cost of earrings packaged this way is usually under $1.

LOOK ACROSS THE PACIFIC. The Orient has become strong competition for domestic costume jewelry manufacturers because low labor costs there can translate into lower prices here. Some industry veterans say that domestic costume jewelry may be as much as 40 percent higher than imports. While there has been some concern in recent years over the quality of these imports, insiders say it is improving, although some merchandise is still not as good as what's made stateside.

HEAD TO RHODE ISLAND. Besides being the capital of our smallest state, Providence is also the costume jewelry capital of the world. The city's Olneyville Square has nearly two blocks of wholesalers, each claiming to sell costume jewelry for less than the next. Some stores require a minimum purchase of about $25, but savings generally run 50 to 90 percent.

Why Providence? Besides having a number of costume jewelry manufacturers in and near the city, it's long been a settling spot for immigrants (many from Italy) who make and sell jewelry.

CREDIT CARDS

The comfortable monopoly on credit cards once enjoyed by banks is dwindling as automakers, clothing stores and even hardware stores plunge into the market. But don't cry too hard for the banks: The difference between what they pay for the money loaned to you for credit purchases and what they charge you averages 15 interest points.

Also, most credit card companies charge an annual fee, some up to $85 or more, just for the privilege of using their card. They also may lure new customers with low initial rates that increase within months and even charge interest on your purchases before you get the bill.

Yet we can't seem to kick the credit habit. Collectively, Americans owe a staggering $340 billion on credit cards—mainly because two of three cardholders carry over their balance from one month to the next. But even if you're the typical American who routinely uses up to three credit cards, here's how to trim the cost of buying on credit.

HAGGLE. Whether you're seeking a new card or just want a better rate on existing cards, you can probably get a lower rate than you're currently paying. That's because Visa, MasterCard and other credit cards are issued independently by 6,000 banks and other institutions, not by centralized companies. In essence, they are private vendors in competition with each other for your business.

So make them compete—by making them realize that they need your business more than you need theirs. Many credit card holders are bombarded each week with phone and mail solicitations promising low rates and other benefits. And while these deals may sound great, you can generally reduce the offered interest rate by 1 to 1½ points by calling the toll-free number on the application form and telling the customer service representative that you've shopped around for new plastic and are giving them an opportunity to "match" the better offer. They may initially balk at your request to

GETTING THE BEST DEAL

With credit card rates and fees in constant flux, how do you find the best deal for you? Your Uncle Sam is a great place to start: The Federal Reserve issues "SHOP: The Card You Pick Can Save You Money," a free twice-yearly list of credit card interest rates charged by banks responding to that survey, along with their telephone numbers. Call (202) 452-3244 for a copy of the list.

Some private companies that are also helpful:

- CardTrak, a consulting service based in Frederick, Maryland, offers a monthly report listing about 500 of the lowest-cost cards and highlighting the best new deals on the market. It costs $5 and can be ordered by calling 1-800-344-7714.
- Bankcard Holders of America is a membership organization that has two dozen different publications, including lists of the lowest-rate cards and descriptions of rebate cards. Membership is $24, but you don't have to join to order any of the publications, which cost $1 to $5 each. Call (540) 389-5445 to order.
- *Bank Rate Monitor*, a weekly newsletter, sells a monthly updated list of the best credit card deals, based on low rates and no annual fee. You can order one for $10 by calling 1-800-327-7717, and charge it to your Visa or MasterCard.

shave off a point or two, but you should offer to leave your name and number with the customer service manager in case they change their mind. Sometimes you'll get a return call within a week offering a better rate.

GO FOR THE GOLD. Although they vary from issuer to issuer, Gold Cards traditionally have lower interest rates than other credit cards—anywhere from ½ to 2½ points. So one of the best ways to instantly reduce your credit card costs is to ask your bank to upgrade you to a Gold Card. (Despite the glamour they once held, you don't necessarily need a high income to qualify for one—only a good credit history.)

As with other cards, you can haggle for lower interest rates with a Gold Card. But don't expect across-the-board savings: Some Gold Cards have higher annual fees because of extra enhancements like auto rental discounts and other perks. Others simply extend your credit line without lowering your interest rate significantly, if at all. So when going for the gold, be specific about your wants—and insist on a Gold Card whose main benefit is a lower rate than what you're paying.

SHOP WHERE YOU'RE KNOWN. Find out about credit card terms offered where you bank, since the bank is likely to have a special deal for its customers. Some of the best rates are available from credit unions, professional associations, special interest groups and alumni clubs. Organizations such as the American Association for Retired Persons (AARP) and the Union Privilege AFL-CIO, for instance, offer particularly good terms for members.

THE LOWDOWN ON FREE AIR TRAVEL

Some credit cards offer fringe benefits like free gas or even money back, but one of the more popular special promotions is for cards that offer free frequent-flier miles. Are they as good as they sound?

Maybe—but only if you're someone who already flies a lot, buys frequently on credit, and most important, pays off that balance at the end of each month. The premise is easy: For every dollar you spend, you get one mileage credit toward a free airline ticket. Also, with some cards, you can rack up extra points for staying in membership hotels—again a plus for those who already do a lot of traveling. But like other reward cards, frequent-flier plastic tends to have high interest rates—typically 40 percent higher than other credit cards with no special deals. So consider that you need to make about $25,000 worth of purchases (the minimum is 25,000 mileage points for one domestic free trip) before you get a free frequent-flier ticket. If you don't pay off your balance each month, you could pay more in interest alone than it would cost to buy airline tickets.

SEEK A CARD THAT SUITS YOUR SPENDING. Of course, interest rates aren't everything—especially if you're the type who pays off your bill quickly or never carries a balance over $1,000. If you are, it may be even more important to get a card with no annual fee. (If you're slow to pay the bill, however, concentrate on getting a lower interest rate.) If your current card requires that you pay an annual fee, ask the issuer to waive it, but keep in mind that American Express never waives its fees.

READ THE SMALL PRINT. Getting the best deal on a credit card has as much to do with dodging hidden charges as it does with finding the best rates. Waiving the annual fee won't help at all if you get stuck with a credit card that has concealed extra costs for such things as cash advances and late payments. Many banks are compensating for lower rates and fees by adding hidden charges or changing the way they calculate the interest. Avoid any credit card that figures interest charges from the date of purchase instead of giving you a grace period of at least 24 days, and preferably up to two months. And if you've been tempted by an "initial low rate," remember that the seemingly attractive introductory interest figure can nearly double within six months.

These short-term offers do have a benefit, however: You can transfer your other debts to your new low-rate card and pay off the balance before the interest rate increases. By doing this, you can save nearly $80 on a $1,000 balance.

CRYSTAL

When it comes to entertaining at home, casual may be in, but it's hard to buck tradition. Most brides-to-be still register for crystal, thus helping to keep fine glassware sales at over $3 billion a year.

But in an attempt to snag even the most informal diners, retailers are offering more choices of crystal than ever before. And designers are experimenting with more colors, simpler lines and glass that has fewer cuts.

OUTSTANDING OUTLETS

If you don't mind driving, factory outlets offer some great deals on certain lines of crystal. Mikasa fans will want to check out factory outlets in Secaucus, New Jersey (201-867-2354) or Long Beach, California (310-886-3700), where they can save up to 50 percent on overruns and discontinued patterns.

For more general discounts, try the China Cabinet in Tenafly, New Jersey (201-567-2711). Its warehouse offers savings of up to 40 percent on selected crystal patterns from Gorham, Orrefors and Baccarat, among others. And Rudi's Pottery, Silver & China in Paramus, New Jersey (201-265-6096) boasts similar discounts on stemware from Baccarat, Belleek, Bernardaud Limoges, Fitz & Floyd, Galway, Gorham, Lalique, Lenox, Mikasa, Minton, Noritake and Orrefors, among others. You can also get price quotes and order by phone from any of these outlets.

THE BEST FOR LESS: BACCARAT

The crème de la crème of crystal, a single Baccarat goblet can set you back $100. For pure elegance and quality, nothing beats it. But while Baccarat is considered by many to be the finest, many insiders suggest Waterford. You can buy either brand for less by ordering by mail from Barrons (1-800-538-6340), Michael C. Fina (212-869-5050) or Ross-Simons (1-800-556-7376), where these brands are sold for 20 percent off retail prices. You also might want to consider Waterford's "by Marquis" economy line, which starts at about $25 per goblet and is also available from these catalogs. This stemware is manufactured under license with Waterford by factories in Portugal and Germany.

Given the fact that a single Waterford goblet can set you back $50 to $65, however, it's still easy to run up a big tab just providing the happy couple with enough crystal for a private toast. Fortunately, there are ways to save, if you know what to look for and where to shop.

DELAY UNTIL APRIL—OR OCTOBER. The best deals on crystal at department stores like Macy's and Marshall Field's are available during their annual housewares sales, when prices are discounted as much as 50 percent. The sales tend to occur in April, just before the busy wedding season, and again in October for the Christmas season, although some stores have sales throughout the year.

BUY BY MAIL ORDER. Unless you've stumbled upon a fabulous promotion at a department store or specialty shop, you'll probably get the best deals on crystal through mail order. Because they buy in bulk, mail-order houses allow you to save anywhere from 50 to 75 percent off retail prices and get goods from nearly every major crystal maker.

There are about a dozen mail-order companies, but insiders say the best deals on top-quality crystal are from Barrons in Novi, Michigan (1-800-538-6340), which features goods from Gorham, Lenox, Waterford and Mikasa; Michael C. Fina in New York City (212-869-

5050), which has Atlantis, Baccarat, Gorham, Lenox, Miller Rogaska, Noritake, Orrefors, Royal Doulton, Sasaki, Stuart and Waterford; Ross-Simons in Cranston, Rhode Island (1-800-556-7376), which carries Lenox, Gorham and Waterford; and Albert S. Smyth Company in Timonium, Maryland (1-800-638-3333), which also offers crystal from several different manufacturers.

ASK FOR A DISCONTINUED PATTERN. One way to save even more at mail-order houses (and a few department stores) is to ask for patterns that have been discontinued. You'll save at least 50 percent—and more during sales. Just be sure you buy enough of the pattern so that replacing a broken piece won't be a problem.

CUTLERY

Professional chefs take only two things with them when they switch restaurants—their recipes and their knives. Good knives are an extension of a chef's hands, and like hands, they should last a lifetime.

The tricky part comes in getting quality carvers for a price that's been sliced below retail. Long-lasting knives tend to carry big prices and a retail markup of between 50 and 100 percent, depending on where you shop. The best knives use high-carbon stainless steel, a nonstaining alloy that holds a sharp and uniform edge. The handles might be wood or a plastic composite, but stick with plastic when you can: Wooden handles can rot, discolor or chip with misuse. They also turn slippery when wet or greasy.

Years ago the pros demanded that a knife's nonblade metal, or tang, run the full length of the handle. But now quality manufacturers like Henckels use high-tech bonding techniques that don't require a full tang. This often makes for a lighter, easier-to-use knife, and it's just as secure as the old full-tang models. While fine knives are never cheap, here's how you can save while outfitting your cutlery drawer.

HOLD OUT FOR THE HOLIDAYS. Your gift for buying knives just prior to Christmas, Mother's Day or Father's Day: a typical 20 percent discount. That's because major knife manufacturers discount their merchandise for these holidays, and retailers invariably pass the good cheer on to you.

SHOP WITH THE PROS. For the best selection and price, head to a restaurant supply store, where cutlery typically sells for up to 70 percent below retail. A case in point: An eight-inch Mundial chef's knife sold for under $8 at a major Los Angeles restaurant supply store, while a comparable Henckels Eurocraft knife went for $23 at a nearby discount chain. Restaurant supply stores also carry brands not typically found in department stores and specialty shops. Look in the yellow pages under "Restaurant Equipment and Supplies."

CUT A DEAL AT AN ESTATE SALE. Since fine knives are practically indestructible, they often outlive their owners—so head to estate sales in

The Best for Less: Victorinox

Quality knives should last a lifetime, so it doesn't make sense to settle for second best, especially since the best knives don't necessarily cost the most. While few doubt the quality of an $80 Wusthof-Trident chef's knife, the lesser-known Swiss-made Victorinox line is just as good (and maybe even better, according to some insiders). Its similar eight-inch chef's knife costs only $30, with either a rosewood or composite plastic handle.

To get it for even less, buy during holiday sales just before Christmas, Mother's Day and Father's Day, when retailers typically discount quality knives about 20 percent.

better neighborhoods for some incredible buys. At these sales, advertised in the classified section of local newspapers, you can pay only pennies on the dollar. But since fine knives are expensive, you'll probably only find them when the wealthy die and their heirs sell off their belongings. One recent sale netted us a Wusthof-Trident eight-inch chef's knife for only $5; its retail value is about $80.

You're usually able to check cutlery before the bidding starts, so take advantage of that. Look for cracks in the handles and large nicks, but keep in mind that small nicks and other imperfections can easily be ground out.

Pass on sets. Most chefs make do with only "the basic four": an eight- or ten-inch chef's knife, a slicing knife for meat, a five- or six-inch utility knife and a three-inch paring knife. So spending a lot for a bigger set is a waste of your money—especially if you opt for those laser-sharpened knives you see on late-night TV. Their edges tend to wear out, and eventually they can only be thrown away.

Your best bet: Stick to well-known European brands like Henckels, Wusthof-Trident, Victorinox and Sabatier. You'll pay between $15 and $80 per knife, but you'll never need to buy another.

Dishes and Dinnerware

The $1.5-billion-a-year casual dinnerware market used to be recession-proof, thanks to the steady flow of gift-receiving newlyweds who were responsible for more than half its revenue. But as more couples plan for married life by registering at hardware stores instead of china shops, the industry is being forced to change dramatically in order to generate new sales.

How? By producing a larger variety of new patterns and lowering prices on everyday dishes and dinnerware. Even so, here's how you can save even more.

Be a post-Yuletide buyer. As with other home furnishings, casual dinnerware sells most briskly from October until the December holidays, while January and February are notoriously slow months. So that's the time you'll find low clearance-sale prices on remainders and returned sets—real discounts of up to 30 percent off regular retail prices rather than the "great deals" advertised in those full-color glossy flyers when the dishes first arrive in the stores.

There is also a spate of specials just before Thanksgiving and around Mother's Day. And to stir up sales, some retailers also tie promotional activities to other holidays you wouldn't expect. For example, manufacturers will add an orange accent to a set of white dishes, throw in a centerpiece bowl that looks like a pumpkin and sell it as a Halloween collection. Holly in the pattern makes for a quaint Christmas set; also look for shamrock highlights on St. Patrick's Day. Generally, the best time to buy these so-called celebration table settings is November 1, December 26 and March 18—the days after the respective special occasions.

Take it to the bank—or supermarket. Remember when local banks passed out sets of dishes to new account-holders or when supermarkets offered table settings to their customers who saved their register receipts? Some still do. And don't assume the merchandise is of poor quality. Respected manufacturers such as Corelle continue to participate in these promotions. You'll need to shop around for these freebies, but a few phone calls can nab you a four-piece setting.

HEAD FOR THE BLUE LIGHT. Mass-merchandise "blue light special" retailers like Wal-Mart and Kmart are the kings of casual dinnerware, accounting for 40 percent of all new dishes sold. And the gap in quality between what you'll find there and what's available from elegant department stores is narrowing. Since most consumers make their purchase based on pattern, there's virtually no difference between the Southwestern, contemporary and traditional designs you'll find at mass merchandisers and those at expensive retail stores. The prices are as low as $20 for a 20-piece set that looks similar to the $60 sets on sale at the fancy mall department stores.

One drawback: The selection is more limited. But if you don't find what you like, here's more good news: Competition from mass mer-

THE BEST FOR LESS: PFALTZGRAFF

Although it's been owned by the same family since 1811, Pfaltzgraff isn't living in the past. While it offers classic patterns that have been in production for as long as 30 years, the company has also introduced fanciful contemporary styles ranging from basic black to art deco. And unlike many other manufacturers, its central distribution center is in the United States and maintains a large inventory of back patterns, so you can replace your chipped or broken dishes years after you bought them. There's even a toll-free number you can call to ask questions such as whether you can put your Pfaltzgraff product in the microwave.

Pfaltzgraff dinnerware starts at about $40 for a 20-piece set and can run as high as $200 for some styles. But you can save anywhere from 20 to 50 percent off retail prices at the company's 60 factory stores from coast to coast. Call 1-800-999-2811 for locations.

OUTSTANDING OUTLETS

You can furnish your entire house at Bed Bath & Beyond, a national chain of more than 80 giant discount stores. You'll find ceiling-high stacks of a huge variety of dinnerware sets and matching open stock for as little as half what the big department stores charge. The displays are customer-friendly and the salespeople tend to be more knowledgeable than their counterparts at other bargain outlets. For the location nearest you, call (201) 379-1520. (In New England, the stores are called BB&Beyond to avoid confusion with a local chain that has a similar name.)

chandisers has forced department stores to expand their dinnerware inventory and reduce prices.

BUY IT DIRECT. To the irritation of their retailers—and the benefit of customers—some major dinnerware makers have opened outlet stores to sell first-quality, slightly chipped and open-stock merchandise at discount prices. Among them are Corning/Corelle (1-800-999-3436), Crate & Barrel (1-800-451-8217), Dansk (914-697-6400), Fitz & Floyd (1-800-243-2058), Lenox (1-800-423-8946), Mikasa (1-800-489-2200), Royal Doulton (908-356-7880) and Villeroy & Boch (609-734-7800); call for the location of the nearest outlet store. Although some of these companies specialize in selling china, they also sell casual dinnerware direct to consumers at prices as much as 40 percent below retail.

Doctor Visits

You may be hurting when you go to the doctor, but your doctor's bank account certainly isn't. More than *$1 trillion* is spent on health care each year—over $18 million alone on routine office visits. Although prices vary depending on your condition and where you live, the average office visit (which usually lasts only a few minutes) costs $53; first-time patients pay nearly $100 to see a doctor or specialist. But there are ways to get top-quality health care for less.

Pay out of your pocket. Even if you have health insurance, sometimes it's in your best interest *not* to use it—especially if you rarely go to the doctor and have little chance of meeting your deductible. In this case, you may be able to cut up to 40 percent off your doctors' visits simply by bypassing insurance and paying out of your own pocket.

Some doctors are willing to negotiate their fees—especially if they can avoid the hassle of paying their staff to fill out insurance forms. Other doctors do this because they would rather get some money up front than wait to get all of it down the road. Advice: When you first get to the doctor's office, ask the receptionist if the doctor offers discounts to patients who pay cash.

Get help from your employer. Besides providing your basic health insurance, many employers allow you to contribute to a lesser-known Medical Reimbursement Account. This account covers what your insurance doesn't; in addition, the money you put into this fund is *not* taxable income. And when you spend money for medical care that isn't covered by your insurance—including costs applied to your deductible—you can be reimbursed. A word of caution, though: Make sure you spend the money in this fund, because it's a use-it-or-lose-it situation; money not taken out during the year is your loss.

See a Jack-of-all-trades. Specialists charge almost twice as much as general practitioners for an office visit, yet family doctors, or primary care physicians, are qualified to treat you for many of the same con-

TAKE ADVANTAGE OF FREEBIES

Health departments in most cities and states may offer some low-cost and free medical tests and screenings for residents—usually the very same tests given by your doctor for a fee. You can learn what's available by calling your local health department. These centers also provide some free or low-cost vaccines for both children and adults.

Nationally, the American Cancer Society offers information on free or low-cost screenings for skin, colon, prostate and other cancers, as well as low-cost mammograms. The availability of tests depends on where you live; call 1-800-227-2345 for more information. If the test turns up something suspicious, however, you will need to see your own doctor.

And if you're over 65, living on a limited, fixed income and don't have access to an ophthalmologist (an M.D. with training in eye care), the National Eye Care Project can refer you to an ophthalmologist who will provide care with no out-of-pocket expense to you. Call 1-800-222-3937 for a referral to the program, sponsored by state ophthalmological societies and the Foundation of the American Academy of Ophthalmology. You can also get written information on eye care and eye disease by calling or writing the National Eye Care Project, P.O. Box 429098, San Francisco, CA 94142-9098.

ditions. So before seeing a specialist for an initial consultation, call your family doctor to see if you need the specialist's care. Many people routinely assume that a proctologist is the best person to treat a new case of hemorrhoids or that an otolaryngologist (ear, nose and throat specialist) can give the best care for a sore throat or earache. Often that specialist will run the same tests and prescribe the same medications as a primary care physician, for 40 to 60 percent more money. Of course, for chronic or more serious conditions, a specialist is your best bet—as your family doctor will likely tell you.

CALL FOR ADVICE, NOT NECESSARILY AN APPOINTMENT. Before you make an appointment that can cost you $50 or more, try to get your answers over the phone. Considering that some doctors see up to 100 pa-

DO-IT-YOURSELF MEDICAL RESEARCH

Free or low-cost information on virtually any health condition may be as close as a local library.

Medline, the National Library of Medicine's database, contains references and abstracts of articles in scientific and medical journals. It's available at most medical libraries and some university and college libraries.

For those seeking more information on alternative as well as conventional medical treatments, the Planetree Health Resource Center at California Pacific Medical Center, 2040 Webster Street, San Francisco, has a well-stocked medical library that's available to the public. Bay area residents can use it from 11:00 A.M. to 5:00 P.M. on Tuesday, Thursday, Friday and Saturday and from 11:00 A.M. to 7:00 P.M. on Wednesday; nonresidents can call (415) 923-3681 for over-the-phone information. The center will, at no cost, refer you to other organizations that provide information, or it can conduct a search for you. There is a charge ranging from $20 to $100, depending on how in-depth a search you seek.

For referrals to condition-specific clearinghouses (nonprofit groups that provide literature on a specific disease or condition), write the National Health Information Center at P.O. Box 1133, Washington, DC 20013-1133.

tients a day, many are happy to answer basic questions or fill prescriptions over the phone for long-time patients—especially those who belong to a health maintenance organization (HMO). That's because HMOs pay the doctor a flat fee per patient, no matter how often he sees you. Although some doctors will insist on an office visit to make sure there are no complications, others will gladly provide answers to your questions over the phone. So if you know you need a prescription refill for allergies or another long-term problem, or your condition has improved before a scheduled follow-up visit, call the office with as many details as you can, and you might get answers without an expensive office visit.

Your insurance company is another place to get free advice. Some companies provide free help lines staffed by nurses who answer health-related questions; others have prerecorded health information lines that can help answer your questions.

CHECK INTO A MED SCHOOL. If there's a health sciences or medical school in your area, a phone call could lead you to low-cost or free programs such as health screenings and information services provided by students under the supervision of licensed professionals. And dental schools may offer the same services as a dentist's office for as much as 65 percent less. One drawback: You may have to wait longer to be seen; plan on spending a couple of hours for treatment that would take about 45 minutes in a dentist's office.

CONSIDER A BIRTHING CENTER. If you're pregnant and have had no complications, you can slice 30 to 45 percent off your delivery charges by choosing a birthing center instead of a hospital. There are over 135 across the country, and all are "associated" with hospitals, meaning that they can transfer you to a hospital if there are complications. Delivery is usually done by a certified nurse-midwife, who works in consultation with a physician. For information on the nearest birthing center, write to the National Association of Childbearing Centers, 3123 Gottschall Road, Perkiomenville, PA 18074-9546, or call (215) 234-8068. The association requests a donation of $1 for the referral.

Drugs and Medications

Americans pay more for medicine than just about anyone—over $50 billion a year for prescription drugs and another $12 billion for over-the-counter medications. And don't expect that to change anytime soon.

Since the 1980s, the cost of prescriptions has increased at more than three times the rate of inflation. One reason behind these skyrocketing prices: We're a captive audience. When you're sick, you need your medicine, and few folks quibble over its price—or are even aware of it until the pharmacist tallies up the cost.

Luckily, 100 million Americans are on some sort of insurance or medical assistance plan to get prescriptions for only a small percentage of the actual cost. But there are still ways to lower the cost of doctor-prescribed and over-the-counter drugs and medications.

Prescription Drugs

Get samples from your doctor. According to industry figures, pharmaceutical companies spend about $2.5 billion each year giving free samples to doctors—about $5,000 worth of medicine to every physician. The companies do this in hopes that the doctor will prescribe or recommend these drugs to their patients.

These samples are usually the newest and most expensive drugs offered by the pharmaceutical companies, so do yourself a favor: Whenever your doctor starts writing a prescription, ask if a trial dose packet is available. Most doctors readily give them to those who ask.

Seek out generics. Nearly 40 percent of all prescriptions are now filled with generic drugs—and with good reason. Generics are typically about half the cost of brand-name medications with the same ingredients. Generics undergo the same rigorous tests of content and quality as brand-name drugs. And according to tests by the Food and Drug Administration, the quality of generics is just as good as that of

GREAT MAIL-ORDER BUYS

In 1981, $100 million per year was spent on mail-order prescriptions. By 1994, the amount soared to $6 billion. The reason: Savings of up to 40 percent on popular prescription drugs, as well as many over-the-counter medications.

There are several mail-order pharmaceutical services, but the biggest and best-known is the AARP Pharmacy Service, based in Alexandria, Virginia, which fills over eight million prescriptions a year. Carrying over 12,000 prescription and drugstore items, this service is a benefit for members of the American Association of Retired Persons (although nonmembers can also place orders if they call the toll-free number). Orders are usually shipped within 24 to 48 hours by UPS or first-class mail.

You can place an order or request a catalog by calling 1-800-456-2277 or get a price quote by calling 1-800-456-2226 from 7:00 A.M. to 7:00 P.M. Monday through Friday and from 7:00 A.M. to 1:00 P.M. on Saturday. (Hearing-impaired persons with access to a TTY can call 1-800-933-4327.)

the brand-name versions. The difference in price is mostly due to higher costs for initial research and discovery of the drug.

Both your doctor and the pharmacist should offer you the option of choosing a generic, but many don't. Doctors usually don't give their patients an option: They write a prescription for the name brand, and the pharmacist follows it. So before you have a prescription filled, ask the pharmacist for the generic version. (While there are some drugs that shouldn't be replaced with generics, in some states, by law, a pharmacist must substitute a generic unless the doctor or patient specifies otherwise.)

GO DISCOUNT. No matter what you buy, get it at a discount chain and you'll typically pay 15 to 35 percent less than drugstore prices. Chains like Wal-Mart and Kmart offer some of the best deals on many drugs, but you'll also save big at regional discount drugstore chains like Drug Emporium and Phar-Mor. These stores can sell for less because they buy medications in such large quantities.

BUY IN VOLUME. Pharmacists charge a professional fee each time a prescription is filled—whether it's for 1 pill or 100. So if you're taking medication for a chronic condition and frequently need refills, ask your doctor to write a prescription for three to six months' worth of medication. This way, you may get a slight discount for buying in bulk, and you'll also save the filling fee.

But if this is the first time you are filling a prescription, it may be wise to just get a week's worth of medicine. That way if you have a bad reaction, you won't get stuck with useless medication. Ask your doctor about this option.

OVER-THE-COUNTER MEDICATIONS

DON'T BE A SLAVE TO NAME BRANDS. Store-brand varieties of vitamins, pain relievers and other over-the-counter products usually contain ingredients identical to those of their brand-name counterparts but can cost up to 60 percent less. Most drugstore chains and even supermarkets have their own store brands of ibuprofen, acetaminophen, allergy medicines and other common over-the-counter products. Read the labels and you'll see no difference—except on the price tag.

ASK FOR A FREEBIE. Besides prescription drugs, doctors also get—and give—free samples of over-the-counter pain relievers and other medications. In fact, the free samples you can get at your doctor's office are sometimes stronger and faster-working than commonly bought store items.

Drugstore Items and Toiletries

The dizzying array of pain relievers, beauty products and other drugstore items and toiletries lining the aisles of drugstores, supermarkets and discount chains is enough to make your head spin—or at least keep it (and the rest of you) looking and feeling good.

Americans spend over $20 billion a year on these items—everything from deodorants and shaving creams to corn removers and bandages. That translates to about $200 worth of these products crowding the bathroom sinks and medicine cabinets of every U.S. household. That's not a lot in real dollars—about $4 a week—but here's how to save even more when buying these products.

Band that soap dispenser. Advertisements have conditioned us to use more of a product than we actually need. Toothpaste ads display a healthy strip of toothpaste along the entire brush, when all that's really needed is a small dab. Shampoo bottles instruct you to wash your hair twice, but a single washing is sufficient. With these products, you can control the amount you use.

When you use liquid soap dispensers, however, the pump is designed to dispense more soap than you need to clean your hands. Try placing a rubber band around the base of the pump so it pumps less. The soap will last twice as long and you'll be just as clean.

Buy like a man. Ounce for ounce, deodorants, shaving creams, hair colorings and other "dual-gender" products targeted for men sell for up to 20 percent less than similar products aimed at women. But read the labels and you'll see that there's little—if any—actual difference in ingredients.

Or like a groomer. The rage in beauty aids right now is animal-care products—not only because they are cheaper but also because some people like the results. For years, horse owners have been sneaking capfuls of equine shampoo and mane detangler onto their own heads—at only 3 cents per ounce—after noticing how the products tamed the coarsest horse hair. In fact, sales of Mane 'n Tail by

GREAT MAIL-ORDER BUYS

Although best-known for its deals on prescription medications, the AARP Pharmacy Service, based in Alexandria, Virginia, offers over 12,000 drugstore items in its catalog for about 10 to 40 percent less than drugstore prices. Despite its relationship with the American Association of Retired Persons, the service is available to anyone, although AARP members are sometimes eligible for additional discounts. Orders are usually shipped within 24 to 48 hours. To order a catalog, call 1-800-456-2277.

Straight Arrow have increased about 10,000 percent since 1989. You may not even have to go to your local tack shop to find it. Large discount chains such as Wal-Mart are now carrying Mane 'n Tail right next to conventional shampoos.

Look for bargains on other animal-care products, such as moisturizer, and you can save up to 40 percent compared to buying "human" products.

CLIP COUPONS—THEN WAIT. Although many savvy shoppers don't utilize coupons for groceries and other products, thinking that the effort isn't worth the savings, this is one area where it pays to clip and save—quite literally.

After clipping coupons *only* for items that you use regularly, don't be tempted to cash in on your savings right away. Instead, stockpile your coupons and wait for a sale, which usually occurs four to six weeks after the coupons are published. Companies that make drugstore items tend to offer generous coupons—usually $1 or more—meaning you can save 50 percent or more off the retail price. When coupons are used in conjunction with manufacturer's rebates, you can get the products almost free—so make sure to check the bulletin boards at your local stores for rebate offers.

GO GENERIC. Nearly all the major drugstore and discount chains offer their own versions of popular brand-name products—everything from mouthwash to plastic bandages to deodorant. The ingredients are nearly always identical, and sometimes the generic product is even manufactured by the same company that makes the brand-name version. But without the fancy label, you can pay as much as 60 percent less.

BUY BIG. It's generally cheaper to buy large sizes. Most drugstore products don't have a unit price readily displayed, so it may take some figuring to see if it pays to buy a product in bulk. But ounce for ounce, the largest size of items such as toothpaste, mouthwash and even shampoo is up to half the cost of the smallest size.

BUY A CRYSTAL STONE. Americans spend $1.6 billion a year on underarm protection. But for only $2.50 a year—about 70 percent less than the average person spends on commercial deodorants and antiperspirants—you can use a deodorant stone made from crystallized mineral salts, which inhibit the growth of odor-causing bacteria.

The three-ounce, egg-size stone, which you rub on your underarms, sells for about $5 and lasts about two years. If you can't find it locally, call the Deodorant Stone Manufacturing Company at 1-800-962-7863 for a list of local merchants that sell it.

EXERCISE EQUIPMENT

We shell out over $2 billion a year to pump up, slim down and otherwise shape ourselves with the help of home exercise equipment. That's quite a figure when you consider that only one in ten Americans exercises regularly—and many of those folks don't use

THE BEST FOR LESS: NORDICTRACK

Some might argue over claims made in NordicTrack commercials that cross-country skiing gives you the best aerobic workout (although research seems to back them up), but there seems to be little argument over the best manufacturer: This company's treadmills, weight machines and cross-country ski machines are top-quality.

But they don't always come cheap, with some costing $1,000 or more. That doesn't mean, however, that the budget-minded have to settle for less. NordicTrack operates 18 factory-direct outlet stores in 14 states, offering scratch-and-dent merchandise at up to 30 percent off regular retail prices. What qualifies as scratch-and-dent? According to NordicTrack officials, their factory-direct merchandise consists of demos and floor models from retail stores. There's nothing wrong with the machines; they've just been used by would-be customers. For information on the nearest factory-direct store, contact NordicAdvantage at 1-800-872-2596.

TRY BEFORE YOU BUY

They usually start with the best intentions but often end up with an expensive coat rack. Half of all people who begin an exercise program quit it within six months, and this dropout rate may be even higher among home equipment users, who don't have the incentive provided by the social interaction at a health club or organized sports program. So before you run out and buy an expensive machine, many experts recommend that you test the waters at a health club to see if your plans to work out will indeed work out.

There's no need to sign on the dotted line, a move that costs an average of $500 and locks you into a one-year membership (and you pay whether or not you play). While the local YMCA or YWCA is cheaper—memberships can be as little as $350—your best bet is to ask for a trial membership of a week or two at the club of your choice. That way you'll have an opportunity to try all types of equipment and determine whether you'll stick to an at-home exercise program. You may have to pay $25 or so for the trial, but many clubs will gladly offer a free week's pass for potential members. To get this freebie, make sure you seem enthusiastic about joining, but say you don't want to make a financial commitment until you try out the club.

weight equipment, treadmills, stationary bikes, rowing machines and other machines. And while the exercise craze that began in the 1960s continues to flex its financial muscle—industry insiders report an annual 20 percent increase in equipment sales—there are several ways for you to be more fiscally fit in this area.

SEEK OUT FLOOR MODELS. Since home exercise equipment is usually heavy, so are the transportation costs back to the factory. That's why sporting goods stores offer even greater discounts on the display models—usually 30 percent. You won't get a box, but you'll save.

CRUISE THE CLASSIFIEDS. Probably the best deals in exercise equipment are in your local newspaper. Statistics show that half of all people who start an exercise program abandon it within six months. So before you dish out big bucks for new exercise equipment, check out the classified ads, and you may be able to buy hardly used machines for a song. Experts say that offering half the retail price is common, and some savvy shoppers buy barely used weight benches, treadmills and other equipment for 60 to 75 percent off new retail prices.

ASK FOR "RETURNS" WHEN SHOPPING AT STORES. The newspaper isn't the only place to find great deals on dust-collecting exercise equipment. People who buy machines they don't use sometimes sell them back to stores—and the stores then resell them at anywhere between 35 and 60 percent off regular retail prices. Simply ask the clerk if the store has any returns and make an offer. Advice: Aim for a 60 percent price break, but figure you'll have to settle for a discount in the 35 to 40 percent range.

OR BUY NEW AT A HUGE DISCOUNTER. National discount chains like Service Merchandise often sell exercise equipment for up to 30 percent less than sporting goods and specialty stores. How? By buying in volume and having less overhead—by locating stores away from expensive malls, for example—they're able to pass the savings on to you. While their selection may be limited, be sure to visit these stores for price comparisons before making your purchase.

EYEGLASSES AND CONTACT LENSES

More than 100 million Americans own some type of eyewear—from contact lenses and designer glasses to protective specs.

But even if you bought a pair of cheap sunglasses, you probably paid more than you should have. Some eyeglass frames cost as little as $1 or $2 to make, yet they retail for many times that much. Contact lenses also cost only a few dollars to manufacture yet are marked up several times.

Whatever the cost, though, don't skimp on eye exams. Folks between 40 and 50 should have an eye exam every two years; after age 60, you should have an eye exam annually. And once you know what you need, here's how to get eyewear for less.

EYEGLASSES

HEAD TO THE DRUGSTORE. Ready-to-wear reading glasses have been available at local drugstores since the 1800s, and you can still purchase a pair of these magnifying specs for $10 to $15—anywhere from 30 to 80 percent less than what you'd pay at a local optician or "frame" shop. Keep in mind that these specs aren't for everyone, especially people who do prolonged reading or close work. But for some cases of presbyopia, a loss of elasticity in the eye lens that makes it harder to focus on close objects, drugstore reading glasses can work as well as prescription glasses.

CLIP THOSE COUPONS. Although there's no official sale season for glasses, manufacturers tend to unveil their new frames at two trade shows, in late March and early fall. While they may not offer bona fide markdowns related to these shows, many retail stores tend to offer coupons in conjunction with the debut of new styles that can save you up to 50 percent off regular prices on selected styles.

THE BEST FOR LESS: ARMANI (EYEGLASSES) AND REVO (SUNGLASSES)

As one of three manufacturers of higher-end eyeglass frames, Luxottica manufactures men's and women's frames for some of the best-known names in fashion—including Giorgio Armani Occhiali, Brooks Brothers and Yves Saint Laurent. Its dozen Armani lines of designer eyeglass frames are considered by some insiders to be the best-made in the industry. Armani frames sell for $100 to $250 at most retailers, but look for deals at Lenscrafters. The reason: Luxottica bought the chain in 1995.

With a pair of Revo sunglasses, you'll get the most technologically advanced sunglasses made—tough, durable frames and optical-quality lenses polished to the same standards as camera and telescope lenses. A pair of Revos averages about $200, and they rarely go on sale. But you'll get a great deal at Sunglass Hut, a chain of more than 1,400 stores that vows to match or beat any price. For a location near you, call 1-800-767-0990.

SHOP THE PRICE CLUBS. Warehouse clubs like Sam's Club and B.J.'s Warehouse Club usually have an optical department, where glasses (and in some cases contact lenses) can be purchased for about 20 percent below regular retail prices. These clubs can pass on the savings by dealing directly with frame manufacturers to get what is currently available, rather than closeout or discontinued items. Don't expect to see high-end designer specs, though. Manufacturers tend to stay away from warehouse clubs because they don't feel the markup is in line with market standards.

An added bonus: More of these clubs are also providing optometric services, usually from optometrists who act as independent contractors and stick with the club's philosophy of keeping the price of eye exams low. If an on-site eye exam isn't available, as long as your current prescription isn't over a year old, you should be able to have it filled. Simply present it or have the retailer call your eye doctor.

BYPASS ONE-HOUR SERVICES. Some companies, like Lenscrafters, have made convenience their drawing card—they'll promise you new eyeglasses in one hour. While the convenience is nice, it comes at a cost: Other optical companies that take longer to prepare your lenses and frames tend to be cheaper, usually by at least 15 percent. So unless you need an emergency pair of glasses, play the waiting game and pocket the extra money.

TAKE ADVANTAGE OF A TWO-FOR-ONE SALE. Pearle Vision Centers and others offer two-for-one specials that can help you save big on your next eyeglass purchase. Simply buy one pair from the general collection of frames—between $39 and $350—and receive a second pair of your choosing from a more limited collection. Lens coating and tinting are extra for both. Since these specials are offered at different locations at different times each year, call ahead.

DON'T PAY TWICE FOR THE SAME SERVICE. Glass and plastic have long been the lens materials of choice. (Glass is usually cheaper and offers the most clarity, but it shatters more easily than plastic and can look bulky for some people who need thick lenses.) Now a third type of lens material is being pitched: polycarbonate (the same plastic used for bulletproof windows), which was first introduced in 1980 and is widely used for sports eyewear and glasses for children.

While a pair of polycarbonate lenses costs about $15 more than traditional plastic, they come with scratch resistance and UV protection at no extra charge. With plastic lenses, you'll be charged extra for those services (and probably more than $15). Be wary of a salesperson who tries to sell you either of these two features with polycarbonate lenses.

CONTACT LENSES

GET CONTACTS AT A MART. About 25 million people wear contact lenses, and unfortunately, most get them from their optician, optometrist or ophthalmologist. With today's technology, all contacts are virtually the same, so why pay a premium price? By going to a discount retailer like Kmart or Wal-Mart, you can save approximately 20 percent or more compared to getting similar (if not the same) lenses through a professional. Warehouse clubs like Sam's Club and B.J.'s Warehouse Club often sell contact lenses at even greater savings. (Note: Some states allow only licensed opticians, optometrists or ophthalmologists to fill contact lens prescriptions.)

OPT FOR THE LONG HAUL. You'll generally pay as much as six times more for daily-wear contacts than for those that you can wear for several months.

Granted, some people can't use extended-wear lenses because of their vision needs. But for most people, the difference comes down to some hard-not-to-see economic realities: Lenses that need to be replaced daily can cost over $500 a year, compared to about $100 for extended-wear lenses that can last up to one year. (Just make sure you clean extended-wear lenses properly. Experts say bacteria growing on a dirty contact lens need only enter your eye through a scratch or some sort of injury to start a serious infection.)

BUY THE OFF-BRAND. Bausch & Lomb and Johnson & Johnson are the two leading manufacturers of contact lenses, but they're certainly not the only ones. Off-brands—sometimes carrying the name of the store where they're purchased—are as good as these big-name lenses, yet they tend to sell for anywhere from 15 to 30 percent less. Not every store carries off-brands, but they may be worth a try if you can find them.

LOOK FOR AN HMO MEMBER. Even if you're not a member of a health maintenance organization (HMO), look for an optometrist or ophthalmologist who is. Experts say that eye doctors with HMO affiliation, as well as those with a close relationship with an optical chain or distributorship, tend to offer discount prices on contact lenses and eyeglasses.

LET YOUR FINGERS DO THE WALKING. Depending on your prescription, you can buy contact lenses for 10 to 30 percent less from Contact Lens Depot in Great Falls, Virginia, simply by making a phone call. After providing the brand of your contact lenses and your prescription, you can receive them by Federal Express in one or two days. For more information, call 1-800-245-5367.

SUNGLASSES

KNOW WHEN TO GO. Sales of sunglasses at department stores boom from February to June, but you can find discounts as high as 50 percent come July and August. That's because retailers receive markdown money from manufacturers—a gift to help absorb price cuts and clear the aisles for incoming cold-weather merchandise.

HIT THE HUT. Your future's so bright you've got to wear shades. But where to buy them? Check out the selection at Sunglass Hut International. With over 1,400 locations around the world, Sunglass Hut promises to match the sale price of any competitor on any pair of sunglasses, including those made by RayBan, Oakley, Serengeti, Giorgio Armani Occhiali, Calvin Klein and Gaultier. And if a pair goes on sale somewhere else within 30 days of your purchase, they'll refund the difference.

TRY A PRIVATE LINE. Produced by some of the big-name manufacturers for department stores and other retailers, private lines offer comparable quality for prices that are generally 10 to 20 percent cheaper. Sunglass Hut International's private line, for example, is called SunGear, while Macy's has Charter Club, and Pearle Vision Center has its Wrangler line.

GET YOUR SPECS FROM A FLEA MARKET. Thanks to overproduction and manufacturers' closeouts, you can often find designer sunglasses at wholesale and below-wholesale prices at large flea markets in major cities, insiders say.

Fireplace Accessories

Even in the television age, the fireplace is still the heart of a home, and it can set the tone for the whole room, if not the entire house. Fireplace accessories—andirons, hearth tools, screens and grates—can therefore be a lot more than just functional afterthoughts.

But with hearth tool sets ranging in price from $25 to $1,300 and fireplace screens starting at $20 and rising to $5,000 for some handcrafted, chrome-plated models, a little common sense and buying savvy go a long way. Whatever you buy for your fireplace, figure you'll spend anywhere from 15 to 300 percent more than the retailer pays the manufacturer or wholesaler. But follow these suggestions to save on fireplace goodies.

Buy at the top of the chains. Many of the top manufacturers of fireplace accessories are now doing business with the discount home warehouses like Home Depot or hardware stores such as True Value. Usually their goods are packaged under different names—even the store's brand name. Buying these brands can net you 25 to 30 percent savings compared to the name brand.

If you carefully check out the house brand, you might find it's identical to merchandise at specialty stores but for less money, because the chains buy in volume and are able to pass the savings on to you.

Get them while it's hot. Since warm weather puts a damper on the fireplace accessory business, retailers tend to discount during the summer—the obvious slow season. Shop during July and August and expect to save 20 to 30 percent off regular prices at larger retailers.

Keep it simple. Most fireplace accessories fuel our fantasies more than our fires. A fireplace specialty shop can become the equivalent of an adult candy store—and you'll pay the price: Chrome-plated, long-handled keys for turning on gas jets and ash scoops tipped with deer antlers can fetch $60 or more, when a more simple model, available at most home centers, can do the same job for as little as

THE BEST FOR LESS: PILGRIM

You can spend more for fireplace accessories, but experts consistently choose Pilgrim Fireplace Equipment Company of Richmond, California, for providing the best quality and value. (Another top name is Sunset, a brand offering similar top-notch quality.)

Pilgrim uses thick rods and solid brass forged into simple, classic designs, all with a five-year warranty. A three-piece set of hearth tools costs about $130—certainly not cheap, but a quality investment that may pay off in the long run. Your best bet for buying Pilgrim products for less may be during summer preseason sales, when prices for discontinued items can be up to 30 percent below retail, and current stock is sometimes discounted 10 to 20 percent. For information on a Pilgrim dealer near you, call (510) 412-9000.

one-fifth the cost. The same is true for bellows, hand-forged damper hooks and screens that depict English hunting scenes. It all looks great, but your logs will burn just as well without them.

Before you shop, experts recommend that you make a list of what you really need. Most hearth tool sets include a poker, a shovel and a broom—and a quality set can run less than $30 at a home center. Some add log tongs for an additional cost, but the tongs are generally superfluous. Fancy andirons, used to hold logs, have been replaced by grates (available for about $10 at most home centers), although some salespeople will try to sell you andirons as a necessity.

SEARCH FOR HANDSOME SECONDS. Swap meets and garage sales are excellent sources of fireplace accessories, as are the ads in local "shopper" flyers. The better-quality ones last a lifetime, and a simple investment of brass polish and elbow grease will bring them up to display quality. Savings will vary along with selection, but you can sometimes buy top-quality merchandise for less than half the retail price of new items. A case in point: We found a hand-carved, solid oak antique mantelpiece advertised in a local "shopper" flyer for $125 or best offer. The same item new starts at $300.

KNOW THE QUALITY DIFFERENCE. Cheaper tools are made with cast iron, which can bleed through over time, or with steel rods placed inside hollow brass tubes that are susceptible to denting. On the other hand, they cost half the price of solid brass tools and may work just as well. The choice is yours.

If you go the more expensive route and decide on solid brass, be aware that the best brass comes from England—and you'll pay for it. Taiwanese brass is fine, since it's made to American tool manufacturers' specifications, and it costs about 30 percent less. Lower-quality Indian brass tends to discolor and flake with use, so avoid it completely. If tools aren't solid brass, ask what base materials were used. Better tools use zinc, triple-plated for a high, durable polish.

STICK WITH THICK. You'll make your money stretch further if you buy thicker stock. Cheaper tools use what's called quarter-inch bar stock, while better-quality tools begin with three-eighths to one-half-inch stock. The difference is minimal come purchase time, but the thicker stock will last longer.

BUY LIVE. Although many home catalogs now offer fireplace accessories, industry insiders caution against buying by mail. The reason: Photos can fib. Only a visual inspection—complete with lifting the items—can reveal the quality and feel of fine tools. What may look nice may not have the weight to survive years in the fire. So before you buy, lift the items to make sure they feel sturdy—something you can't do by mail order.

Flatware

You'll find fewer newlyweds filling their buffet drawers with sterling silverware these days. The high cost of silver is one reason, but perhaps more important, the quality and variety of stainless steel flatware has vastly improved over past years.

There are literally thousands of patterns to choose from—including many that look and feel similar to sterling silverware. But along with better quality come higher prices: Retailers tend to mark up their inventories of stainless steel flatware by as much as 50 percent. Here's how to buy flatware without flattening your budget.

Shop with the pros. If you have simple tastes, you can save up to 70 percent off retail prices by buying flatware at a restaurant supply house. Most larger towns and cities have restaurant supply stores—check the yellow pages under "Restaurant Equipment and Supplies." While the selection of cutlery may not be vast, you can be sure the pieces are sturdy and reliable. After all, the goods must stand up to lots of use. Some larger restaurant suppliers also sell used flatware at even bigger savings.

Know when to shop department stores. If you are looking for brand-name flatware and want to go the traditional retail route, there are three months each year when sales at department stores bring you the biggest across-the-board savings—usually between 20 and 35 percent off regular prices.

January is probably the best time, as stores try to clear out inventory and lure shoppers back after the holidays. But November is also a good time to buy, when retailers need to move their goods to make room for the Christmas merchandise. And in May, stores tend to mark down flatware to entice summer wedding shoppers.

Buy used. Estate sales, garage sales and auctions are all excellent places to buy flatware at drastically low prices. But unless you want to scour the neighborhood for these homeowner grab-bags, try heading right to the source: auctions that liquidate restaurant supplies.

SILVER OR STAINLESS—WHAT'S BEST FOR YOU?

The price difference between an average eight-place setting of sterling silver and a setting of stainless steel flatware is at least $1,000. Before opting for both, ask yourself these questions.

"How often do I entertain formally?" If your get-togethers are homey, friendly affairs—Dockers and grilled fish instead of suits and salmon en papillote—consider forgoing the fancy stuff. For that once-in-a-blue-moon affair, you can always rent sterling.

"Am I prepared to polish?" If not, consider that silver will look dingy and forlorn over time, even if it's kept in a sliver drawer. Silver tarnishes on contact with just about everything, including moisture in the air—and over time, you'll have to polish.

"Will two sets of stainless do the trick?" You may want to consider buying an everyday set of flatware and a more upscale set for special occasions. Even high-end stainless doesn't carry the price tag of low-end sterling, and you'll solve the problem of what to put out when the in-laws come to visit.

The sad fact is that many restaurants go out of business within the first couple of years of operation. Often their inventories of dishes, glasses and flatware are sold in business auctions for just pennies on the dollar: Look for these auctions under "Public Notices" in the classified section of your local newspaper.

You can also get the finest in new and used flatware for huge savings off retail prices from Replacements Ltd. in Greensboro, North Carolina. Although they specialize in silverware, you may be able to get great deals on quality stainless by mail order. The company can be reached at 1-800-REPLACE.

HIT THE DISCOUNT CHAINS. Stores like Lechters and Kmart offer savings in the 50 percent range compared to department stores on complete sets of flatware in prepackaged boxes. The metal will be lighter, the pattern choices fewer and the brand names all but unknown. But if you're looking for no-nonsense yet sturdy flatware, why pay more?

FLOORING

If he were alive today, eighteenth-century economist Adam Smith would see his laissez-faire theories in good working order in the cutthroat, competitive marketplace of noncarpet flooring. Thousands of manufacturers worldwide pump out every conceivable pattern of vinyl sheet goods, ceramic tile and wood for the ever-voracious $27-billion-a-year American remodeling industry.

What works well in economic theory, however, can leave consumers overwhelmed. Some types of flooring have retail markups of up to 300 percent over manufacturing costs. But by making a few informed choices, you can get the flooring of your dreams at bargain-basement prices.

HEAD TO A HOME CENTER. Stores like Builders Square and Home Depot are usually good places to buy vinyl sheet goods (commonly but incorrectly called linoleum) and ceramic tile—two popular types of flooring for kitchens, bathrooms and other "nonformal" areas. Selection is more limited than at other stores, but because home centers buy in such large quantities, prices are usually at least 25 percent less than at retail flooring stores—and even cheaper than at some flooring outlet centers. In fact, Home Depot often sells some ceramic tile at what would be wholesale cost at other stores. And most home center chains promise to match or beat any competitor's price.

An added bonus: These stores frequently hold do-it-yourself workshops to teach customers how to do the work themselves—and hiring a professional to install your floor can be as expensive as the goods themselves. Actually, sheet goods and tile can be laid easily enough by most do-it-yourselfers, although laying a wood floor takes more expertise.

PIECE TOGETHER REMNANTS. Since sheet goods are usually sold by the square yard—and can run anywhere from $10 to $50 per yard, de-

WHAT TO CHOOSE

A new kitchen floor averages about $700 when professionally installed, while a new bathroom floor is about $500. Do the labor yourself and it'll cost half as much. While there are literally thousands of patterns and styles available for kitchen and bathroom floors, the choices usually come down to three possibilities—sheet goods, tile and wood. Here are some things to remember about each type of flooring.

Sheet goods. Often called linoleum, these products are usually made of vinyl. Because of their relatively low cost (although higher-quality products can cost more than tile or wood), they are the most popular choice for kitchens.

Benefits: Easy on your feet and legs, forgiving on dropped dishes and glasses and safer for young children.

Drawbacks: Can dent, tear and scuff easily, and colors may dull with age or exposure to sunlight. Some sheet goods can be slippery when wet, so think twice before installing them near showers and bathtubs.

pending on the style and quality—it's usually cheaper to piece together several remnants. Generally you can save between 25 and 40 percent by heading directly to the remnants roll section and getting enough to cover the room. Just be sure that the remnants you choose have the same lot number—a numerical system used to ensure that similar-looking patterns are made with the same dyes—for a perfect color match.

Remnants tend to be sold in two ways, either as prepackaged goods in established sizes, like 9 by 12 feet, or as "leftover" pieces from square-yard orders. You're likely to save more with the leftover pieces (usually available at floor-covering stores), but even prepackaged rolls sold in home centers tend to be cheaper than buying on a square-yard basis.

CHOOSE THE RIGHT WOOD. If you want a wood floor, which are growing in popularity for living rooms, dining rooms and even kitchens

Ceramic tile. This is the favorite choice for bathrooms, and it's becoming more popular for kitchens and other areas.

Benefits: Low-maintenance, extremely durable and long-lasting, it keeps cool in warm climates.

Drawbacks: Takes longer to install, is cold in the winter, can be hard on your feet and legs after long periods of standing and is dangerous for toddlers or other accident-prone children—as well as dropped glasses and dishes.

Wood. This material is gaining popularity in less formal rooms like kitchens and family rooms.

Benefits: Beautiful and durable, warm in the winter and cool in the summer and easy on your feet and legs.

Drawbacks: A poor choice for bathrooms, since water and moisture are wood's mortal enemies. Wood floors also require more maintenance than sheet goods and tile, and crumbs and dirt may collect in plank grooves.

(but are a poor choice for the bathroom because of dampness), you can save up to 30 percent by choosing oak over maple. Both wear very well, and oak actually has more grain for a nicer appearance.

And because of higher labor costs in the United States, wood flooring that's manufactured in China, Malaysia and Thailand tends to be about 25 percent cheaper, yet quality and durability are similar to those of American-made goods.

SHOP IN THE SPRING. While the flooring industry has no official sale season, it seems as though prices dip slightly in the spring as more homeowners turn their attention to outdoor improvements. Don't expect huge savings, but figure you can get vinyl, tile and wood flooring for about 10 percent less from April though the early summer.

CALL THE MANUFACTURER. The best selection for all types of flooring is usually available at specialty shops. Unfortunately, these shops also

THE BEST FOR LESS: ARMSTRONG DESIGNER SOLARIAN II

If you're looking for a kitchen floor that won't need to be replaced in a few years, look to Armstrong Designer Solarian II. Available in a wide variety of styles and colors, this tough-as-nails vinyl flooring is the best the leading floor manufacturer has to offer.

It's not cheap, retailing for around $34 a square yard, but it's less than what you'd pay for wood flooring and about the same price as ceramic tile. And it's money well spent, since Designer Solarian II colors won't fade like cheaper sheet goods, and its thicker-than-usual padding will hold up for years—especially in hard-traffic areas like the kitchen. For the best deals, look to home centers like Home Depot, which typically sell top-quality Solarian and other Armstrong flooring products for less than you'd pay even at discount flooring outlets.

generally sell their flooring at the highest prices.

Not to worry. Industry insiders say that once you've found the flooring of your dreams, write down the style and lot number and call the manufacturer for a list of retailers that stock it, then call at least six for the lowest price. Retailers tend to be more willing to offer discounts to shoppers looking for a specific style because they know those customers have been shopping around. Most flooring manufacturers have toll-free numbers, which you can obtain by calling 800 directory assistance (1-800-555-1212).

FIND YOUR OWN CONTRACTOR. If you're not a do-it-yourselfer and want a professional installation, you're better off finding your own contractor first and buying the flooring directly from him. You can usually save in two ways: Professional contractors tend to get industry discounts from either the manufacturer or retailer—usually 30 percent less than what you would pay yourself. (Most contractors charge a 10 percent "service fee" for placing the order, but you'll still save 20 percent compared to buying retail.)

Second, a contractor you hire tends to charge a flat rate for the job, while a store-provided installer will likely charge by the hour—generally a more expensive option. Of course, you'll have to do your own shopping so you can tell the contractor exactly what needs to be ordered.

You can find flooring contractors in the yellow pages and local "shopper" flyers. As with the goods themselves, it pays to shop around and get several contractor bids.

FORMAL WEAR

Formal wear usually signals a happy occasion—until it comes to paying for it. A wedding gown is probably the most expensive dress a woman will ever buy, retailing for anywhere from $400 to ten times that amount. And tuxedos, bridesmaids' dresses and ball gowns also cost two or three times the price of other men's suits and women's "better" dresses.

Manufacturers typically sell formal wear to retailers for about 30 percent over their cost, but the real jump comes once the retailer displays it. Markups to customers often double the original cost, and some department stores even triple it. But here's how you can buy formal wear for less.

SEEK OUT A "LEFT-BEHIND." When a wedding is called off, one couple's misfortune can be another's bargain, since bridal salons are sometimes stuck with wedding gowns, bridesmaids' dresses and even tuxedos that have been ordered but never picked up. Generally, these items have been fitted and even partially paid for (usually with a deposit), but at the eleventh hour, the wedding plans changed.

So when you go shopping, ask the salon owner if there are any of these "left-behind" gowns and suits available. Since the store has already received half the payment—the typical deposit on a wedding gown—you may be able to get the clothing for 50 to 80 percent off the original price.

NEGOTIATE. Competition in the bridal wear business is a lot stiffer than you might imagine, as salons try to outbid each other for sales. Your best bet: Look at consumer bridal magazines to find a gown that you like, then note the model number and call various salons for a price on that gown, letting each one know the low bid you've gotten. By shopping around, you can save as much as 20 percent off the regular price.

BUY USED—BUT WITH CAUTION. In these tough financial times, more

OUTSTANDING OUTLETS

David's Bridal is a 38-store chain that stocks wedding gowns, bridesmaids' dresses and other apparel for all female members of a wedding party. Each store stocks up to 1,000 dresses at a time, in sizes 4 through 26.

You don't get the service you'd find in a full-price bridal salon, but the prices make up for that lack: Gowns sell for anywhere from 20 to 50 percent less than regular retail prices, starting as low as $99 (although the average is $300). Most of the stores—located primarily in the East—do tailoring and alterations, which cost extra. For more information or to learn of a store near you, call 1-800-399-BRIDE.

In addition, Massachusetts' Manhattan Bridals and Tux Store stocks wedding gowns at up to 50 percent off regular retail prices and carries men's tuxedos at the same great savings. They'll also ship anywhere. Call (617) 326-9888 for more information.

brides are taking their worn-only-once wedding gowns to consignment shops to be sold; the shop owner and the bride usually split the proceeds 50-50. You can get a great deal this way: Consignment shops offer some great bargains, often selling their wares for half the retail cost or even less, but don't expect to get alterations at a consignment shop. And since some bridal salons add a $100 surcharge to the actual cost of alterations for gowns purchased elsewhere, it's best to seek out a private tailor for alterations if you buy a used gown.

And if you're in the market for a tux, check out tuxedo rental shops, which often sell off part of their inventory—usually at substantial savings. Although the timing of these sales varies from store to store, look for them in midsummer, after the busy prom and wedding season. You'll save between 40 and 80 percent compared to buying a new tuxedo.

RECONSIDER SILK. Fabric is the most costly component of a wedding dress, and a pure silk dress is the most expensive. To save at least

$200, choose a gown made of polyester shantung—a fabric that looks like silk but costs a lot less. An added bonus: This "imitation silk" is more durable than the fragile real McCoy and is less likely to snag.

Even less costly is acetate polyester satin, which can save you between $250 and $500 on a wedding gown and up to $100 on bridesmaids' dresses compared to all-silk gowns. It's thin and very shiny, though, and it might show alteration marks since it's so fragile.

FURNITURE

Goldilocks had it easy—she had just three chairs to choose from. But today's stores are crammed with an almost overwhelming array of choices in furniture, with prices ranging from bargain-basement to astronomical.

Actually, you can figure that the latter is more common. The average retail markup on furniture is between 200 and 250 percent, but some items cost customers as much as 700 percent more than what retailers pay. If you decide to buy a custom-made sofa or chair—meaning that you select the fabric and style you want and have the piece made for you—your costs will be even higher.

Of course, the best way to *not* pay retail is to negotiate for a better price. With such high markups, some retailers in competitive markets are willing to shave 10 to 25 percent off the price of furniture for those who ask, or they may offer other incentives like free delivery or accessories.

Sorry, but those so-called holiday sales—offering recliners for Father's Day or dining room sets for Thanksgiving—offer more lip service than actual savings. Often the price is raised and then "discounted" to the regular selling price. But here are some real ways to save when buying furniture.

ORDER DIRECT FROM THE MANUFACTURER. North Carolina is the furniture capital of the United States, with hundreds of manufacturers based in or near the cities of High Point and Hickory. Many operate giant furniture outlets offering deals of up to 50 percent off top-quality case goods—merchandise that is sold in sets (like dining room furniture) or storage items like bureaus and bookcases—and upholstered pieces like sofas and chairs. Other retailers sell merchandise from various manufacturers at similar savings. In fact, the offerings in North Carolina are so good that these outlets now do $750 million in sales each year.

Your best bet for adding to this figure—and getting top-quality goods for the same price you'd pay for lesser-quality items in other stores—is to go to the Tar Heel State, since shipping can add several hundred dollars to the purchase price. For information on outlets and hotels in the High Point area, located off I-85 near Greensboro, write to the High Point Convention and Visitors Bureau, P.O. Box 2273, High Point, NC 27261. For information on offerings in the Hickory area, located between Winston-Salem and Asheville, you can get a free *Furniture Shopping Guide* by calling 1-800-849-5093 or writing the chamber of commerce at P.O. Box 1828, Hickory, NC 28603.

HEAD TO A CLEARANCE CENTER. If you can't go to North Carolina, check out a local furniture clearance center. Most larger retailers run these centers, where they sell merchandise that was brought back by customers as well as overstocks and older-model furniture for up to 60 percent less than you'd pay at the main store.

Selection is usually limited and could include scratch-and-dent merchandise, but usually the items are top quality and were returned for decorating reasons—the color didn't match other furniture, for in-

THE BEST FOR LESS: GEORGE SMITH

Located in New York's trendy SoHo district, George Smith Sofas & Chairs has gained a national reputation for its meticulously handmade custom upholstered furniture. Construction and materials are first-class, with eight-way hand-tied springs, kiln-dried hardwood frames and luxurious cushions filled with a combination of down and feathers. Prices are top of the line as well: George Smith sofas average $1,000 per linear foot.

But twice a year this company sells its returns and floor samples at 50 percent off retail price. The pieces are strictly what-you-see-is-what-you-get, but the quality is pure George Smith. Sales are held in May and November at the company's showroom at 73 Spring Street. Call (212) 226-4747 for details.

stance, or the item didn't fit in the room. Call local furniture stores to see if they operate clearance centers, which are usually located in industrial parks and other off-the-beaten-path locations.

GET A DESIGNER'S DISCOUNT. While anyone can visit a retailer's clearance center, it's hard to walk into those "open-to-the-trade-only" showrooms frequented by professional decorators and interior designers. That's too bad, because there you'd have access to top-quality goods for about 40 percent less than regular prices.

A growing number of interior designers, however, now offer a shopping service in which they take customers through these design centers and let them pick out furniture, then buy it with their professional discount. The designer usually tacks on a 10 to 15 percent service fee, which still leaves you with an average 25 percent discount. In larger cities, check the classified ads under "Home Improvements" or "Interior Decorating," or call designers to ask if they offer this service.

And don't forget to ask designers about the buys in the back room. Both at showrooms and at designers' warehouses, there may be some even better buys—usually upholstered furniture that was custom-made but wasn't accepted by the client. The quality tends to be first-rate, and the price can be wholesale or even below.

HIT THE "CHARITY" CIRCUIT. Yet another way to get furniture from a designer for less than retail is to capitalize on designer "show homes" that raise money for charity. Interior designers are hired to decorate homes (usually those of prominent local residents), and people are charged a fee to view the homes. The money then goes to a local charity, and the decorator gets publicity.

But when the tours end, decorators are left with yards of draperies and pieces of custom-made upholstered furniture. To recoup their expenses, they may sell these pieces at just 25 to 30 percent above their cost—still a fantastic buy for retail-shopping consumers. So if you visit these homes and see something you like, make a deal on the spot.

Designer show homes tend to be featured in the spring or fall, when the weather is nicest, and usually are advertised in local newspapers. Or call well-known local decorators to see if they're participating.

BUY A RENTAL. Don't overlook rental companies as a source of furniture. Like retail stores, rental companies constantly get new products, so they need to move older, overstocked furniture. Occasionally, Rent-a-Center and other furniture rental companies sell these goods

GREAT MAIL-ORDER BUYS

Maybe "seeing is believing" is what motivates thousands of people to go to North Carolina each year to find fantastic furniture buys, but you can get the same great deals through mail order. Just be prepared, as you may be required to pay a deposit of up to 50 percent. And be sure to check on shipping costs. They are figured by weight and distance, but if you ship outside North Carolina, you won't be charged sales tax.

While some of these outlets offer catalogs, some don't. If you want to order from a company that doesn't have a catalog, first do some shopping at a local furniture retailer, then call the outlet and give them the stock number to get a quote. If possible, pay for your order with a credit card, so if there's a problem, your credit card company may help with its buyer protection plan.

Here are some of the best places in the Tar Heel State to get furniture by mail: Boyles Furniture (910-889-4147), Classic Leather Gallery (704-324-1776), Edgar B. (1-800-327-6944), Furnitureland South (910-841-4328), House Dressing International Furniture (1-800-322-5850), Hickory Park Furniture Gallery (704-322-4440), Loftin-Black Furniture Company (1-800-334-7398), Priba Furniture Sales and Interiors (910-855-9034), Rose Furniture (910-886-6050), Shaw Furniture Galleries (910-498-2628), Utility Craft (910-454-6153), Windsor Furniture Galleries (910-883-9000) and Wood-Armfield Furniture Company (910-889-6522).

You also might want to check out *The Fine Furniture and Furnishings Discount Shopping Guide* by Michigan interior designer Kate Gladchun. The book provides information on more than 250 discount furniture, fabric and accessory resources that sell merchandise by phone. To order your copy, send $12.95 plus $2 for shipping and handling to Resources, Inc., P.O. Box 973, Bloomfield Hills, MI 48303-0973, or call (810) 644-3440.

at significantly below retail cost. Look in the yellow pages under "Furniture—Rental" to see if anyplace near you is offering these sales.

One caveat: Be sure to carefully inspect all pieces before buying, and feel free to negotiate if you notice scratches, tears or dents.

TAKE THE "STRAIGHT" TO NARROW YOUR SPENDING. Wherever you buy, figure that subtle design features can drive up the price of a piece of upholstered furniture 30 percent or more compared to a similar item with a more simple design. Curves in the arms, legs and back of a chair or sofa, for instance, require more man-hours during the manufacturing stage as well as more fabric—and as a result, a piece with these features tends to cost substantially more. The same is true of furniture with claw feet and "ball" carvings on exposed wood components.

GET THE FABRIC FACTS. Up to 40 percent of the cost of an upholstered piece is for the fabric. With the average three-cushion sofa requiring 10 to 14 yards of fabric, a savings of $10 per yard can shave $100 or more off the total price of your sofa. So try to avoid fragile fabrics such as silk or linen, which are often more expensive than more durable covers, as well as dressmaker details such as pleats, welts, fringes or braids.

And the larger the "repeat"—the amount of fabric it takes for a pattern to recur—the more an upholsterer will have to waste to get the design to match up. That means you can save by sticking with smaller and simpler patterns rather than large plaids and other "hard-to-fit" fabrics.

HIRE AN UPHOLSTERER. One way to cut fabric costs is to let an upholsterer do the work instead of getting a custom-made sofa from a retailer or manufacturer. Just buy the style of sofa you like and then buy your own fabric—it tends to be cheaper at upholstery shops and discount fabric shops than at furniture retailers. You can find upholsterers listed in the yellow pages.

PROTECT IT YOURSELF. Furniture stores make a huge profit on the stain-protection treatments and warranties they sell to their customers, but the coverage they offer doesn't cover much. Pass on the expensive warranties—which cost $50 to $75 at many stores—and insist instead on fabric that has been treated with stain protection at the mill. This treatment is just as effective as the stuff the furniture store would spray on, and it's free.

Or you can do it yourself with a can of Scotchgard or a similar product, which will cost you less than $5 in most cases. Just be sure to ask the retailer about stains or other possible effects of the spray.

INVEST A LITTLE SWEAT EQUITY. If you can use a paintbrush or a screwdriver, you can save up to 20 percent on wood furniture like tables, chairs, bureaus, entertainment centers and armoires simply by buying it ready to assemble (RTA) or unfinished. RTA furniture is just that: You assemble it yourself, usually with a screwdriver or hex-wrench that comes in the carton. Because it's shipped compactly in boxes, the manufacturer and retailer can save hundreds in shipping and warehousing costs—savings that are passed along to you. Unfinished furniture, meanwhile, costs less because you paint or stain it yourself.

While RTA furniture has had a less-than-sterling reputation in the past—it was often made of cheaper veneer-covered particleboard—more manufacturers are now making RTA goods of more upscale veneers and even solid wood. Still, stay away from RTA bureaus, because they tend to not hold up well.

Unfinished furniture is usually made of solid pine, maple or oak, and its quality is often comparable to that of "ready-finished" goods that cost much more.

FURS

After years of sluggish sales due to the recession and opposition from animal rights groups, furs are regaining popularity—with a vengeance. Americans now spend over $1 billion on minks, sables, chinchillas and other pelts.

One reason for the comeback: Furs are more economical to own than ever before, and there are more choices. While a full-length Russian sable coat might cost $250,000 at some trendy shops, you can get other furs for as little as $200. Retailers insist they're not discounting as much as in previous years, but if you know where and when to shop, you can still get a bargain. Here's how.

BUY WHEN THE WEATHER'S HOT. Furriers make 60 percent of their annual sales and nearly all of their profits between Thanksgiving and Christmas, during the four-week period when bad weather prompts thoughts of furs and people are shopping for gifts.

Since retailers have a harder time moving furs in the spring and summer, they often discount their wares up to 50 percent—especially during the dog days of July and August.

ASK FOR A DISCOUNT. Prices can be negotiable, particularly when you're talking about a big-ticket item like a mink. Over the last few years, discounting has become more common, and insiders say furriers are often willing to knock up to 20 percent off the asking price for those deemed "serious" buyers. So don't be shy about asking for a better price or dropping hints that you'll be pricing elsewhere.

HAVE YOUR OLD COAT RESTYLED. If your old fur is out of style, you can have it restyled for a lot less than the cost of buying a new one. Just take your fur to a tailor, who will restyle it and usually charge only the cost of labor—about one-quarter of the price of a new fur.

FAKE THEM OUT. New styles and fabrics are making it harder to tell the difference between real and faux fur, and some designers like Karl Lagerfeld are mixing both in the same coats. If you buy something less than real, you'll notice a big difference in the price tag—as

THE BEST FOR LESS: VALENTINO

It's no surprise that this designer's furs are revered as the best in the business—especially when you consider that some styles fetch as much as $200,000, and people are willing to pay it.

Fortunately, you don't have to pay that much. Valentino minks start at around $13,000, and most other furs can be purchased for under $100,000. But you can save up to 30 percent off those retail prices by buying in the late spring, when retailers are trying to get rid of excess stock prior to getting the new fall line. Call Valentino's U.S. manufacturer, Alixandre, at (212) 736-5550 to find out which stores in your area carry these furs.

Or try your luck buying used. The Ritz Thrift Shop in New York City sells a good selection of preowned furs—including used Valentino designer coats—at prices as much as 50 percent less than you'd pay retail.

All Valentino coats carry a Valentino label that lists the name of the fur, its origin, whether it's been dyed or otherwise processed and sometimes even the part of the animal skin (paws, sides, tails and so forth) that went into the coat. Reputable dealers will also usually guarantee a 100 percent refund if you're not completely satisfied.

much as 80 percent—and you'll probably notice no difference in the actual garment.

HEAD TO NEW YORK. If you can make it there, you'll find some of the best deals on furs anywhere—especially at the furriers along Seventh Avenue, between 28th and 30th streets. Most New York furriers will deal with you, particularly on slow-moving styles, and you can save 30 percent or more off what you'd pay at a retail store.

GIFT WRAP AND RIBBON

You need it. You buy it. You give it—and then it quickly gets tossed in the trash. Such is the saga of wrapping paper and ribbon, a $2-billion-a-year business that includes everything from fancy imported paper whose patterns rival the finest wallpaper to second-rate Christmas wrap so cheap that it tears as you cut it.

Whatever you buy, you usually pay between 40 and 70 percent more than the retailer did. More colors and designs mean an even higher markup for gift wrap, as do the thickness of the paper and its country of origin. For ribbon, the amount of ribbing and the type of materials used are what determines its price. But here's how to save on all types of gift wrap and ribbon.

SHOP THE DISCOUNT CHAINS. It's easy to fall for the floral charm of those individual sheets of gift wrap or the fancy bows available at stationery stores. But by heading to discount drugstore and retail

GREAT MAIL-ORDER BUYS

Current, in Colorado Springs, Colorado, offers a catalog featuring a fun selection of wrapping paper, gift bags and bows—often in prepackaged sets so you don't have to fuss about what goes with what. Price breaks are offered depending on the number of items you order; the more you order, the more you save. But you can cut up to 45 percent off retail prices and get some items that are not available elsewhere. For a catalog, call 1-800-525-7170.

OUTSTANDING OUTLETS

There are hundreds of so-called dollar stores across the country that sell overstocks of gift wrap and ribbon for a song, but for the best selection of top-quality goods, head to any of the 25 Current factory outlets in California, Colorado, New Hampshire and Oregon. There you'll find discontinued items from the company's popular catalog at up to 80 percent off retail prices.

You can buy single-sheet gift wrap for as little as 49 cents. And the stores stock seasonal wrap year-round, so you don't have to worry about fighting crowds the day after Christmas. Special sales at certain times of the year offer up to another 40 percent in savings. To find a store near you, call 1-800-525-7170.

chains like Drug Emporium and Kmart, you can save 40 percent. The reason: Their buying power allows them to get better deals from manufacturers, but they also specialize in large-quantity packages. True, the selection may not be what's hot on the Hallmark shelves, but the paper and ribbon are multipurpose and suitable for any occasion.

SHOP AT STORES WITH FREQUENT-BUYER PLANS. If you want to frequent the fancy shops, be sure to benefit by asking for a store discount card. Hallmark Gold Crown stores, for instance, track customer purchases with bonus points, which accumulate as you buy products in their stores and can be used to purchase Hallmark merchandise. Customers are notified every few months of the number of points they've earned.

Not every stationery store has jumped on this bandwagon—it's unlikely you'll find this feature at independently run Mom-and-Pop businesses—but many of the better-known chains have it.

BE A POSTHOLIDAY BUYER—ALL YEAR LONG. You already know that the best time to buy Christmas gift wrap is on December 26, when prices are slashed by half or even more. But the same applies to other gift-giving holidays—Easter, Valentine's Day and even Mother's Day.

Since wrapping paper and ribbon don't go out of style like clothing, it makes sense to buy them and put them away for next year's holiday.

BUY IN BULK. Wherever you buy, you can save up to 40 percent by buying multiroll packages of gift wrap and mega-rolls of ribbon instead of gift wrap in skimpy 15-foot rolls or packages with just a few sheets and small amounts of ribbon. On a per-foot basis, you tend to get more for your money if you buy the largest packages of paper and ribbon you can find.

Golf Equipment

Hey, they don't call them "the greens" for nothing. Besides being one of the most popular sports—especially among aging baby boomers—golf is also among the most expensive. A set of clubs can run as much as $1,500, with a retail markup of about 40 percent, and balls can be over $20 a dozen—and that's just to have the equipment to play. After that initial outlay, it will cost anywhere from $20 to $65 per round just for greens fees. And then there are the extras: Clothes and gloves typically have a 100 percent markup, as do shoes, which can cost over $100 a pair for better brands.

But there are ways to play this country club game without having to spend the type of money it costs to join one. Here's how.

Golf Clubs, Shoes and Bags

Shop in the fall. Although golf is a year-round sport for many people, it's considered a summer sport by retailers. Because of this, many sporting goods stores and pro shops try to unload much of their equipment after Labor Day. That's why golf clubs typically go on sale at sporting goods stores for about 20 percent off their regular price, while accessories like bags, clothes and shoes may be featured at 30 percent discounts. Pro shops may also discount their wares up to 30 percent, but since these shops are more expensive generally, you'll still usually pay more.

Check out a "golf town." Since golfing resort towns like Myrtle Beach, South Carolina, and Palm Springs, California, have so many retailers selling golf equipment, the stiff competition brings the prices down—often by at least 10 percent compared to other places. But for even bigger savings, find a discount retailer like Nevada Bob's, which operates over 300 stores worldwide, some in or near golf meccas. Although there may be slight price differences in certain areas, most offer savings of as much as 40 percent below retail on

THE BEST FOR LESS: HENRY-GRIFFITTS

While Ping has the reputation, advertising budget and price tag to continue its reign as the "best" name in golf (it's also the equipment of choice for many pros), industry insiders say that it's Henry-Griffitts that truly deserves the honor of being the best in the business.

Established 15 years ago in Idaho by golf pros Randy Henry, Ross Henry and Jim Griffitts, the company specializes in custom-fitting (by a golf pro) and manufacturing clubs specifically for your measurements, swing *and* golfing style. (Some other "custom" manufacturers take only height into consideration.)

Like Ping clubs, which are also very respected by those in the know, Henry-Griffitts clubs don't come cheap, but they can be slightly less expensive than their better-known rival: Prices start at $90 for a single steel-shafted club and $130 for a metal wood. They are sold exclusively in pro shops, and because they are custom-fitted, they are not discounted. For information on local dealers, call Henry-Griffitts at 1-800-445-4653.

many products—with a "guaranteed lowest price" policy.

GO WITH THE BASICS. If you're just getting started in golf, experts say that you don't need the entire set (typically eight irons, three woods, a pitching wedge, a sand wedge and a putter). All beginners really need, they say, are four clubs: a number 1 driving wood, two irons (preferably a 3 and a 7, 8 or 9) and a putter. By scaling down, you can save several hundred dollars up front, and then slowly add the clubs you need. (A wedge would be the next logical purchase.) These four clubs, custom-fitted, will cost you about $360, and a basic "beginner" mass-produced set will run about $150—about half the cost of a full set of comparable clubs.

BUY USED. Considering that the cheapest set of new golf clubs costs about $200, you'll usually get more for your money if you buy used clubs, which can sell for a fraction of the cost of a similar new set. A

DO IT YOURSELF AND SAVE

If you're serious about golf as well as about saving money, you shouldn't be without the Golfsmith catalog. It sells components—everything from shafts, grips and club heads to the tools needed to put them all together—at prices that allow you to get a custom-made set of clubs for less than the price of decent-quality generics.

If you're handy, you can learn to make your own clubs (although it's not recommended for beginners). But you can also order the parts and take them to an independent fitter. (Check the yellow pages under "Golf Equipment and Supplies" or ask at a pro shop.) Either way, you'll save up to 60 percent compared to buying a custom set through a pro shop and get the set of clubs you've always dreamed about at prices you can afford. For a copy of Golfsmith catalog, call 1-800-456-3344.

case in point: We bought a complete set of used left-handed irons (which are harder to find used) at the local Goodwill store for $35—only 15 percent of the cost of a comparable new set. Although golf clubs are not a popular item at thrift stores, you're most likely to find them in the spring and fall, when golfers tend to replace older clubs. Check the pro shops and the classified ads in your local newspaper as well. You can also find used golf equipment periodically at garage sales, auctions and flea markets.

For the best selection, try sporting goods stores that specialize in selling used equipment, such as Play It Again, Sports, a national chain that caters to golfers. Its staff can help you pick the right set of used equipment. And while you probably won't be able to negotiate a deal when buying used equipment at a pro shop or sporting goods store, you can usually get clubs for 10 to 15 percent less than the asking price when buying through a classified ad or at a thrift store or flea market.

BUY CLONES OF NAME BRANDS. You can save over 50 percent by buying generic or off-brand clones of the big-name clubs. These clones can be found at sporting goods stores, large discount stores like Kmart and even some pro shops. For each of the popular top-of-the-line trade names—Ping, King Cobra, Titleist and Tommy Armour—there are a number of knockoffs or clones. The differences between the two are subtle, such as the type of metal used or the way the club head is attached. If you buy a set of clones, you may end up compromising on quality and fit, and some clones have been known to break more easily, but many weekend duffers can't tell the difference.

GOLF BALLS

BE A COMPANY MAN. You can save at least 50 percent on golf balls by buying overruns—bulk packages of brand-name balls that were produced as part of a promotion and imprinted with a corporate name, logo or message. These overruns are sold at sporting goods stores, large discounters like Kmart or warehouse clubs like B.J.'s Warehouse Club or Sam's Club.

SAVE $ WITH X-OUTS. While perfect balls may cost $25 a dozen, a dozen X-outs can be had for about half that amount at sporting goods stores and pro shops. These balls are usually perfectly good except for cosmetic blemishes, such as smeared ink.

ASK FOR LEFTOVERS. Probably the best way to save on golf balls is to buy "second chance" balls, which are balls salvaged from the links—those lost in bushes or in water—by professional ball retrieval companies, then washed and resold. Sometimes the courses themselves sell these balls at the front desk, usually for 50 to 80 cents each. You can also find them at some sporting goods stores, discount chains and buying clubs.

Most of the balls sold this way have been hit only a few times and are in very good condition, but they sell for anywhere from one-third to one-half the price of new balls.

Gourmet Foods

Free association: What's the first word that pops to mind when somebody says "gourmet"? If you're like most people, you think "expensive."

It's true—you could stop in at the Caviarteria in New York or Beverly Hills and shell out $140 for about two bites of salty fish eggs. But you don't have to.

Outstanding Outlets

For some, shopping at Trader Joe's is a religious experience—and it's easy to see why. The 74-store chain, based in South Pasadena, California, offers breathtakingly low prices on private-label gourmet items ranging from wild dried Italian porcini mushrooms—for 35 percent less than what others charge—to dried apricots, wines, nuts and imported condiments at 50 percent off retail. Trader Joe's also carries its own line of private-label frozen and ready-to-eat foods, breads, pastas, supplements, coffees and juices, generally at 30 to 50 percent less than supermarkets charge.

How? By dealing directly with manufacturers instead of going through wholesalers, by buying in massive quantities and by keeping advertising to a minimum. Long known in California and Arizona, Trader Joe's has opened new stores in Seattle, Las Vegas and Portland, Oregon, and the chain is expanding to Boston and other eastern locales. To learn of a store near you, call 1-800-SHOP-TJS.

DO-IT-YOURSELF "GOURMETING"

Considering that many of what we consider gourmet foods were once the foodstuffs of peasant folk, it's not surprising that you can pocket a small fortune by making them yourself.

Consider smoked salmon. You can pay up to $38 per pound for it at a New York deli—or you can hit the wholesale fish market, buy an entire salmon for $7 and spend another $2 on brown sugar, salt and smoking chips. Follow the recipe in *The Great American Seafood Cookbook* by Susan H. Loomis (which you can borrow from the library), and you've got brunch at a fraction of the cost.

Sun-dried tomatoes? Make these flavor-packed Italian kitchen staples yourself by buying several pounds of summer's best plum or Roma tomatoes. Cut them in half lengthwise and sprinkle them lightly with sea salt, then dry them on cake racks in a 200° oven for 6 to 12 hours. You've saved anywhere from 50 to 90 percent off store prices.

Check your local bookstore or the cookbook section of the library for more recipes for making your own gourmet foods.

One of the bonuses of the "foodie boom" of the 1980s has been the widespread availability and lower price of upscale foods in the 1990s—these days, even the neighborhood supermarket is likely to have fine bottles of extra-virgin Italian olive oil shelved beside tubs of Crisco. Best of all, you can sometimes find pantry-perking goodies at a fraction of what you'd think gourmet foods should cost. Here's how you can downsize your spending even more when buying upscale eats.

OVERCOME THE MAIL-ORDER URGE. Unlike other items, it's tough to find mail-order bargains on gourmet foods. Those glossy pictures of glazed hams and quaintly bottled maple syrups in mail-order catalogs may be tempting, but you'll pay dearly: The cost of producing and mailing catalogs and shipping merchandise can boost the price of mail-order gourmet foods by at least 25 percent over what they cost in stores.

Mail order also costs more because in order to make products look more appealing, catalogs offer them in large quantities or "bundle" them with other gourmet items like fancy canisters or serving boards, adding significantly to the price. At a store, of course, you buy just what you need.

WAIT UNTIL DECEMBER 26. They've become a popular holiday gift, so gourmet items tend to carry their highest prices before the gift-giving season. And like other items, they end up in the sale bins after the holidays—often at savings of up to 50 percent off regular prices.

Don't expect the seasonal price drops you'll find with other foods, though, because gourmet food growers and distributors have such sophisticated storing techniques.

CHECK OUT WAREHOUSE CLUBS. They may cater to the common man (and woman), but take your gourmet shopping list to warehouse clubs like Sam's Club and PriceCostco and you'll be surprised at how many items you can find. Along with T-shirts and bulk detergents, you're likely to see a wide range of gourmet foods, from imported pasta to Nova-style lox, at drastically reduced prices.

While the standard retail markup for gourmet foods is between 25 and 60 percent, the markup at warehouse clubs is a scant 5 to 7 percent. In fact, many owners of gourmet food shops go to warehouse clubs for some of their store's inventory.

BULK UP. If you have unused cellar space, you can save 20 percent or more by buying some items in bulk and storing what you don't use right away. While imported produce, seasonal fruits and fresh cheeses are extremely perishable and must be eaten soon after purchase, items like dried pasta, olive oil, dried fruits and maple syrup can keep almost as well as a can of Spam in a cool, dark, dry place in your home.

A freezer also comes in handy: Nuts, dried fruits and most cheeses will keep for months in the freezer, so if you find a good buy, snap it up. The key to freshness is to double- or triple-wrap each item in plastic wrap or foil.

BE A LATECOMER AT EARLY-BIRD MARKETS. Most towns have fish and produce marts that open before sunrise and offer the freshest and best selections at wholesale prices. In fact, these markets are where most gourmet food retailers buy foods like meat, fish, produce and other perishables for about 60 percent less than what they charge.

USE COMMON SENSES

With their often tremendous markups and high desirability among the yup-and-coming, gourmet foods can attract their share of rip-off artists. One common ploy: Some importers buy cheap, flavorless dried wild mushrooms and spray them with salty vegetable stock. After a second drying, the flavor-enhanced mushrooms are sold as pricey authentic "forest-fresh" produce. So before you buy these gourmet foods, take a tip from Grandma and ask for a sniff, a poke or even a taste.

Sniff smoked fish. It should look bright and smell salty and smoky, not fishy.

Poke fresh fish and game birds. The skin should spring back; if it's mushy or an indentation remains on the skin, the fish or fowl isn't fresh.

Sip olive oil. Avoid any that tastes musty or acrid.

Although these markets are technically only for licensed retailers, the reality is that most wholesalers won't turn away cash—especially if you go right before closing (usually before 7:00 A.M.) to snap up their leftovers. You could go earlier, but you might not get the same great deals or even be allowed to shop. (The wholesalers must first satisfy their retail customers.) You'll have to pay sales tax, and be prepared to buy larger quantities, such as whole fish.

To find out about wholesale markets in your area, ask a retail gourmet food vendor or local restaurateurs where they shop. Or check the yellow pages under "Wholesale Meats" or "Wholesale Produce."

SHOP ETHNIC. *Gourmet* usually means *exotic*, which in turn often translates to *ethnic*. So whether it's a special brand of soy sauce, canned Italian tomatoes or fresh tortillas, chances are you'll find it for anywhere from 30 to 80 percent less than gourmet food store prices at one of the ethnic markets that can be found in most larger cities—like Philadelphia's Italian Market, where part of the movie *Rocky* was filmed.

Although such markets are not common in smaller towns, most ethnic neighborhoods in metropolitan areas have one that's usually open on weekends (if not daily). Shopping at these markets isn't just economical: It's an education in ethnic cuisine and a great place to pick up some cooking tips from those who really know. Check your local bookstore for ethnic food guides or consult the yellow pages under "Markets." (Southern Californians should get a copy of *A Guide to Ethnic Food in Los Angeles* by Linda Burum.)

GRILLS

All you really need for a barbecue is fire and meat. But today your grilling options include charcoal and scented woods, natural gas, liquid propane and electricity. Grills range from $12 tailgate hibachis to $2,000-plus BBQ islands, with a vast and confusing array in between.

Before you shop, remember to factor in operating costs: Natural gas and liquid propane grills—chosen by about 85 percent of grillers—are the least expensive to fire up, consuming only about 7 cents' worth of fuel per use. Charcoal grills, while cheaper to purchase, cost about 55 cents per use; add some "gourmet" hardwoods and the cost goes to about $10. Electric grills rate somewhere in between, depending on the cost of electricity in your area. But whatever you choose, here's how to buy it cheaper.

THE BEST FOR LESS: DUCANE

You may save $200 by buying an inexpensive grill, but for quality that lasts, the experts advise that you spend now to save later. Case in point: the Ducane Model 1202S. This American-made, twin-burner gas grill costs around $400—about half the price of other much-ballyhooed grills like the Weber Genesis. Available with Ducane's lifetime warranty for an additional $10, this or the slightly larger Model 1504S is a grill that can last a lifetime of barbecues. For the Ducane retailer nearest you, call 1-800-382-2637.

QUALITY CHECK

The most important component of the grill is its shell—the only part that cannot be easily or inexpensively replaced. Cast-aluminum shells cost more, but they're a better buy than the more common pressed metal because they will last for decades. Also check the burners: American-made cast-iron and brass burners found in costlier gas grills outlast stainless steel ones by at least five years. And while wire racks wear out easily (although they are easy and inexpensive to replace), cast-iron or stainless steel ones usually last the life of the grill.

CONSIDER WHAT YOU COOK. Steak-eaters will pay more for the 40,000-Btu (British thermal unit) burners and cast-iron racks required for premium searing. But if you're primarily grilling chicken, fish or vegetables, you can make do with a less expensive 22,000-Btu unit. The same is true with regard to the number of people you're cooking for. If you have a family, you'll need a larger grill—around 350 to 400 square inches. But if you're cooking for two (or just yourself), stick with a smaller and less costly unit.

GO STRAIGHT TO SECONDHAND. The secret among grill retailers is that secondhand grills are clean, safe and priced up to 75 percent less than new units. In addition, older grills, made before the widespread use of cheaper imported components, will often outlast brand new ones. So before you buy, ask at local grill specialty stores if they have any used grills for sale. To find a small retailer that sells used grills may require some detective work, but you could save big. Most stores that sell used grills perform leak tests, repaint old parts and replace regulator hoses and burners before selling the units. (Sorry, but discount stores like Kmart don't sell used grills.)

Bassemiers' Fireplace and Patio sells used grills by mail order; call (812) 479-6388 for more information. Another way to buy good grills for less is to check the classified ads in your local newspaper; these items often go for a song, and for about $25, a local shop will clean and check your purchase.

AVOID THE FRILLS. Grills are bell-and-whistle intensive. Add-ons like thermometers, fuel gauges and side burners can boost the price tag by up to 20 percent—even though these features are notoriously unreliable. Another extra to avoid: see-through tempered windows. After three cookouts, the glass is a greasy, opaque mess that requires a lot of elbow grease. And although a rotisserie attachment may cost up to $200 more, most people rarely use it.

DUST OFF THE SCREWDRIVER. Even if you're the type who confuses lug nuts and doughnuts, try to put your grill together yourself—and pocket the $35 to $50 installation fee charged by most stores. What some retailers don't tell you is that most of today's gas grills are up to 90 percent preassembled anyway, so you're only looking at tightening a few nuts.

BUY AT A BUYING CLUB. National chains like Kmart tend to sell middle to lower-end grills at a markup of about 25 percent, while warehouse clubs like Sam's Club and B.J.'s Warehouse Club typically sell the same grills at about a 10 percent markup. Both types of stores tend to discount their inventory in late April or late August—just before or after the prime grilling season.

BARGAIN WITH A SPECIALIST. If you go to a specialty store, you can expect to find higher-quality grills with a higher price tag. One reason is that smaller specialty stores deal with middlemen who distribute goods and take a chunk of the profits. On the bright side, these stores provide more services for their customers than mass retailers do.

Not to worry, though. At these specialty stores, you're in a better position to make an offer and get a lower selling price. Your best bet: Offer the lowest price you've seen for a similar model, then bargain for an extended warranty and free delivery and assembly as well. You may not get a top-notch grill at Sam's Club or Kmart prices, but many people who ask get discounts in the 20 to 25 percent range.

GROCERIES

Some thought for food: The typical family spends upwards of $10,000 each year buying groceries—more than any other single expense except your home or car. And as with a house or car, many people feel their grocery bill should be a "fixed" expense.

So why is it that about one-third of your grocery spending—up to $70 a week for some families—is wasted money that goes to overspending or buying unplanned or "impulse" items not on your shopping list? Like other retailers, grocers want to part you from your money, and they apparently do this very successfully. Besides a 25 percent retail markup on most grocery items, their strategic stocking, tempting displays and pricing gimmicks are responsible for Americans spending 25 percent more on groceries today than they did during the 1980s. But here's how you can save at the supermarket.

EAT THE SALES. While it's always important to stick to a grocery list when shopping—it helps avoid impulse purchases and excess spending—most people rely on their list too much and don't take advantage of sale items that they can store and freeze. While this may require more flexibility with your shopping list so you can substitute sale items for items on your list, industry insiders say that by planning meals around sales, you can cut up to 25 percent off your weekly grocery bill.

SHOP BIG. The bigger the chain, the bigger its buying power—and as a result, the more you can save. Since large chains buy groceries from wholesalers and manufacturers in greater volume for *all* their stores, they're able to sell groceries for less than a smaller chain or independent grocer. So while it's important to shop different supermarkets for select sale items, item for item, the average family can save up to 20 percent by shopping at a larger chain with lower prices.

CASH IN AT A CLUB. For even greater savings, buy big—at a warehouse club like Sam's Club or B.J.'s Wholesale Club. True, you have to buy larger quantities, but the markup on grocery items at these warehouse clubs is only 10 percent above wholesale (compared to about 25 percent at supermarkets). Add in the cheaper-by-bulk factor and surveys show that you can save 25 percent by buying at warehouse clubs compared to getting the same items (and quantity) at the supermarket. But take note that B.J.'s Wholesale Club takes manufacturer's coupons, while Sam's Club doesn't.

ADD YOUR OWN EXTRAS. You'll usually pay more for products that contain "added" ingredients like sugar, eggs and seasonings than if you buy the same item and mix in these extras yourself. Frozen vegetables in their own sauce can cost as much as 60 percent more than sauceless varieties. And some presweetened cereals, like "frosted" flakes, can be twice the price of their regular corn-flake counterparts.

CAN THE NAME BRANDS. You may notice a difference in taste between some generic products and their brand-name counterparts, but you'd have a hard time distinguishing among most canned goods. Most house-brand canned fruits, vegetables, beans and similar products are grown and manufactured by the same companies that provide the name brands—but they typically sell for about 20 percent less. The higher price for those name brands usually goes for advertising and more attractive packaging. Quality-wise, however, the items are usually identical.

WISE UP TO END CAPS. The ends of supermarket aisles are a consumer booby trap—and grocers know it. But you should realize that these end-cap items are usually not discounted. Rather, they're the same price as usual, only with brighter banners that are designed to make you think you're getting a deal.

USE COUPONS ONLY FOR A SALE. Only one-third of people ever use coupons, even though those who do save about $4 billion a year on grocery and personal care items. The real savings come if you use coupons at the right time—usually two to six weeks after the coupons are issued in the newspaper. Many people use coupons the week they are issued, but usually if you wait a while, you'll notice that coupon items have been discounted. By playing this waiting game, instead of saving a flat 25 or 50 cents per item, you can increase your savings as much as 50 percent on some items if your supermarket doubles coupon values.

IGNORE THE "SELL-BY" DATES. Stuck with a warehouse full of some items stamped with a fast-approaching sell-by date, some wholesalers offer them to local grocers at a significant discount just to get rid of them. Your grocer in turn puts them on sale, offering you a similar chance to save money. Unfortunately, most people panic when they see a sell-by date a week or less away and decline to make the purchase.

That's a big mistake. These items can sell for as much as half off and, if frozen, can last for months. (Remember, "sell by" means that the grocer needs to unload them; they don't go bad for up to two weeks.) Look for these sales on meats, canned goods, baked goods, dry goods and other items.

Guns and Ammo

The shooting industry has enjoyed robust growth in recent years—much of it, ironically, driven by the threat of gun bans. As anti-gun forces push for laws that would outlaw certain firearms, people are buying additional firearms at a rate not seen since the early 1980s. So much for gun control.

Whether acquired for protection, hunting, target practice, an investment or to beat the government clock, there is at least one gun in 51 percent of American homes. And since the average gun owner has at least four guns, that puts over 200 million in American hands.

Retail prices can go as high as $10,000 to $12,000 for a handmade, fully engraved, gold inlaid, hand-carved firearm, but the typical gun sells for between $300 and $900. Most guns have a retail markup of

The Best for Less: Remington 870

When it comes to firearms, "best" doesn't always mean most expensive. Gun experts agree that probably the best sporting gun you can buy is the Remington 870 12-gauge pump gun. For quality of construction, longevity of design, durability and accuracy, you can't beat it. The design has been around for ages, and the gun has a proven track record. The 870 Wingmaster 28-inch model generally sells for around $325, but you can save 10 to 20 percent if you buy at the end of hunting season, which is the end of January in most parts of the country.

12 to 15 percent. But here's how you can get them for less.

DRAW ON THE USED MARKET. Since guns are generally made to last for decades, a good used gun will provide years of service—often for 35 percent less than you'd pay for a new one. Most reputable gun dealers sell both new and used guns. And unlike cars, gun models change very little from year to year. A Ruger Red Label 12-gauge, 28-inch, over-and-under shotgun—one of the most popular sporting guns sold in the United States—costs about $1,170 new and $750 to $850 used.

You can find a reputable dealer who specializes in better-quality used guns through *The Gun List.* Call 1-800-258-0929 for the name of a local distributor or to order a subscription to this biweekly publication. To educate yourself about the current market values of used guns, there's also *Modern Gun Values*, a reference book available at most bookstores and gun dealers that has a complete listing of used gun prices. For general information on guns, browse through *Gun Digest* for a historical and technical account of firearms and ammunition as well as a bibliography of arms books.

STRIP IT DOWN AND SAVE. Most consumers don't know that guns, like cars, have options that can affect price. For instance, opting for a field-grade wood rifle stock over a fancier version could save you up to $400. If you find a gun you like that's loaded with extras, ask the dealer if he can order a model without them to bring the price down. Generally, buying a stripped-down model can save you as much as 40 percent. If you like the performance of a gun, go for the simple model, not the one with all the bells and whistles.

ARM YOURSELF A CASE AT A TIME. Like many products, ammo is cheaper when purchased in bulk—usually a case of ten boxes. You can usually save at least $1 a box this way. A case of Remington Premier target loads 2¾ 3 Dram EQ No. 7½ 12-gauge shotgun shells costs $45, for instance, while a single box costs about $6, which adds up to a $15 savings if you buy by the case.

But remember: Accuracy is affected by the ammunition you choose. Beware of imported brands, particularly those from China—which racked up sales of 52 million rounds in one recent year—because they may contain corrosive gunpowder that will eat up the barrel of your firearm. The best ammo, according to gun experts, is Hornady, which averages about $2 more a box than brands such as Remington and Federal.

SHOOT FOR AN ESTATE SALE. If you know your firearms, you can save

GREAT MAIL-ORDER BUYS

There are more than 100 catalogs that sell firearms, accessories, supplies and hunting equipment. But because of registration requirements and servicing problems, experts generally discourage people from buying guns from a catalog.

Like an item of clothing, a gun is a personal item that has to be fitted to its owner—something that can't be done by looking at a picture and reading the dimensions in a catalog.

Some catalogs, however, offer hard-to-find accessories, such as gun cases, hunting clothing and reloading supplies, at discount prices. Among the best is the Gander Mountain catalog, which offers a full line of hunting and outdoor equipment, including many hard-to-find items, at prices 10 to 20 percent below retail. Call 1-800-558-9410 for a free catalog or write Gander Mountain, Inc., P.O. Box 6, Highway W, Wilmot, WI 53192.

Cabela's also has reasonable prices on brand-name merchandise. Its fall catalog features hunting and firearms supplies; to order yours, call 1-800-237-4444 or write Cabela's, 812 13th Avenue, Sidney, NE 69160. Some experts say you should avoid pricey catalogs like L.L. Bean and Orvis, because they say their prices on hunting accessories are marked up 40 to 300 percent.

50 percent or more on guns sold at estate sales and auctions. The best ones are those held at private family homes rather than at an auction center. You'll find these sales listed in the "Public Notices" section of the newspaper's classified section.

BECOME A REGULAR CUSTOMER. Like most small businesses, gun shops will sometimes offer special deals to regular customers. Although these deals aren't generally advertised, industry insiders say that discounts can be as much as 30 percent on selected items—usually when manufacturers offer a special deal for retailers. Besides, the owner may throw in a holster or attach a scope for free for his regular customers.

HANDBAGS

Whether dressed in the finest leathers or tough-as-the-streets vinyl, adorned with fancy clasps or no-nonsense zippers, handbags are as much about fashion as they are about function. What's in today may be collecting dust tomorrow.

That may help explain why women spend $4 million each year on new handbags. But while styles come and go, some things about handbags never change. First, basic black still reigns supreme, ac-

GREAT MAIL-ORDER BUYS

Even if you don't live in cowboy country, bargains on leather handbags may still be only a phone call away. The Deerskin Place in Ephrata, Pennsylvania, offers handbags and other accessories in cowhide, sheepskin and deerskin for about 50 percent less than retail. You can get your catalog (which costs $1) by calling (717) 733-7624.

For look-alike designer handbags, you can save up to 80 percent by shopping by mail order from J. Tiras Classic Handbags in Houston. Its catalog costs $2 and features the look of top brands like Bottega Veneta, Louis Vuitton, Ferragamo, Bally, Donna Karan, Judith Leiber and Chanel. You can order a catalog by calling 1-800-460-1999.

And New England Leather Accessories in Rochester, New Hampshire, has a catalog offering its brand of leather bags and accessories. The catalog costs $5, but prices are about one-third less than retail. Call (603) 332-0707 for more information.

THE BEST FOR LESS: COACH

You'd need a mighty big handbag to accommodate all the quality manufacturers of this essential accessory. Unfortunately, when you consider that Chanel handbags can run over $1,000 and others are in the high three figures, you might also need a mighty big bank account.

But you can still get top quality for a fraction of the price. Sure, they're expensive—starting at about $100 and going as high as $400—but Coach handbags, with a lifetime warranty, are some of the best-looking and most durable in the business. Even if your bag wears out from years of use, Coach will replace hardware and straps and resew seams at no charge. All you have to do is take the handbag to a retailer that carries Coach, and in a few weeks, your bag will be delivered to your door looking like new.

To get Coach handbags for 15 to 30 percent below retail (and sometimes even less with special sales), check out the company's 28 outlet stores in 20 states. Some of the bags at these outlets may be slightly irregular, but not to worry: These "defects" are virtually undetectable, and the bags are still covered by the company's lifetime warranty—if there is a flaw, you'll get a new bag or a refund from the outlet. Call 1-800-444-3611 to find out about an outlet near you.

counting for seven of every ten handbag purchases. And second, even on sale, the typical handbag is costly, with an average 50 to 60 percent retail markup. But no matter what you buy, here's how to keep more money stored in your handbag than you spent on it.

LOOK FOR THE HOUSE BRAND. Most department stores sell a house brand of handbag, usually for 20 to 30 percent less than big names of similar quality. Some of these are obvious: Saks Fifth Avenue offers handbags with its "Exclusively for Saks Fifth Avenue" label, but Macy's own-label bags carry the less recognizable Charter Club label.

Wherever you shop, ask the store about its in-store brand.

SHOP WHEN THE PROS DO. The best time of year to buy handbags is immediately after store buyers make their purchases. This occurs twice a year, in late summer near the end of July and August and then again just before Christmas. Handbag prices tend to be 20 to 50 percent less at these times, as retailers try to move slow-selling merchandise to make room for new shipments.

HEAD TO A CHAIN STORE. Discounters like Wal-Mart and Marshalls typically sell handbags for 20 to 60 percent less than department stores because they buy huge volumes.

BUY BIG TO STRETCH YOUR SAVINGS. The quickest way to destroy a good bag is to overstuff it. While those petite bags look cute, consider what you carry before buying. If it's a lot, you're better off with a big bag with room to spare or even a backpack. Otherwise, you'll be likely to need a new bag in less than a year.

CHECK THE WARRANTY. The best way to tell you're getting quality is to check the warranty. Most authentic leather handbags carry a warranty of at least five years and some as long as ten. Top-of-the-line manufacturers like Coach offer lifetime warranties on their goods.

While most warranties don't cover ordinary wear and tear or leather discoloration, they come in handy in the event a strap or fastener breaks. A warranty is also your best insurance that you're getting the real McCoy: Knock-offs are a big problem in the industry, but impostor designer brands *don't* have good warranties, if they have them at all.

Hand Tools

Shopping for hand tools can be intimidating if you don't know the territory: A 20-ounce claw hammer ranges from $3 to about $35, and a 60-piece socket wrench set can cost $30 or three times as much. The contrast in price can mean the difference between getting a good set of tools and getting a good set of tools for a great price.

Most hardware stores have retail markups averaging about 80 percent, which is lower than just a few years ago. Larger home centers like Home Depot have a much lower markup and often sell hand tools for just a fraction above their wholesale costs. But whatever your needs or shopping preference, here's how to find the best deal possible.

The Best for Less: Craftsman

You can't argue with success: In nearly 70 years of producing hand tools, Sears Craftsman has made over one billion tools—and guaranteed every one of them forever. Since Sears makes its selections based on the criterion that the tool must consistently do its job better than any competitive tool in its price class, the quality is usually top-notch.

And during special sales—usually around Christmas and Father's Day—prices are often reduced up to 30 percent, making Sears *the* place to shop for hand tools. You can also order through the free 150-page Craftsman Power & Hand Tools Catalog, which can be yours by calling 1-800-948-8800.

BUY AFTER NEW YEAR'S. Whether it's a Mom-and-Pop hardware store or a mass-market giant, most tool retailers order heavily for the Christmas holidays and are more than likely to be sitting on a surplus of items in January. Managers are very eager to get rid of this carry-over inventory to make room for the new line, which usually comes out in February or early spring.

During the month of January, expect discounts of 20 to 30 percent or more off retail. Although your choices may be somewhat limited, the selection should still be broad enough to satisfy even particular bargain-hunters.

LOOK FOR THE CHANGES. In today's competitive markets, even hand tools go through model changes. Some lines may be discontinued, a new style or color may be introduced, or a retailer may decide to carry different brands. When these changes occur, you're in a great position to pick up the "older" models for up to 70 percent below retail—especially at mass-market home centers like Home Depot, where these changes mean that the old items must go to make room for the new.

BUY IN BULK. Many hand tools lend themselves to group packaging—mechanic's tools like combination wrenches, sockets and punches; household tools like screwdrivers and pliers; and woodworking tools such as chisels, files and drill bits. All of these tools are available individually, but when purchased as a set, savings can be considerable—anywhere from 15 to 50 percent less than the same items individually, depending on the type of tool and its "set" packaging.

READ THE WARRANTY, NOT JUST THE PRICE TAG. Don't make price alone the deciding factor in making a tool purchase. Most quality tools have a replacement guarantee—the best tools have a lifetime warranty. The exception: Some importers of inexpensive, no-name "offshore" brands don't stand behind their products, and these tools tend to be less expensive and easily breakable.

You can recognize a good hand tool not only by its name and packaging but by such signs as its overall finish, its feel and balance in your hand and the way it functions in use. Avoid at any cost bargain-priced tools with doubtful lineage—they're not bargains in the long run and could cost you in frustration and possible injury.

DON'T COUNT ON FREQUENT-FLYER DISCOUNTS. Or to put it another way, don't assume items are on sale simply because they're advertised in a flyer. A significant number of tool sales are made by large home center chains using a marketing strategy that's now quite common

GREAT MAIL-ORDER BUYS

There are two good reasons to order hand tools by mail: The tools can be less expensive, especially if there are no large home centers in your area, and there's often a better selection than local stores can offer.

One good source for discount woodworking tools is Trend-lines of Revere, Massachusetts. Besides offering a broad selection of power tools, Trend-lines has a lowest-price mail-order guarantee on all nationally advertised brand-name hand tools and accessories. And the company will match any mail-order competitor's advertised price. Trend-lines also offers special pricing and multiple-item discounts on selected tools at 40 percent less than regular retail prices. To get your catalog, call 1-800-366-6966.

but still relatively unknown to the consumer. Rather than the traditional markup-then-discount system, which offers price breaks to tradesmen and during special sales, the current "everyday low price" system discounts everything: Prices are set at just below wholesale costs, with the cost of the flyers and other advertising built in. Actually, the best bargains are usually *not* those advertised in the flyers but rather other items on the shelf that are marked with a special price tag because they're targeted to move for one reason or another.

BUY USED IN THE NEIGHBORHOOD. While the best prices on new hand tools are usually found at larger home centers like Home Depot or Builders Square because of their vast buying power, the best *deals* on hand tools are probably found at neighborhood auctions and flea markets because somebody wants to get rid of them. Hand tools are one of the more popular items at neighborhood sales, and with good reason: You can get quality used tools for just a fraction of their new cost. Local "shopper" flyers often advertise these sales; just go early for best selection.

HARDWARE

Those 3-cent screws and 89-cent boxes of nails may seem a lot less painful on your wallet than a hammer-blackened thumb is on your nerve endings. But considering that hardware represents about 25 percent of the total cost of materials for most home repairs and improvements, it certainly adds up.

So much, in fact, that Americans spend nearly $130 billion each year buying fasteners, mounting devices, brackets, hinges, drawer pulls and other hardware. Generally, the retail markup for hardware is much lower than for other home improvement products—usually no more than 40 percent at smaller Mom-and-Pop hardware stores and much less at larger retailers. There are literally hundreds of different types of hardware items in dozens of sizes, but whatever you need, here's how to get it for less.

BULK UP. You'd be surprised at the difference in the unit price between a single item and a large quantity of the same thing. As an example, the hardware store asks 4 or 5 cents for an individual 6 × 2 Phillips-drive woodworking screw. Buy the same size in a 100-piece box and the price drops to an average of 3.5 cents each, and by the pound—about 200 screws—the price drops to about 2 cents each.

In general, you'll usually pay up to 45 percent less if you buy a box of nails or screws than if you buy them from the "single-item" bins.

DON'T OVERBUY QUALITY. As with other products, hardware and fastener items come in different grades and finishes to suit various needs. Using brass hinges where zinc-plated steel will do or buying hardened alloy bolts for common repair jobs, for example, can be very expensive—adding 100 percent or more to the cost of the project. So whenever possible, stick with standard-quality hardware.

If you're not sure about the right kind of hardware for a job, check the box or ask store personnel for guidance—some manufacturers

GREAT MAIL-ORDER BUYS

A mail-order catalog is probably not your best source of rock-bottom prices for hardware, unless there's a special sale going on. But it may save you some gas money if you tend to drive all over town searching in vain for hard-to-find hardware items, since most catalogs include a broader selection of fasteners and hardware than the average retail store is able to offer.

Catalogs also tend to offer better quantity discounts on many hardware items, and money-back guarantees are normally a condition of sale. Though shipping and handling costs do add some expense, they are offset to some extent by the lack of state sales tax (unless you live in the same state as the company from which you're ordering).

For some of the best catalog prices and an excellent selection, call Woodworker's Supply in Graham, South Carolina (1-800-645-9292), Trend-lines in Revere, Massachusetts (1-800-366-6966) or the Woodworkers' Store in Medina, Minnesota (1-800-279-4441). For good bulk prices on quality screws—especially square drive screws—call McFeely's, a mail-order outlet in Lynchburg, Virginia, at 1-800-443-7937.

have a toll-free customer service line to answer questions about their products, and it can be the quickest and most effective way of getting the right information.

LOOK FOR LOOSE. You see them everywhere: hardware items like shelf brackets, hinges and other items sold in pairs or sets in neat plastic see-through blister packs. These packages may be convenient, but they're more expensive than getting the same items individually.

Consider a pair of packaged shelf brackets that retails for about $2.10. If you buy the same items from a bin at the bottom of the shelf, you'll pay 75 cents each or $1.50 for the pair. That 60-cent difference may not seem like a lot, but it amounts to a savings of 30 percent.

BUY AMERICAN. Watch TV shows like *This Old House* and you'll hear contractors rave about those fancy European hinges and other hardware products. What you won't hear them mention, however, is that European specialty hardware typically costs 30 to 50 percent more than equivalent domestic screws, fasteners, hinges, handles, drawer pulls and brackets.

THINK BIG. While the local hardware store typically has a 40 percent markup, those large discount home centers like Home Depot and Builders Square are able to sell their hardware for a mere 10 to 15 percent above the same manufacturer's cost—and sometimes less. The reason: They buy so much of it that they're able to buy it for less and pass the savings on to you.

HEALTH FOODS

If recent trends in sales of natural foods are any indication, we're clearly getting the message—loud and clear—about the hazards of the traditional high-fat, high-sodium, convenience food–oriented American diet.

In recent years, sales of natural and health foods have skyrocketed. Americans now spend an estimated $6 billion each year on natural food products. That's particularly impressive when you consider that many of these foods—grown and manufactured without chemical additives or preservatives—have a history of being among the most expensive options in the marketplace, generally costing between 10 and 15 percent more than similar conventional items. But here's how to get healthy savings when buying health foods.

STORE RIGHT TO MAKE SAVINGS LAST

Because most natural foods are made without preservatives, additives and synthetic chemicals, they tend to spoil more quickly than conventional food products. To preserve your savings, here are some tips on how to store natural foods.

- Produce should be stored in the refrigerator in a tightly sealed container.
- Dry goods like seeds, nuts, flour, cereals and dried fruits should also be stored in airtight containers and refrigerated until you're ready to use them. Flour, nuts and seeds can also be frozen. Refrigerated or frozen, these items can last up to a year.
- Oils should be refrigerated and used within three months of purchase.

BUY FROM THE BIN. Most health and natural food stores feature a large selection of bulk items—including flours, beans, coffees, oils, peanut butter, grains, pasta, teas, baking mixes and granola cereals—that are kept in large bins; you package them yourself. By doing this, you can save between 10 and 30 percent on a per-pound basis compared to buying the same items prepackaged. Some stores will supply reusable containers or bags, while others offer a rebate to customers who bring their own bags or containers.

TAKE HOME THE HOUSE BRAND. Just like conventional supermarkets, many natural food stores now sell their own line of products. Alfalfa's Markets, for instance, a chain of natural food stores based in Boulder, Colorado, has its own line of products that sell for less than other brands of equal quality. While this is more common with the bigger health food chains, these in-house brands can be anywhere from 10 to 40 percent cheaper than competitors' products.

KEEP YOUR EYES ON THE SHELF TAGS. Many health and natural food stores mark certain items with brightly colored shelf tags that say "everyday low price," or EDLP. Through the EDLP program—which operates industry-wide—retailers purchase products at a discount and pass the savings on to you. These EDLP items tend to average 10 to 40 percent below competitors' prices.

GET THE SPECIAL STORE CARD. Some stores have their own discount plan. Fresh Fields, for example, a natural food chain based in Rockville, Maryland, marks its monthly specials with FreshShopper tags. To cash in on these discounts, customers need to use their free FreshShopper Card.

JOIN A FOOD CO-OP. You can save at least 20 percent just by becoming a member of a neighborhood co-op supermarket. These community-based operations typically feature an extensive selection of natural food items and function like a retail supermarket—except that members commit to working at the store for an hour or so each month. Most food co-ops require a one-time joining fee or annual fee and a time or work commitment.

To locate a food co-op near you, send a stamped, business-size envelope to Co-op Directory Services, 919 21st Avenue S, Minneapolis, MN 55404. Or send $6.95 (which includes shipping) to Co-op America, 1612 K Street NW, Suite 600, Washington, DC 20006 to order the National Green Pages, a yearly directory that lists hundreds of socially and environmentally responsible businesses, including dozens of food co-ops nationwide. Co-op America also publishes the

GREAT MAIL-ORDER BUYS

The nation's oldest and largest organic mail-order food company is also the best—offering an incredible inventory at rock-bottom prices. From organically grown fruits and vegetables to whole-wheat sticky buns, Walnut Acres Organic Farms features hundreds of organic food products that can be sent directly to your home. A "parcel stuffer" accompanies each order, listing about 100 items that have been reduced by as much as 50 percent. An added bonus: No matter how large your order, shipping and handling costs are only $4.90. For a catalog, call Walnut Acres at 1-800-433-3998.

Co-op America Quarterly, which includes information on how to start a food co-op in your neighborhood; to order a copy, send $4 to the above address.

FORM YOUR OWN BUYING CLUB. You'll need to assemble a group of family members, friends, neighbors or co-workers so you'll have enough resources to place a minimum order, but you can buy directly from a distributor and save up to 60 percent on certain items—or cut a deal with a store manager and shave 10 percent or more off larger orders.

Deliveries from distributorships can usually be made to wherever the group designates, and then the group divides the goods. But sometimes you may need to find a wholesaler who can accept delivery. To locate a supplier near you, consult the National Green Pages.

READ ALL ABOUT IT. Many stores try to distinguish themselves from the competition by publishing newsletters and flyers that not only educate customers about various food products and health issues but also advertise price-reduced items. Wild Oats Markets, another Colorado-based chain, publishes *Wild Times*, a monthly newsletter that advertises around 50 items that have been reduced by approximately 30 percent. To maximize your savings for the long haul, pick up the in-store newsletter before you shop and preplan your meals around sale items.

HEARING AIDS

About 60 percent of people over age 65 have some degree of hearing loss, and a growing number of younger ears have also suffered from exposure to amplified music and other noise. That translates to nearly two million people who ultimately resort to hearing aids each year—usually at a cost of anywhere from $300 to $5,000 and with a retail markup of up to 100 percent.

If you suspect you have a hearing problem, you should go to a physician or certified audiologist, who is specifically trained to test for problems. A hearing aid dealer or audiologist can help you select a model, either one that fits behind the ear (about 40 percent of hearing aids sold are this type) or one that is placed directly into the ear canal. And remember that while hearing aids amplify sound, they cannot clarify unclear speech or eliminate background noise.

Medicaid covers hearing tests for everyone and hearing aids for children, and most private medical insurance plans will pay for hearing examinations but not hearing aids. So when buying an aid, it's especially important to search for the best deal possible. Here's how.

BUY THE TECHNOLOGY, NOT THE NAME. Many hearing aids use components that are similar or exactly the same—the only differences are the name and the price. For example, a behind-the-ear hearing aid by Oticon costs about $700, while a similar type from a franchise dealership may cost twice as much.

In fact, industry insiders say that no fewer than 24 different brands use the same patented K-Amp technology, which amplifies soft sounds without increasing louder ones. So when buying, ask the dealer for the cheapest model with this technology.

AVOID MAIL ORDER. Calling the toll-free numbers advertised by hearing aid companies such as Beltone and Miracle-Ear costs more in the long run because the only information you usually get is the tele-

THE BEST FOR LESS: RESOUND

While conventional hearing aids merely amplify all sound, digitally programmable hearing aids can be adapted to a wide range of settings and fit individual hearing losses more specifically. And insiders say that some of the best hearing aids of this type on the market are made by ReSound Corporation of Redwood City, California.

Based on a patented sound-processing technology that automatically adjusts volume 22 times per second, ReSound's devices seldom need volume adjustments. Its Sculpture model, from its Premium line, which permits adjustments for separate listening situations like a noisy environment, is cosmetically matched to your ear—and the battery door is on the inside, making it virtually invisible. The volume settings can be altered by an optional remote control instead of by tiny, unwieldy dials on the hearing aid itself. Of course, a pair of ReSound Sculpture hearing aids costs as much as a used car—about $4,000.

But you can get the same sound-processing technology in ReSound's new Encore line, which sells for about $1,400 for a pair of behind-the-ear or in-the-ear models. The one drawback is that the Encore has no remote control; the settings have to be adjusted by the dealer or an audiologist.

phone number of their franchise dealer in your neighborhood. Instead ask your doctor to recommend a certified audiologist or hearing aid dealer who isn't affiliated with a single company.

SEEK A RETAILER WITH "FRIENDS IN THE BUSINESS." Hearing aid retailers and audiologists often buy large quantities of hearing aids from manufacturers collectively, reducing their costs by up to 50 percent and usually passing a substantial portion of these savings on to you. Some even sell hearing aids purchased this way under their own private labels. So when you're shopping for a hearing aid, ask the re-

GETTING INFORMATION

Many organizations offer purchasing tips for hearing aids. Call the Federal Trade Commission in Washington, D.C., at (202) 326-2222 and ask for the brochure *Hearing Aids*. You can also call the Hearing Aid Helpline of the International Hearing Society (1-800-521-5247), the League for the Hard of Hearing in New York City (212-741-7650—voice; 212-255-1932—TTY), the American Speech-Language-Hearing Association Helpline (1-800-638-8255) or Self-Help for Hard of Hearing People in Bethesda, Maryland (301-657-2248—voice; 301-657-2249—TTY). Or send a postcard to the Department of Veterans Affairs, Audio and Speech (126), 50 Irving Street NW, Washington, DC 20422 for a copy of its yearly test results on a few brands of hearing aids.

Keep in mind that using a new hearing aid requires weeks of adjustment, and it may even turn out to be the wrong type for you. So saving money starts with knowing what you need and why a particular type is recommended. Avoid purchasing a hearing aid from anyone who sells only one brand, no matter how familiar; that's like going to a clothing store that sells only one size. Expect to return for several tests and adjustments, and make sure they're all included in the price. Demand at least a 30-day trial period; in some states, that's the law. And check to see if your dealer also will repair your hearing aid, since these devices break down frequently.

If there's a nonrefundable "restocking fee" for hearing aids that have to be returned, walk out and look somewhere else. The only nonrefundable charges should be for custom-fitted parts and a hearing test.

tailer about his buying power—does he purchase inventory only for his store, or as a part of a larger buying group?

PROFIT FROM A NONPROFIT. Some nonprofit organizations offer hearing tests and hearing aids without the high markup that commercial dealers get. You may find them by looking in the yellow pages under "Hearing Aids" or "Audiology"; also check the listings under

"Deaf Services" for organizations listed as noncommercial.

In South Florida, for example, you can call United Hearing and Deaf Services of Broward County at (954) 731-7200 for hearing tests and hearing aids without big markups. There is also a national nonprofit group called Hear Now based in Denver that sells previously owned hearing aids; call 1-800-648-HEAR. The group requests $25 if you can afford to pay but will provide a hearing aid even if you can't.

The Boston Guild for the Hard of Hearing, at (617) 267-4730, offers free or cut-rate hearing examinations and hearing aids. In addition, the Lion's Club, Kiwanis Club and other service organizations also sometimes offer financial assistance to help people on fixed incomes pay for hearing aids.

HEATERS AND HEATING EQUIPMENT

The type of heater you buy will help determine the comfort level of your home—and finances—for the next 15 to 30 years. That's because heating and cooling account for up to 70 percent of the energy used in the average American household.

Depending on where you live, energy bills can be a big part of your monthly budget, so it pays to consider your options carefully when selecting a new heater. One key consideration is efficiency: An inefficient model may save you a few hundred dollars initially but will add thousands in heating costs over its lifetime.

Most central heating units are normally purchased through the contractor that you select to do the installation, and industry insiders say you should always get estimates from at least four reputable con-

GREAT MAIL-ORDER BUYS

You can't order a new furnace through the mail, but you can get some good deals on portable space heaters and heating equipment by mail order. Damark International is a Minneapolis-based mail-order company that specializes in discontinued and overstocked merchandise. We found savings of up to 60 percent off retail prices on kerosene and electric heaters, fireplace blowers and even wood stoves and fireplaces. The best deals can be found in the spring catalog, when winter items go on sale, and customers can always save an additional 10 percent by joining Damark's Preferred Buyers' Club. To order a catalog, call 1-800-729-9000.

BUYING SPACE HEATERS

Space heater prices run from $20 to well over $200. So what's the difference? Generally, as with central units, the less a portable electric space heater costs to buy, the more expensive it is to operate.

All portable heaters are designed to add *supplemental* heat to an area, so don't expect them to efficiently heat a room that has no other source of heat. Convection heaters—which blow air around the room—will heat a room more quickly than radiant heaters, which are best suited for spot heating.

To figure out what size is best, calculate 40 Btu (British thermal units) per square foot of room space for a radiant heater and 50 Btu per square foot for a convection heater. The maximum wattage for *any* model is 1,500 watts.

tractors. Portable space heaters to take the chill out of a cold room or help boost a less efficient system can be purchased at most home centers and hardware stores. When buying either type, here's how to get the most for your money.

SHOP WHEN IT'S HOT. Installation cost is the real budget-breaker when it comes to central heating systems, comprising anywhere from one-half to two-thirds of the total cost of a new system. But you'll likely get the best deal on installation (as well as the total cost) if you hire a heating contractor during the "slow" season, between April and August.

Generally, most contractors lower their bids about 10 percent—or at least $200—during these months compared to the rest of the year. An added bonus: Your installer will also be able to pay more attention to your job during his slow time.

THEN ASK ABOUT PRESEASON DISCOUNTS. To get their "clients" hot on new heaters, distributors typically offer contractors a 15 percent preseason discount on heating equipment when they order units in August and September. Since the cost of the furnace, boiler or heat pump can be up to half the total cost of the job, the contractor could pass $100 to $200 in savings on to you—as long as you ask. Your best bet: Get an estimate first and *then* ask the contractor to redo the bid, incorporating preseason savings on parts and labor.

If you're shopping for a portable space heater, you can also take advantage of preseason savings. Retailers such as Sears begin stocking space heaters in September and soon run preseason sales of between 10 and 15 percent off to begin moving the merchandise. And by February, retailers are thinking spring and want to move what's left of their stock. So if you can hold out, you'll likely find space heater prices dropping up to 25 percent below retail then—unless, of course, there's a sudden cold spell.

SEEK OUT THE SLIGHTLY DAMAGED. Just as with scratch-and-dent sales on appliances, you can usually save up to 20 percent by asking a contractor for a new central heating unit that's been slightly dented. These units usually work fine, but they've been damaged during shipping. The only problem with scratch-and-dent heaters is that they sometimes come with compromised or more limited warranties.

STICK WITH YOUR EXISTING FUEL. Experts advise against trying to save money by switching fuel—going from an electric system, for instance, to gas or oil. The reason: This year's cheapest fuel may be next year's most expensive—and the cost of converting can be several thousand dollars. Since heaters are long-range investments, the year-to-year fluctuations of fuel costs should not be considered a savings strategy. You're better off if you upgrade to more efficient equipment instead.

Herbs and Spices

America is discovering that the spice is right. Increasing interest in both healthy and hot foods has led to a surge in herb and spice sales. As a result, for the first time, we're now downing over 800 million pounds of spices a year. Experts say that at this rate, we'll be eating over a billion pounds by the year 2000. Any way you flavor it, that's a lot of salsa, hot chicken wings and Cajun shrimp.

The hottest sellers? Not surprisingly, those that add a little flame: dehydrated onion and garlic, mustard seed, red pepper, sesame seeds (as in fast-food buns), black pepper and paprika.

Herbs, which also can give meals a special taste boost in lieu of salt and butter, have become a nearly $2-billion-a-year industry, with sales rising at an annual rate of 20 percent.

Although the United States is a significant spice producer—we grow 38 percent of what we consume—we import from countries as far away as Indonesia, China and Guatemala. And then there's retail markup, which can add 50 percent or more to prices.

Outstanding Outlets

You can save at least 15 percent off retail prices by buying herbs and spices at cooking stores located in outlet malls. Among the best is Le Gourmet Chef, which has a great selection of seasonings with this markdown. To find a Le Gourmet Chef near you, call (908) 782-0139 during business hours.

GREAT MAIL-ORDER BUYS

The San Francisco Herb Company has been selling herbs and spices to food co-ops at wholesale prices for over 20 years. With a minimum order of only $30, you can get the same great deals, and this is one of the few companies that also offer discounts for smaller orders—a 5-pound order is discounted 10 percent off the typical per-pound price, while orders of 25 pounds net you 15 percent savings. (Depending on the specific herb or spice, most 5-pound—and even 25-pound—orders come packed in separate 1-pound cellophane bags to maintain freshness.) Shipping is free on orders of $200 or more. For a free catalog, call 1-800-227-4530. People who live east of the Mississippi can get similar savings by calling its sister company, the Atlantic Spice Company, at 1-800-316-7965.

Chef Paul Prudhomme's Magic Seasonings Blends, created by the famous chef at K-Paul's Louisiana Kitchen in New Orleans, are available at retail stores throughout the country. But you can get these spice blends at reduced prices if you order the 24-ounce canister through K-Paul's mail-order catalog. (Most of the other items in the catalog are priced at retail.) Each of the Magic Seasonings Blends, which are specially formulated for meat, poultry, seafood, vegetables, blackened redfish, blackened steak, pork, veal, pizza and pasta, contain 10 to 12 different herbs and spices to enhance the flavor of these foods. For a free catalog, call 1-800-457-2857.

But you can enhance the flavor and character of foods without putting the pinch on your wallet. Try these tips.

SHOP ETHNIC. The most common place to buy herbs and spices—your neighborhood supermarket—is the worst place. That's because most supermarkets sell factory-ground herbs and spices in small containers for full retail. Your best bet is to buy herbs and spices at ethnic markets, especially Middle Eastern markets. For the one nearest you, check the yellow pages under "Grocers."

BUY A LOT. You can save as much as 70 percent off retail if you buy in bulk from ethnic markets, food co-ops, natural food stores and specialty stores such as Aphrodisia, a spice and herb boutique located in New York City. To store fresh herbs so they'll retain their freshness, put them in a plastic bag (squeeze out the air) and keep them in the refrigerator. When moisture forms on the inside of the bag, turn it inside out.

AGREE TO GRIND YOUR OWN. Whole herbs and spices not only cost less but also tend to be fresher, since grinding them causes them to lose the essential oils that contain their flavor. You can crush them yourself with a mortar and pestle or in a coffee grinder, or you can grind spices in a pepper mill immediately before adding them to a recipe.

JOIN A WAREHOUSE CLUB. Herbs and spices are not exempt from the typical 15 to 40 percent savings that warehouse clubs like Sam's Club and B.J.'s Wholesale Club offer on a variety of products. National

THE BEST FOR LESS: SAFFRON

No wonder saffron is one of the most expensive spices: It takes 70,000 hand-picked flowers to produce just one pound of this wonderfully earthy ingredient.

But because Penzeys Limited Spice House imports directly from India, they're able to offer quality Spanish saffron—the most common type—for 50 percent less than retail stores. They also sell kashmir saffron, which is often hard to find, at discount prices: A gram of saffron that costs between $10 and $11 at most stores is only $5.95 from Penzeys. (Fortunately, just 15 cents' worth is enough to provide that distinctive, light yellow saffron color and flavor to dishes.)

Penzeys also publishes a free 36-page catalog with a selection of over 300 herbs and spices. Call (414) 574-0277 for more information or write Penzeys Limited Spice House, P.O. Box 1448, Waukesha, WI 53187.

brands such as McCormick's are usually featured at these supersavers, sold in sizes that begin at one pound. Although they're usually preground, they can retain their flavor for up to a year if you store them in a cool, dry place such as an enclosed kitchen cupboard or the freezer rather than in a spice rack over your stove.

FORAGE AT A FARMERS MARKET. Besides fresh produce and cheese, farmers markets—typically located outside major cities—tend to offer fresh herbs and spices for up to 25 percent below retail. Many, like the New York Farms Market at Woodbury Common Factory Outlets in Central Valley, New York, also carry brand-name packaged seasoning blends such as Spice Hunter. To find a farmers market near you, call the U.S. Department of Agriculture's Wholesale Market Development Branch at (202) 720-8317 and ask for a copy of the *1994 National Farmers' Market Directory*, which lists farmers markets across the country.

DON'T BUY DIRECTLY FROM THE COMPANY. Many manufacturers and sellers of retail herbs and spices, such as Flavorbank, based in Tampa, Florida, sell directly to customers—but at prices that are typically 20 percent higher than what you'd pay retail. That's because most manufacturers want to avoid competing with the retail outlets that carry their products.

However, if you buy in bulk from a manufacturer—in quantities greater than one pound—you can get slight savings compared to buying at an ethnic market or farmers market. If you're interested in bulk savings, ask for Flavorbank's Home Catalog by calling 1-800-835-7603. A tip: The best deals in the bulk section are in the middle of the catalog.

Home Computers

In 1970 a computer cost nearly $350,000, and it occupied an entire room. Today a personal computer costs an average of about $1,500, and it's smaller than a TV set. Best of all, you can expect prices to fall even lower, thanks to manufacturing efficiencies and technological advances.

About 15 million personal computers are sold each year, and industry insiders predict that rate should double every seven years. The result: intensive price wars and a flood of perfectly serviceable used computers. But in the meantime, here's how you can save when buying a home computer.

Stay one step behind. You may notice that computers are advertised by numbers such as 486/33 or 586/66. The first number represents the style of microprocessor; the higher that number is, the newer and more high-tech the microprocessor is. The second number is the megahertz, or speed; a higher number means it's a "faster" computer.

Whenever a new "breed" of computer—the 586, for instance—is introduced to the market, the previous models go on sale. This usually occurs twice a year, in the spring and in the fall. Although many shoppers assume they should buy a personal computer with the most recent microprocessor because it's the latest and greatest, by sticking with the previous year's model you can save up to 30 percent compared to the same model before the new line was introduced—and have a computer that just may serve all of your needs.

Think big. One of every eight computers is sold in large retail electronics stores like Circuit City and Best Buy, office products superstores like Staples and OfficeMax or warehouse clubs like Sam's Club. True, their sales staff may not be as knowledgeable as the staff at a computer specialty store, but the larger stores make up for this in price—usually 15 to 20 percent below what you'd pay at a retail specialty store.

Because of their buying power, these large stores are able to pur-

GREAT MAIL-ORDER BUYS

You'll find only a sample of the items available from PC Connection/MacConnection in their monthly catalog. Otherwise it would be roughly the size of a telephone book: They carry over 15,000 products in stock.

A five-time winner of *PC World* magazine's Best Mail-Order Company award, PC Connection/MacConnection carries everything from computer systems and peripherals to the hottest new home and business software programs—all priced below retail. What's more, any order that weighs 10 pounds or less costs just $5 for overnight delivery. Shipments that weigh 11 pounds or more are $1 per pound. A toll-free technical support line and a manufacturer's authorized service center provide prompt, helpful information. And unless you live in Ohio, there's no sales tax.

For more information, contact PC Connection/MacConnection, 6 Mill Street, Marlow, NH 03456 or call 1-800-795-1111.

chase vast quantities of the more popular brands and pass the savings to you with frequent sales—usually a model or two each week. You may have to do a little more homework before shopping to make sure you're getting the right computer for your needs, but you can figure you'll save about $300 in the process.

LOOK TO THE SECOND STRING. Rather than shelling out top dollar for a big name like IBM or Apple, check out the smaller computer companies. Though their computers are not generally stocked in some large retail outlets like Circuit City or warehouse clubs like Sam's Club, companies like Dell Computer Corporation and Gateway 2000 make computers comparable to the bigger names—usually for about 20 percent less. Call 800 directory assistance (1-800-555-1212) to get toll-free numbers for these companies so you can comparison-shop at home.

BUY USED. Used PCs can be a great deal, generally going for about 30 percent or less of the original price. And with computers now in one of every three households, a new subindustry of computer bro-

THE BEST FOR LESS: COMPAQ PRESARIO AND MACINTOSH PERFORMA

Home computer styles and prices seem to change more often than Liz Taylor's marriage partners. But one thing in this high-tech world seems to be rock-solid: The reputation of Compaq and Macintosh computers.

Sure, there are more expensive products on the market, but insiders say few give you more "byte" for your buck than these brands.

A computer and 14-inch color monitor in a single unit, the Presario is only 15 inches tall and takes up 14 inches on your desk. But don't be fooled by its compact size. For the price of a standard personal computer you get an all-in-one multimedia PC with a built-in quad-speed CD-ROM drive, fast modem, high-fidelity speakers, stereo sound, Super VGA monitor, SpeechMail voice recognition for remote mail retrieval, a 75-megahertz Pentium processor and a one-gigabyte hard drive.

The company includes an understandable operating manual with the Presario; the preinstalled Presario Gallery includes software for the whole family, from Launch Pad for the kids to Windows 95 for experienced users, and offers easy access to America Online and other major on-line services. All you really have to do is plug it in.

You can buy it for less than retail at electronics stores like Circuit City, or for even greater savings on a refurbished system, contact the Compaq Works Factory Outlet at 1-800-318-6919.

If you prefer a Macintosh, look no further than the Performa. It too offers the convenience of an all-in-one multimedia system, quad-speed CD-ROM drive, stereo sound, a variety of preinstalled software, 75-megahertz processor and a one-gigabyte hard drive. Price is comparable to the Presario.

kerages has emerged to take the guesswork out of buying used computers. Some of these companies occasionally have great buys on dealer overstocks.

The oldest such brokerage, the Boston Computer Exchange, maintains a $2 million inventory of used IBM, Macintosh, Toshiba, NEC, Hewlett-Packard and Compaq computers that it buys directly from the company and refurbishes. Call 1-800-262-6399 for information on their inventory. Other computer brokerages include the American Computer Exchange (1-800-786-0717) in Atlanta, the National Computer Exchange (1-800-622-6639) in New York City and Practical Computer (703-321-3003) in Springfield, Virginia.

Again, the best time to shop these brokerages is during price wars or after new introductions in the spring and fall, when retailers are clearing out their inventories. You'll also find used computers advertised in the local classified ads and on the electronic bulletin boards of most on-line computer networks.

OUTSTANDING OUTLETS

Compaq Works Factory Outlet sells refurbished Compaq computers for about 25 percent below retail from a 20,000-square-foot outlet store in Houston. It also stocks accessories, software and printers made by other manufacturers. Compaq personal computers sold there come with a 90-day warranty—considerably shorter than warranties available on new systems sold through authorized resellers, such as large electronics stores. They also offer 24-hour technical support. You can find out what's available, and at what price, by calling 1-800-318-6919.

The IBM PC Factory Outlet sells for 20 to 50 percent below retail on most IBM lines, including Aptiva, PS/1, Valuepoint and the ThinkPad portables. This outlet offers a 15-day money-back guarantee as well as the original warranty. Call 1-800-426-7015 for more information.

In addition, Micron Electronics Factory Outlet offers additional savings on its already low prices in its Minnesota outlets. You'll also get a 30-day return policy, three-year parts and labor warranty and technical support by phone. Call (612) 486-1900.

CHECK OUT A BUSINESS AUCTION. While businesses consider their computers indispensable commodities, creditors consider them disposable assets—and as a result, few products are as easy to find on the auction circuit. Look in the auctions section of your Sunday paper or call an auctioneer and ask to be notified of business auctions, sales that are held when a business goes under or is refurnishing its inventory. These auctions almost always have a preview day when you can test the merchandise, and computers are sold for as much as 60 percent below regular retail prices.

DON'T BUY . . . LEASE. Another way some businesses unload their computers is to lease them to consumers. In fact, a long-term leasing deal could be a cheaper way to get computers if you operate your own business. Generally, these computers are leased from one to five years, then sold to you for anywhere from $1 each to 10 percent of the retail price. Leased computers come with service warranties and software.

CALL THE COMPANY DIRECTLY. The mail-order market for computers and accessories is approaching the $20-billion-a-year mark—and it is no wonder: Mail-order houses charge as much as 40 percent less than retail stores for some models and include some "extras," from software to warranties, that you'll find buying retail.

You'll find a slew of mail-order houses listed in the back of popular computer magazines, but it's probably safest to buy directly from the manufacturer. Some even have clearance sales offering better savings. Call for a catalog of their products, and then call back to talk with a sales representative to put together the system you need. Among the best: Compaq DirectPlus (1-800-888-5858), Dell Computer Corporation (1-800-879-3355), PCs Compleat (1-800-642-4532), IBM PC Direct (1-800-426-2968) and Micron (1-800-554-7172).

Home Health-Care Equipment

In a bid to cut costs and improve patients' quality of life, the health-care industry is turning to home-based care. Medicare spending on home health benefits has increased fivefold since 1988, to about $10.5 billion a year. And that figure is expected to double by the end of the decade.

Advancements in medical care products play a key role in this trend. In addition, equipment that was once confined to hospitals is now available for home use, allowing even people with chronic conditions to receive treatment at home.

About 75 percent of the products classified as home-care equipment—walkers, ostomy supplies, diabetes supplies, lifts, wheelchairs, special beds and chairs—are covered by insurance. Items such as bath seats and bathroom-related items, grab bars and blood pressure cuffs are not. Patients are also often expected to pay for upgraded or spare equipment. Insurance may cover the cost of a heavy, traditional hospital wheelchair, for example, that costs between $450 and $665. But if you'd prefer a sleeker, ultralight model for increased mobility, you'll likely have to pay $2,000 to $4,000 for one. In short, your insurance company isn't going to buy you a Cadillac when a Chevy will do.

Most home-care equipment is prescribed by a doctor or physical therapist, in some ways limiting your choices. But you can still get top-of-the-line equipment on a modest budget—which is particularly important if you're one of the estimated 10 to 15 percent of people not covered by any type of insurance. Here's how.

Check the mail. Virtually all home-care equipment can be purchased for about 50 percent below retail through mail-order catalogs. Specializing in everything from fashionable clothing for the disabled to ostomy supplies, wheelchairs and general equipment, there are over 100 catalogs offering home equipment. Among the best are Bruce Medical Supply in Waltham, Massachusetts (1-800-225-8446),

HELP FOR THE WHEELCHAIR-BOUND

There are several resources available to help you choose a medical equipment dealer and select home-care equipment, particularly wheelchairs.

The National Association for Medical Equipment Services (NAMES) has a pamphlet called *Health Care in Your Home: A Shopper's Guide to Home Medical Equipment* that's available free at dealers affiliated with NAMES or by calling (703) 836-6263.

Choosing a Wheelchair System is available free from the Department of Veterans Affairs, Veterans Health Administration, Washington, DC 20420. Write and request Clinical Supplement #2, *Journal of Rehabilitation Research and Development*, March 1990.

A detailed, feature-by-feature comparison of lightweight wheelchairs is done each year in the March/April edition of *Sports 'n Spokes* magazine.

Packets of information on choosing wheelchairs and other home health-care equipment are available for $5 from Abledata (a federally funded project developed to maintain a database of information on assistive devices for people with disabilities) by calling 1-800-227-0216.

AARP Pharmacy Service in Alexandria, Virginia (1-800-456-2277), Creative Health Products in Ann Arbor, Michigan (1-800-742-4478) and Care Catalog Services in Portland, Oregon (1-800-443-7091).

The only drawback when ordering through the mail: Assembling, adjusting and servicing items like wheelchairs and lift chairs can be a problem. Wheelchairs in particular need to be fitted properly, and if you buy a wheelchair that doesn't suit your needs from a mail-order firm, you may have to pay a 25 percent restocking fee to return it.

SNATCH SOME SEASONAL DISCOUNTS. In the months before national trade shows held in November and April, medical equipment dealers offer their distributors special deals—a golden opportunity for you to save up to 30 percent on equipment they're trying to promote. Remember to ask your home-care equipment supplier what kind of special deals the manufacturers are offering so you can cash in.

These vary from retailer to retailer, but the special discounts are most likely in August through October and then again in February and March.

STOCK UP. If you're going to continue to need supplies, you can usually save by buying in bulk. Most dealers discount orders between 5 and 20 percent for customers who buy in quantity, although the definition of *bulk* may vary from product to product. For many items, it means any order of more than one case.

MAKE USE OF USED STUFF. Medical suppliers routinely sell rental equipment for up to half the price of the same item new, so consider this option if you are temporarily disabled or plan to use the equipment only occasionally. Most suppliers have plenty of used equipment, but be sure to ask for it: Some retailers don't display it, since the profit margin is smaller.

BUY WITH A GROUP. For some items, like wheelchairs, distributors typically offer an across-the-board discount on purchases of four to five chairs at a time. Depending on the chair you order, that could add up to \$100 to \$800 in savings. These discounts are typically offered to sports teams, such as wheelchair basketball teams, but you don't need to be a member to get a discount. Ask a local team if they're ordering new equipment, since you all save.

RENT UNTIL THE HEALING HAPPENS. If you're out of commission only temporarily, it's probably better to rent medical equipment than to buy it. A standard wheelchair that costs over \$500 typically rents for about \$50 a month. This option is only available for mechanical, nonpersonal equipment, such as beds, crutches, wheelchairs and walkers. Items such as bedpans, bath seats and bathroom accessories must be purchased.

HOME SECURITY SYSTEMS

Name the nation's largest manufacturer of security systems. Bet you can't. That's because America's 10,000-plus home alarm dealers rarely sell the reputation of the equipment itself. Instead they woo your business by trying to establish an ongoing relationship with you.

But as in marriage, if you don't choose your partner carefully, you could be headed for an ugly and expensive breakup. That's because once you *buy* a home security system, it's only the beginning. Installation can be another $250 or so. And if you want your system monitored—where an agency responds to attempted break-ins or notifies police—you can figure on at least another $25 a month.

All told, a home security system can be a huge investment. And there's no way to tell if you're really getting a good deal, because the industry is extremely secretive and close-knit, there's no seasonal sale time, and retail markups range from 10 to 100 percent. But we found these tips to help make buying a home security system a little easier on your wallet.

FORGO THE FRILLS. You'll need some kind of siren, but do you really need attack-dog response? Skylight protection? Armed second-story windows? You can save up to 50 percent simply by choosing a system that steers clear of the dealer's most profitable hardware—the fancy stuff that most homes never need.

Home security systems divide the house into zones, or places where an intruder might enter. While you need to ensure that all potential entry points, like windows and doors, are protected by a zone, don't allow an unscrupulous dealer to sell you many more than you need, thus jacking up the price considerably. Talk to neighbors and local police before you decide what system will work best for you. Industry insiders suggest that you avoid control panels that can be used by only one company, and before signing, ask to

THE BEST FOR LESS: ITI

If you're shopping for a home security system, ask for the brand that industry distributors and police officers say is the one they'd buy for their own homes: ITI, manufactured by Interactive Technology.

According to industry experts, ITI systems have the fewest malfunctions and are considered to be among the most dependable in the business. Unfortunately, like other security system companies, ITI sells only to licensed dealers—and doesn't operate outlets. So your best bet for getting a system for less is to shop around. ITI systems are about the same price as other types, but many experts say you get more for your money. Call ITI at 1-800-777-1415 for more information.

see proof that the company is licensed for fire alarm installation, uses only certified installers and has error and omission insurance.

SHOP AROUND—AND LET THEM KNOW IT. You can save 20 percent or more on an alarm system just by pitting the dealers against each other. Increased competition has meant that prices have been cut in half in the last ten years, so before signing with anyone, get bids from at least three dealers—and let them know you're shopping around.

You'll want their estimate to include prices for equipment, installation and monthly monitoring. Dealers who buy in bulk get discounts from the manufacturer, and they'll usually pass on savings of up to 50 percent if you agree to sign a monitoring contract—the real bread and butter of the industry. But this is a also great bargaining tool: Ask for several months of free monitoring if you agree to buy from one dealer over another. Some dealers will also give free monitoring if you provide them with the names and numbers of several friends or neighbors who are interested in security systems.

CALL RADIO SHACK. Nearly every burg has at least one of these electronics stores, which sell burglar alarms as well as home security systems for less than you'll pay elsewhere. Granted, they're not the fanciest systems on the market, but they certainly are a good buy, starting at about $200 (plus a $15 monthly monitoring fee). Best of all, you may be able to install one of these over-the-counter systems yourself.

JUST SOUND OFF. A siren is usually enough to keep your home from being burglarized, and if police in your area agree, you may want to bypass a monthly monitoring system altogether. This is where dealers make their biggest profits, and monitoring costs you about $25 a month. But you can save that money by using the system's siren warning only. Few burglars stick around long enough to complete the job once a siren has been activated—whether or not your home is being monitored by a security agency.

Hotel Rooms

The mainstays of the hotel industry—business travelers—are taking shorter trips, so hotels are having to work a little harder to fill their rooms. Of course, they haven't worked too hard at lowering their prices—the average cost for a hotel room in a big city like New York is $144 per night.

Still, at any given time, 84 percent of those rooms are booked, earning hoteliers about $60 billion a year. Here's how you can keep a little more of that money in your pocket the next time you're sleeping away from home.

Make your reservation from the lobby. The easiest way to get a discount if you're a walk-in—someone who seeks a room without a reservation—is to call the hotel's toll-free number from the lobby. Hotels offer various rates for the same room, and walk-ins tend to be charged the full price. But if you phone and ask if you're entitled to any discounts, you can usually save up to 25 percent.

Call a broker. For even better deals, especially on extended stays, call a hotel broker beforehand. These brokers, who often get access to rooms that hotels say are booked, get large numbers of rooms at low prices and sell them directly to customers through travel agents at rates of up to 50 percent off. Some rooms also come from tour operators whose package tours don't sell.

For broker-assisted accommodations in the United States, call California Reservations (1-800-576-0003) or Quikbook (1-800-789-9887). For rates in the United States, Canada, the Caribbean, western Europe and Asia, call Room Exchange (1-800-846-7000), VacationLand (1-800-245-0050) or Hotel Reservations Network (1-800-964-6835). For rooms in Asia and the South Pacific, there's Travel Interlink (1-800-477-7172 or 1-800-888-5898); for Europe and Asia, call Hotels Plus (1-800-235-0909). If you're traveling to the Hawaiian islands, try All About Tours (1-800-274-8687), and in Mexico, there's Pleasant Holidays (1-800-448-3333).

JOIN A HALF-PRICE HOTEL PROGRAM. When hotels sense that they're approaching a slump, they'll offer rooms through this program for half the usual price instead of letting the rooms sit empty. The programs sell memberships, usually for around $50 a year, and provide directories of participating hotels to let you make your own arrangements. The memberships often include discounts on car rentals, cruises, movie tickets and even film processing. Half-price rooms are available only during periods when business is slow, and a minimum stay is occasionally required.

Some half-price programs include America at 50 Percent Discount (1-800-248-2783), Encore (1-800-638-0930), Great American Traveler (1-800-331-8867) and Quest (1-800-638-9819). Meanwhile, ITC 50 (1-800-342-0558) is a travel program available free to members of major auto clubs. And Entertainment Publications offers regional guides listing hotels that have agreed to provide deep discounts on available rooms. Most of the books cost $33, while a bed-and-breakfast guide goes for $22; call 1-800-285-5525 to order.

Keep in mind that while you may be paying a rock-bottom price for a room, the food, services and tips in these hotels are pegged at the full cost. And it's generally necessary to book 30 days in advance.

CALL IT A BUSINESS TRIP. If you don't want to join a club or buy a guidebook, the easiest way to save around 15 percent off the full price of a room at check-in time is to ask for the corporate rate—usually your business card is all you need to prove you're gainfully employed in a professional capacity. And if you work for the government, mention that: Uncle Sam drops more than $1.5 billion each year on hotels, giving you the leverage to get at least 10 percent off on your room. Some state and municipal employees also qualify for the government rate.

BE A CARD CARRIER. Besides the corporate rate, many hotels offer dozens of special discounts based on age, union or club membership and even residence. For example, if you're over 50 and a member of the American Association of Retired Persons (AARP), mention it to the desk clerk. AARP has arrangements with 31 national chains that give members a 10 to 50 percent discount. The Marriott and Omni chains give up to 50 percent discounts to AARP members, Howard Johnson takes 20 percent off, and Ramada offers a 15 percent discount. Other chains don't require AARP membership—just show your driver's license or other proof that you are over 50 when you check in to qualify for a discount.

50 PERCENT OFF, ZERO EFFORT

Want to save between 10 and 50 percent off your hotel bill without the hassle of even having to ask? Instead of making your reservation with the hotel itself, make it with a local hotel reservations service.

These services get great deals by promising a steady flow of guests to the hotels. They supply the people, and the hotels supply the news of last-minute cancellations, special discounts to fill empty rooms, wholesale rates once offered only to well-known tour operators and a commission. By calling these services, you can enjoy savings of from 10 to 40 percent off, but they can go as high as 50 percent when hotel business is slow. Most of these services act like travel agents and don't charge, but be sure to check first. Here's a list of some reservations services for specific cities.

Boston: Meegan Hotel Reservation Services, 1-800-332-3026.

Chicago: Hot Rooms, 1-800-468-3500.

Kansas City: Kansas City Hotel Reservation Service, 1-800-877-4386.

Las Vegas: City Wide Reservations, 1-800-733-6644.

London: Hotels Plus, 1-800-235-0909; RMC Travel Centre, 1-800-782-2674.

Los Angeles: Express Reservations, 1-800-356-1123.

Miami: Central Reservation Service, 1-800-950-0232.

New York: Central Reservation Service, 1-800-950-0232; Express Reservations, 1-800-356-1123.

Orlando: Central Reservation Service, 1-800-950-0232.

San Francisco: Central Reservation Service, 1-800-950-0232; San Francisco Reservations, 1-800-677-1550.

Washington, D.C.: Capitol Reservations, 1-800-847-4832.

In addition, membership in auto clubs and labor unions may entitle you to discounts, usually in the 25 percent range. And if you're a resident of a tourist-dependent state, like Florida or Hawaii, tell the desk clerk: Many chains also give price breaks to encourage "domestic" travel.

ASK YOUR TRAVEL AGENT ABOUT THOR24. When some of these great deals are hard to find—and they may be during busy times for the hotels—ask if your travel agent belongs to the THOR24 travel consortium. The reason: Members of THOR24 can get you room discounts of 20 percent or more even during peak periods and blackout dates when other discounts can be tough to find. Call 1-800-862-2111 to find a member of THOR24 near you. American Express Travel, Carlson Wagonlit Travel, Uniglobe and B.T.I. Americas are other names to look for when selecting a travel agency.

SLEEP IN THE SUBURBS. One in three hotel rooms is in the suburbs—and for good reason: They tend to be less expensive than similar hotels in the heart of the city. You may have to drive a little further, but you'll get reduced room rates because the hotel doesn't have to pay a big-city tax. Besides, parking is more convenient.

STAY ON CAMPUS. A conventional hotel room isn't the only place to sleep while traveling. Many universities now rent dorm rooms in the summer; some even provide access to all university facilities as part of the deal. Call the school's housing office for more information. In addition, some schools provide an Elderhostel program for people 55 or older that offers university courses, sightseeing and entertainment along with a dorm room. Call (617) 426-7788 for more information. And if you're traveling to England, write the British Universities Accommodation Consortium, Box 996 ATW, University Park, Nottingham, England NG7 2RD.

Jeans

Nothing came between Brooke Shields and her Calvins. But today, hefty price tags come between many shoppers and the jeans they want to buy.

Sure, you can get a pair for about $15 at a discount store or outlet. Or you can spend $100 or more for designer denim at a fancy shop. Jeans prices run the gamut, but no matter what the price, Americans spend more than $8 billion on them each year—buying a total of about 1.2 million pairs each day.

No matter what your price range, look for features like sturdy denim and stitching and snaps, rivets or buttons that are attached securely. Fit does vary from one manufacturer to another, so always try on *each* pair—don't assume that a size in one brand will fit like the same size in another.

Great Mail-Order Buys

Don't expect any fancy-shmancy designer labels, but if you want rugged, no-nonsense jeans at outlet prices (or less), check out the Sierra Trading Post catalog. Jeans and other outdoor wear sell for between 30 and 70 percent less than retail, with prices as low as $14.95 for 14-ounce preshrunk denim; pleated chinos by Columbia Sportswear Company sell for $17.95.

Most merchandise is first-quality or irregulars with minor cosmetic flaws, and shipping is prompt and reasonable. You can order a catalog by calling (307) 775-8000.

THE BEST FOR LESS: LEVI'S

Although designer jeans no longer enjoy the "must-have" status they had in the 1980s, Calvin (Klein), Donna (Karan) and others are still dropping their names on jeans—and charging premium dollar. But to take the . . . ahem, *Guess*work out of your next purchase, stick with the most demanded name in denim: Levi's.

They may not carry the fancy name or price tag—a pair of Levi's typically sells for about $35, about a third of the cost of some other brands—but they do what jeans are supposed to do: provide comfort and durability that will last for years. And industry insiders say that dollar for dollar, they do it better than just about any other name in the business.

To get Levi's for up to 60 percent less than regular retail prices, check out the County Seat and, in western states, Miller's Outpost. The stores sell mostly irregulars—jeans whose stitching or seams don't meet standards—but the average shopper can barely tell. You'll also find other Levi's items at less substantial savings, but still below retail. To find a store near you, call Levi Strauss & Company at 1-800-872-5384.

Most retailers sell jeans for about twice their wholesale cost. But here's how to pocket some savings the next time you're shopping for jeans.

GET YOUR BEST DEALS IN OCTOBER OR NOVEMBER. The back-to-school shopping season—late August through early September—is one of the most popular times to buy jeans. Some retailers offer "value prices" of 10 to 25 percent off during this busy shopping season, but it's smarter to wait. A month or two later, you can net real savings, as jeans may be marked down as much as 50 percent to clear them out before the Christmas merchandise comes in. Besides, waiting gives your kids a chance to see what everyone else is wearing so you won't spend money on a closet dust-collector.

SHOP AT A STORE'S LESS EXPENSIVE COUSIN. If you like Gap style, you'll like jeans from its "value-priced" Old Navy Clothing Company stores. These are not outlets—the clothing is specially designed for Old Navy—but prices begin at $12 for kids' denim jeans and $16.50 for adult-size jeans.

GO WITH THE HOUSE BRAND. Some department stores put a new label (or no label) on jeans made by well-known manufacturers and sell them as their own house brand. Except for the label (or lack of it, as the case may be), they're the same jeans—for up to 20 percent less than the well-known name.

SHOP ARMY-NAVY. If your heart is set on covering your legs with names like Levi's or Lee, head to your nearest Army-Navy store. You may find jeans for up to 20 percent off department store prices—especially during spring and summer, when you can avoid the autumn rush of hunters and students.

BYPASS THE PREWASHES. Those acid, stone and other "washes" may provide a more faded look, but these manufacturer's treatments can add 15 to 30 percent to the cost of a typical pair of jeans. After a few washings, your new jeans will have an older look anyway.

OR BUY THEM USED. Want the faded look without the price? Shop at a vintage boutique or consignment store and you can pocket the $20 or more you'll save by not buying a new pair. Jeans like Levi's 501s have become a hot item at many secondhand and vintage clothing stores, where they sell for as little as $5 to $10 a pair. Used jeans often are more comfortable, since they're already broken in. Just be sure to check for tears, seams that are coming apart or missing rivets, which might be hard to replace.

Jewelry

Silver and gold, baubles and jewels—luxury items that never seem to go out of style. Last year Americans spent $13 billion on diamond jewelry alone and another $8 billion on the always-coveted gold.

Meanwhile, a push for value has led to a resurgence of platinum, which is considered the finest of all metals. Over the last three years, sales of platinum jewelry have tripled. And thanks in large part to the television shopping networks, pearls and other gemstones—particularly tanzanite, citrine and garnet—are becoming popular as more

Outstanding Outlets

If you're looking for a good diamond at a reasonable price, check out Diamonds by Rennie Ellen in New York City. She's been cutting gems since 1966 and has an impeccable record within the industry, selling diamonds of all shapes and qualities at prices up to 75 percent less than you'd pay retail. Call (212) 869-5525 for more information. Also in the Big Apple is Maurice Badler Jewelers, which offers men's and women's jewelry at savings of 25 to 40 percent below retail. To order a catalog, call 1-800-M-BADLER.

In Chicago, check out S.A. Peck & Company, which sells diamond jewelry and some gold jewelry at 10 to 15 percent below wholesale prices. The company will have the stone that you choose appraised and give you a gemologist's certificate that documents the diamond's quality. Call 1-800-922-0090 for their catalog.

GREAT MAIL-ORDER BUYS

If you know what you're looking for, you can find some of the best jewelry deals by mail order. For gemstones, Hong Kong Lapidaries is a great place to start. Its 60-page catalog includes a wide range of precious and semiprecious stones for as much as 50 percent below retail. You can order a catalog by fax or mail for $3. Fax them at (305) 755-8780 or write to 2801 University Drive, Coral Springs, FL 33065.

For a more general assortment of fine jewelry at outstanding prices, try Ross-Simons Jewelers in Cranston, Rhode Island. Through its free catalogs, the company offers a wide selection of necklaces, gold bands, bracelets and chokers at prices about 20 to 40 percent less than retail. Call 1-800-556-7376 for a catalog.

economical substitutes for sapphires, emeralds and rubies.

What hasn't changed, though, are the prices. A one-karat diamond engagement ring with a gold band, for example, can still set you back at least $7,500 at a retail jeweler. But here are some ways to cover yourself with fine jewelry without breaking the bank.

GO WITH 10 TO SAVE 20 OR MORE. Once considered the poor stepchild of big daddy 14-karat gold, 10-karat gold is now considered a good buy in jewelry. Not only is it sturdy, it's often indistinguishable from its heavier relative—and sells for 20 percent less than 14-karat.

STAY AWAY FROM THE MALL. Those mall jewelry stores, with their high rents and other overhead costs, are the most expensive places to shop for jewelry and gemstones; they charge anywhere from 20 to 50 percent more than you'd pay for similar jewelry found in "Jeweler's Row" sections of major metropolitan areas or discount jewelry warehouses across the country.

When buying from a discounter, however, you should be aware that some have been accused of selling second-rate or even used goods at new prices. So when buying anything—especially precious gems—be sure to get a certificate of replacement—an appraisal letter from a certified gemologist or a guarantee that you can return the jewelry if it turns out to be worth less than the discounter promises.

SPEAK UP FOR A BETTER DEAL. Jewelry is priced with negotiations in mind—especially for higher-end pieces. Since jewelers make their money on quick turnover, many are willing to cut the sticker price by 10 to 40 percent in order to make a sale, especially during slower months like July and August. Don't expect as great a markdown between November and June, since jewelry is a popular holiday gift and jewelers are busy in the pre-wedding season of the spring and early summer.

SHOP FOR YOUR STONES WHOLESALE. Although they're technically not supposed to sell to the public, many wholesalers will let you select a stone from them and then steer you to a jeweler who will give it to you for a discount; some might even sell it to you "under the table." With stone in hand, you've got 90 percent of the value of your ring. To find wholesalers in your area, look in the yellow pages under "Jewelers—Wholesale."

BUY SECONDHAND. Pawn shops may not have the glamour of fancier jewelry stores, but don't let their reputations fool you: Pawn shops are heavily regulated and offer some of the best deals on jewelry. You can save 30 percent or more compared to buying new wholesale. Of course, you're buying used.

And many jewelers also sell secondhand jewelry. As with cars and other items, jewelry is sometimes traded in when a new piece is purchased. Your deals won't be as good as at a pawn shop, but you'll save at least 25 percent compared to buying new.

MAKE YOUR PURCHASE A FEDERAL CASE. The U.S. Customs Department periodically holds auctions to sell jewelry and other valuables that have been confiscated, usually from lawbreakers. This isn't the most reliable way of shopping, since it can be a virtual gold mine (quite literally) or offer nothing. But when there are jewelry and gemstones to be sold, it's usually at a great bargain, sometimes just pennies on the dollar. To find these sales, contact the department directly; it is listed in the blue pages section of your telephone directory.

These auctions can be closed-bid (where you submit your offer in a sealed envelope) or open. Often government auctions will allow attendees to inspect the merchandise the day before the sale. And estate sales are also worth a look-see, as an old piece of jewelry will often sell well below its appraised value. They're listed in the classified section of most newspapers.

KITCHEN CABINETS

New kitchen cabinets cost anywhere from a few hundred dollars to well over $50,000. But no matter what you spend, they seem to be a good investment: Along with bathroom renovations, kitchen makeovers are the most cost-effective home improvements you can make—raising your home's value as much or even more than the cost of the actual renovations. And nearly half of all money spent on kitchen renovations goes into new cabinets.

Of course, right now you're probably thinking about what those cabinets will *cost*—not what they'll bring in come sale time. While there's less room for negotiating a better price on cabinets than there is on other retail goods—retail markups tend to be a scant 10 percent—here's how to get the most for your money.

SHOP AROUND—AND LET 'EM KNOW IT. New cabinet lines are introduced in the spring and fall, but the average consumer would never know it: Cabinet prices rarely fluctuate because of seasonal inventory changes. And you can't believe those promises of up to "70 percent off the suggested retail price" that grace newspaper ads and cabinet displays as you enter a home center. That "suggested" price is usually meaninglessly inflated, with real savings amounting to only pennies.

So how do you really get the best deal? For custom cabinets, your best bet is to comparison-shop, just as you would for a new car. Salesmen count on you falling in love with those raised oak panels or that sleek brass hardware, but they also know that the competition can offer something very similar, if not identical. So the more places you visit, the better you'll be able to compare prices and negotiate a better deal.

Visit various kitchen and home centers like Home Depot and Builders Square and you'll notice a wide variance in prices, so there *is* room to haggle (even though salespeople say there isn't). Your

GETTING DESIGN HELP

While most experts suggest that you hire a designer to help arrange your dream kitchen, the cost can be a nightmare: A designer can double the cost of your kitchen renovation. So if you're replacing what exists or have simple needs, you can save the design costs and do the layout yourself. And home centers like Home Depot offer free, in-store kitchen design services. (Home visits cost about $50 for the first two hours and $35 for each subsequent hour.)

The National Kitchen & Bath Association has a free pamphlet, *40 Guidelines of Kitchen Design*; write to 687 Willow Grove Street, Hackettstown, NJ 07840, or call 1-800-367-6522. And Merillat, one of America's biggest cabinet manufacturers, has a Kitchen Planning Kit for $8, packed with ideas to help consumers with design problems. Order yours by calling 1-800-624-1250.

best bet: Choose the cabinet style you like and ask the clerk to help you devise a floor plan (also called a cabinet layout). Map out every detail—including hardware and extras. Then ask him to write it up. Take the estimate, thank him for his time and move on to the next store—with that paper in hand.

Once you've visited about five kitchen and home centers, you'll be in a good position to say what the other stores are offering—and watch the "estimate" price come down between 10 and 20 percent.

TAKE STOCK. For real savings, bypass custom cabinets altogether. You'll save at least 40 percent in real dollars by passing those fancy cabinet displays when you enter a home center and going straight to the storage aisle.

There you'll find stock cabinets, which get their name because they're in stock and already assembled. The main difference is that stock cabinets are built by the manufacturer to meet general demand—meaning they're available in a few standard sizes and a limited selection of styles and colors. The more popular (and expensive) "custom" cabinets are supposedly built to the customer's individual specifications, but in reality, they also come in fixed sizes—the only difference is that there are more sizes to choose from.

Don't expect to find dozens of stock styles: Most stores carry only one or two styles of stock cabinets, usually the popular raised-panel oak cabinets, but other styles can usually be ordered. But other than style and cabinet width, stocks can provide the same quality (and cabinet frills like kitchen islands, pantries and wine racks) as customs costing twice the price or more.

OR ASSEMBLE THEM YOURSELF. You may already know that 60 percent of the cost of any home improvement is for the labor—not materials. The same goes for cabinets. By buying ready-to-assemble (RTA) cabinets (they arrive in flat boxes) and putting them together yourself with a screwdriver or Allen wrench, you can save 40 percent off the price of already rock-bottom stock cabinets—about 80 percent less than the retail price for custom cabinets.

American manufacturer Mill's Pride of Ohio has come to dominate the American RTA kitchen cabinet market (although Ikea, a Swedish-based company with 13 stores in the United States, is probably the best known RTA retailer in the country for all home furnishings). Keep in mind that if you go for lots of extras—roll-out trays, microwave cabinets and hutches, for instance—your savings shrink, since these items on RTAs can be even more expensive than on stock or custom cabinets.

RETHINK YOUR WOOD. Since over 80 percent of people choose wood cabinets over laminates or other surfaces, remember this fact: You can instantly cut about 15 percent or more by choosing oak over more expensive woods like cherry or maple. But don't expect the same savings by going with pine: It's very similar in price to oak, but it scratches more easily and doesn't wear as well.

CHECK OUT SCRATCH-AND-DENT SALES. Like appliances, cabinets are subject to scratch-and-dent sales—only these specials are meant to unload overstocks and discontinued lines (the cabinets aren't really scratched or dented). Some dealers specialize in scratch-and-dent cabinets, which can sell for up to half off regular retail prices. To find a scratch-and-dent sale, look for "Kitchen Dealers" in the yellow pages and call around.

GO WIDE WHENEVER YOU CAN. Inch for inch and dollar for dollar, you'll save 15 percent or more by going with wider cabinets. All things being equal, try to order 36-inch-wide cabinets over 24-inchers

QUALITY CHECK

No matter what the price, it pays to shop for quality when buying cabinets, since they're expected to last for several decades. Here's how to tell you're getting great goods.

- Frames ideally should be constructed of plywood, or at least five-eighths-inch particleboard. If they're a half-inch thick or less, they won't hold up as well.
- If the exterior finish is wood, make sure the face frames, drawer fronts and door frames are solid, not veneer. The most durable solid-color finishes are catalytic varnishes, lacquer and polyester—without the cross-sanding marks that occur from machine finishing. Fine finishes have a rich luster and a satiny texture.
- High-quality plastic laminate cabinets are very durable, but check door and drawer edges for irregularities or scratches before you buy them.
- A durable drawer should have a four-sided box with side-mounted slides made from epoxy-coated steel with nylon rollers. Press down firmly on drawers to make sure they have little give. Ask about the load rate: 50 pounds is the bare minimum; most are 75 to 150 pounds.

whenever possible, and 24-inchers over 18- or 12-inchers.

BUY DIRECTLY FROM A CONTRACTOR. Installing new cabinets is usually a two-man job, so even if you have an accomplished do-it-yourselfer in your household, you'll probably need an extra set of hands to hang the cabinets. The problem is, many folks buy the cabinets first and then hire a contractor to install them.

Since contractors get a discount—which is about half the retail price—you might be able to buy the cabinets directly from the contractor you hire. He'll probably add a little something for his trouble (usually 15 percent), but you'll still get cabinets for a fraction of what you'd normally pay.

FIX UP BEFORE YOU RIP OUT. The cheapest alternative to new cabinets, of course, is to keep your old ones. The cost of equipping a typical kitchen with new cabinets averages about $7,500. But for about 10 percent of that cost, you can get a different look with new "fronts"—doors that are placed over existing frames to make them look like new cabinets. Or you can spend about $100 on materials to strip, sand and refinish your cabinets, assuming they're wood (and you have both time and a tolerance for sawdust). For about $30, you can get new knobs and other hardware for a cheap fix-up.

Lamps and Lighting Fixtures

Here's some enlightening news to keep in mind the next time you go shopping for lamps or lighting fixtures: Discounts are a joke.

The retail markup on most lighting fixtures is so high—usually twice the wholesale or manufacturer's cost—that it's become customary for retailers to knock a quick 10 to 20 percent off the price for any schlump who walks in the door. The real trick to saving money, say industry insiders, is to be able to dig a little more to reach the "second" level of savings, which can amount to up to 40 percent off the full retail price. And here's what they recommend.

Buy after the trade shows. Twice a year—in January and July—buyers for lighting stores converge on Dallas for trade shows to order their inventory. Between two and three months later, the new shipments arrive—and in that time, retailers need to move the old stuff out to make room for the new. So shop between January and March and again between July and September, when prices can be cut as much as 40 percent. The worst time of the year to buy is in the fall and early winter.

Close in on closeouts. Among the goods displayed at these trade shows are discontinued styles of lamps and fixtures sold at drastic discounts—a $120 lighting fixture, for instance, selling for a mere $30. Even when the retailer doubles his price, it's still selling for half the original price. So in the months after these trade shows, ask retailers to see any closeouts they bought. You'll be buying an outdated style, but you'll get an incredible deal.

Open a store account. While just about everyone can get discounts of 10 to 20 percent, only the best customers tend to get the next level of markdown—the "commercial" or "trade" discount of about 40 percent. One way to get it is to open an account with the store by filling out a form on which you list credit references. The paperwork is a bother, but it's well worth your time if you anticipate putting together a big order, such as for a major remodeling job.

THE BEST FOR LESS: LIGHTOLIER

One of the brightest names in residential lighting is Lightolier. The company has earned a reputation—and quite rightly—for its innovative product line, solid construction and quality materials.

Unfortunately for bargain hunters, Lightolier products don't often find their way into home center chains and discount catalogs. The company aims its line at architects and more educated consumers and distributes through lighting specialty stores. A basic three-light track fixture will run about $80; you'll find a similar product by another manufacturer at Home Depot for about $60, but it's not made in the United States.

Although Lightolier products are less likely to be marked down than those made by other companies, try to shop after the trade shows that are held in January and July. That's when most lighting retailers discount their stock.

BUY FROM A PRO. Another way to get lighting fixtures for less is to buy them from a licensed electrician, who normally gets trade discounts from wholesalers or retailers. While an electrician may tack on a service charge—10 percent is the standard—his cost was probably about 40 percent less than other customers pay, so you'll still save 30 percent.

HEAD TO AN OFFICE SUPPLY STORE. You can spend a small fortune for the high-tech design of halogen desktop lights—but you don't have to. Office supply stores like Staples and OfficeMax sell basic desktop lamps—including halogens—for up to 50 percent less than you'd pay at some specialty lighting stores.

Lawn and Garden Equipment

If you tend your own lawn or garden, you know the beating your equipment takes. Hours of digging, raking, mowing, mulching, clipping, snipping and shearing are enough to send any second-rate piece of equipment to that Great Compost Heap in the Sky. Maybe that's one reason that Americans spend over $22 billion each year on everything from hand tools like rakes and shovels to gas-powered edgers, trimmers and lawn mowers.

Professional landscapers and horticulturists advise investing in quality equipment because it will save you money in the long run. The trick is to buy solid equipment without digging yourself into a financial hole. And here's how.

Do your shopping in February. In most parts of the country, you can save 20 percent or more on carry-over motorized merchandise during preseason sales in February. Although dealers won't go out of their way to suggest last year's mowers or chain saws, most of the inventory available during the dead of winter is left over from the previous season. (From March until mid-June, you can expect to pay top dollar for gardening equipment and tools.)

February is also a great time to save 10 percent on equipment tune-ups. With lawn equipment, just as with a car, tune-ups extend the life of the product. A tune-up on a lawn mower typically runs between $45 and $50 and includes changing the air filter and oil, sharpening the blades and checking the adjustments and belts.

Or buy in midsummer. Another time to stock up on gardening equipment—including hand tools—is after July 4, when prices typically drop about 20 percent. Prices spike again in September and October, as folks venture back into the yard and gardening stores. November brings substantial savings, but the selection is spotty.

Go big. Warehouse-size stores such as Home Depot and warehouse clubs like Sam's Club and B.J.'s Wholesale Club tend to mark up garden tools like rakes, shovels and hoses by 20 percent or less, while

GREAT MAIL-ORDER BUYS

Published between seven and ten times a year, the catalog from Langenbach Fine Garden Tools in Stillwater, New Jersey, carries top brands like Felco, De Van Koek, Garant and Ryobi. Order yours by calling 1-800-362-1991.

And *Walt Nicke's Garden Talk* of Topsfield, Massachusetts, is a direct import mail-order catalog published in January and August that offers an excellent opportunity to pick up selected British, German and Danish tools. Plus, with their twice-yearly sales catalogs, you could save 10 to 15 percent over retail. You can order a copy by calling 1-800-822-4114.

A lesser-known company that also provides good value, at least according to gardening writers, is A. M. Leonard of Piqua, Ohio. You can order a catalog, published four times a year, or get quotes on gardening equipment by calling 1-800-543-8955.

the markup at smaller hardware stores and specialty shops is traditionally 35 to 45 percent. The bigger stores are able to buy in higher volume and pass their discounts to you.

BYPASS THE BELLS AND WHISTLES. For most gardeners, ergonomic hand tools and top-of-the-line weed whackers are an unnecessary expense; the extra features can add 40 percent or more to the price. Simpler, high-quality tools are a better buy, but be careful: Spending too little—buying those $1 hand pruners, for instance—is no bargain in the long run, because the tools tend to break after a couple of uses.

PURCHASE PREOWNED. You'll find used and reconditioned lawn mowers, lawn edgers, backpack blowers, rototillers and chain saws priced 50 to 60 percent less than new models at most lawn mower repair shops or through company-run repair shops or hardware stores that allow customer trade-ins. Look in the yellow pages under "Gardening Equipment" or "Lawn Mowers."

BUY DIRECT FROM THE MANUFACTURER. Several power equipment manufacturers—makers of lawn mowers, rototillers and leaf blowers—will sell directly over the phone or from a factory store for about 10 per-

THE BEST FOR LESS: FELCO

When gardeners talk about reliable hand pruning tools, the name heard over and over again is Felco. Sure, these tools are expensive—pruners range from $40 to $75, depending on the style—but the handles (made for right- and left-handers) rotate to prevent blisters, and the pruning blades are made of lightweight cast aluminum and easy-to-sharpen stainless steel. Felco parts are also replaceable, unlike those of cheaper hand tools.

It's difficult to find Felco products on sale in retail stores, since demand for them is so high, but you can save up to 30 percent off retail prices on some models by buying them from A. M. Leonard in Piqua, Ohio. Call 1-800-543-8955 for a quote or to order a catalog.

cent less than retail. Mantis has one factory store, and Troy-Bilt has numerous stores throughout the country. Some manufacturers (like Troy-Bilt) also offer premiums and discounts on attachments, if they're purchased with the main piece of equipment. For more information, call Mantis at 1-800-366-6268 and Troy-Bilt at 1-800-828-5500.

LIGHTBULBS

The average home contains about 60 lightbulbs, so it's no wonder that one-quarter of all electricity produced in the United States is used for lighting. And while the cost of those bulbs may seem incidental—after all, you can buy them for as little as 25 cents each—some prices can be as blinding as a watt-heavy specialty bulb.

Actually, the true cost of a lightbulb is not so much what you pay for it as how much light it can deliver—and for how long. So here are a few bright ideas about how to shop smarter for the best value in bulbs.

CLUE IN TO LUMENS. You can't begin to save money unless you understand lightbulb lingo. To start, a bulb's wattage is only one way to measure its performance. Actually, the bulb's "lumens per watt" output is a far better gauge of its efficiency.

A lumen is simply a scientific unit of measurement that indicates the intensity of one candle of light over a certain distance. More lumens equal more light, so a higher number is better. But the number of watts, or electrical power, it takes to create those lumens is also critical: An energy-saver bulb that generates 400 lumens using 34 watts is a better choice than a standard bulb that gives 445 lumens using 40 watts. (The former delivers 11.8 lumens per watt, while the latter furnishes only 11.1.) When shopping, compare standard incandescent bulbs to the more expensive energy-saver incandescent variety. If the price difference is more than 20 percent, your energy savings may not be worth the extra cost.

READ THE BOX. When it comes to money, a bulb's life expectancy is just as important as its efficiency. The next time you go bulb shopping, read the specifications label on the box. It will not only tell you how many lumens each bulb delivers, it will also indicate the bulb's typical life. Standard hardware- and grocery-store incandescent bulbs are good for somewhere between 750 and 1,500 hours. Generally, with these consumer-quality bulbs, the higher the wattage, the lower the life expectancy.

GREAT MAIL-ORDER BUYS

You can get inexpensive compact fluorescent bulbs in many discount stores, but you may be buying a bill of goods. Poor workmanship and low-quality parts have found their way into even this new market, and often the price reflects the quality. Name brands such as Panasonic and Philips Lighting have a good reputation, but names like Fluorever and Dulux (to mention only a couple) are building their own reputations as well.

Two mail-order companies—Seventh Generation in Colchester, Vermont (1-800-456-1177) and Real Goods in Ukiah, California (1-800-762-7325)—carry a comprehensive line of compact fluorescent lamps that will last, as well as other types of energy-efficient and healthful light sources, including halogen and full-spectrum bulbs. Prices are competitive, but you'll get quality that's not always offered by retailers.

If there's a meaningful difference in price, you can figure the bulb's hours-per-penny performance by dividing the price of the package by the number of bulbs inside to get the unit price, then dividing the unit price (without the decimal point) into the average life in hours. The higher that number, the greater the bulb's value to you.

BUY COMMERCIAL. Made to last considerably longer than residential bulbs, commercial or "industrial-grade" bulbs aren't usually that much more expensive than standard incandescent bulbs. In fact, a 4,000-hour, 100-watt frosted commercial bulb can cost as little as 61 cents, compared to the 57 cents you might pay at the grocery store for a 750-hour bulb, which will last only one-fifth as long.

The only problem with commercial bulbs is that you'll have to buy in quantity—usually a minimum of a dozen, and more likely up to ten dozen, depending on how they're crated.

Your best source is a local industrial lighting supply house, listed in the yellow pages under "Lighting Supplies." Be aware that some suppliers accept only wholesale business.

USE FLUORESCENTS. All things considered, you're better off using fluorescent lighting. Over 90 percent of the energy consumed by common tungsten-filament bulbs is wasted as heat. Not only is this inefficient, but it increases the use of summer air conditioning, which wastes more energy.

These days, fluorescent bulbs aren't used only in long overhead fixtures. They're now designed as replacements for incandescent bulbs. These compact fluorescents include a ballast built into the base of the bulb. Don't be put off by the initial cost of these bulbs, which can be between $15 and $27, because, on the bright side, they are four to five times more efficient and last about 10,000 hours—up to 12 times longer than standard incandescent bulbs.

LINENS

First the good news: Because of fierce competition, technological advances and increased manufacturing efficiency, the price of towels, tablecloths and bedding materials had been dropping by as much as 30 percent in recent years compared to the 1980s. Unfortunately, those days seem to be over, as the cost of raw materials is increasing—and retailers are passing on their added costs to you.

Still, it hasn't seemed to hurt sales. With more Americans "cocooning," we're more willing than ever to dig deep into our pockets to make the home nest more comfortable. Nearly $3 billion is spent

THE BEST FOR LESS: FIELDCREST CANNON

Fieldcrest Cannon's Charisma line is considered the Rolls-Royce of bath towels. Made from pima cotton, the towels are as soft and luxurious as any you'll find anywhere. But as with its automotive counterpart, expect to pay for this quality: Charisma bath towels usually retail for more than $25 each.

You can get these and other high-end towels for 20 to 60 percent off list price by ordering through Harris Levy in New York City at 1-800-221-7750 or (212) 226-3102 for New York residents. Or for similar savings, call the Eldridge Textile Company, also in New York, at (212) 925-1523.

In addition, Fieldcrest Cannon offers great deals at its more than 60 outlet stores nationwide.

each year on bath and kitchen textiles, and with an average wholesale-to-retail markup of 100 percent or more, that figure is likely to grow. But here's how you can buy linens for less.

KNOW WHEN TO BUY. It's virtually impossible to walk into a department store and not find linens on sale. White sales, once held primarily in January, have become common as stores tend to rotate products and put them on sale every few weeks. While January is still a good time to buy linens—especially tablecloths—the best sales tend to be in April and October, when prices drop as much as 40 percent. That's because these two months are when manufacturers usually introduce new lines and urge retailers to move out their existing inventories.

AND WHERE TO BUY. Generally, you'll find the largest selection of top-quality towels and tablecloths at department and specialty stores like Strouds. But unless you're looking for specialty colors, you can get good-quality linens at a warehouse club like Sam's Club or the Price Club or discount chains like Kmart or Target Stores for about 20 percent less than department store prices. For specialty items, try a dis-

GREAT MAIL-ORDER BUYS

Designer Secrets in Fremont, Nebraska, offers a complete line of linens at discounts of up to 25 percent below manufacturer's suggested retail prices. You can get a catalog by calling 1-800-955-2559.

The Eldridge Textile Company sells medium- to top-quality bedding, towels and tablecloths at or near wholesale prices—about 30 to 35 percent below retail. The catalog costs $3 (which will be refunded with your first order) and is available by writing to the company at Dept. M, 277 Grand Street, New York, NY 10002.

And Harris Levy in New York City specializes in top-quality towels for 20 to 60 percent below retail costs. Get your catalog by calling 1-800-221-7750; New York residents can call (212) 226-3102.

OUTSTANDING OUTLETS

The best linen outlets tend to be in the South, where most manufacturers have their manufacturing plants. But two of the top outlets—WestPoint Pepperell and Fieldcrest Cannon—have scores of stores in outlet malls throughout the country.

At WestPoint Pepperell Bed, Bath & Linens Factory Outlets, you can figure on paying up to 50 percent below retail on a day-to-day basis, but these outlets tend to have periodic sales throughout the year where you can save even more on top-of-the-line items. Be sure to buy all you need, though, since outlets rarely carry a continuing assortment of merchandise.

You can also find exceptional values at the more than 60 Fieldcrest Cannon stores nationwide.

count specialty store like Linens 'n Things, a national chain, where everyday prices tend to be 20 to 25 percent below department store prices.

SEEK OUT SECONDS. You can cut your linen spending in half by looking for irregulars—goods that fail to meet the manufacturer's quality standards. Often these so-called flaws are minimal—a stitch was missed or a few extra loops were added—but they don't affect appearance or quality. Mass merchants such as Marshalls or T.J. Maxx tend to be the best places to find these seconds, and they offer deep discounts.

Also look for special-purchase sales, most often found at discount chains like Kmart. From time to time, manufacturers offer retailers special bargain-basement prices on one-time purchases they want to unload. Make sure you buy all you need the first time you shop, however, because these special purchases are rarely restocked.

KNOW THE SIGNS OF QUALITY. People often overpay for linens because they have no idea how to judge quality. High-quality towels have woven sides and lock-stitching that looks even and tight. Make sure the towel folds evenly—lesser-quality towels are off-size by two or three inches. The larger the towel, the more it should cost. Even two or three inches can make a difference in price, so be sure to compare towels of the same size when shopping for savings. And top-quality towels should be 100 percent cotton; some lower-end products contain polyester.

For tablecloths, avoid buying permanent-press cotton, since the chemical used to make it permanent press also makes stains harder to remove. And you don't have to buy vinyl to have a stain-resistant tablecloth; manufacturers make treated cotton and polyester blends that resist stains as well. A true linen tablecloth, made from flax, is expensive. A jacquard pattern gives the cloth a glossy sheen; the higher the texture of jacquard, the better the quality. And for bedding materials, look for smooth stitching that's free of snags.

LINGERIE

Sigh! If only buying lingerie were as uplifting as the Wonderbra—or offered as much promise. Sure, they may be great for your ego, but those silk teddies and other undergarments can often be more than your finances can bear.

Each year, about $8 billion is spent on women's lingerie—nearly $3 billion alone on bras. And retail markups average more than 50 percent industry-wide for bras, panties, slips, camisoles and lingerie sets. Items with fancy designer names can be marked up even more. But no matter what you buy, here's how to get it for less.

BUY WITH THE BOYS. Lingerie is to Valentine's Day what turkeys are to Thanksgiving, and you'll find more sales in late January and early February, when prices are typically discounted in the 20 to 30 per-

GREAT MAIL-ORDER BUYS

If you don't mind finding a color catalog loaded with scantily clad models in your mailbox every other week, Victoria's Secret is for you. But the real eye-openers are the prices: at least 20 percent less than what you'd pay in Victoria's Secret stores for most items, ranging from pajamas and night-dresses to panties and Miracle bras.

The best catalog savings are offered at the end of the season or right after Christmas. Orders over $75 can be discounted $7.50, and each catalog has its own special discounts. To order your Victoria's Secret catalog (assuming that your husband hasn't already), call 1-800-888-8200.

cent range. Lingerie sales are also common right after Valentine's Day, during the Christmas shopping season and in May, just before Mother's Day.

But the *best* sales—at least at smaller specialty lingerie stores—are held for men at Gentlemen's Night parties where the latest fashions are modeled in an effort to sharpen Cupid's arrows. To encourage men to buy, these pre-Valentine's Day events typically offer additional discounts—usually 10 to 15 percent off. So during these sales, you can save as much as half off normal prices.

These "boys' nights out" are equal opportunity functions—women can usually also attend and reap the same savings. Keep an eye peeled for advertisements, usually in the sports section of the local newspaper, for these Gentlemen's Nights in early February; you may also find them in May and December.

PLAN YOUR OWN PARTY. Who needs the boys to have a lingerie bash? Several home party companies offer their wares for 10 to 15 percent less than you'd pay in stores. What's more, women who hold an event in their homes and invite friends who buy products are entitled to free stuff. One such company, Colesce Coutures in Dallas, features custom-fitted bras in 249 sizes as well as a wide variety of lingerie, among other items. For more information, call 1-800-487-4697.

THE BEST FOR LESS: JOSIE BY NATORI

Christian Dior and Flora Nikrooz may get the press, but the lingerie preferred most seems to be Josie by Natori. This brand is known for its charmeuse and lever lace, and you could pay $150 or more for one teddy.

But there are three times a year when you might find Josie by Natori lingerie for 33 percent off at Nordstrom's: the retailer's "half-yearly" sales in June and November and its anniversary sale in mid-July. For information on these sales and to find a Nordstrom's near you, call (206) 628-2111.

OUTSTANDING OUTLETS

Jockey is a name synonymous with quality underwear, and now it has a chain of outlet stores. Jockey outlets sell women's underwear and panty hose as well as underwear and socks for all members of the family at 25 to 75 percent off retail Jockey prices. Check the yellow pages for stores in Castle Rock, Colorado, Michigan City, Indiana, and Lancaster, Pennsylvania.

And if you're a fan of Bali, Olga, Vanity Fair or other well-known names in lingerie, you don't have to wait for department store sales. Lingerie for Less, a chain with 23 stores in California and 16 others across the country, sells designer and brand-name lingerie at 30 to 65 percent off department store prices—all the time. If you don't live in the Golden State, call 1-800-755-4535 to find out how you can take advantage of these golden savings.

TRACK THE NUMBERS. Some department stores—including Macy's, Bullock's and Robinsons-May—offer free lingerie after the purchase of a certain amount. At Macy's, for instance, if you buy six bras, the seventh is free; buy six pairs of panties and the next is on the house. You get a card to keep track of your purchases, and you usually don't have to buy them all at once. But for the best savings, stock up during department store sales, which are also usually held just before Valentine's Day, Mother's Day and Christmas. A 30 percent discount is common during these sales.

GET ON A MAILING LIST. If you have a department store credit card, you're probably aware of the advance notices and special coupons for lingerie (and other items) that are mailed to you, usually offering between 10 and 25 percent off regular prices. Independent lingerie stores may not have credit cards, but you can just as easily get on their mailing lists and enjoy the same perks just by asking. Some even send out "thank-you coupons" to those on a mailing list after they've made a purchase, entitling them to another 10 to 20 percent off their next purchase.

LUGGAGE

Luggage is one of those products that's destined for abuse. It's going to be kicked by baggage handlers, jammed in tiny compartments and overstuffed with junk. Still, we're especially picky about the bags and suitcases we buy, and we expect them to withstand the most abusive rigors of traveling.

We also expect ourselves to be able to withstand the cost, which helps explain why luggage prices have dropped in recent years. But with a retail markup of up to 100 percent that keeps prices sky-high—a top-brand tote bag can start at $115, while a pullman can top $1,000—it's sometimes hard to find a good deal. But here are some ways to pack on extra savings the next time you're shopping for luggage.

BUY LAST YEAR'S MODELS. A new color or different liner fabric may be

OUTSTANDING OUTLETS

For economy lines, American Tourister has more than 100 outlets where you can pick up luggage and travel accessories for 30 to 50 percent less than you'd pay retail. Call 1-800-547-2247 for a location near you.

The Luggage Center (1-800-626-6789) has 20 outlets in California that sell brands like Halliburton, High Sierra and Samsonite for up to 50 percent off. And Bentley's Luggage & Gifts has six stores in the Washington, D.C., area that offer up to 30 percent off on certain lines of higher-end brands. Call 1-800-330-0050 for the location of a store near you.

THE BEST FOR LESS: TUMI

Hartmann Luggage Company has a distinguished history—its Walnut Tweed line has long been a classic. But these days, insiders say Tumi is the luggage of choice for those who would rather pay for quality than reputation.

Built to last, all Tumi bags have reinforced handles, ballistic nylon fabric that won't rip or tear and pockets that can hold more than most other brands. Tumi garment bags retail for about $250 to $450, while its 29-inch "wheelaway" suitcase has a sticker price of about $550.

While Tumi doesn't have its own outlets and limits what it sells in other outlet stores, you can get Tumi products at a discount at some outlet shops: Bentley's Luggage & Gifts, which has six stores in the Washington, D.C., area, sells Tumi outlet merchandise for about 25 percent below retail, as do California Luggage Outlet stores in the West. Another good stop is Innovation Luggage, with stores in New Jersey, Connecticut, Massachusetts and New York. Your best bet: Call Tumi at 1-800-322-TUMI for the location of a distributing dealer near you.

all that separates the new styles from the existing ones, but opt for the "old" and you can save 30 to 50 percent—especially if you shop in the late summer or early fall, when retailers hold closeout sales as they try to move their existing inventory to make room for the new shipments.

Actually, August to November is the best time to buy the new styles, too. That's when sales of 10 to 25 percent are most frequent, although you'll get bigger savings during closeout sales.

CAPITALIZE ON THAT CHRISTMAS SPIRIT. Another good time to buy luggage is during the Christmas shopping season, particularly if you're shopping for more than one piece. Most retailers don't offer substantial across-the-board price reductions during this season—it is, after

GREAT MAIL-ORDER BUYS

There's a grab-bag of mail-order opportunities when it comes to luggage. Some of the best offerings are from Ace Luggage and Gifts in Brooklyn. Its catalog comes out once a year around Christmas, but the prices—up to 50 percent off retail for featured brands like Boyt, Hartmann, Jansport and Tumi—are good throughout the year. Call 1-800-342-5223 to order your copy.

Another good bet is A to Z Luggage Company, which sells luggage by Andiamo, Boyt, Delsey, Hartmann, Samsonite, Tumi and other manufacturers for 20 to 50 percent off retail. You can order a catalog by calling 1-800-342-5011. And Altman Luggage offers discounts from 20 to 50 percent on brand-name luggage and leather goods; call 1-800-372-3377 for a catalog.

all, their busiest selling season—but that's when manufacturers are most likely to hold special promotions, such as discounts on a second bag if you pay full price for the first.

In fact, whenever you're shopping around Christmas, ask if the store is holding any special promotions. Some stores readily advertise these manufacturers' incentives to bring people in; others don't.

GO FOR THE SET. It generally costs 30 percent less to buy a complete set of luggage than to buy similar pieces separately. But you may be able to negotiate additional savings if you downplay your need for an entire set, because retailers prefer to sell sets and many are willing to give you a price break on a four-piece set.

Don't expect huge additional discounts, but depending on how anxious the retailer is, ask for and you may get an additional 5 to 15 percent break on a complete set of luggage.

BANISH YOUR FEAR OF IRREGULARS. With some items, *irregular* means "reject." But with luggage, irregular goods often have only minor scratches and other cosmetic flaws.

Retailers usually sell these irregulars for 40 percent off or more, and after a few trips, spanking new luggage usually shows the same wear and tear anyway.

FORGO THE FRILLS. Unless you're planning to travel to Beruit and need to use your luggage to protect you from gunfire, pass on ballistic materials, which are supposed to be bulletproof. This material costs at least 25 percent more than others, and since your luggage isn't likely to be shot at, it's little more than a marketing gimmick. Most other luggage coverings are strong enough to withstand rough handling without ripping or tearing.

READ THE LABEL. All bags are not created equal. Luggage that's manufactured in Europe and the United States is considered to be the best quality, while suitcases made in Mexico or the Far East aren't considered as well-made. So while you may pay a little less for the latter, some insiders say that there may be a bigger difference in quality than price suggests.

Magazine Subscriptions

It may not get the publicity of Romeo and Juliet's hardcover hankering or Tracy and Hepburn's reel romance, but we seem to have an anything-but-mediocre love affair with another medium: magazines.

Americans buy over 11 billion magazines each year—enough to fill every household in the country with 2,088 pages (and that doesn't include advertisements). There are now 3,500 different magazines published in the United States, about twice as many as in 1980. That number swells to over 11,000 titles if you count trade publications and academic periodicals.

But while the number of magazines is growing—or rather, *because* it is—those glossy pages pose some crystal-clear realities that affect our wallets. With so many magazines competing for readers, newsstand sales have declined across the board each year for more than a decade. This makes the nearly $6 billion in subscription revenue the publishers get each year vital, prompting them to try a variety of strategies to get as many of your dollars as possible. But here's how to save when ordering magazines.

Listen to Ed McMahon. While it's very unlikely that you'll actually win the multimillion dollar jackpot (so don't quit your job just yet), Publishers Clearing House of Port Washington, New York, and American Family Publishers of Tampa, Florida, actually provide the lowest magazine subscription prices in the business.

Since their market penetration is so great—Publishers Clearing House alone has annual sales well over $100 million—they're able to force publishers to guarantee the best available subscription prices, up to 30 percent lower than rates from other offers.

Both Publishers Clearing House and American Family send out one big mailing and several smaller ones throughout the year. But you can order any of about 350 major magazines at any time (you'll be billed later) by calling Publishers Clearing House at 1-800-645-

9242 or American Family Publishers at 1-800-237-2400.

RENEW IN A DIFFERENT NAME. Magazine publishers make their money on renewals, so you may be surprised to learn that instead of rewarding loyal readers with lower prices, they discreetly raise the price when it's renewal time—while offering lower rates to new readers to "hook" them in.

The strategy: Stay a first-time subscriber by renewing in a new name—your maiden name or your spouse's or child's name. You may miss an issue or get a duplicate, but you'll still save in the end—anywhere from 10 to 25 percent off the rates offered to loyal customers. Just be sure to use the subscription card in the magazine instead of a regular renewal notice to reap these savings.

TAKE FIVE. Don't want to use another name? You can still save—by playing the waiting game. Although some publishers really offer lower renewal prices up front to dodge the rising cost of sending you additional appeals, most send a total of five renewal notices to subscribers who don't renew immediately.

While each renewal notification claims to be your "last chance," you'll notice that each one gets increasingly desperate and offers a sweeter deal than the last. By holding out until the fifth notice, you can sometimes save up to 15 percent compared to the original offer.

TAKE A HARD LINE ON SOFT OFFERS. Many magazines try to set themselves apart from the crowd by offering a free introductory issue to would-be subscribers—what's called a soft offer in the business. In

GO ON-LINE FOR FREE SUBSCRIPTIONS

More than 200 magazines are now available on your computer through the online networks. Some even come with sound and graphics, and all are included with the regular monthly access charge.

And while magazines have long been included with membership in particular organizations, such as the American Association of Retired Persons (AARP), some subscriptions, such as the *Disney Channel Magazine*, *Chevy Outdoors* and *Baby Talk*, are now free when you buy a product or use a service.

LET THE READER BEWARE

A common practice in the magazine business is "back-starting," in which subscribers are sent several previous issues after ordering a subscription. If you order in December, for example, you may receive the September, October and November issues before you receive the current edition.

This practice allows the magazine to count you in its circulation audit for the prior period, satisfying advertisers who are guaranteed a minimum distribution. But don't let this affect you: If you demand to have your subscription adjusted, the magazine will usually extend your subscription for the entire 12 months and still give you the "bonus" issues.

fact, the publishers will usually send you six issues free before cutting you off as a bad debt.

While the free mags are nice, the problem with soft offers is that many magazines bill you before your "free" issue shows up. Don't pay that bill, since that rate isn't the lowest. Instead call the magazine's toll-free number and say you want to subscribe, but for a lower price than the billed rate. Chances are you'll get a discount of between 10 and 35 percent.

ACT LIKE A PRO. One of the best-kept secrets in the business is the professional rate offered to those who need general-interest magazines for their business—teachers, journalists, business executives and others who need to be in the know about the magazine's subject matter. (Sorry, but most trade and specialty magazines don't offer professional rates, since they are geared to that particular profession.)

These rates are anywhere from 30 to 50 percent less than regular subscription rates, and once you're on the professional list, chances are you'll stay there and avoid the other renewal shenanigans. But you'll have to call the magazine directly to ask the customer service rep for their professional discount rate. Best of all, you don't necessarily have to be a teacher or hold another approved job if you can make a solid case for your request.

MAJOR APPLIANCES

It's tough to build a home appliance in your garage, and they weigh too much to economically import from overseas. So you're pretty much stuck with buying one of the 19 major domestic brands of refrigerators, dishwashers, washing machines, dryers, stoves and other major appliances.

If that seems like a lot of choices, think again. Those 19 brands are made by just five companies, which together control the major appliance market, with annual sales of $14 billion. Maytag owns Jenn-Air, Magic Chef and Admiral. Whirlpool makes the KitchenAid and Roper brands. Amana, owned by the giant defense contractor Raytheon, manufactures Speed Queen and Caloric as well as the Amana line. Frigidaire, a division of a Swedish company, owns White-Westinghouse, Gibson, Kelvinator and Tappan. And General Electric makes the RCA and Hotpoint brands. The popular Sears Kenmore line is made by some of these manufacturers under contract.

The newest trend in home appliances is to add more features than you'll ever need in an attempt to convince you to buy fancy new models before your old machines wear out—the way some consumers buy cars. So the first way to save money when buying major appliances is to steer clear of the bells and whistles you don't really need. Here are some others.

TIME IT RIGHT. October is National Kitchen and Bath Month, and some retailers get into the spirit of the festivities and offer discounts of between 10 and 20 percent. But probably the biggest push to sell appliances is from late December through late April, as factories rush their latest models off the assembly line in time for the two big annual industry trade shows: the National Homebuilders Show in January and the National Kitchen and Bath Show in May. During these times, some retailers offer discounts of 30 percent or more on older models they want to move off the floor.

In addition, retailers tend to offer little-known promotions on re-

THE BEST FOR LESS: WHIRLPOOL

This company has set the standard for responsiveness to the consumer, and its appliances are consistently rated among the best, both by consumer groups and industry insiders.

Maybe that's why Whirlpool products aren't always the cheapest. But you can get a first-quality Whirlpool product for less at warehouse clubs such as Sam's Club and B.J.'s Wholesale Club, which carry a line that Whirlpool makes especially for them to avoid offending its full-price dealers, who don't want their customers to cross-shop. Called Estate by Whirlpool, these appliances have the same motors, pumps and other internal machinery as the products sold across the street. What they lack, however, are features you probably don't need anyway and materials and styling that have only cosmetic value. The warranty is exactly the same as the one that applies to Whirlpool's other products.

You can get an 18-cubic-foot Estate refrigerator for about $480, compared to $630 for the baseline Whirlpool model. An Estate washer sells for $330, compared to $350 for a name Whirlpool; a stove is $300 versus $550; an Estate dryer goes for $250 compared to $290 for a Whirlpool; and you'll pay $240 for a dishwasher instead of $290. The only downsides are that the Estate selection is limited, and the warehouse clubs don't deliver or install appliances.

frigerators at the beginning of the summer, when compressors tend to fail.

HEAD TO A RESTAURANT SUPPLY STORE. Some "professional-quality" kitchen appliances—most notably refrigerators and stoves or ovens—can cost as much as a used car, but there's no need to pay full price for these heavy-duty units. By buying a used model from a restaurant supply store, you'll save about 75 percent off new prices and still enjoy years of use and power. You'll find these stores, which take used merchandise when restaurateurs upgrade or go out of business, listed in the yellow pages under "Restaurant Supplies."

FIND ONE WITH DINGS. You can save 25 percent or more by shopping at a scratch-and-dent outlet. Such outlets, operated by Sears and other manufacturers, have all types of major appliances with minor scrapes, dents or dings—usually on the sides or back, so they're not visible once the unit is installed. Most scratch-and-dent offerings come with complete warranties; often they're floor models or left-overs from appliance shows. Check the yellow pages under "Appliances" for stores that specialize in slightly damaged items.

AVOID THE EXTENDED WARRANTY. Besides pushing the multispeed cycles and automatic doohickies that are often unnecessary but usually expensive, most retailers will try to sign you up for an extended warranty, which can add over $100 to your purchase. These warranties are seldom used and are mostly profit for stores that have been forced to trim their markup to compete. Instead, pay for your purchase with a credit card that has automatic extended-warranty protection.

OUTSTANDING OUTLETS

The Appliance Outlet is the nation's largest scratch-and-dent dealer, offering new and damaged appliances for 8 to 25 percent less than retail stores. Its stores, which carry various brands, are located in Massachusetts and are little more than warehouses crammed with so many rows of home appliances that you have to walk in single file. But what the Appliance Outlet saves in overhead, you save in price.

Most of the damaged appliances have only scratches, though some have corner dents and noticeable blemishes. Still, all are covered by their original warranties. And brand-new, undamaged goods also are on sale in the showroom for up to 10 percent below retail, thanks to the chain's high-volume sales. Credit cards are accepted, and there is a delivery fee unless you opt to take your purchase with you. For a location near you, call (617) 740-1111.

BUY FROM A BUILDER. Homebuilders and other contractors get a price break on appliances because they buy in volume—especially when they're developing a new subdivision. If you're constructing a home or plan to, you can get in on this by asking your builder to buy appliances for you, usually at up to half the regular retail cost. Even if you're not building a home, some builders may make purchases for you. They'll add a service charge—usually 10 to 15 percent—but you can still save hundreds of dollars.

BE A VOLUME BUYER. Many retailers are willing to give you a price break—usually only 10 percent or so, since the markup on most appliances is very low—but you're in the best position to get a better deal if you buy more than one appliance at a time. So if you're remodeling your kitchen, opt for getting the new refrigerator, range and dishwasher at the same time rather than buying them separately. The same is true if you buy a washer and dryer.

Other retailers are willing to throw in the tiny extras, like range cords, separate icemakers and the like when you make a large purchase—for yourself or with a friend.

CHECK OUT SEARS. Only one manufacturer—Sears—sells its major appliances directly to the public. Its Kenmore appliances also happen to be rated extremely high, probably because they're actually made by Whirlpool and other manufacturers to Sears' specifications—not by Sears itself. You'll notice that Sears obligingly displays its Kenmore appliances side by side with Whirlpool's so you can see how much alike they are.

One difference is the price. Without a middleman, Sears avoids at least one layer of markup, which results in its appliances often (though not always) being $50 to $200 cheaper than competitors'. That may be one reason Kenmore appliances are in six out of ten homes in the United States. Sears also has frequent sales with deep discounts and free delivery specials and is the only major large appliance dealer that has a chain of outlet stores. There you'll find discontinued, surplus and slightly damaged Kenmore and other brands of appliances at up to 70 percent less than in Sears stores.

Maternity Wear

If you're pregnant, your midsection isn't the only thing that's going to grow in the next few months. So is the amount you spend on clothing.

Although there's never been a more fashionable time to be pregnant—with designers inspired by the throngs of women who have continued to hold jobs throughout their pregnancies—a stylish maternity wardrobe can be costly, especially when you consider the relatively short period of time you wear it. Like other articles of women's clothing, maternity wear can have a retail markup of 100 percent or more, meaning you pay twice the amount the retailer paid the wholesaler or manufacturer.

And since it uses more fabric and is more of a "niche" item, maternity wear tends to cost more than a similar piece of clothing for a woman who isn't pregnant. All told, just one week's worth of maternity wear at full retail price—everything from nightgowns to dresses—can cost big. Besides looking at consignment shops and neighborhood garage sales, where the best buys often are, here's how to get maternity wear for less.

Outstanding Outlets

From oversize tops to maternity career dresses, it's all available at Mother's Works, a 40-store outlet chain that offers great styles at prices anywhere from 30 to 70 percent below retail. To find an outlet near you, call (215) 625-0151.

SHOP THE END-OF-SEASON SALES. Maternity wear is like other apparel—the best deals tend to be available at the end of the fashion season. You can typically save between 30 and 50 percent on maternity clothing by shopping in January and February for winter clothing and in July for summer items. The worst times to shop are in March, September and October, when prices tend to be highest.

CHECK OUT THE MEN'S DEPARTMENT. Who says you have to shop in the maternity department? If it fits, wear it—and the odds are you can find plenty that fits in the men's department of your favorite retailer or off-price store. Men's shirts and sweats tend be about 10 percent less expensive than ladies' garments.

BUY OVERSIZE. Nonmaternity cotton dresses, stretch pants and roomy cotton tops—which often fit women during various stages of pregnancy and are available in the women's department—can be as much as 25 percent less than a similar item specifically made for a mother-in-waiting.

And because it's difficult to anticipate how high, low, big or small you'll carry, avoid wasting your money on clothes that won't fit comfortably in months to come by buying as you grow, not for the future.

SEEK OUT SEPARATES. For better value, build your wardrobe around a few choice cotton/Lycra separates rather than getting matching sets. Two-piece suits are among the most expensive items of maternity wear (and of women's clothing in general); by concentrating on separates, you'll get more wardrobe for your money. Generally, you can save at least 20 percent compared to buying traditional maternity sets.

Experienced moms-to-be recommend skirts with elastic waists, baby doll–style dresses, oversize tunics and a few pairs of solid-color leggings that will expand and contract with your shape and allow you to mix and match. Stay away from styles that you wouldn't normally wear. And don't forget to baby yourself with accessories like colorful scarves, a funky hat, bangle bracelets and comfortable, snazzy flat shoes, to take the focus away from your expanding midsection.

HONE IN ON THE HOLIDAYS. Whatever you buy, look for price reductions of between 10 and 20 percent on maternity clothing around holidays like Columbus Day, Veterans' Day, Presidents' Day and other times when clothing is usually discounted. Since value-priced

GREAT MAIL-ORDER BUYS

Garnet Hill in Franconia, New Hampshire, offers a wide selection of maternity clothing—as well as such diverse products as bedding, towels and hosiery—in natural fiber lines and other comfortable fabrics. Shop by mail during its end-of-season sales in January and June and you can get between 30 and 70 percent off regular prices. Sale catalogs are sent only to previous customers, so call 1-800-622-6216 to get on the mailing list.

And recognizing that special clothing needs don't end when your baby is born, Motherwear in Northampton, Massachusetts, offers comfortable and fashionable nursing garments that help make breastfeeding simple and discreet—for at least 35 percent off regular retail prices. Selections range from economical basics as low as $15 to spectacular seasonal fashions, and sizes from XS to XXL are available. The best time to buy is in July and January, when prices are discounted even more. The catalog also has a complete selection of breastfeeding support products: nursing bras, breast pumps and pads, milk coolers, nursing pillows and stools. Call 1-800-950-2500 to order your catalog. Shipping is free for your first order.

retailers like Sears tend to be promotionally driven, most holidays provide ample sale opportunities.

Check your Sunday newspaper for special inserts advertising these sweet deals. Keep in mind, however, that some price reductions aren't advertised, so it pays to browse frequently at your favorite retailer.

BUY MATERNITY AT THE MART. Discount chains like Kmart and Wal-Mart and off-price stores like T.J. Maxx and Marshalls usually offer maternity clothing for anywhere from 10 to 40 percent less than department stores and other full-price retailers. And since they cater to families, these discounters also tend to have extensive maternity departments, with lines that feature the latest fashions. In addition to sizable savings, expect to find everything from maternity denims to dresses.

ASK YOUR OBSTETRICIAN. Some doctors' offices have information and coupon books for maternity clothing from select retailers. Mimi Maternity and Mother's Works, for example, distribute information to some doctors' offices—as well as hotels, tourist information centers, day care centers and other locations believed to be frequented by lots of women. Look for their discount brochure displays, which contain \$5 certificates good for first-time purchases of \$50 or more.

MEAT AND SEAFOOD

With most Americans consuming more than six ounces of meat or seafood each day—a total of about 140 pounds per year—it's no wonder that surf and turf have become an $80-billion-a-year industry. In fact, meat and seafood purchases account for about 16 percent of our total supermarket spending. Retail markup is usually about 50 percent.

While Americans have been eating less red meats like beef and pork in recent years, we're not necessarily eating less flesh: We're just substituting more fish, chicken and turkey. Whatever your choice, though, here's how to spend less on meat and seafood and still eat high on the hog.

GO TO A RESTAURANT SUPPLIER. Most people shop for meat and seafood at their local supermarket chain for convenience—and with the mistaken notion that the chain's larger buying power delivers lower prices. Actually, the best retailers are those that sell to restaurants and Mom-and-Pop butcher and seafood shops—and they often give the same wholesale prices to other customers.

At some of these restaurant suppliers, like Empire Purveyors in New York City, consumers can buy custom-cut chicken and beef at as much as 30 percent off butcher prices. Buy at least ten pounds of some cuts of beef and chicken and you can receive the wholesale price—a 50 percent discount. One caveat: Many of these establishments accept cash only. To find this kind of butcher in your area, check the yellow pages under "Meat—Wholesale."

DO YOUR OWN CUTTING. Generally, the more a butcher or fish retailer uses a knife, the more you pay. For example, if you buy whole strips of steak and cut them yourself, you'll save an average of 35 percent compared to buying individual steaks that are prepared by a butcher. For the greatest savings, however, buy the whole thing—an entire lamb or a whole fish like salmon. Cut it yourself at home and you'll save up to 55 percent on a bite-by-bite basis compared to individual cuts.

GREAT MAIL-ORDER BUYS

Dakin Farms is a mail-order merchant in Ferrisburg, Vermont, that features turkey, baby back ribs, pork chops and lean, maple-cured, cob-smoked ham produced on its own farms, as well as cheese and other products. Although most of its business occurs during holiday time, if you buy during the "postseason"—from January 1 to February 28—you'll get an average of 10 percent off most items, in addition to free items such as a half-pound of bacon and a half-pound of Cheddar, a $7 value. Similar deals can be had from September 1 through October 30. To get a catalog, call 1-800-993-2546.

And Jamison Farm in Latrobe, Pennsylvania, specializes in selling lamb to restaurants but will also sell to the public for about 20 percent below regular prices. For a catalog, call 1-800-237-5262.

GET THE MORE EXPENSIVE CUTS. Strange as it may sound, getting more expensive cuts can actually be cheaper if you're buying smaller quantities—at least for meat. That's because the cheaper "bone-in" cuts weigh more; even though they're cheaper on a per-pound basis, they can actually cost up to 25 percent more because you wind up throwing away half of what you pay for. Pay the higher price for boneless cuts instead, and you'll save because there's little or no waste.

An added bonus: Most boneless meats are trimmed so they have less than one-eighth inch of external fat. In general, compared to bone-in cuts, you can get double the number of servings from boneless cuts, saving you about 25 percent.

BUY THE VALUE PACKS. Most larger supermarkets sell larger quantities of precut meat and seafood in "value" or "family" packs. Compared to getting the same cuts in smaller quantities, you'll save an average of 10 percent and possibly as much as 20 percent, depending on the cut. Butcher shops and seafood stores also offer these quantity discounts because it gives them a more steady cash flow.

KNOW THE "SEASONS." Unlike chicken, pork and beef, which come from farm-raised animals and therefore are in steady supply all year, most seafood is harvested by commercial fisherman, who are at the mercy of Mother Nature. Consequently, seafood prices tend to fluctuate according to the weather, the season and fish migration patterns. As with most retail items, when fish supplies dwindle, prices tend to rise. Likewise, when fish are plentiful, prices tend to be lower, usually about 10 percent. So watch for fresh salmon specials in the summer, cheaper shrimp in the fall and price reductions on blue crab in the spring and summer.

While meat prices don't fluctuate as much, there are "best" times of year to shop for certain items—but because of demand, not supply. In summer, for instance, porterhouse and New York strip steaks are more popular (and higher-priced) because it's grilling season. Roasts, meanwhile, go down in price then because they're considered a "winter" cut. April is best for stockpiling grilling meats such as steaks and lean ground beef that are popular summer fare, while August is a good time to stock your freezer with winter meats such as rump roast, eye of round and pork chops. Ham and smoked turkey are popular in December and at holiday time—but you'll save up to

THE BEST FOR LESS: OMAHA STEAKS

Omaha Steaks, a mail-order and retail operation that features succulent cuts of corn-fed Midwestern beef and a variety of specialty beef, poultry and seafood offerings, is perhaps the best-known name in meat.

The company will ship its products to customers in a reusable cooler, packed with dry ice, via Federal Express. Special introductory offers are available for new customers, and unadvertised specials are often available to both mail-order and retail customers. Retail customers are invited to use a Frequent Buyer card to earn a free selection from the product list. To receive a catalog or to find a store near you, call 1-800-228-2778.

15 percent if you buy them in January and February or September and October.

CHECK THOSE LOCAL VAL-PAKS. Although it's tempting to throw away those envelopes filled with dozens of coupons for local retail products that frequently clog your mailbox, it might be worth your while to open them. They often contain deals of at least 20 percent off on seafood and meats from local retailers. New local seafood and meat markets are especially likely to resort to this method to build their customer base. Look for a Val-Pak in your mailbox at least every other month. They're distributed throughout the United States.

Men's Shirts and Neckties

It's not the shirts off our backs that we're giving up—it's the $3 billion each year we spend to buy them. And enough ties are sold in the United States each year—over 100 million—to stretch from New York to Los Angeles and loop back to Chicago.

No doubt about it, men's dress shirts and neckties are big business—especially when you consider that most retail for at least twice the cost of manufacturing them, and some have markups much higher. But here's how you can dress for less.

Know the name game. Like other clothiers, most shirt and tie manu-

Outstanding Outlets

There are literally thousands of outlets selling shirts and neckties, but for sheer variety of inventory, few can beat the outlets operated by the Salant Company, which manufactures Manhattan, Perry Ellis and John Henry shirts and ties. Discounts can be as high as 50 percent off regular retail prices at Manhattan, Perry Ellis and John Henry outlets. For locations near you, call 1-800-922-0614.

In addition, most top-brand manufacturers run their own outlet stores, usually selling overstocks, returns, irregulars, the previous season's styles and merchandise from canceled orders. The prices vary significantly from store to store but can be as much as 70 percent off. For locations near you, call Brooks Brothers (1-800-444-1613), J. Crew (1-800-932-0043) and Van Heusen (1-800-388-9122).

facturers produce several brands, and often there's very little difference between them—except price. Manhattan, Perry Ellis and John Henry shirts, for example, are all made by Salant, but Manhattan shirts run $10 to $20 cheaper. Hathaway and Christian Dior both come from Warnaco, but the Hathaway line costs 30 percent less. Hartmarx makes Henry Grethel, Pierre Cardin, Nino Cerrutti and Austin Reed of Regent Street dress shirts; you'll generally find that the Austin Reed and Henry Grethel lines are least expensive.

Shirts carrying a store brand are often made by these brand-name manufacturers; sometimes they cost more, but usually they're discounted better during sales. Even off-price chains now carry house-brand dress shirts: Filene's Basement's Saddles line, for instance, comes from the same factories in Asia as the higher-priced name brands.

SNATCH SOME SAMPLES. Most designers manufacture sample shirts and ties to show store buyers. What happens to the samples? They're sold for half price or less at sample sales. Most sample sales are in New York City, capital of the apparel industry, but with the industry taking root in other U.S. cities, like Los Angeles, Dallas, Atlanta and Chicago, you may find a sample sale in a city near you. Check the newspaper or look in the yellow pages under "Designers—Apparel" to find out dates and locations of sample sales in your area.

TIE ONE ON AT THE RIGHT TIME. Neckties are more likely to be offered at specific seasonal sales than dress shirts, and during these times you can expect savings of up to 25 percent off regular prices. The prime times are just after Christmas, in early June just before Father's Day and in late July and August, when clearance sales are common for men's dress clothing.

SHOP A DISCOUNTER. You can avoid specialty men's shop and department store prices and save 30 percent or more by heading to off-price stores like Filene's Basement, Marshalls, T.J. Maxx and Syms. These stores get shipments of new in-season dress shirts directly from manufacturers a mere 8 to 12 weeks after they arrive in the full-price department stores—and the lag is steadily growing shorter. How can discounters offer such savings on new merchandise? One reason, insiders explain, is that they don't pay advertising fees to vendors who supply their stores. The only downside is that they aren't able to mention brand names outside their stores.

In addition, when the men's departments of full-price retailers start to overflow with ties, they shovel the excess to these discounters,

THE BEST FOR LESS: GITMAN

Gitman & Company is hired to make private-label shirts for such top-end retailers as Barney's New York, Nordstrom, Paul Stuart and Saks Fifth Avenue—and with good reason.

You'll find no polyester in these shirts—only the finest domestic and imported cotton and other natural fabrics. Seams are sewn with 22 stitches per inch, far more than any other shirtmaker uses.

Gitman's private-label shirts retail for $38 to $70 at finer men's specialty and department stores, but you can buy the same shirts under Gitman's own label for $38 to $58 at the Oak Hall store in Memphis, Tennessee, and the Parisian chain in the southeastern region of the country. Or buy from the factory store in Somerville, New Jersey (call 908-412-1800 for information, but don't expect much, since the company doesn't advertise its factory store). For the best deals, though, check out the Off 5th–Sax Fifth Avenue Outlet, where Gitman shirts sell for up to 70 percent off retail. Call (914) 771-3880 for a location near you.

where prices can be as much as 80 percent lower. Department stores buy huge quantities (and then ship off the excess) because the markup on neckties is among the highest of any apparel product, meaning the stores can buy ties cheaply and reap big profits.

TRAVEL A LITTLE, SAVE A LOT. You'll usually find the best selection of dress shirts and ties—and sometimes the best prices as well—at discount chain locations in blue-collar suburbs or rural areas. The reason: Most people tend to shop close to where they live, and those with blue-collar jobs tend to not need a whole wardrobe of dress shirts and ties. So even though these discount chains often offer the best prices across the board, you might save an additional 10 to 15 percent by shopping at one in a blue-collar neighborhood.

Men's Shoes

Saving money on shoes once meant stuffing them with cardboard insoles or going barefoot. But the average Joe travels 115,000 miles on foot in a lifetime, and that's a long way to walk in substandard moccasins.

Don't let puffed-up promotions and sales teams catch you flat-footed. Here's how to save on men's footwear.

Know when to go. Stride over to a semiannual clearance sale and you'll save 20 percent or more on men's shoes. But don't be fooled by those so-called sales that are held nearly every week. The real savings happen when wholesalers dump their leftover stock on retailers, and that occurs twice a year, during June for spring and summer shoes and in October for fall and winter merchandise.

Outstanding Outlets

Famous Footwear offers savings of up to 50 percent—prices lower than at the shoe companies' own outlet stores—on everything from Hush Puppies to cowboy boots at over 750 stores scattered from Maine to California. Besides, there's a better selection, with Nunn-Bush, Rockport, Dexter and other major brands being offered.

The merchandise is stacked in boxes in the showroom, so there's no waiting for a harried salesperson to find your size. This also keeps the company's overhead low, which means more savings for you. Call 1-800-888-7198 for the location of a Famous Footwear outlet near you.

THE BEST FOR LESS: ALLEN EDMONDS

There are many men's shoes that are arguably the "best": Bally, Cole-Haan and other brands are all known for their fine quality—and high price tags. But insiders say that Allen Edmonds likely reigns supreme.

While many manufacturers of high-end men's shoes have moved their factories overseas and started using cheaper leather due to tough economic times, Allen Edmonds still manufactures only in the United States and uses only the finest soft calfskin for its dress shoes. But it's the craftsmanship that sets these shoes apart. They are stitched 360 degrees and contain no metal shank, leaving them flexible enough to conform to your foot rather than forcing your foot to conform to them.

A pair of Allen Edmonds shoes retails in the $240 range, but you can get them at one of the company's 14 factory outlet stores for a flat 25 percent discount. Call (414) 284-7158 for a location near you. (If you must shop in a full-price men's shoe store or department store, go in January or July. That's when Allen Edmonds ships its summer and fall lines and the current inventory is placed on sale.)

LOSE THE LABEL. One of the best ways to save on first-quality shoes is to ignore the label altogether. Many department stores and independent retailers buy direct from the same factories that make expensive brand-name shoes. A case in point: The ultrafancy Scott Shoe chain in the Washington, D.C., area buys direct from the same factories in Italy that make Bally shoes. In most cases the Ballys sell for almost twice as much as the virtually identical private-label shoes.

BE HIP TO THE NAME GAME. Some famous shoe companies don't actually make any shoes—they only market shoes made by other manufacturers under their brand name. Until recently, for instance, Cole-Haan had no factories of its own. Now it produces some of its shoes—the rest are made by other manufacturers. Hanover also makes Bostonians, but you can get Hanover wingtips for $70, while the Bostonians cost up to $249. And Nashville-based Genesco makes shoes under the elite Nautica brand as well as Dockers, which cost half as much. Looking for work boots? E.J. Footwear Corporation makes Lehigh boots, which are sold at retail prices, and also manufactures Georgia Boots, which are often sold at wholesale prices. Northlake is its line of outdoor footwear.

OPT FOR AN OUTLET. Virtually every major men's shoe brand has off-price outlet stores that sell excess inventory direct at deep discounts. You'll find first-quality, in-season shoes generally at 10 to 40 percent off, past-season shoes at half price or less and irregulars at up to 80 percent off. Call to find the locations of outlet stores for these top brands: Bally (1-800-825-5030), G.H. Bass & Company (1-800-777-1790), Cole-Haan (1-800-633-9000), Dexter (1-800-852-2336), Florsheim (312-559-2500) and Timberland (1-800-445-5545). Two companies, Allen Edmonds (414-284-7158) and Rockport (1-800-762-5767), sell only factory irregulars in their outlet stores.

Hanover (1-800-444-2115) sells Bostonian, Clarks of England and Hanover shoes in its off-price outlets and also stocks Timberland and first-quality Rockports. Call the same number for information about the separate chain of discount outlets that sell Bostonian shoes exclusively. Genesco (615-367-7000) operates discount stores that carry Dexter, Florsheim, Rockport, Nunn-Bush and other brands and runs a second chain of off-price outlets (615-367-7401) that sell only Johnston & Murphy shoes.

SEARCH THE DISCOUNTERS FOR DRESS SHOES. How does 60 percent off retail sound? That's what off-price stores like Marshalls, T.J. Maxx, Filene's Basement and others charge for fancy-label dress shoes once offered only at overpriced department stores and exclusive men's shops. The overstock from these stores goes to jobbers, who resell the stock at a lower price to discount chains or other, cheaper shoe stores and shoe outlets.

Men's Sportswear

Even before casual Friday came to the workplace, men were working hard at dressing down. Now they're acting like Type-A beavers about it—spending nearly $9 billion a year on knit and woven sport shirts (about three times as much as they shell out for dress shirts) and close to $6 billion on shorts and casual pants.

Like other pieces of clothing, men's sportswear can have a retail markup of 100 percent or more. But here's how to spend casually for dressing that way.

Take a clue from Uncle Sam. One thing the government does well is buy clothing for its armed forces, and it purchases so much that contractors provide plenty of extras. The result: Clothing not needed for the military winds up at Army-Navy stores—along with surplus brand-name jeans, sweaters, shirts and other men's casual clothing at just a fraction of its retail price.

Since the government buys directly from manufacturers, it avoids a middleman, or jobber, in business lingo. So while you'll certainly find fatigues and other military garb at Army-Navy stores, you'll also pay as little as $10 for a sturdy wool sweater that sells for four times as much in mall department stores. European governments are also selling their surplus military clothing to Army-Navy stores, and you'll find a wide selection of general merchandise as well—everything from durable T-shirts to other casual sportswear. The range of sizes may be limited, but Army-Navy retailers have been broadening their lines to stay competitive, and they are offering more variety and keeping their markups lower than other retail stores.

Make it at a mart. Another place to buy casual clothing for less is at discount chains like Kmart, Wal-Mart and Target Stores. These mass retailers carry the same men's basics as department stores—often from the same manufacturers—but because they have lower overhead and do more volume buying, they're able to sell them for about 15 percent less. Besides carrying brand-name casual wear, some stores also stock their own store-brand spinoffs of comparable quality for even less money.

OR GO A CASUAL SPECIALIST. Full-price retailers have also responded to America's new value-consciousness with new lines of lower-priced casual clothing, and some even sell them at their own lower-priced branches. The Gap, for instance, has 50 Old Navy Clothing Company stores, which carry casual wear at prices 20 to 25 percent lower than those at the chain's traditional retail stores. While no one would accuse the Gap of not selling casual clothing, Old Navy sells it for less.

CHECK OUT A DESIGNER OUTLET. There are more than 10,000 outlet stores in the United States, and there's no excuse not to buy your casual clothes at one. Designers such as Ralph Lauren and companies such as J. Crew sell their overstocks, returns, irregulars, previous-season styles and sample inventories in their own stores at outlet centers, often near vacation spots. There's no middleman, so the deals are good—usually 25 to 60 percent off regular retail prices—but there are ways to get even better deals.

OUTSTANDING OUTLETS

Filene's Basement practically invented the bargain—and it hasn't let up. Founded in 1908 in Boston, the anchor store has become that city's second most popular tourist attraction, where 20,000 shoppers daily jostle their way through bins of brand-name clothing that costs anywhere from 30 to 75 percent below department store prices. There are 48 outlets, mostly in the Northeast and Midwest.

Less well known is the fact that the company has vastly expanded its men's line, so much so that *Men's Wear* magazine proclaimed it "the father of fashion apparel discounting." The store's ruthless buyers go to any lengths to get top brands at a cut rate, once even raiding the haberdasheries aboard the *Queen Mary* when the luxury cruise ship was stranded in New York by the outbreak of World War II. The biggest annual markdowns come just after Labor Day. Call 1-800-666-4045 for store locations.

THE BEST FOR LESS: EDDIE BAUER

For casual clothes and sportswear, it's tough to do any better than Eddie Bauer—especially during its frequent preferred-customer sales, which are open to anyone who buys something. The company's classic styling also means its clothes will stay in fashion for as long as they last, and they last for years. Every item is unconditionally guaranteed.

A division of the Spiegel Company, Eddie Bauer posts annual sales of $1 billion, but it's the only company in its class that's down-to-earth enough to operate an extensive chain of outlet stores—40 in all. During sales, for which customers get advance notice, you'll get polo shirts for $9.99 and chinos for $14.99—and they're first-quality, not irregulars or out-of-style surplus. Another tip: If you order from the catalog, use the phone in any Eddie Bauer store and get free delivery. Call 1-800-645-7467 for outlet store locations.

Get on the mailing lists of outlet stores so you're notified of "preferred customer" sales—or shop with a friend to cash in on the two-for-one specials. But be sure to examine the merchandise and check that it's the size that's indicated on the tag or box. Also, some outlets may not take credit cards, so be sure to inquire about any payment restrictions before you shop.

For the location of an outlet store near you or to find out what brands an outlet carries, call Outlet Bound at 1-800-336-8853. The company will answer questions over the phone and send you brochures with discount vouchers from any of about 170 outlet centers. Outlet Bound also publishes a guidebook by the same name for $7.95 (plus $3.50 shipping and handling) that's available in the spring and fall. It lists outlet stores around the country and in Canada and includes about $1,000 worth of coupons.

MEN'S SUITS

Descended from enormous nineteenth-century English frock coats, men's suits slimmed down to something closer to their current incarnation during World War I—thanks in part to shortages of fabric.

Another watershed event of sorts has led to a dramatic reduction in the number of suits sold over the past decade: the rising acceptance of casual work clothes. Suit sales numbered 20 million annually about ten years ago; today fewer than half that many are sold.

The dramatic drop in the suit market hasn't stopped most full-price

OUTSTANDING OUTLETS

If you're looking for a deal on a suit, it helps to live in the South. S&K, started by two traveling salesmen in Richmond, Virginia, has 172 stores in 26 states, mostly in the South and Midwest. Stocking end-of-season excess inventory from department stores such as Bloomingdale's and Lord & Taylor, S&K also carries in-season overstocks from major manufacturers—all for 30 to 50 percent off. S&K provides alterations and other services and is experimenting with mail-order and custom-tailored suits in collaboration with the Botany 500 label. Call 1-800-644-SUIT for store locations.

In addition, the Houston-based Men's Wearhouse owns 234 stores in 27 states, also mostly in the South. Besides selling brand-name suits for 25 percent off or more, the stores offer free pressing—forever—for any suit that they sell. Call 1-800-777-8580 for more information.

retailers from adding the traditional 100 percent markup over wholesale. But you don't need to pay full retail for a suit anymore. Here's how to suit yourself for less.

SEEK OUT THE SECONDARY LINE. Top-name designers have a strategy for selling suits in this tighter market. Besides the well-known name brands, they also offer less pricey secondary lines that use less expensive fabrics and machine stitching but are otherwise close in quality and fit. Andrew Fezza's secondary line is called Assets, and Armani has its Le Collezioni and Mani lines. They're sold in most department stores for 30 percent less than name designer offerings and eventually make their way to discount houses at an additional 50 percent off.

GET EXTRA CREDIT. Fill out an application for a store credit card and you'll get 10 to 20 percent off. The stores make this offer hoping you'll use the discount on a pair of socks, which costs them only pocket change, but if you can apply it to the average suit, you could save $45 to $80. Retailers like Neiman Marcus and Sears run these offers as promotional campaigns, while Macy's offers this benefit year-round. Remember to pay off the balance immediately, though, since store credit cards usually carry hefty interest rates.

DO A DISCOUNTER. Don't want to wait for a sale? Off-price stores such as Marshall's, Filene's Basement, Syms and T.J. Maxx get some of the same suits as department stores, but they sell them for less because they offer fewer customer services and take a smaller markup. Discount chains receive their suits 8 to 12 weeks after the full-price retailers do. Department stores start having sales by this time, but discounters reduce their prices faster. Mass retailers such as Sears and JCPenney sell separates for a lot less than you'll spend on brand-name two-piece suits, although the quality may not be as high.

TRAVEL AND SAVE. Here's an excuse to visit Europe. In Paris, pick up the "Gault Millau" or "Paris Cher" guide, which list stores with "permanent sales"—actually outlets selling the best French suits at up to 50 percent off regular prices. To avoid the exorbitant French sales tax, take your purchase with you rather than having it sent. When in Rome, hit the half-price Armani Emporium near the Piazza di Spagna or the Loehmann's-style Discount System on Via del Viminale. Both advertise in Rome's English-language publications.

BE THRIFTY. America's thrift stores are bulging at the seams with perfectly good men's suits—"vintage" clothing that's become as trendy as it is cheap. Two of the best places to prospect are the Salvation

THE BEST FOR LESS: ARMANI

Giorgio Armani's familiar classic tailored suits and sportcoats earned him the name the Blazer King during the 1980s. He still makes arguably the world's best men's suits. And Giorgio isn't lowering his standards—or his prices. A new Armani suit will run you $1,800.

But there are two sure-fire ways to get one for a lot less. First, Armani has a high-quality secondary line called Mani. Mani suits are handmade of 100 percent virgin wool from 100 percent Italian sheep, and the patterns are even a little snazzier than the traditional Armanis. Yet they'll cost you less than half as much—about $750 at a full-price retailer.

Then you can cut the price in half again by shopping at a discount store like Filene's Basement. The latest season's shipments of Armani suits show up at the discount stores within two months of the time they make their debut in the full-price men's shops.

Army and Goodwill Industries. The Salvation Army runs more than 1,560 thrift stores, and Goodwill has over 1,400 nationwide. The merchandise turns over frequently; the biggest selection comes in at the end of the calendar year, when people make donations so they can deduct them from their taxes, and during spring cleaning time.

For the best selection, go to thrift stores in affluent areas and those with an older population. Since most people tend to donate in their neighborhoods, the former will net you higher-quality merchandise; the latter get some of their suit inventory in great condition from family members when someone dies.

There's even a for-profit thrift-store chain: Value Village, which has more than 100 stores located mainly in the central and western United States. The stores are filled with secondhand clothes that are purchased by the pound from charities. A new department in the Value Village, called Labels, features manufacturers' overstock, often with the original tags still hanging from the sleeves. Items that haven't sold after two weeks are discounted 30 percent; after three weeks, they're marked down 60 percent. Unlike nonprofit thrift stores, Value Village has a seven-day refund policy. And don't rule out yard sales, flea markets, swap meets, rummage sales and estate sales, where canny consumers have been known to find clothing that was never even worn by its original owners. Shop early or volunteer to help; you'll get first dibs on the best stuff, especially in common sizes.

COMB A CONSIGNMENT STORE. You'll find good-as-new castoffs in consignment shops for 50 to 80 percent less than the original retail price. Found in the trendy parts of major cities and in wealthy suburbs, consignment shops make sure that clothes are dry-cleaned or washed before they're sold—unlike thrift stores. Some consignment shops buy from thrift stores and clean the merchandise up, so check it carefully. It's okay to negotiate, especially if there's a button missing or some other defect or if you notice that the item has been in the store for a while. You can also sell your old clothes there; the store usually gets 50 to 60 percent of the sale price and you get the rest.

MOTORCYCLES

The lure of the open road has long appealed to the young at heart. Now record numbers of Americans of all ages are discovering the joys of motorcycling. In fact, the Motorcycle Industry Council says over 31 million people—about one of every eight Americans—ride a motorcycle, scooter or all-terrain vehicle.

There's no doubt that there are less expensive hobbies: The average price of a new motorcycle is about $3,500, and the deep-throated growl of a Harley Davidson touring bike can cost up to $19,000 or more. But here's how to ride for less.

LOOK AT THE ENGINE, NOT THE FRILLS. Those low-slung sport bikes may be more visually appealing, but take away the fiberglass fairings and clip-on handlebars mounted on individual front fork stanchions and you often have just a dressed-up version of a standard or touring bike—for up to 25 percent more. What's more, these trendy sports bikes usually command—and get—the full retail price. Plus, they are more expensive to operate.

Instead of falling for these frills, look for the same engine and other appealing mechanical components in the brand's touring or standard bike models.

GO TO A MULTIBRAND DEALER. The deal you get on a new motorcycle has a lot to do with the dealership itself. Low-volume and single-brand dealers—those who stock only one brand of cycle—often demand full price, especially if they are the only franchise in town. After all, retail markups for new bikes are just 10 to 20 percent. But multifranchise stores—a dealer that stocks Suzuki, Yamaha and Kawasaki bikes, for instance—are more willing to discount off list price. You should be able to negotiate 10 to 15 percent off on slow-selling bikes from such dealers.

CHECK OUT THE FLOOR MODELS. Cycle dealers usually order from the factory just four times a year, and they can misjudge how many of a specific model they will sell. But this much is clear: They'd love to

THE BEST FOR LESS: DUCATI

Sorry, bikers, but you already know about Harley Davidson—and how these premium bikes sell for a premium price, if you can buy them. For the most sought-after models, you could be on a waiting list for up to two years.

What you may not know is that there's an Italian-made motorcycle called a Ducati that some experts believe is even better. Like Harleys, these bikes have big V-twin engines that can rattle your bones. But Ducati doesn't make touring bikes—its bikes are strictly racing motorcycles.

Although quality-control problems in the past marred its image, Ducati has corrected them in recent years. And while a high-end Harley can cost $17,000 or more, the most expensive Ducati is $15,490.

There are 180 Ducati dealers in the United States. To find one near you, call the Ducati importer at (201) 839-2600.

see you ride into the sunset on a bike that's been sitting around the showroom for a while. This is because dealers usually "floor plan" new motorcycles, meaning they buy them from the factory on credit at an interest rate several points above the prime rate. The sooner they sell those floor models, the more quickly they recoup their money—or cut their losses. These floor models may be the attention-getting "hot" bikes, but in many cases they're also the ones whose prices are most likely to be negotiated.

ASK FOR THE INVOICE. Unlike automobile dealers, motorcycle dealers in many states aren't required to use uniform price stickers supplied by manufacturers, similar to Monroney window stickers on new cars. So the price you see on the tag dangling from a new motorcycle may be higher than the manufacturer's suggested list price—in other words, retailers mark 'em up just to mark 'em down. This is how some dealers add profit to new sales and give themselves bargaining room for customers who want to negotiate prices. So don't trust the

BEFORE YOU BUY: CHECK INSURANCE RATES

Hear that roar? It's not a new motorcycle racing down the highway, it's someone's insurance rates taking off.

Before you slap down big bucks for a new bike, consider the impact your choice will have on your insurance costs. A motorcyclist with a clean driving record may pay $2,000 or more just for basic coverage on a sport bike, while the same policy on a more conservative touring bike might cost only $600 or $700. In other words, call your insurance agent before you buy.

To save even more on insurance, take a course approved by the Motorcycle Safety Foundation and you may qualify for a 10 percent discount. To get more information on these courses, call 1-800-447-4700.

price tags; ask to see the invoice or manufacturer's price list.

GO BY THE BOOK. You can save hundreds by sticking to the prices listed in the Kelly Blue Book or NADA motorcycle appraisal guides. In addition to new and used values, these guides include the amount a bank would lend on the bike.

LOOK AT THOSE SUBURBAN "SHOPPERS." The best deals on used motorcycles aren't at dealerships but in garages in upper-middle-class neighborhoods, courtesy of affluent middle-aged men who were bitten by the motorcycle bug but lost interest after a year or two, leaving their premium models—with low mileage and up-to-date servicing—collecting dust. When it comes time to sell them, they tend to place classified ads in local newspapers and those freebie "shopper" flyers given away by local merchants.

You can often get used cycles for a song compared to what a dealer will charge, since people who tire of their motorcycles are often more interested in having them gone than in recovering every dollar they can. You can tell if a classified ad is placed by someone in a nice neighborhood by checking the phone prefixes (the first three digits of the phone number). The front of your white pages phone directory should have a map of your city that shows the prefixes for each section of town.

BEWARE OF "HARDLY USED" BIKES. Come across a used motorcycle only ridden to church on Sunday by a little ol' lady? Forget it—and any other motorcycle that's been sitting around, even for a few months.

Some mechanical components in motorcycles, especially in the fuel systems, may become dysfunctional quickly if they are not used regularly. Water condenses inside the gas tank and rusts the inside lining, and deteriorating gasoline gums up carburetors and fuel injectors. And it's common to underestimate the cost of parts and repairs for a used motorcycle. Even common parts like starter motors and piston rings can be extremely expensive, sometimes even more than corresponding parts for automobiles.

TALK CASH—EVEN IF YOU WANT TO FINANCE. When price shopping, either by phone or in person, ask for a *specific* quote of the full cash sales price. Don't accept a vague answer like "I can sell it to you for $1,500 down and $200 a month."

If you need to finance, try to get a loan through a credit union, which generally offers the lowest rates on motorcycle loans. Pass on dealer loan programs sponsored by the manufacturer of the bike you're buying—they tend to be several interest points higher than credit arranged through a lending institution and will cost you several hundred dollars more over the life of the loan.

And also forget "limited buyer programs"—loans for those with little or no credit history. The down payment is hefty and interest rates can be as high as 20 percent, or up to the highest rate your state's credit regulations allow.

Musical Instruments

With the abundance of brands and quality levels, just choosing the right musical instrument can be tougher than mastering one.

Still, our need to make music is powerful—and costly: Americans shell out $5 billion each year on musical instruments and their accessories. Retail markups range from about 10 to 100 percent depending on the instrument, but here's how you can play those tunes without singing the financial blues—whether you're buying a grand piano or just getting the young'uns started on a school music program.

Band and Orchestra Instruments

Delay until May. A standing joke among school band directors is the correlation between the time student musicians lose interest in practicing and the time they discover the opposite sex. And when spring is in the air—or maybe just the freedom of summer—many a would-be musician's thoughts turn to getting rid of that saxophone or oboe, leaving you with an opportunity to buy these hardly used student rental instruments for up to 40 percent or more off retail prices.

Call the music teacher or band director of your local school and ask which music store they deal with, then call that store as the school year is ending. Don't wait too long, however, since prices tend to escalate in August—and stay high.

Head to the big city. If you want a new instrument, you can save up to 40 percent by taking advantage of the highly competitive business in America's major cities. Small-town shoppers may find themselves a captive of full retail markups or nominal discounts at best—and most instruments in tiny burgs are available only at smaller Mom-and-Pop music stores, where markups are highest. The best cities to shop are New York, Chicago and Los Angeles, but an abundance of musicians in Las Vegas, New Orleans and Nashville keeps prices down in those cities as well.

OUTSTANDING OUTLETS

Sam Ash Music Stores is a nine-store chain in the New York City area that claims to beat all other prices and offers over-the-phone quotes (and shipping) on a full line of instruments. Count on savings of at least 40 percent compared to other retailers—with a two-week money-back guarantee and a 30-day exchange policy. Call (212) 719-2299 for a quote or the location of a store near you.

And in Texas, Swords Music Company of Fort Worth (1-800-522-3082) offers similar savings and carries all types of instruments; it specializes in matching or beating others' deals and offers a two-week exchange policy.

In New York, the first stop should be West 48th Street and Broadway. That's the heart of the retail music industry, and price competition can be fierce, so you'll be in the best position to negotiate a lower-than-sticker-price deal.

ASK FOR A BETTER DEAL. It may sound obvious, but keep in mind that some instruments are actually priced slightly higher than the manufacturer's suggested retail price because music store owners *expect* people to negotiate with them. Unfortunately, many buyers don't even try, and they wind up paying top dollar. A good rule of thumb: Offer between 15 and 20 percent less than the asking price for new instruments and expect to settle for a 10 percent discount. For used instruments, offer 20 to 25 percent less and settle for 15 percent off.

READ THE TRADES. Experienced musicians have a secret—where to buy instruments at deep discounts through mail order. Discounters often advertise only in trade magazines, the newsletters of musicians' guilds and by direct mail. While the latter two may not be options for the nonprofessional, go to any well-stocked bookstore or newsstand and check out the offerings. In the back of *Modern Drummer* magazine, for instance, are listings for mail-order houses that sell drum equipment; the same is true for other specialty titles. Some of these advertisers are full-line retailers, selling all types of instruments, and most have toll-free numbers and will send free catalogs to callers.

GREAT MAIL-ORDER BUYS

Manny's Music Store in New York City offers 40 percent off regular retail prices on Gibson and Martin guitars and varying discounts on other instruments. Call 1-800-448-8478 for a catalog.

And Thoroughbred Music in Tampa, Florida, sells just about every type of instrument except wind instruments—including hard-to-find items—at an average of 40 percent off list price. Plus, it offers a 30-day return policy. Call 1-800-800-4654 for more information.

Another place to look for great deals is the classified section of the local newspaper. Generally, you'll save up to 30 percent on used instruments compared to buying used at a retail store. That's because most people who place ads are more interested in getting rid of that unused horn or violin than in making a profit.

TRY IT BEFORE YOU BUY IT. Some stores rent used instruments as well as new, cutting your spending even more. Another option is to ask about a rent-purchase deal on new instruments, in which you buy a new instrument after trying it out for a while. But be aware that rent-purchase agreements on new instruments may be based on the full retail price, so avoid a long-term plan. Most rental purchases offer extraordinarily low payments for the first three months but then require a balloon payment of the remaining balance or immediate return of the instrument. And keep in mind that many student instruments are generally of lower quality to start with.

CHECK OUT A PAWN SHOP. Some of the best deals can be found in pawn shops, where you can buy used instruments at rock-bottom prices. On average, about 10 percent of a pawn shop's inventory will be in musical instruments, although you may have to do some legwork to find the instrument you want.

Pawn shops typically lend about 20 percent of the pawned item's value, which pawnbrokers determine by checking industry price guides. If a mandolin is worth $500, for example, the loan amount would be $100, and the selling price may be $200. If the owner doesn't pick up the instrument when the loan is due, the pawn shop has a relatively small stake in the mandolin for sale on the shelf.

Another advantage: Many pawnbrokers want to clear out their instruments to recoup their cash, so there's more room for bargaining than at a retail store. In fact, pawnbrokers *expect* customers to negotiate prices. But don't expect to get answers to your questions: You need to know what you're looking for.

PIANOS

BE A SUMMER BUYER. Interest in piano-playing tends to wane during the summer months; in fact, many piano teachers take time off from late May through August as kids focus their attention on other activities. So if you're looking to buy, pounce during these months: Discounts on both new and used pianos tend be in the range of 10 to 20 percent. Prices spike again in September.

BUY USED. A good used console piano will usually cost between $850 and $1,000. The same model will generally start at around

THE BEST FOR LESS: STEINWAY MODEL M

Unless you're a Rockefeller, you probably wouldn't be able to touch a Bösendorfer grand piano, the type that has long graced musical concert halls. The cheapest one costs $60,000—used.

But although a Bösendorfer may be priciest, industry insiders say the best grand piano is actually a vintage Steinway Model M. Bought new, this model costs over $30,000. But you're better off buying used for about $20,000—and not only because of price. The aged wood found in an older Steinway enhances tonal quality, and the heavier cast iron that was used in older models is another plus for enhancing sound.

To locate these vintage Steinways, call A.C. Pianocraft in New York City at (212) 957-9268 or your local Steinway dealer.

$2,500 new. So all things being equal, buy used for greater savings—especially if you're testing the waters of piano-playing. Look for names like Kimball or Wurlitzer, and for best results, buy only from a reputable used piano dealer.

RENT TO OWN. You could save yourself hundreds by renting a piano for a few months to see whether you or your kids are budding Mozarts or are bored by the whole thing. It's also common to negotiate a deal in which the rent can be applied toward the purchase price, experts say. (You shouldn't pay much more than $100 a month to rent a piano, though, and as with other instruments, avoid balloon payments at the end of the rental period.)

PAY A PIANO TECHNICIAN. Here's a piano horror story that you should avoid duplicating: A woman buys a beautiful concert grand piano at an auction for $195. Upon having it inspected by a piano technician, she discovers that it must be restrung—to the tune of $2,500. The moral: You can sometimes save thousands by paying $35 to have a professional take a look—before you buy.

Office Furniture

The $9 billion market in office furniture is healthier than ever, thanks in part to the trend toward working at home. What can be sickening, however, is the incredible retail markup for office furniture—anywhere from 200 to 700 percent, depending on the item.

So with furniture prices obviously padded more for profit than for comfort, buyers need to be especially careful in order to get the most for their money. Shopping at an office superstore like OfficeMax or Staples is the obvious route for buying desks, chairs and other office furniture for home use. While selection may be more limited, their prices are anywhere from 30 to 60 percent below those of smaller specialty retailers, who sell closer to the manufacturer's suggested list price. But no matter where you shop, here's how to save.

Spring into action. Office furniture retailers tend to try to unload their inventory during the spring, when business typically falls off and they need to make room for the new merchandise introduced at the industry's annual trade show held in June. From March to June, you'll likely find across-the-board markdowns of up to 20 percent, especially at smaller specialty stores.

But for the best deals, seek out floor models. The desks, chairs, filing cabinets and other pieces displayed on the floor are usually discounted up to 35 percent because retailers are particularly interested in selling them. Besides, they're already assembled.

Be hip to the name games. Like other manufacturers, some companies that make office furniture produce their wares under several different names. Steelcase, the leading producer of desks and other office furniture, has its Turnstone line. A subsidiary of Herman Miller offers the Miller SQA line, and the Knoll Group has its Parachute and SoHo lines of chairs. These products are designed with simpler features and manufactured to be more affordable, yet they meet or exceed industry standards for quality and durability.

Buy used. Corporate downsizing has helped trigger an $800-million-

THE BEST FOR LESS: STEELCASE

Famous for its high-quality, durable office furniture, Steelcase is perhaps the best-known and most respected name in the business. What's more, it manufactures select products specifically designed for home office use.

Just want the basics? Look to the Turnstone line of ergonomic chairs, stackable storage units and desks in laminate or veneer. All products are sold through authorized Steelcase dealers. Call 1-800-TURNSTONE for the location of one near you.

a-year market in used office furniture that's growing at a rate of 20 percent a year. Buying used furniture in "as-is" condition can save you up to 80 percent compared to buying the same item new. And you'll pocket up to 60 percent when you buy used goods that have been refurbished or remanufactured. (A refurbisher improves the look of used furniture with new fabric or paint; a remanufacturer improves its mechanical condition with new springs, screws and so on.)

You can find used furniture dealers—including some of the 3,000 refurbishers and remanufacturers who operate in the United States—in the yellow pages under "Office Furniture." "As-is" furniture is usually sold by companies to employees on a first-come, first-served basis, but you can call a company's facilities manager for information on upcoming sales. Some companies also advertise auctions under "Public Notices" in the classified section of local newspapers.

MAKE AN OFFER TO UNCLE SAM. Dozens of federal, state and local agencies routinely sell off office furniture at public auctions that are advertised in local newspapers. Some items are available at these auctions for as little as 3 cents on the dollar.

The quality of the furniture—which includes both used government furniture and goods seized from drug dealers, tax evaders and other criminals—varies considerably, so be sure to inspect it before the auction. Of particular interest are the offerings of the Federal Deposit Insurance Corporation, which is charged with auctioning off furniture from failed banks and financial institutions—items that are often new and of high quality.

For information on these auctions and others, contact the U.S. General Services Administration at 1-800-472-1313 or the specific agency, such as the Internal Revenue Service. Or call the Federal Information Center at 1-800-688-9889 to order *The Federal Government Sales* for $1.75. This booklet lists auction-holding agencies and their numbers.

BYPASS THE FRILLS. An office chair with all the ergonomic bells and whistles can list for up to $1,500, but you can spare yourself such prices if you buy only the features you need. For example, get a good swivel chair with a pneumatic lift, but pass on the tilt lock option and you'll save 30 percent. Get stationary arm supports instead of the "3-D" supports that move in all directions and you'll pocket 50 percent. And passing on something as simple as fire-resistant fabric can save up to $100 on some chairs.

CUSTOM-BUILD YOUR DESK. Even if you're all thumbs, you can put together an attractive and practical desk for about half the cost of a ready-built model—by piecing together materials available at most building supply stores. A 30-by-60-inch Formica top sells for about $100 at home centers such as Home Depot and is more attractive and far more durable than the melamine tops found on most inexpensive desks. To support the desktop, consider two-drawer oak laminate or metal cabinets, available for about $25 to $40 each. Or if you don't need drawers and would prefer more leg room, support the Formica top on legs made of cut PVC piping (painted any color you choose) that cost about $2.50 each. The information booths at home centers can give you complete details about what you'll need and how to piece it together.

Office Supplies

Good news for those who shop for office supplies: Catalogs and superstores like Office Depot, Staples and OfficeMax are buying office supplies in greater volume than ever before—and passing on savings that used to be available only to the corporate giants.

And rightly so, since it's the everyday person—not corporations—who shells out two of every three dollars spent on office supplies. And that amounts to about $100 billion each year.

The most obvious way to save money on office supplies is to buy from these superstores and catalogs, whose prices tend to be as much as 40 percent below those at small specialty retailers. But there are other ways to save, too.

Ask for the house brand. Just like supermarkets, most larger office supply distributors—including most superstores—carry their own brands that are identical to brand-name supplies, except they sell for 25 to 35 percent less. At OfficeMax, look for the MaxBrite line of copy paper, printer paper, legal pads and adhesive tape. At Office Depot, look for Office Image copy paper and legal pads.

The major catalogs also have private-label products for similar discounts. Quill, Viking and Reliable, three leading office supply catalogs, have house brands of everything from typewriter ribbons and paper to computer disks and labels.

Or look for the private brand. Even the big brand-name companies play this name game—or a version of it. A 12-pack of 100-sheet, three-by-three-inch Post-it Notes by office supply giant 3M sells for $8 at OfficeMax. The same number of Highland brand notes—also manufactured by 3M—sells for about $5, a savings of over 35 percent. The reason: Highland is the economy line made for light use; the notes have less adhesive than the higher-priced Post-it Notes, but they are fine for most people.

Fall into savings. September and October are the best months to

GREAT MAIL-ORDER BUYS

If you want to buy office supplies through mail order, three companies stand above the rest. Chicago-based Reliable offers some prices that are slightly higher than you'll find at superstores like Staples, OfficeMax and Office Depot but discounts other items up to 80 percent and has superior customer service. It also offers free, same-day shipping on all orders and a no-risk, no-hassle guarantee. To order a catalog, call 1-800-735-4000.

Viking Office Products, based in Los Angeles, is another excellent mail-order company. With prices and service similar to Reliable's, it offers free shipping on orders over $25 and a one-year guarantee on its goods. And like Reliable, Viking will pay return shipping regardless of the reason for the return. Its catalog is available by calling 1-800-248-6111.

Quill, of Lincolnshire, Illinois, offers free same-day shipping on orders over $45 and sells at prices comparable to those of the other two companies. It offers a no-risk guarantee and a Customer Bill of Rights. A Quill catalog can be yours by calling 1-800-789-1331.

No matter where you order, however, be careful of so-called sale catalogs. The prices in these catalogs aren't necessarily better than those in regular catalogs and are mostly a ploy to sell slow-moving inventory.

buy many office supplies. Calendar goods, appointment books and items like paper and pens tend to be 10 to 25 percent less expensive when they first hit the stores just as the school year begins. (Calendars are most expensive just after the New Year, when people flock to buy them.)

Also think of buying during the Christmas season, since it's the slowest time for office supply retailers. You may find few bona fide sales, but that's when retailers are most willing to negotiate a lower price—especially for larger orders.

BYPASS BANKS FOR CHECKS

Go to a check-printing specialist rather than a bank and you can save 50 percent on the purchase of new checks—whether for business or personal use. Banks usually mark up the cost of the checks they provide, keeping a healthy profit on the transaction.

Typically, check-printing specialists—which frequently advertise in Sunday newspaper coupon supplements—offer a good selection of designs, and their checks are accepted by all banks. Among the best are Checks in the Mail in New Braunfels, Texas (1-800-733-4443), Current in Colorado Springs, Colorado (1-800-525-7170), Designer Checks (1-800-239-9222) and Image Checks in Little Rock, Arkansas (1-800-562-8768).

LOOK TO UNCLE SAM. Government agencies, hospitals and schools tend to buy their office supplies by contract—an agreement to buy a certain amount for a set price. Often these contracts are for huge volumes of goods, and the agencies wind up with more office supplies than they need, so many hold auctions to unload their extra inventory. Look under "Public Notices" in the classified section of the local newspaper to find auction times and locations.

THINK GREEN. You can save up to 75 percent by buying recycled computer disks instead of new ones. And there's no problem with quality: Most computer disks are manufactured to last for 200 years. Even though they've been used, once they've been demagnetized, reformatted and relabeled, they're as good as new. Office superstores haven't caught on to this recycling trend, but you can call Computer Recyclers in Orem, Utah, at (801) 226-1892 for recycled, high-density 3½-inch disks for about 30 cents and 5¼-inch floppies for about 24 cents each—about 75 percent off the manufacturer's suggested retail price for new disks and about 60 percent less than you'd pay from the best catalogs.

The same is true for toner cartridges for photocopy machines. Buy remanufactured cartridges and you'll save 40 percent compared to new ones. But we found that their quality isn't as good as that of recycled disks, so it's especially important to buy from a reputable manufacturer. Try Nashua in Nashua, New Hampshire, at 1-800-258-1724 or Nu-Kote International in Franklin, Tennessee, at 1-800-448-1422. Both companies guarantee their work. If you want to return their used cartridges, they will pay for the shipping, and depending on the type of cartridge, they may even buy it back from you for up to $15. Call them for details.

Paintings, Prints and Posters

Artists might say that you can't put a price on art. But if you've been shopping for paintings, prints and posters, you may feel comfortable using an adjective for it: expensive.

True, buying art can be costly—and confusing. There's no way to comparison-shop when buying original artwork, and there's no recognized system for calculating retail markups. Dealers simply set prices based on what they think the market will bear for that particular artist. But there are ways to save money, whether you're buying an original painting, a reproduction print or a poster. Here's how.

Deal directly with the artist. A gallery is a wonderful place to develop your eye for art, but it tends to be an expensive place to buy because of the owner's high overhead. So do what industry insiders suggest: Cruise the galleries—then call the artist directly to make a deal. You'll usually find complete biographical information, sometimes including an address, posted with the displayed pieces.

Many galleries take an artist's works on consignment—when the piece sells, the artist is given a commission, usually between 40 and 60 percent. But even if the gallery buys the artwork outright, it tends to double the price to cover its overhead. So don't be shy about offering the artist a lower price: Even if it's half of the gallery's selling price, it's still approximately the same as what the artist would be paid by the gallery owner.

Look to the unknown. Prices for original artwork are often based on the cost of previous works sold. The works of well-known artists—even the "bad" ones—will cost more simply because they've sold their work before, and dealers believe there is a market for them. With newer artists, however, the waters are untested, and galleries are willing to sell their works for a lot less—often whatever they can get. All things being equal, expect to pay at least 30 percent less for an unknown artist whose talent is on a par with that of a more accomplished one.

THE BEST FOR LESS: POSTER ORIGINALS

Posters are the least expensive form of artwork, with an average price of less than $30. And few companies offer more in the way of selection and quality than Poster Originals, which was responsible for starting the popularity of posters in America over three decades ago.

Poster Originals in New York City sells mostly to museums and galleries, but for the best selection—over 1,000 posters, all on top-quality 80-pound paper—you can order the company's 160-page catalog for $25 by calling 1-800-638-0008.

GO BACK TO SCHOOL. Don't assume that galleries are the only place to look for artwork—especially by new artists. University art departments frequently have shows displaying the works of their more promising students. A phone call to the local university's art department can alert you to these shows, where pieces by tomorrow's stars often go for a song. If the price isn't as low as you'd like, make an offer. Starving artists rarely refuse to part with their work.

PAY CASH. Wherever you buy, most sellers can work out a payment plan. After all, most original paintings can sell for several thousand dollars. But if you pay cash, you will likely get a 10 percent discount. If it's not offered, ask for this industry standard.

BE A LATECOMER. When it comes to paintings, prints and posters, it's the early bird who pays full price. Flea markets and yard sales are great places to buy artwork, but it's best to shop near the end of the day when people are ready to close down and unload whatever they haven't sold.

And wait until the end of a traveling museum exhibit to buy a poster at the gift shop. Once the show is over, you're more likely to get a discount—usually 10 to 15 percent.

BECOME A JOINER. To save even more at a museum gift shop, get a membership to the museum. Besides free or reduced admission, membership (which can be as low as $5 per year at some art museums) typically qualifies you for an additional 15 percent discount on all purchases made in the gift shop.

ASK ABOUT A CHARITY SALE. On occasion, smaller art museums will sell off some of their inventory in order to display new works. These works are usually sold in either a silent or open auction, with the money benefiting a local charity. Sometimes this is a great way to get a deal; other times, bidding fever can cause you to actually pay more than retail. But either way, the amount you pay for the artwork is usually tax-deductible.

At other times, these museums may just have a liquidation sale, where you can usually find better deals (but not get a tax deduction). You can learn about these sales by calling the museum directly or asking to be put on their mailing list.

Party Decorations

Americans spend over $1 billion a year on party decorations. Everything from paper cups to paper napkins to streamers is bought in the name of celebration.

What's not so joyful, however, is the retail markup: up to 80 percent. Fancy designs on paper goods like plates and napkins, seasonal appeal and hot new theme characters push prices up even more. While a streamer is pretty much a streamer, look for sturdiness, a wax coating and thick ply on plates and napkins so that the cake won't land in someone's lap. Certain brand names such as Hallmark usually assure quality—and a higher price. But here's how to celebrate with some savings.

Switch seasons. There are floral prints in spring and earth tones in the fall, berries at Christmas and bunnies at Easter. But if you take one season's look for another occasion—like Easter bunnies for a child's birthday party—you can save up to 50 percent off regular prices. And while using "fall" earth tones for an outdoor summer

Outstanding Outlets

In outlet malls from coast to coast you'll find a chain of more than 120 stores under different names—the Paper Factory, the Paper Outlet, Paper Chase and Paper Galore. But whatever they're called, all offer a complete line of party decorations for up to 50 percent below regular retail prices. The stores are in 37 states throughout the country; for the location of a store near you, call (414) 738-3600.

GREAT MAIL-ORDER BUYS

Paradise Products offers party decorations with unique international and seasonal themes at prices that won't make you want to leave home. Call 1-800-227-1092 for shop-at-home convenience for everything you need for your next party—from fortune cookies to packets of beach sand for your luau. You have to spend a minimum of $30 per purchase to save on shipping and handling charges; otherwise these charges will be about 10 percent of the total bill. To order your catalog, call the company or send a check for $2 to Paradise Products, P.O. Box 568, El Cerrito, CA 94530.

party won't disturb the rules of etiquette, it will leave you with more cash for food.

THINK "SPECIALIST." You're more likely to get a discount—and a bigger selection—at a store specializing in party goods than at a department store, toy store or drugstore that also sells party decorations. The 130-store chain Party City, for instance, discounts most of its goods up to 60 percent, and because of its large inventory, it runs frequent sales that save you even more.

If there are no party goods stores in your area, check out the nearest "dollar store." These stores—where everything sells for $1 or less—frequently get discontinued and overstocked party decorations and sell them at discounts of up to 60 percent off their original retail cost, or even more.

LOOK FOR THE BASICS. Card shops and other stores where party goods are displayed in fancy racks and shelves have higher overhead—and higher prices. Instead look for stores with basic fixtures and bins of party hats that are off the mall maps, such as the Pic 'N' Save or MacFrugal's, a chain where party goods sell for 40 to 70 percent below retail prices.

SEEK OUT FADING STARS. As Barney and the Teenage Mutant Ninja Turtles fade from glory—as they eventually will—retailers are left with all the paper plates, party hats, streamers and everything else from which they smile. As a result, store owners tend to mark down yesterday's childhood celebrities by up to 50 percent to move them out. Keep your eyes peeled for their replacements. One way is to keep tabs on the newest Disney or cartoon introductions—and you'll see the current lineup quickly become "has-beens."

BUY BIG. As with other retail items, you save more by buying in bulk. An eight-pack of party paper plates or hats (the standard size) costs about 15 percent more on a per-piece basis than the next largest size. But for the biggest savings, seek out the largest packs available, usually sold in bulk at party decoration specialty stores. You may be eating off decorative paper plates for a while, but the savings can amount to as much as 35 percent over buying smaller packages.

PATIO FURNITURE

It used to be that buying outdoor furniture on a budget meant sacrificing style for savings. No longer. Thanks to mass merchandisers like Target Stores, Wal-Mart, Kmart and Home Depot, you can buy wrought-iron, wood and resin deck furniture that looks like the stuff displayed on the well-appointed pages of the Smith & Hawken or Gardeners Eden catalogs—at half the price or even less.

Generally, you can get whatever you want for less—anywhere from 5 to 60 percent lower than the prices in showrooms, retail catalogs or advertisements—if you shop around. The reason: Competition. Thousands of domestic and foreign manufacturers sell to retailers all over the country, including many low-overhead, high-volume dealers that buy directly from the factory and ship to you. Here's how to shop for the best deals in patio furniture.

HEAD TO A HOME CENTER. For the basics—the very familiar green or white resin furniture and canvas umbrellas—few stores can beat prices offered by Home Depot, Builders Square and other large mass-merchandise home centers. Chairs cost as little as $5 each, and you can save 80 percent compared to regular retail prices on other patio furniture.

Home Depot has a slight edge over other home centers because it promises to beat any price by at least 5 percent. Just take in a competitor's receipt or advertisement and a clerk will refund the difference. In fact, Home Depot's prices are often lower than those offered by manufacturer's outlets because it buys in such large volume.

OR TARGET TARGET OR WAL-MART. For fancier stuff, like wrought-iron rocking chairs and better-quality aluminum chaise lounges, discount chains like Target and Wal-Mart offer prices that are between 50 and 80 percent lower than those you'll find in department stores, catalogs and specialty shops. Again, the discounts are a result of volume buying. Other places to get substantial savings include trendy yuppie re-

THE BEST FOR LESS: SUMMER CLASSICS

The Summer Classics line of high-quality outdoor furniture appears in the pages of Neiman-Marcus, Gardeners Eden and Horchow catalogs, often at four-figure prices that would make you think you're furnishing your living room—not an outdoor deck.

But you can get these $1,500 five-piece patio sets for up to 50 percent less by buying from the factory in Pelham, Alabama, throughout the summer months, when the factory sells its overrun inventory of seconds, discontinued lines and one-of-a-kind designs at drastic savings.

tailers like Crate & Barrel in Northbrook, Illinois (1-800-451-8217), Gardeners Eden in San Francisco (1-800-822-9600) and Smith & Hawken in Florence, Kentucky (1-800-776-3336), which offer cedar gliders and other items for about 25 percent less than retail.

BUY IN MARCH—OR WAIT UNTIL SEPTEMBER. If you go the home center route, shop in March—when patio furniture first starts arriving in the stores. Although Home Depot and similar stores rarely have sales then, their "everyday" prices tend to be the same as or even better than other stores' sale prices. It's best to shop early, though, because patio furniture tends to move quickly.

If you shop elsewhere, you'll probably find the best deals after Labor Day. In the cold North and Northeast, stores begin outdoor furniture sales as early as the Fourth of July, when prices begin to drop, but they continue a downward spiral to clearance prices around Labor Day. In other parts of the country, where the weather stays warmer longer, some sales don't start until Labor Day. Either way, look for discounts up to 80 percent off regular retail prices.

CALL NORTH CAROLINA. If you're interested in the really fancy stuff, you can get classic outdoor furniture for half what you'd pay at department stores simply by shopping at the dozens of deep discounters who work out of various stores, primarily in North Carolina and throughout the South.

GREAT MAIL-ORDER BUYS

There are scores of great places to buy patio furniture by mail order; some of them are based in North Carolina and also sell furniture for *inside* your home. Among the best—offering savings up to half off department store prices as well as prompt and helpful service—are Adirondack Designs (1-800-222-0343), Holiday Patio Showcase in Hudson, North Carolina (704-728-2664), Priba Furniture Sales and Interiors in Greensboro, North Carolina (910-855-9034), Rose Furniture in Highpoint, North Carolina (910-886-6050) and Wicker Warehouse in Hackensack, New Jersey (1-800-274-8602).

Here's what you do: Visit your local retail showroom or thumb through garden catalogs for what you want. Get the name of the manufacturer and the model number, usually listed on the back of the tag in a showroom or with the item listing in a catalog. Then call furniture outlets in the Tar Heel State (see "Great Mail-Order Buys" and the Furniture chapter for a list).

Savings vary from 40 to 50 percent less than regular department store prices, depending on the item. Shipping is extra, and some companies require a cash payment, but you usually don't have to pay the state sales tax.

GO FOR A MODEST WOOD. One of the most popular items of patio furniture is the classic Adirondack chair. Buy it in teak or another fancy wood and you'll pay dearly—up to $300 per chair. But if you settle for pine, you can spend less than one-third the price and get the same great styling. Coppa Woodworking in San Pedro, California, offers its chair and ottoman combos, unfinished and unassembled, for about $90 plus $8 for shipping and handling. But for an extra $15 the company will stain or prime them for you to make them weather-resistant. You can get a Coppa catalog by calling (310) 548-5332, but you can get similar prices for pine Adirondack chairs at the Door Store and other retailers.

PENS

Time was when hardly a graduation or executive promotion wasn't commemorated with a fine fountain pen or other classy writing instrument of near-heirloom quality. Then came the nearly indestructible ballpoint refill, the 19-cent Bic and the personal computer—and the once-mighty pen became a mere tool instead of a treasure.

But fine pens are on the rebound, with some modifications. These days there are basically three classes of pens: the very finest, with gold nibs, platinum inlay, "piston" filling systems and price tags as high as $1,000; more moderately priced executive pens in the $25 to $150 range; and everyday pens selling for less than $20.

Whatever you buy, you can figure on a typical 100 percent retail markup, so it pays to shop around to get the most for your money. Here's how.

GREAT MAIL-ORDER BUYS

Buying pens by mail order is no guarantee that you'll pay less. In fact, you're often better off just waiting for a seasonal sale or shopping at a discount office supply store.

There are a few exceptions, however: Fahrney's Pens in Upper Marlboro, Maryland, occasionally offers savings of up to 50 percent off retail on closeouts found in its summer catalog or in special sale flyers. Its catalog is available by calling 1-800-624-7367. Artlite Pens and Gifts in Atlanta offers discounts in the 20 to 25 percent range on many items. Call 1-800-327-PENS for its catalog.

THE BEST FOR LESS: MONT BLANC MEISTERSTUCK SOLITAIRE COLLECTION

Mont Blanc makes some of the best and most expensive pens in the world, and its Solitaire Collection is no exception. With prices ranging from $535 to $985 retail, these pens are custom-fitted, have 18-karat nibs (instead of the more traditional 14-karat) and other special touches not found in a typical ballpoint. There are various models in sterling silver and with platinum inlay. And by the way, they write pretty well, too.

These are not pens you'll find in discount catalogs or office supply stores, but you can occasionally find them on sale—for 10 to 20 percent below retail—at exclusive pen shops, such as Arthur Brown & Brothers in New York City (1-800-772-PENS).

SHOP WHERE THE PROS DO. Although many people shop for finer pens at fancy specialty gift shops and department stores, you'll get more for your money at a *real* specialty shop—a commercial office supply house (listed in the yellow pages under "Office Supplies") or stores like Staples, Office Depot and OfficeMax.

Because of their tremendous buying power, these stores can sell top-of-the-line pens for prices that are about 30 percent less than you'll find elsewhere. Of the three office superstores, OfficeMax is the best place to buy top-level pens, boasting an impressive selection of Cross, Mont Blanc and Waterman Laureat pens—the Cadillacs of the industry—as well as more moderately priced Sheaffer, Lodis and Parker pens. Office Depot and Staples have less to offer on upper-end pens but have a good selection of more moderately priced items at savings of up to 25 percent off regular retail prices.

DELAY UNTIL MAY. The one-two punch of the graduation season coupled with the fact that some manufacturers introduce their new inventory in late spring or early summer results in May and June being the best time of year to snag a deal. Look for discounts up to 30 percent. Another good time to shop is around Christmas, although the savings may not be as great.

KNOW YOUR TIPS. If you're buying a gift for someone who has no real preference, think ballpoint. You'll save anywhere from 10 to 20 percent compared to the same pen with a fountain tip. Rollerball tips fall in the middle.

TUNE UP BEFORE YOU BUY NEW. If you've already received a fine pen that's seen better days, you might want to refurbish it rather than replace it. Some companies specialize in tuning up antique and better-quality pens, usually for $10 to $25—a lot cheaper than buying new. Among them are Fahrney's Pens in Upper Marlboro, Maryland (301-568-6553), the Fountain Pen Hospital in Kingwood, Texas (713-359-7367); Good Service Pen in Somerville, Massachusetts (617-666-2975), the Southern Scribe in Montgomery, Alabama (334-263-4169) and Vintage Pens in Columbus, Ohio (614-267-8468).

Perfumes and Fragrances

With the typical price of fragrances ranging from $25 to $100 per bottle, you usually need plenty of dollars for a few good scents. But apparently Americans are willing to dig deep into their pockets—to the tune of over $5 billion each year—to smell like citrus, lavender, jasmine or even baby powder (a common albeit subtle ingredient in many women's fragrances).

And it's not just women who buy these fragrances. Men's and unisex colognes are the fastest-growing segments of the industry, now accounting for one-third of all sales.

Good luck trying to figure out the retail markup of perfumes: It's a closely guarded secret, and the range varies widely, since some per-

Great Mail-Order Buys

If you know the scent for you, there are a handful of mail-order companies where you can buy your favorite perfumes for up to 70 percent below retail prices.

Holbrook, based in New York, sells designer fragrances like Chanel No. 5 and Shalimar. Discounts vary depending on the quantity. Call 1-800-347-3738 for a free catalog.

New York Cosmetics and Fragrances in San Francisco offers discounts from 10 to 70 percent on men's and women's fragrances. Call (415) 543-3880 for more information.

And Wynnewood Pharmacy in Wynnewood, Pennsylvania, boasts savings of up to 50 percent on perfumes and colognes. Call 1-800-966-9999 for a quote.

fumes sell for only a few dollars, while others cost a small fortune. But whatever you buy, here's how to get it for less.

TURN UP YOUR NOSE AT FANCY FRAGRANCE COUNTERS. From the saleswoman in the white lab coat to those free samples, the fancier trappings of a department store fragrance counter sure are nice, but you'll pay the price—up to 50 percent more than buying perfumes at a drugstore or discount chain. True, larger department stores may have a better selection than the neighborhood pharmacy, but drugstore superstores like Phar-Mor and discount chains like Kmart and Wal-Mart tend to have a similar inventory for a lot less money. You may have to weed through lower-quality fragrances to get to the good stuff, but it's there.

ASK FOR SOME SAMPLES. Department store perfume counters do serve a purpose, however—they're a great source of free "tester" samples. Simply approach the counter and ask for some samples: You may get only a few at a time (and they're good for only one or two applications), but asking for handful might get you more.

SHOP DUTY-FREE. When you're headed out of the country on an expensive vacation, blowing money on expensive perfume isn't exactly foremost in your mind—but maybe it should be. Duty-free shops sell perfume—along with other merchandise—for 15 to 20 percent less than department store prices, and perfume is one of their biggest items. Selection may be limited, but most larger airport shops carry enough inventory to make the stop worthwhile. A tip: Make your purchase when you return so you don't have to haul it around as you travel.

FAKE 'EM OUT WITH A FAKE. For even greater savings, avoid expensive brand-name perfumes and buy designer duplicates instead. These fragrances smell like the real thing (at least to most people) but cost up to 75 percent less. You'll find designer duplicates at fragrance counters at most drugstore and discount chains, or if you know what you want, you can order them directly from Essential Products in New York City at (212) 344-4288.

BUY THE BIGGER BOTTLE. You can usually save between 20 and 40 percent by buying a bigger bottle, since the per-ounce cost tends to decrease as the size increases. The department store price of a 100-milliliter bottle of CK One, for example, is $35, but you can get twice as much—200 milliliters—for only $15 more.

GET INTO OUTLETS. A handful of perfume designers operate their own outlets. Calvin Klein has a number of stores in New Jersey, New

THE BEST FOR LESS: JOY

It may be Joy on your skin, but it's certainly no joy to your finances: An ounce of this hot perfume costs over $200, making it the most expensive mass-market perfume. And according to its fans, it's also the best.

Joy may be hard to find at a discount: Discount houses often don't carry it, and it's not a popular choice in some duty-free airport shops. But New York Cosmetics and Fragrances in San Francisco does sell Joy—for about 10 percent less than retail. Call (415) 543-3880.

York, Maryland and Michigan that sell its fragrances and fashions for at least 10 percent below retail. Ralph Lauren has about 60 outlets across the nation and sells fragrances for about 20 to 30 percent below retail. Liz Claiborne also sells her fragrances at 65 outlets across the country.

There are also several national chains that sell fragrances from various manufacturers for up to 70 percent below retail prices. For the best selection, check out Perfumania, which has stores in 33 states. For a location near you, call 1-800-3-FRAGRANCE.

PETS AND PET SUPPLIES

With at least one pet in more than half of all households, it seems as though Man's Best Friend has certainly found a loyal and generous pal in us. First there are the pets themselves: The cost of a typical dog or cat purchased from a breeder is anywhere from $200 to $700, while top show-quality critters can set you back as much as some cars. Even a pound-found pet can cost about $100.

And then there's the care and feeding of your four-legged friend: Americans spend an estimated $15 billion each year on pet-care supplies, collars, toys and other accessories—nearly $9 billion annually on food alone. Veterinary care adds another $13 billion to the yearly tab: an average of $132 for each dog, $80 per cat and $35 per bird.

All told, pet ownership is our country's top leisure expense, costing about $800 a year per family. But here's how you can trim the bill without sending your pet's care to the dogs.

GETTING NEW PETS

TRY A BREED RESCUE INSTEAD OF A BREEDER. Other than getting a freebie, going to the local animal pound or humane shelter will provide the best deals—dogs and cats usually can be adopted for between $30 and $100, which includes some shots and spaying or neutering. But if you have your heart set on a particular breed—and a specific purebred may be hard to find at the local pound—then save some of the $200 or more a breeder will charge by adopting your pet from a breed rescue league. These volunteer groups operate like traditional shelters, except they specialize in particular breeds. The greyhound breed rescue, for example, takes dogs that are retired from racing (at one or two years old). Or when a litter of purebred Irish setter pups is abandoned in a parking lot, the local pound may turn it over to the setter rescue league.

GET A MUTT AND SAVE A LOT

They may lack the paperwork of their purebred counterparts, but mixed breeds make up for it by saving you a different kind of paper—the green kind you keep in your wallet. Besides the initial low cost of getting a mixed breed at the local pound, which can be as little as $30 (shots included), mutts tend to be healthier than purebreds, and as a result, cheaper to own.

That's because overbreeding and inbreeding have resulted in some breeds' being more prone to health problems, including hip dysplasia (German shepherds), bone disease (Labradors), vision-threatening eye problems (bulldogs, Yorkshire terriers, collies and others) and breathing problems (Persian cats). Over the past few years, unscrupulous breeders, pet stores and puppy and kitten mills have been investigated and closed down for churning out unhealthy—though "pedigreed"—animals without regard to the animals' health or welfare.

"The very same thing that makes a particular breed so attractive may be what causes problems," says Janet Hornreich of the Companion Animals Section of the Humane Society of the United States in Washington, D.C. "We often receive calls from unsuspecting pet owners who purchased their pets from greedy breeders who were only interested in making money, and now these heartbroken pet owners have very sick animals," she says.

You'll pay more at a breed rescue than at the pound: Puppies and adult dogs cost about $100, including some shots and spaying or neutering (kittens and cats cost less, but feline breed rescues are rarer), but it's still just a fraction of what you'd pay at a breeder. To find out about a rescue league in your area, contact a local shelter or the library of the American Kennel Club chapter that specializes in the breed you want.

TRAIN A DOG FOR THE BLIND. If you want to test the waters of pet ownership, prefer a dog only for the short term or like puppies more than adult dogs, there are ten guide dog schools across the country that provide top-quality dogs to willing families for a year at no charge—even health care is free. The dogs, purebred Labrador and golden retrievers that are to be trained as guide dogs, are sent out to "puppy-walker families" at eight weeks of age. The families keep them until they are 14 months old, training and socializing them, then return them to the agency, where they undergo specialized training before they are given to the blind. In return, the families get a great dog—albeit for only a year.

This program isn't for everyone; it can be tough to return the dogs at 14 months, and some agencies require that families attend monthly meetings. But it's a great way to get an excellently bred dog worth up to $600 at no charge (other than food). To find out more about this program, call the Guide Dog Foundation for the Blind in Smithtown, New York, at 1-800-548-4337 or The Seeing Eye in Morristown, New Jersey, at (201) 539-4425 or contact the nearest social service agency that provides resources for the blind.

SAY YOU WANT "PET QUALITY." If you don't mind paying big bucks to a breeder, you might as well get a premier pooch at a fraction of the cost. To do this, tell the breeder, "I want pet quality, not a show dog." Top breeders tend to sell their blue-blooded dogs in two categories—pet quality and show quality, with the latter costing about three or four times more.

Both have full AKC or affiliated paperwork; both come from champion bloodlines. But unless you're planning to display your pet in dog shows, don't pay for those finely tuned features. You'll get the same dog—minus perfect hindquarters or snout—for about one-fourth the price.

HEALTH CARE

VACCINATE YOUR PET YOURSELF. Among the most expensive costs of pet ownership is that trek to the vet for Fido's or Kitty's vaccinations. A puppy requires up to five shots during its first 18 weeks, and cats require three, with two feline leukemia shots strongly recommended—and veterinarians usually charge $25 or more for each injection. Rabies vaccination must be done by a veterinarian (it is the law in most states, and failure to administer the vaccine correctly can cause serious harm to your animal). But it's relatively simple and inexpensive to give a dog or cat most other vaccines yourself.

A note of caution, however: Check with your vet before you vaccinate your pet. Some vets don't accept home-administered vaccinations and require revaccination before they board, groom or perform surgery on your pet. Some kennels also require proof from a vet that your pet's vaccinations are up to date. If home-administered vaccinations are an option in your area, you can get detailed instructions in the pet supplies catalog from Doctors Foster & Smith in Rhinelander, Wisconsin (1-800-826-7206).

Omaha Vaccine Company in Omaha, Nebraska (1-800-367-4444), a major supplier to kennels, animal shelters and veterinarians, sells single-dose vaccines to the public at a huge discount—about 70 percent less than what a vet charges. A seven-in-one shot, for instance, which should be given once a year and protects dogs against most major canine diseases, costs only $2 to $4 plus shipping and handling; syringes cost less than a quarter. The Doctors Foster & Smith catalog also sells a complete line of vaccines for dogs and cats at similar discounts and provides a complete vaccination timetable.

OR GO TO A CLINIC. Don't want to administer the shots yourself? Then take your pet to a clinic like those run by Pet Vaccine Services, based in Sarasota, Florida. You'll pay $1 or $2 above cost for veterinarian-administered vaccines, but that's still 65 percent less than having your own vet do it. To learn about such clinics in your area, contact your local humane society or call Pet Vaccine Services at 1-800-336-4228.

DO THE ROUTINE STUFF YOURSELF. You'll pay a vet up to $20 to clip your pet's nails, which should be done every six weeks for "inside" dogs and every month for housebound cats. You can do the job yourself in 15 minutes with a pair of $8 clippers. Ask your vet to show you how to clip your pet's nails and which clippers to use. Be sure to keep the clippers sharp and don't cut the nail too short—you could cut the quick, the blood supply that runs through the middle of the nail, which can hurt your pet and cause bleeding. You can easily avoid the reddish quick if your pet has white nails, but it's harder with dark nails, so trim only the curved tip.

In fact, there are several "maintenance" checks you can provide for your pet to cut your veterinarian bill. Although susceptibility varies from breed to breed—and your vet is the best judge of your animal's individual needs—all dogs and cats are prone to dental problems, particularly gum disease, which can cost hundreds to treat. But you can avoid most of these problems by brushing your pet's teeth once a week. You can use a sprinkle of baking soda on a moistened gauze pad or washcloth or the special toothpastes and brushes available at your vet's office or in pet stores, but be sure not to use human toothpaste.

Even a five-minute body scan every now and then can help you notice unusual bumps, lumps and other changes at their earliest stage, when they're easiest and cheapest to treat.

FOOD AND SUPPLIES

CAN THE MEAT. Consider that a 13-ounce can of dog food can cost over 50 cents and that cat food costs about 30 cents for a 5.5- to 6-ounce can. Premium brands in those cute little cans cost even more per ounce. And then consider this—your pet doesn't really need canned food if he is getting a good-quality dry food, and meat should make up only a very small percentage of his diet.

GREAT MAIL-ORDER BUYS

Save as much as 40 percent off regular pet store prices and those in other catalogs by ordering your pet supply needs through Cherrybrook, located near Washington, New Jersey. This mail-order company, which began in 1969 to service the dog show trade (and also supplies your cat's needs), carries everything from catnip to crates. Shipping and handling costs are between $2.75 and $4.25 but are free for orders over $75. Cherrybrook offers all major brands and ships orders within 24 hours of receiving them. To get a catalog, call 1-800-524-0820; New Jersey residents should call (908) 689-7979.

Another big money-saver is R.C. Steele. Its prices are comparable to Cherrybrook's, but you must order at least $50 in merchandise, and shipping charges are 10 to 15 percent of the amount of your order. Call 1-800-872-3773 for a catalog or directions to its Brockport, New York, warehouse, which offers the same great prices—with no shipping and handling costs.

If you still want to feed your pet some meat, however, an occasional treat of canned food or even a little cooked, skinned, boneless chicken won't break the bank.

DO THE MATH. Check the serving size. Some premium foods are more digestible than the cheaper brands, so you can feed less of them. One premium brand suggests feeding a medium dog up to 3¼ cups, while the cheaper supermarket brand suggests up to 6 cups. But you'll need to do the math to figure if more servings per bag will make up for the difference in cost between the two.

FEED YOUR PET FEED STORE FARE. If you use commercial pet food, you'll usually save about 20 percent compared to supermarket or pet store prices by buying top brands at large discount stores like Kmart and Wal-Mart; you can save even more at warehouse clubs like Sam's Club and B.J.'s Wholesale Club. But for even greater savings, do what farmers do—head for the nearest commercial feed store. Even in urban areas, stores like Agway sell a full range of pet food, from brands like Science Diet to its own brands like Big Red and Buster, at prices anywhere from 30 to 65 percent below regular pet store prices.

BUY BIG TO SAVE BIG—ON ALL YOUR PET NEEDS. It's no surprise that buying the bigger bag can save you money. Ounce for ounce, you'll generally pay anywhere from 10 to 15 percent less for a 50-pound bag of dry critter chow than for a smaller bag of the same brand. But did you know that if you buy the really big bag, you can slash that much off your total pet supply bill? Petco stores, for instance, offer discounts of 10 percent or more on everything you buy when you buy 200 pounds or more of dry cat or dog food. While that may seem like a lot, the average medium-size dog eats well over 200 pounds a year, so you'll reap the food savings and get a discount on your other pet supplies.

If dry food isn't your pet's preference, you can still buy in bulk and save at warehouse clubs like Sam's Club. Alpo dog food costs about 30 cents a can there when purchased by the case—about half the cost of buying on a per-can basis at the local supermarket. You'll get similar savings on cat food, too.

TRAINING

CALL CITY HALL. Many communities offer dog-training classes through their parks and recreation departments. The cost is usually one-third to one-half the cost of using a private or semiprivate trainer—and the classes are often given by the same people who command big bucks for private lessons.

RENT A VIDEO. Many public libraries have a wide selection of videos—including tapes on how to train your pet—that are available free to anyone with a library card. There are some advantages to getting these tapes from the library as opposed to taking a class. With just you and your pet, there are no other animals to distract Fido from his studies, and using a video lets your pet learn at his own pace. Besides, the videos are free.

Photography Equipment

They say a picture is worth a thousand words. They also say that talk is cheap (especially overused clichés). So where does that leave photography equipment? Unfortunately, it's hard to tell: From $10 disposable cameras to $75,000 electronic digital systems that do just about everything but say "cheese," there's a wide range of prices for getting those priceless snapshots.

Common sense says that the best way to save is to resist the gimmicks and buy the best camera that fits your needs. And that's become easier for the amateur shutterbug, since advances in technology and stiff competition have made point-and-shoot cameras even cheaper than the manual focus jobs that used to be the industry standard. But no matter what type of photo equipment you're buying, here's how to get it for less.

Do your homework. Your inability to understand "camera-ese" can cost you plenty come checkout time. But you don't have to stay in the dark. There are several guidebooks on the market that list prices for both new and used photography equipment, such as *McBroom's Camera Bluebook*. It's available from Amherst Media, 155 Rano Street, Suite 300, Buffalo, NY 14207.

The Price Guide to Antique and Classic Cameras by Joan McKeown lists price ranges and includes black-and-white photos of many cameras. Just prior to the publication of a new edition, you can order the current edition of the book for 20 percent off the cover price from Centennial Photo, c/o Pre-Pub Club, 11595 State Road 70, Grantsburg, WI 54840. To learn when a new edition is expected, write to Centennial Photo and get on its mailing list. These books may also be available at your local library, or ask at a local camera shop.

Consider a camera swap meet. One of the best ways to save big on a good used camera is to attend a camera swap meet in your area. Free from the costs of advertising and monthly rent, dealers, professional photographers, hobbyists and bargain-hunters get together to buy

GREAT MAIL-ORDER BUYS

There's no shortage of mail-order houses that offer deals far below the suggested retail price of photo equipment, but unlike the others, B&H Photo/Video in New York City doesn't charge extra for accessories that the manufacturer meant to be included in the package—like a lens cap, straps and batteries.

It also offers some of the lowest prices you'll find for everything from cameras for amateur shutterbugs to professional lighting equipment. B&H offers technical support and a 14-day, money-back guarantee as long as the equipment is returned in the original packaging. Shipping and handling costs start at $7 for the first three pounds, plus 60 cents for each additional pound. Call 1-800-947-9970 for more information.

each other's gear—usually for prices at least 25 percent below what retailers charge. While you might not be able to get a warranty at such a confab, most sellers provide their business card in case there's a problem. *Shutterbug* magazine often lists dates and locations of upcoming swap meets, or you can contact your local camera club. For more information about *Shutterbug* magazine, call (407) 268-5010 or write 5211 South Washington Avenue, Titusville, FL 32780.

CLICK WITH A USED CAMERA SHOP. Because well-kept cameras seem to last forever, some camera shop owners are able to make a living just by selling preowned equipment. Some of the biggest names in the used camera business, like KEH Camera Brokers in Atlanta and Brooklyn Camera Exchange in Rockville Centre, New York, even send out catalogs listing their best buys. Many offer a money-back guarantee. How much can you save? One recent purchase netted a used lens that sells for $900 new for only $600. Contact KEH at (404) 892-5522 for a free 70-page catalog. You can also get a catalog from A&I Camera Classics by calling 1-800-807-2813; the $2 cost of the catalog can be applied to the cost of your first order.

BUY BY MAIL. The lowest prices on new mid- and upper-end cameras, film, flash units and other photo equipment are offered by mail-order companies. They keep their prices 30 to 50 percent below retail by shaving their profit margin to a scant 5 percent. Most mail-order companies are very competitive with each other, but they will negotiate if you've called around and can quote a lower price.

Your best bet: Buy magazines like *Popular Photography* and *Shutterbug* to check the ads in each issue. The *New York Times* also has advertisements for these stores in its Sunday edition, since many are based in the Big Apple. But don't expect a lot of advice about finding the best camera or long answers to your technical questions.

Ask if the camera has a U.S. warranty; some don't, and you're stuck without one. And don't let someone tell you that an international warranty is just as good—it's only valid if you've bought the camera outside the United States. Other concerns: postage and handling charges and returns. Some mail-order houses charge a 15 percent return fee or won't accept returns at all. Also ask if there's an extra fee for credit card orders—if there is, buy elsewhere. And steer clear of expensive extended warranties; they're not worth the money.

OR SHOP AT AN "EVERYTHING" STORE. If you're not the shop-by-mail type or are looking for a more basic camera, such as the smaller point-and-shoot Canon Sure Shot model, you'll do better at a large discounter like Kmart or Service Merchandise than at a camera shop. These buy-by-volume retailers sometimes offer the same range of savings you'll get at mail-order houses—especially during the busy camera-buying season before and after Christmas, when there are sales nearly every week. You won't get the expertise you'll find at a camera shop, but you will save 30 percent or more.

BYPASS THE EXTRAS. Beware of deals promising accessories at "no additional charge." Usually, these extras are things like a strap and a lens cap, which add only a few bucks to your purchase if purchased separately but add significantly more to the cost of the package.

You should be on your guard when buying camera equipment by the piece, however. Lenses, bodies and even flashes made by different manufacturers aren't always interchangeable. Because even low-cost, fast-focusing cameras have precise technology, most experts recommend buying the same brand lens and body together; besides, you'll save about 10 to 20 percent—especially by mail order. The bottom line: If you do buy by the piece—which can also help you save sometimes—make sure the parts are compatible first.

BUY THE GRAY WAY. Gray-market cameras are brought into the United States by unofficial importers, not the manufacturer's official designee. They're completely legal importers, and their wares tend to be cheaper. However, your actual savings depend largely on the ex-

THE BEST FOR LESS: OLYMPUS INFINITY STYLUS

The Nikon F series has long been the choice of most professional photographers, and with good reason: These cameras are extremely rugged and relatively easy to use, and their sophisticated metering system ensures top-quality photos. While older models in the F series cost a lot less, a new top-of-the-line Nikon has a suggested retail price of over $2,000 for the body alone (lenses cost extra) and is out of the range of many nonprofessionals. Even a used one sells for $1,500 in good condition.

Enter the Olympus Infinity Stylus. Many professional photographers use this compact, automatic 35mm camera for those situations when there isn't time to dig in the camera bag or change lenses. In fact, many pros say that the Stylus, with its optical glass lens and four-mode flash, takes pictures that are just as good as those taken with more complex cameras that cost far more. With a list price of $235, it's within the price range of just about anyone. But you can find it for under $200 at some camera shops and stores like Best Buy. Also look for the Infinity Stylus Zoom, which has a 35mm to 70mm zoom lens. It's weatherproof—resisting rain, dust and mud—and it's affordable.

change rate between the dollar and the yen—the more favorable the exchange rate, the more you save.

One caveat: With some but not all gray-market cameras, the warranty for repair and replacement won't be honored. Also, check before you leave the store that the instructions are in English. Larger camera stores and mail-order companies sell gray-market cameras but don't always tell customers. By asking for them by name, you can usually knock 10 percent or more off your best deal.

MAKE AN AUCTION APPEARANCE. Although they're not for the faint of heart, insiders say you can find great buys on photography equipment at auctions. Be sure to take your guidebooks, and carefully inspect anything you're interested in before bidding. Shake a camera to make sure it doesn't rattle (a sure sign something is broken), look through the viewfinder, try the shutter and check the winder.

Picture Frames

An inside joke you may hear at the local frame shop: The picture is worth a thousand words and costs only a few bucks. The frame for it is worth few words but costs . . .

Well, it may not be completely accurate, but you get the general idea—especially if you've been shopping for picture frames. Four pieces of wood or metal, a sheet of glass and some sturdy backing can add up to $100 or more when they're sold together to frame a standard-size poster. While framing will never be cheap, here's how to make it cost less.

Do it yourself. Recently, more frame shops are allowing you to do your own framing—you put together pieces that are custom-cut for your work. Even an all-thumbs art lover can complete an average-size poster in about 20 minutes, all under the watchful eye of a trained professional framer.

Compared to having the store do custom framing, you'll save anywhere from 25 to 40 percent for this do-it-yourself job, depending on the size of your artwork. Usually, bigger posters result in bigger savings.

Great Mail-Order Buys

For near-wholesale prices on a complete line of preassembled, ready-made and sectional frames in metal and wood, contact Graphik Dimensions, a mail-order house based in High Point, North Carolina. Call 1-800-221-0262 for a catalog.

THE BEST FOR LESS: FAST FRAMES

Framing may never be cheap, but it can be less expensive at Fast Frames, which operates 150 stores nationwide. Besides a one-day turnaround on custom framing, it also offers a number of money-saving incentives, including gift certificates, coupons and membership in its Fast Frame Privilege Club, which is good for a 10 percent discount every time you order a frame. Because of its buying power, Fast Frames is able to buy its inventory in huge volume, so even without the savings incentives, expect to pay at least 15 percent less than you would at smaller Mom-and-Pop frame shops.

BUY IN FEBRUARY. There are no official seasonal sales in the framing business. Instead, individual shops tend to discount their merchandise as they deem necessary. Right after Christmas you're likely to find framing discounts of between 20 and 30 percent in some stores.

But one of the best sales is courtesy of Deck the Walls, one of the largest artwork and framing chains in the country, with 200 stores nationally. During the entire month of February, it offers a half-price sale on all framing accessories—matting board, glass and everything else but the frame itself.

TEST YOUR METAL. Most frame shop offerings come down to two options—wood or metal. Both come in a wide variety of designs and colors, but dollar for dollar, you tend to get more for your money with metal.

First be aware that frame shops determine price not by the size of the artwork but by the amount of material needed to make the frame. So the wider the frame, the more material is needed—and because wood frames are usually wider, they can cost twice as much as metal frames. But it doesn't end there. Because of the way metal fames are cut, there's less waste. With a wood frame, as much as one foot of material can end up in the scrap heap. And remember:

Whether it's a custom or do-it-yourself framing job, you are charged for materials on a per-foot basis.

PASS ON PLEXIGLAS. If you buy at a frame shop, chances are the salesclerk will try to sell you Plexiglas, which doesn't shatter like glass. Unfortunately, Plexiglas costs nearly twice as much as regular glass and tends to scratch easily, and some types can make the picture look distorted. So unless you're planning to drop your artwork frequently, save your money and opt for regular glass. For pieces that will be displayed under a light, pay the extra money for nonglare glass; otherwise regular glass is fine for most pieces.

But insiders do advise spending the few extra bucks for conservation matting. A regular mat is made of acidic wood pulp, and acid can eventually leach through to your art or memento. Conservation mats won't leach acid.

HEAD TO KMART—OR A YUPPIE FURNITURE STORE. Actually, you can get some of the best deals on framing by avoiding frame shops altogether. Discount stores like Kmart and Wal-Mart offer a good selection of smaller frames (up to 11 by 14 inches) for as little as $5 each. And for larger frames, head to furniture stores like Ikea or Pier 1 Imports. These havens for the yup-and-coming have an incredible selection of poster frames for a fraction of what you'd pay in a frame shop.

Plants and Trees

They help purify the air by removing carbon dioxide. They lower heating and air-conditioning costs by up to 30 percent. They can even increase your property values: Studies show that for every dollar spent on landscaping, you'll recover $2 when it's time to sell your home.

No doubt about it, plants and trees have lots to offer. Unfortunately, it can take plenty of green to get plenty of green. Retail markups vary depending on the size, type and availability of the foliage, but it's not uncommon for nurserymen to make four times their cost on the sale of plants or trees. Here's how to keep a little more money the next time you go shopping.

Shop in the fall. Popular wisdom suggests that you do your planting either in the spring before it gets too hot or in the fall before it gets too cold. Unfortunately, most folks opt for the spring—and they pay dearly for it.

Spring fever aside, you'll save between 25 and 60 percent by shopping for plants and trees from September through early November, as nurseries prepare to close for the winter. Besides getting some great deals, you'll be doing your new plants and trees a favor. Many experts believe fall is actually a better planting time, since foliage is just going into its dormant period and the shock of replanting (or transplanting) won't be as great.

Buy in bulk. The unwritten rule of shopping for plants and trees is, the more you buy, the better deal you should get. Nurseries need to move their inventory quickly, and customers who buy in bulk are valued—and rewarded for it.

Experts advise that you ask for a 30 percent discount on each tree after you buy the first two at regular price or request one free tree for each three you buy. Seek a 10 to 15 percent discount on each plant after paying full price for the first two.

Head to a mart. While you'll probably want to buy trees at a nurs-

THE BEST FOR LESS: RED MAPLE TREES

They offer beautiful color and great shade, grow quickly and are the most underrated trees in the nursery: A potted three- to four-year-old red maple tree might cost you about $30, and it already has enough branches to look attractive. By contrast, other trees of the same age and size—a live oak, for instance—will have no branches yet, or only a few. Yet they can cost twice as much and take more than a decade longer to fully mature.

ery, you can save up to 25 percent off retail prices by buying flowers and other small plants at discount chains like Kmart and Wal-Mart. These larger discounters buy annuals, perennials and small shrubs from the same nurseries that supply plant shops and other retail stores, but because they buy in such large volume, the marts are able to get their inventory at a much lower price—and pass some of their savings on to you.

Since plants come in different grades, sometimes the savings result from buying an inferior grade—but that is true at nurseries as well as the marts. No matter what the grade, though, don't expect a minimum-wage salesclerk to have the expertise in caring for plants that you'll find among the salespeople at a nursery. If you want to save by buying flowers at a discount chain, try to get them directly off the truck, which is usually parked in front of the outdoor display, since new deliveries are brought in every few days during planting season.

OR INVESTIGATE WHOLESALE NURSERIES. Once open only to greenhouse owners, developers and other professionals, more wholesalers are now opening their gates to the general public, offering typical discounts of between 25 and 45 percent below retail prices for most purchases and up to 75 percent below retail for complete landscaping jobs.

You may have to shop around for a wholesale nursery that sells to the public, since some still deal only with pros, but the local agriculture extension agent may have a list of wholesale nurseries in your area. Or check the yellow pages under "Wholesale Nurseries."

CHECK THE ROOTS, NOT THE LEAVES. Since most plants sold in retail stores are "imported" from nurseries, they can go into shock once they arrive at the store—resulting in falling, drooping or discolored leaves. An untrained salesclerk may write the plant off and offer huge discounts to move it out—anywhere from 25 to 75 percent.

But plants with yellow or brown leaves (or falling or drooping ones) can be restored as long as the root system is healthy. To determine that, remove the plant from its container and look for roots that are a light cream color—not brown or black—and free of wrapping or "girdling." If the plant hasn't been discounted for looking unhealthy, ask for a price break: Many salespeople are anxious to move them out.

BUY SMALL TO SAVE BIG. Trees over ten feet tall tend to carry a tall price tag—usually over $100. But get a tree half that size and it will cost you only 25 to 30 percent as much. While most people would prefer a mature tree (or one that's close to it), if you opt for smaller trees—especially fast-growing types like pines, weeping willows, sycamores and tulip poplars—you'll cut your spending by at least 65 percent. Besides, it will take only a few years for the trees to double or triple in size.

CALL CITY HALL. Assuming you live within city limits, you might want to call city hall before going shopping for trees. Many municipalities have beautification programs that pay for the trees and for planting them along sidewalks and other common-use areas. These programs are usually more common in the spring and fall; you can learn more about them from the city manager or municipal forester.

Plumbing Supplies

Four out of every ten toilets, sinks and faucets are installed, replaced or repaired by do-it-yourselfers. That means a lot of muttered expletives, but it also means a lot of plumbing supplies purchased by the average homeowner.

And with good reason: Besides the fact that plumbers charge an average of $35 per hour, the once-complicated business of buying everything from new toilets and faucets to pipes and valves is now easier—and cheaper—as a result of the do-it-yourself craze that started in the 1980s. Here's how to get plumbing supplies for less.

Shop the big home centers. Not too long ago, about the only reasonable number on a plumber's bill was the charge for supplies: Most plumbers received a professional discount, and some (but definitely not all) passed these savings on to the customer. But these days even a novice handyman can do the job better—at least financially—when it comes to buying supplies.

Although the typical retail markup is between 33 and 40 percent, depending on the item, insiders say that most plumbing supplies are considered "loss-leaders" at larger home centers like Home Depot and Builders Square—they are sold for less than cost in an attempt to get people into the store. That's why you occasionally see some plumbing supplies for as much as 50 percent below the regular price—and why so many plumbers now shop these giant home centers.

But even the everyday cost is usually similar to (if not less than) the typical professional discount that plumbers get from smaller suppliers—usually about 20 percent below suggested retail prices.

Or head for a wholesaler. If there's no home center chain near you, reach for the yellow pages and look up "Plumbing Supplies—Wholesale." Because of the stiff pricing competition from the large home center chains, small plumbing supply wholesalers that once catered only to professional tradesmen have begun selling to the public, usu-

THE BEST FOR LESS: MOEN (FAUCETS) AND ELJER (FIXTURES)

With scores of high-quality faucets on the market, everyone has a different opinion on which is the best. However, ask plumbers and you'll hear one name repeated again and again: Moen.

While it's true that Moen makes some "budget" faucets that will probably not last more than a few years, its midrange line is a tremendous value, with most models retailing for about $85. You can spend three times that amount on fancier models, but the extra money goes for bells and whistles most folks don't need in their quest for water.

To spend less, check out the advertisements and in-store circulars at home centers like Builders Square and Home Depot. Moen and other faucets are featured in these circulars fairly regularly—once every month or so—for anywhere from 10 to 40 percent off regular retail prices.

For toilets, sinks and bathtubs, American Standard and Kohler are . . . well, the American standards. But insiders whisper another name: Eljer. This line may not be as widely available as others—you may have to go to a specialty shop—but plumbers say it offers top-notch quality and supreme value.

To save up to 50 percent off showroom prices—which start at about $90 for a toilet and can run as high as $600—find a showroom that's changing displays, which is usually done once every two years. The display models are usually sold at great discounts and come with complete warranties, if you're savvy enough to negotiate. Keep in mind that dealers get a 50 percent discount on their cost from the manufacturer when they agree to display the fixtures.

ally for about 20 percent less than you'd pay in a hardware store. A bonus: The wholesaler can offer better product and parts selection, and the sales staff has technical know-how.

DON'T BE A TRENDSETTER. Once there's a hot new color in toilets, sinks and bathtubs, retailers are anxious to get rid of bathroom fixtures in the "old" colors. If you're willing to stick with the pinks, greens and powder blues of yesterday, you can save as much as 75 percent compared to what you'd pay for the same item in a new, bolder color. You'll probably find these older items on display, but it pays to ask: Sometimes they're kept in the storeroom.

CHECK OUT A SALVAGE YARD. Though not as common as the more traditional auto junkyards, some salvage yards now carry bathroom fixtures (and other household items) that were discarded because of a remodeling project. Often these items are in fine working order but wind up in salvage yards because of landfill restrictions and a poor resale market for bathroom fixtures. Selection may be spotty, but prices are just a fraction of regular retail: Sinks, toilets and bathtubs can be purchased for as little as $5 each.

It's best to call local salvage yards and junk dealers before you head out there, since bathroom fixtures are hit-or-miss items. Or contact local remodelers to find out where these leftovers are taken.

Pottery and Ceramics

They say you can't put a price on art, but if you've been shopping for pottery or ceramics lately, you might beg to differ. While basic clay gardening pots start at about 30 cents, more decorative pieces can cost several hundred dollars.

It's hard to gauge exactly how much Americans spend on ceramics and pottery, since so many of these pieces are made and sold by private craftsmen and artists. Industry officials say they don't keep tabs on retail markups, but we found some local pottery galleries charging twice their wholesale cost—a 100 percent retail markup. Add hand-paintings, elaborate designs and other special touches and the cost skyrockets even more. But whatever your tastes or needs for pottery and ceramics, here's how to buy them for less.

Buy by the case. The traditional terra cotta flower pot, unadorned with paint or applique, is hard to beat for appearance—and price. But you can save even more when purchasing these mass-produced gardening staples by asking for a "case break." If you buy an entire case—usually 8 to 12 pots—you can get a discount of 10 to 20 percent off the cost of buying them individually. For even better savings (and even larger orders), you may be able to get wholesale prices by ordering direct from a wholesale florist or regional growers' supply firm.

Go to an art school. Art schools frequently hold exhibits, often in the spring, that provide good opportunities to find one-of-a-kind pottery and ceramics at reasonable prices. The students tend to price modestly, since they haven't yet made a reputation for themselves, and they are also more inclined to discount their work for the asking. Insiders say that offering 10 to 25 percent less than the asking price is not insulting, especially if the art show is nearing a close and the work hasn't been sold. The same is true for local art shows: Even better-established artists are more willing to give a price break during the closing hours.

Look for scratches and nicks. Pottery and ceramic pieces can be

GREAT MAIL-ORDER BUYS

Hummel figurines are never cheap—they're usually at least $100—but they can be 10 to 15 percent less expensive when you order them through Worldwide Collectibles & Gifts in Berwyn, Peensylvania,, which sells a wide selection of decorative ceramics and other gifts.

Worldwide also offers glass and porcelain statues and other fine gifts. The company has a 30-day money-back guarantee on all its products and offers next-day shipping. Call 1-800-266-1664 to order a catalog.

very fragile, and they sometimes get nicked, scratched or otherwise damaged during transportation. Although it's not widely advertised, some pottery shops will discount their flawed pieces by as much as 50 percent. Expect smaller discounts for harder-to-notice imperfections, though.

SPRING INTO LATE SUMMER SAVINGS. Although "art" ceramics usually don't have a sale season, pottery purchased for gardening does. As the growing season winds down, usually in late July or August, so does the level of business at garden centers. Along with plants, pottery and ceramics for planting tend to be discounted about 20 percent. Wait until November and the prices decrease another 10 percent or so, since many garden centers close for the winter.

VISIT A VOLUME BUYER. The cheapest prices on the basics in pottery for home or garden can be found at a volume dealer—whether it's a home center like Builders Square, a discount chain like Kmart or a furniture specialty shop like Ikea. Because they buy so much, these stores are able to get their inventory of pottery and ceramics for less than the corner florist, Mom-and-Pop garden center or art gallery; their goods also tend to be mass-produced.

While the selection may not be as unique as what you'll find at a specialty shop, prices tend to be up to 15 percent less than at smaller shops selling similar goods.

Power Tools

Even if the only tool you can master is the TV remote, you probably realize that power tools offer the most productive bang for the buck. The ability to punch a hole through a board or cut a stud down to size in minimal time—and with minimal frustration—is usually worth the extra investment in power hand tools.

Not surprisingly, do-it-yourselfers make up a large part of the market for power tools. One manufacturer's survey indicates that nearly half of all Americans do some type of do-it-yourself work, and one reason is that economy-conscious homeowners want to save the 60 percent of repair and renovation costs that would go toward labor if they hired a contractor. And running a power tool is no great strain on your electric bill—a full hour of continuous use (and few people use power tools continuously) consumes less than 4 cents' worth of power.

Electric drills are the most frequently purchased type of power tool and are in 90 percent of American households. Circular saws are second, in 75 percent of homes, while jigsaws and electric sanders have a place in about half of all households. But whatever you buy, here's how to save.

Go to a home center. Forget those flyers and advertised specials at the local Mom-and-Pop hardware store. For the best deals—week after week—head to large home centers like Home Depot and Builders Square.

Because of their large buying power and close relationship with major manufacturers, these superstores are able to sell most power tools for up to 40 percent below the retail prices at smaller operations. Even these home centers play off each other: Home Depot, for instance, offers to beat any competitor's price; if not, you get an additional 10 percent off.

Another advantage: While smaller stores may not display their power tools, home centers often place them so you're able to handle

THE BEST FOR LESS: PORTER-CABLE

Porter-Cable is one of the oldest names in the American portable power tool industry—and for good reason. The secret to its success is sticking to its established market: professional woodworkers. All Porter-Cable tools are top-notch and come with a factory-backed, 30-day, performance-certified guarantee, which allows the buyer to try out the product for balance, feel and operation. If not satisfactory, it can be returned to the dealer within the return period for a full refund.

Porter-Cable manufactures a complete line of portable power tools, and often you can find the best price deals through mail order, but if you want service and instructions, which are the hallmarks of Porter-Cable, go to a local distributor, hardware store or home center. Its Model 693 plunge router is among the best buys in anyone's book: Its list price is $320, but call the Porter-Cable folks at 1-800-487-8665 for the names of dealers or mail-order houses where you can get it for less (as low as $174).

them—and grip, weight and balance are important considerations before you buy.

BE A MAY-DECEMBER BUYER. Whether at the local hardware store or a larger home center, there are two times each year that provide the best opportunities to buy power tools—the weeks before Father's Day, starting around Memorial Day weekend, and the two weeks before Christmas. During these times, regular prices are lowered as much as 30 percent, since tools are still the most often purchased gift items for men.

SEEK A PROFESSIONAL DISCOUNT. Professional craftsmen—and in some cases those who pretend to be—can buy tools at some retail stores for up to 20 percent below the regular price, including items that are already marked down. At some chains, you may be required to show proof that you're a pro, such as a union card, but other stores simply sell their wares to those who look the part.

So before heading to the power tool aisle, wander over to the contractors' booth—usually near the exit at large home centers—and price those wares. If you don't have to prove you're in the business, you may get the same tools at the contractors' table for less than they sell for on the tool aisle. But be warned: It's best to look like a pro, so shop in jeans and work boots and even wear a tool belt if you own one.

GET SOME R&R. When something goes wrong with power tools, they're usually sent to a manufacturer's-affiliated repair shop, where they are refurbished or reconditioned. Some of these tools eventually are sold at prices up to half off the price of a similar new tool. Look for these repair shops in the yellow pages under "Tools" or contact the manufacturer for a list of authorized service centers in your area.

SHOP AT HOME. If you can't go to a home center, go to a newsstand—and pick up a copy of magazines like *American Woodworker* or *Fine Homebuilding*. Besides running frequent tool reviews, these magazines are loaded with ads for mail-order houses that typically sell power tools for 40 to 50 percent below the suggested retail price.

GREAT MAIL-ORDER BUYS

With the exception of occasional special sales in stores, mail-order companies offer the deepest discounts on power tools of any single source. Price breaks of 50 percent from list are not uncommon, and unless you live in the state from which you order the tool, you can avoid state sales tax as well.

While your best bet is to check out woodworking and do-it-yourself magazines, some of the best mail-order buys are from Whole Earth Tool & Supply in Berkeley, California (1-800-829-6300), Tools on Sale, the catalog division of Seven Corners Hardware of St. Paul, Minnesota (1-800-328-0457) and Tool Crib of the North in Grand Forks, North Dakota (1-800-358-3096).

Many mail-order tool companies ship tools by UPS ground for free or a nominal fee, depending on the cost of the total order. For between $9 and $13 more, you can have your purchase delivered by Federal Express two-day service.

Many of these tools have the same warranties as tools purchased in home centers and other retail stores.

DON'T HORSEPOWER AROUND. They don't call them "power" tools for nothing, and few things can be as confusing as electrical terms. As a rule, horsepower figures alone can be misleading because of the way in which the ratings can be misused. Some manufacturers claim "rated" rather than delivered horsepower, which implies a bench test that may or may not have much to do with reality.

A more accurate measure of whether or not you're getting the most tool for your money is the motor's actual amperage draw, which is printed on the data tag on its housing. By using this number—it'll be somewhere between 1.2 and 16 amps, depending on the tool—as a point of comparison between similar tools, you can gauge the machine's ability to do meaningful work. Generally, drills and jigsaws should be at least 3 amps, while table saws and circular saws should have at least 15 amps.

Likewise, depending on what job the tool does, other technical factors come into play. Revolutions per minute (RPM) are important to a drill's function, the number of teeth per inch (TPI) is a measure of a saw's cutting characteristics, and the total surface feet per minute (SFM) is critical to the performance of a belt sander. The higher those numbers, the better the tool.

BEWARE OF BARGAINS. The power tool market is deliberately stratified to target the needs of a variety of customers—hobbyists, carpenters, do-it-yourselfers and serious woodworkers. But even if you need to use a tool only occasionally, you're usually better off spending a little more to get quality. Low-end drills that sell for under $30 may sound like a bargain, but they probably won't last more than a year or two. By going to the middle range, you'll spend only about 25 percent more, but you'll get a tool that will probably last longer and perform better.

Industry insiders say that besides price, you can spot an inferior tool by giving it a good examination. Look for cracks, dents or other imperfections on the casing or rough surfaces and corners. And always stick with well-known brands.

PRODUCE

Medical research shows that it pays to eat plenty of fruits and vegetables. And we're buying it.

Americans spend about $6 billion a year on produce—up 13 percent over the last decade. How much you spend depends on several factors that are out of your control—consumer demand, weather conditions during the growing season, even the amount of labor needed to cultivate crops. But here are some things you can do to eat more fresh produce without forking over so much green.

PASS ON PICTURE-PERFECT PRODUCE. Many produce marketers, especially those who promote their inventory as gifts, pride themselves on the perfection of their product. But you can save as much as 20 percent if you buy produce that offers superior quality on the inside but has slight superficial imperfections—pears, for example, that aren't exactly pear-shaped or apples that aren't the same shade of red all over. Many fruit merchants and mail-order companies are willing to negotiate a lower price for this special inventory on a case-by-case basis. Some even offer a line of products that are slightly imperfect.

GET IT STRAIGHT FROM THE GROWER. Those roadside and farmers market fruit and vegetable stands have lower overhead than commercial growers, and as a result, they tend to sell their wares for 10 to 20 percent less than the same produce at the supermarket. Keep in mind, however, that some farmers market stands aren't actually run by bona fide farmers but by retailers who get their inventory from commercial growers.

A giveaway: If the items have a stamp or are wrapped in cellophane, it's a good bet that they were purchased from a big grower rather than grown on the family farm—and they may not be the bargain you expect.

BE A LATECOMER. If you like the better-quality produce usually offered at a large farmers market—like those in most big cities—you'll

GREAT MAIL-ORDER BUYS

Orange Blossom Groves in Seminole, Florida, is a grower and shipper of top-quality, seedless, Florida-grown navel, Valencia and Temple oranges; pink seedless grapefruit; honey tangerines; and honeybelles (a cross between tangerines and grapefruit). If you sign up for its Taste of Florida Sunshine program before October 15, you'll get a 5 percent discount off its already competitive prices. Prices depend on where you'd like your fruit shipped, but generally ¼ bushel (12 to 16 pieces) of your choice of fruit is about $20 (plus shipping and handling), while ½ bushel (24 to 32 pieces) costs about $23. For an Orange Blossom catalog, call 1-800-237-9880.

And for California-grown artichokes that are generally up to 10 percent less than supermarket prices, Giant Artichoke in Castroville offers fresh artichokes in five different sizes—extra-small, small, mediium, medium-large and large—as well as marinated artichoke hearts. Call (408) 633-2778 for more information.

get the best price break if you arrive in the closing hours. Most of these markets are open a few days a week; by going in the closing hours of the last day, you'll find vendors anxious to unload their wares before they go bad.

Discounts of up to 50 percent are not uncommon during the closing hour or two, especially on fresh fruits like bananas, pears and strawberries. But even goods with longer shelf-life—like apples, onions and potatoes—are usually discounted up to 30 percent so vendors don't have to take these leftovers back home or to a warehouse.

SEEK OUT PEAK-SEASON BARGAINS. Don't be tempted by colorful, beginning-of-the-season supermarket produce ads. To get the best savings (which vary per individual fruit and vegetable), buy in the middle of the season, when produce tends to be the most abundant.

Strawberries, for example, are in season from April through July but tend to be discounted up to 25 percent toward the end of May, when inventory is at its peak. Look for similar discounts on oranges and grapefruit in January, while asparagus and cherries tend to be cheapest in June. For lemons, melons, nectarines and tomatoes, July is the month to buy, and for corn and peaches, it's August.

For broccoli, plums, grapes and green peppers, September is when you'll find the best prices, while October is prime time for pumpkin, cauliflower and brussels sprouts. And November and December are the peak months for apples, pears, sweet potatoes, winter squash and cranberries.

FORAGE FOR THE "FIELD RUN." Many produce outlets offer what's called field run—fresh-from-the-field fruits and vegetables that are displayed in bins and sold by the bag instead of hand-packed in boxes. In general, this more casual packaging results in savings of anywhere from 10 to 50 percent compared to boxed produce.

Larger farm stands and specialty produce outlets, especially those affiliated with a farm or orchard, usually have field runs. So do some mail-order houses, like The Fruit Tree in Hood River, Oregon (1-800-827-6189).

JOIN A FOOD CO-OP. As with other foods, you can save at least 20 percent off your produce bill by joining community-based co-op operations, which typically feature an extensive selection of fruits and vegetables. Co-ops operate like retail supermarkets except that their members contribute a one-time joining fee and/or pledge a certain amount of time working as employees—usually one hour per month. In exchange, they get discounts on produce and other foods.

To locate a food co-op near you, send a stamped, business-size envelope to Co-op Directory Services, 919 21st Avenue S, Minneapolis, MN 55404. To order the National Green Pages, a yearly directory that lists hundreds of socially and environmentally responsible businesses, including dozens of food co-ops nationwide, send $6.95 (which includes shipping) to Co-op America, 1612 K Street NW, Suite 600, Washington, DC 20006. And for $4, Co-op America will send you a copy of the *Co-op America Quarterly*, which includes information on how to start a food co-op in your neighborhood.

GET YOUR FRIENDS TOGETHER. Most produce distributors who regularly sell fruits and vegetables to food co-ops, supermarkets and restaurants will also sell to consumers at wholesale prices. One caveat: You'll need to buy in bulk, as in a 40-pound box of apples or a 24-head box of lettuce.

The answer: Form a buying club—a group of family members, friends, neighbors and/or co-workers who buy together and share

THE BEST FOR LESS: HARRY AND DAVID

This Medford, Oregon, mail-order company is known for its photogenic, gift-quality fruits. But for those who are willing to endure an occasional blotch or bump on their peaches, pears or apples, Harry and David offers a less-than-perfect line called Maverick. And the price? While a five-pound box of Ongold peaches costs $22.95, you can get five pounds of Maverick peaches for $19.95 (and ten pounds for just $35.95). To obtain a catalog, call 1-800-547-3033.

the cost. To locate a wholesale produce distributor near you, check the yellow pages under "Produce Distributors" or consult the National Green Pages. You can save up to 50 percent by buying in bulk, especially if you call produce distributors about one month before the height of the season and arrange to buy from the farmers themselves. To find out which are the best buying seasons in your area, contact your local agricultural extension agent.

Quilts and Comforters

Dressing up the bedroom can be dramatic—in cost as well as looks. Markups on quilts and comforters are often *twice* the manufacturing cost. And with retail prices of some top-quality quilts reaching four figures, it's easy to see how Americans spend over $1 billion each year on comforters and nearly half that amount on quilts.

Of course, this is an area where it pays to spend. While you can get quilts and comforters at the nearest discount store, a higher price often means better quality: higher thread counts, solid stitching, cotton fabrics and superior down—factors that translate into a longer-lasting product. But no matter what your price range, here's how to avoid paying full price.

Go to a show. The best bargain in quilts isn't at a retail store, it's at any of the dozens of quilt "trade" shows across the country. At these shows you can buy a genuine antique quilt top for as little as $75—and then add the batting and backing yourself or hire someone to do

Quality Check

A quality down comforter costs several hundred dollars, while a synthetic quilt or bedspread is much less. But it's money well spent in the long run, since down can last a generation with proper care.

Most experts agree that goose down is superior to duck down because it's larger, loftier and stronger. But when buying, don't go for a comforter that's too thick, because it may be too warm to use except on the coldest winter nights.

OUTSTANDING OUTLETS

There's no shortage of outlets that sell quilts and comforters at below-retail prices, but many agree that among the best are WestPoint Pepperell Bed, Bath & Linens factory outlets. Savings range from 40 to 70 percent off retail on brand names like Martex, Utica, Lady Pepperell and Stevens, and there are over two dozen outlets in 18 states—from Latham, New York (518-782-0085) to Las Vegas (702-361-5542). While there's no toll-free number to call to find the one nearest you, WestPoint Pepperell stores tend to be in bigger outlets.

it for you. Ordinarily you couldn't touch a beautiful piece of quality Americana like that for less than $700 or $800.

If you're even more ambitious, for about $50 you'll also find packs of precut fabric blocks ready for sewing. And if you're not the least ambitious but feel lucky, nearly every show has an inexpensive raffle featuring a quilt as the grand prize.

The monthly *Quilter's Newsletter* features a list of shows by location and month. For more information, write *The Quilter's Newsletter*, c/o Leman Publications, P.O. Box 4101, Golden, CO 80402 or call (303) 278-1010.

CUT OUT THE MIDDLEMAN. You can also save by going directly to a manufacturer's outlet or retail specialty store (look under "Bedding and Accessories" in the yellow pages). That's because these places tend to buy directly from the manufacturer, meaning a savings of 20 to 30 percent compared to department store prices. You're also in a better position to bargain at specialty stores, which can knock another 5 or 10 percent off the price. While department stores will offer some price breaks, they're often on inferior quilts that are mass-produced in China.

DON'T DEPEND ON JANUARY. If you go the department store route, you may assume that you'll get the best deals on quilts and comforters in January, the traditional time for white sales. January is a good time to save 20 to 50 percent off the original price, but fierce competition in the bedding industry has prompted department stores such as Macy's and Mervyn's to offer sales of some kind almost monthly.

In fact, the best time to buy may not be in January but in early November, before the Christmas shopping season starts. The savings are about the same as in January, but the selection tends to be better. Also watch for big markdowns in June and July, as cold-weather bedding is cleared out. And since bedding sales are often tied to major holidays, look for advertised discounts around Presidents' Day and Memorial Day.

GO MAIL ORDER. Quilt and comforter outlets are common, but there's no need to travel to get a good deal. Various mail-order houses offer the same savings—usually 30 to 60 percent below retail, and even more on selected items. But do your homework: While they are inexpensive, imported quilts don't use up-to-date fabrics and have loose weaves that experts have nicknamed toe-catchers (because they're likely to lasso your toes). For more information, call Alden Comfort Mills in Plano, Texas (1-800-822-5336), The Company Store in La Crosse, Wisconsin (1-800-323-8000) and Domestications in Hanover, Pennsylvania (1-800-782-7722).

READ ALL ABOUT IT. For those who like their quilts as artwork rather than bedspreads, Quilts Unlimited, based in Virginia, offers a

THE BEST FOR LESS: CUSTOM QUILTS

Visit a fancy decorator and you may be able to have a quilt made to your color and fabric specifications for $500 or more.

If you'd like to save hundreds on a quilt of comparable quality, however, contact one of the dozens of quilt-makers who advertise in *The Quilter's Newsletter*. After you let them know the color and fabric you want (you can send a swatch in the mail if you like), the artisans start sewing. Your completed quilt is often only $300.

For a free copy of *The Quilter's Newsletter*, write Leman Publications, P.O. Box 4101, Golden, CO 80402 or call (303) 278-1010.

monthly subscription to its 16-page catalog, which includes photos of several featured quilts. Prices are up to 30 percent less than antique dealers charge, and customers are often more serious quilt collectors. To learn more about its offerings, call Quilts Unlimited at (804) 253-8700.

DO IT YOURSELF. If you're handy with a needle and thread, you can make your own quilts for just a fraction of what you would pay retail. Although there are several supply houses, those in the know say that Hancock's in Paducah, Kentucky, offers the best mail-order prices—from 20 to 50 percent below retail—on everything you need for do-it-yourself quilting. For less than $100, you can get all the materials you need—quality fabric included—to make a queen-size quilt. To get a catalog, call 1-800-845-8723.

If you lack quilt-making experience, experts recommend picking up a guidebook like *Patchwork Quilts Made Easy* by Jean Wells. With plenty of easy-to-follow directions and illustrations, you can learn how to make quilts of all sizes. Call 1-800-848-4735 to order a copy. Need sewing lessons? For a beginner's class in your area, see the yellow pages under "Sewing." Up to three lessons shouldn't cost much more than $30. All you'll need to add is your time: It should take roughly six hours a week for six to eight months to make a full-size bed quilt.

Radar Detectors

It seems Smokey isn't the only one out for money from lead-footed drivers. Radar detectors, those gizmos that let you know when police officers are using radar equipment to catch speeders, are a $350-million-a-year business. Of the nearly 180 million cars on the road, as many as 15 million are equipped with one of these devilish little devices, and motorists are buying them at the rate of nearly 2 million each year.

The retail markup on detectors can top 35 percent, bringing the price of some models to about $400. But here's how you can race ahead of those high prices and save when buying one.

Shop with your TV. Unlike many other retail items, radar detectors aren't part of seasonal sales—even though some retailers claim they're discounted in the spring and after Christmas. (These so-called sales are frequently more lip service than reality.)

So don't count on your local electronics store for a good deal. But you can get new radar detectors for as much as 25 percent less by buying through television home shopping networks. These networks

Great Mail-Order Buys

Although it tends to feature only one model per issue (if any), the catalog from Damark International, based in Minneapolis, offers great deals on radar detectors—usually about $190 for models that retail for about 30 percent more. Shipping is usually free. To order a copy of the catalog, call 1-800-729-9000.

WHAT YOU NEED TO KNOW

Radar—an acronym for Radio Detecting and Ranging—was adapted from military uses to help nail speeders in the 1950s. But drivers didn't like being defenseless, prompting the invention of radar detectors that would beep, bleep, chirp and squawk when they sensed a radar ray. Lawmen fought back by shifting the radar beam to different frequencies.

And so it continues. Although more sophisticated lasers and other methods of catching speeders are now being used, most police departments still use one or more of the three radar bands—called X, K and Ka. Most departments don't use all three, but knowing what they do use can help you decide which radar detector will be most effective.

For that information, call R.A.D.A.R. (513-667-5472), a Florida-based industry association that can reveal which bands local law enforcement agencies use. If they employ only the basic X and K bands, for instance, a less expensive detector may be all you need to avoid speeding tickets. Of course, this is all academic if you live in Virginia or the District of Columbia, where radar detectors are illegal.

buy huge volumes of detectors from the manufacturers, so they're able to sell them for less than a retailer. True, radar detectors are not the type of item that's available each time you turn on the TV, but they are sold frequently enough to keep you from channel surfing. If you're not a video hound, call the Home Shopping Network in Florida at 1-800-284-3900 for information on its next electronics show, when you might find radar detectors.

BUY DIRECT FROM THE FACTORY. Some manufacturers sell their wares directly to consumers, and some have distributing outlets with prices 15 to 20 percent below what you would find in a store. Among those worth a call are B.E.L.-Tronics in Covington, Georgia (1-800-341-1401), Cobra Electronics in Chicago (1-800-262-7222), The Escort Store in Cincinnati (1-800-433-3487), Radar & Electronics America in Bensenville, Illinois (1-800-723-2788) and Valentine Research in Cincinnati (1-800-331-3030).

GET SOME R&R. For even greater savings, ask these manufacturers if they're selling what are called R&R models—reconditioned and remanufactured. Since radar detectors are so sophisticated, little things often go wrong with them that necessitate sending them back to the factory for an overhaul. The companies refurbish these units and sell them directly back to retailers and, in some cases, consumers. But it's worth a few toll-free calls to check on availability, since you can buy an R&R from the factory for as much as 40 percent less than a new item would cost you through retailers. Plus, most R&R detectors come with the same one-year warranty you'd get from traditional retail stores.

CALL FOR A QUOTE. If you know what you want but aren't sure that you're getting the best deal from a retailer, try to improve your savings by calling the LVT Price Quote Hotline in Commack, New York. This company carries about 4,000 different appliances and other items, including four different brands of radar detectors. Savings vary depending on the model, but LVT usually beats retailers by at least 10 percent. Call (516) 234-8884 for your quote, and have the model number and other information handy when you call. And LVT doesn't accept credit cards; you must pay by postal money order or cashier's check.

School Supplies

Maybe we're just too fatigued from a long, long summer of kvetching kids to comparison-shop. Or maybe we're too busy jumping for joy around Labor Day to belabor the price of school supplies. But do the math (hey, why should the kids be the only ones?) and you'll learn that those 50-cent boxes of pencils and $6 lunch boxes add up pretty quickly.

The mere basics—pencils, pens, crayons, notebooks, highlighters and erasers—could easily cost $35 per child, plus $6 for that lunch box and about $20 for a backpack to carry the stuff. With school enrollment topping 50 million kids in 1995, Americans easily spent nearly $2 billion on school supplies. And with a projected school enrollment of about 55 million in 2000, it's a safe bet that figure will grow. But here's how you can whittle down the cost of school supplies.

Buy in August. Just before the start of the school year, retailers tend to drop their prices in an effort to move merchandise. So wherever you shop, buying in the four weeks before the post–Labor Day rush can net you savings of between 25 and 50 percent compared to the rest of the year.

Don't assume bigger is better. The newer office superstores like OfficeMax and Staples seem like logical places to buy school supplies—they have aisle after aisle of everything needed for the classroom and promise "unbeatable" prices. But do your own cost comparisons and you'll learn that you'll pay up to 50 percent more for certain items than you would at Wal-Mart.

On any given day, Wal-Mart has the best prices on a wide variety of school supplies—even beating its own Sam's Club and other warehouse clubs. The prices can be so low that some items sell for half of what they go for at discount drugstore chains like Drug Emporium and other places where school supplies are usually purchased. And while Wal-Mart may not have the selection offered at an

THE BEST FOR LESS: DIXON TICONDEROGA

The best pencils are manufactured by Dixon Ticonderoga. They're made of cedar and contain a high-quality core to ensure that they move smoothly over the paper and sharpen slowly and evenly in an electric pencil sharpener. The best-known model is their classic, the Ticonderoga, but the company makes an alternative, the Oriole, for the budget-minded that sells for 25 percent less. (In one spot check, 72 Ticonderogas were priced at $8.99, while the same quantity of Orioles was just $3.99.) Look for Orioles at Wal-Mart, Staples and other stores where pencils are sold.

office superstore, most parents will find everything their kids need in the one or two school-supply aisles.

SHOP GREEN TO SAVE GREEN. When it's time to buy pencils—the most needed item for school-age children—reach for a less expensive new breed of pencils. Sanford Corporation's Ecowriters, which are widely available where school supplies are sold, are made of recycled cardboard and newspaper fiber instead of the more traditional cedar, and always-improving manufacturing techniques mean they move across the paper nearly as well as the best-quality cedar pencils and aren't likely to be eaten by an electric pencil sharpener.

STAY WITH THE CLASSICS. Fashion pencils and designer notebooks may catch your children's eye, but their real effect is on your wallet. The trendy appeal has no bearing on their quality, and the extra cost—which can be six times that of their more modest counterparts—pays for additional processing, artistic services and royalty fees.

PUT THE EXTRA MONEY WHERE IT COUNTS. There is one item for which it pays to spend a little more: a backpack. Though backpacks retail for anywhere from $20 to $60, a well-made one can last for years, while those cheaper plastic models likely won't survive the school year.

Just make sure that whatever you buy, its pockets are large

enough to hold a lot of books (when shopping, it pays to carry three or four books to the store to test it out), the shoulder straps are adjustable and padded, and it's made of tough vinyl or other waterproof material. A leather bottom is a nice feature—especially if your kids tend to fling their backpacks on the floor or schoolyard.

For the best deals on top-quality backpacks, save 30 to 40 percent off retail by going to any of the 45 Eddie Bauer outlet stores around the country. Call 1-800-426-8020 for the location nearest you. Or try any of the 6 L.L. Bean outlet stores in Maine, New Hampshire and Delaware, where standard savings are in the 30 to 50 percent range. Call 1-800-341-4341 for more information.

Sewing Supplies and Craft Items

In nine of ten American households, someone is sewing, doing needlepoint, turning wood, making a quilt or practicing another craft or hobby. All told, we spend nearly $10 billion each year buying the tools of these trades—a 30 percent increase from just a few years ago. Here's how to get them for less.

Link into chains. Those smaller Mom-and-Pop stores may be where you're used to shopping, but the real deals are at national and regional specialty chains. Because they can buy directly from manufacturers, often overseas, stores like Frank's Nursery & Crafts can undersell traditional smaller retailers—usually by 20 percent or more.

Act like a pro. Although only 16 percent of crafters ever sell their wares—most make things for themselves or for gifts—it might benefit you to join that elite group. Even if you don't actually sell anything, if you buy a lot of craft items you might qualify for discounts by

Outstanding Outlets

The Interior Alternative in Newark, Delaware (302-454-3232), sells a wide variety of year-old seconds of Schumacher and Waverly home decorating fabrics for as much as 60 percent off retail prices. There's also the Washougal Mill Store in Washougal, Washington, which sells seconds of Pendleton wools and other goods at about 35 percent below typical prices. Call (360) 835-1118 for more information.

ing an at-home business. Specialty-ribbon maker MPR Associates, located in Highpoint, North Carolina (910-861-6343), for instance, offers a 25 percent discount to crafters who have a tax identification number, available from your state's Division of Taxation. Some other companies also offer discounts for woodworkers, potters and other crafters.

These business startup costs are minimal: A tax ID or business license can be had for under $50 in many states; a box of business cards costs about $15.

GLIDE INTO GUILDS. Some craft guilds arrange for their members to get discounts from national retailers, while the guilds' local chapters can also get discounts from local merchants—usually in the 20 percent range. Two guilds that can get their members bargains include the American Sewing Guild in Medford, Oregon (503-772-4059), and the National Quilting Association in Ellicott, Maryland (410-461-5733). The guilds can give you more information about their requirements for membership and discounts.

BUY IN BULK. The more you buy, the more you save. Muslin that sells for $2.49 a yard costs as little as 99 cents a yard if you buy it on a bolt—50 yards. (Discounts are also available for other craft materials.)

GREAT MAIL-ORDER BUYS

The Buffalo Batt and Felt Company in Depew, New York, offers its high-quality fiber-fill stuffing, quilt batt and pillow inserts for as much as 40 percent below retail on bulk orders. Call (716) 683-4100 for a catalog. The Earth Guild in Asheville, North Carolina (1-800-327-8448) sells everything from basket tools to spinning wheels and weaving supplies; it also has yarns and dyes. Discounts depend on the size of your order.

And sewers should note that the Mill End Store in Milwaukee offers better-quality dress goods and notions purchased as closeouts or end lots from designer back rooms. While discounts vary, one recent offering was a Ralph Lauren fabric that sold at retail for about $50 per yard for only $14.99. There's no catalog, but call (503) 786-1234 for more mail-order information.

BETTER DEALS ON SEWING MACHINES

Sewing machines are a mainstay of home crafting. The best machines—Bernina, Pfaff, Elena and top-of-the-line Viking (which offers the widest variety of stitching options)—start at about $1,500.

But there's a way to get these top-notch machines in your home for a lot less money: Simply offer a lower price, as you would when buying a car. Some of these machines can be purchased for up to 35 percent below the list price—especially if they've been used as demos. And many high-end dealers are willing to bargain with prospective buyers, especially in large cities where there's a lot of competition.

So after you've shopped around and know what you want, pick a dealer and ask for the list price of the model you want. Then make an offer 40 percent below that price. Don't be afraid to go too low; the markup on these machines is very high, and you can always raise your offer.

Resell what you don't need to friends or a local craft organization.

BE A LATECOMER. The best deals at craft and hobby shows and traveling sewing expos are available at the last minute—just before exhibitors are ready to pack up. They'll usually sell their goods at a better-than-average discount rather than haul them home. This is especially true of machinery, such as sewing machines, which has been used intensively for several days and can no longer qualify as new. Some advice: If you see something you like, make a low-ball offer. The exhibitor will likely counter and expect to strike a deal in the neighborhood of 20 to 30 percent off.

SEEK OUT "FIRST-QUALITY" SECONDS. When textile manufacturers make a mistake in their products, it can be either glaring or hardly noticeable. The glaring errors rarely make it to retail stores, but the problems in other seconds are so unnoticeable—the wrong background hue or tiny imperfections that can't be seen unless you examine the fabric closely—that the materials can be sold. By asking the salesclerk for the reject bolts, you could save 50 percent.

SILVERWARE

Consider yourself lucky: In Victorian times, all proper families had *two* sets of sterling silver knives, forks and spoons—one setting for luncheon and a heavier one for dinner. And they didn't bring it out only on special occasions—they used it every day, at every meal.

Maybe the Victorians were on to something. Silver is a soft, pure metal that doesn't react well with the acids in food, which is why the Victorians also had servants to polish it. But it has one major advantage over the common tableware we modern folk use—it retains its value extremely well.

Don't let its beauty or utility fool you: Silver cutlery is a solid investment, one that can be passed on for many generations. Follow these simple tips and you'll save up to 70 percent on your initial investment, making a wise buy even better.

BUY THE BEST—SECONDHAND. With one phone call, you can find huge savings on the finest American and imported silverware. Just dial one of the nation's large secondhand tableware dealers. These dealers field small armies of buyers to scour the world's estate sales and major auction houses. They verify the silver's worth and do all the cleaning. They can even provide single pieces to replace some you might have lost from an old set.

Consider these savings: A four-piece sterling Chantilly place setting by Gorham is $225 in most department stores, and discount suppliers sell it for $129. Buy it used and you'll pay about $99.

Many say the best places to buy used sterling silverware are Beverly Bremer Silver Shop in Atlanta and Replacements of Greensboro, North Carolina. Both companies guarantee satisfaction.

You can also buy secondhand goods closer to home—at estate sales and auctions and even from upscale caterers—but no matter where you shop, check for existing monograms or old monograms that have been erased; either will lower the resale value. And if you

POP THE QUESTION

Before you commit to a set of silverware—wherever you buy it—you'll need the answer to one important question: "Does the manufacturer make discontinued patterns available?"

Most of the larger silversmiths do. Oneida, the world's largest tableware manufacturer, keeps discontinued upper-end silverplate and sterling patterns in inventory for two years. But many smaller companies don't, and you may end up having to track down your missing teaspoon through expensive replacement services—or invite one less guest to your dinner parties.

doubt the authenticity or quality of the silver you want, take it to a reputable silver appraiser before you buy.

HIT THE OUTLETS. Factory outlets offer direct-from-the-manufacturer savings of anywhere from 20 to 70 percent off retail prices. You won't even have to sacrifice selection or convenience, since outlets are kept well-stocked by manufacturers who have caught on to their popularity—and profitability.

Once upon a time you had to drive far and wide to find silverware outlets. Reading and Lancaster, Pennsylvania, Barstow, California, and Orlando, Florida, have long been popular outlet cities, known for their good deals on silverware (and other items), and the tableware capital is still in and around Lawrenceville, a tiny town in central New Jersey. With the factory outlet industry booming, however, silverware outlets are springing up closer and closer to major cities. To find one near you, check the yellow pages under "Silverware" or call the manufacturer directly.

The downside: Many manufacturers are using outlets simply as alternate retail stores, and sometimes prices at department store sales can be cheaper. To get the most for your money, know the typical cost before trekking to outlets.

ORDER BY PHONE. There are many mail-order houses that offer fine silverware, as well as flatware, for up to 65 percent less than department store prices. Most even allow you to open a bridal registry over the phone and will gladly send catalogs to help you make your selections.

OUTSTANDING OUTLETS

In addition to offering great catalog prices, Ross-Simons operates three outlets—in Las Vegas, Kittery, Maine, and Warwick, Rhode Island. You'll find catalog surplus and discontinued silverware, china, crystal and giftware from its Ross-Simons and Gift and Home Collection catalogs. Prices are from 20 to 70 percent below regular catalog prices. Call 1-800-556-7376 for more information on these outlets.

These companies buy directly from leading silverware manufacturers such as Gorham, Kirk Stieff, Lunt, Towle and Reed & Barton. Along with silverware, they offer china, crystal and giftware. Among the best dealers are Albert S. Smyth Company in Timonium, Maryland (1-800-638-3333), Barrons in Novi, Michigan (1-800-538-6340), the China Cabinet in Tenafly, New Jersey (1-800-545-5353), Corson's Glasshouse in Hingham, Massachusetts (1-800-533-0084), Geary's in Beverly Hills (1-800-243-2797), Michael C. Fina in New York City (1-800-288-3462), Michael Round Fine China & Crystal in Lorton, Virginia (1-800-752-6622), Midas China & Silver in Chantilly, Virginia (1-800-368-3153), Nat Schwartz & Company in Bayonne, New Jersey (1-800-526-1440), Ross-Simons in Cranston, Rhode Island (1-800-556-7376) and Thurber's in Richmond, Virginia (1-800-848-7237). Prices vary slightly from dealer to dealer, but they are competitive. Expect your order within one to two weeks—longer if an item is out of stock.

SHOP RETAIL IN MAY AND NOVEMBER. These two months are the best times to buy silverware in department stores, as retailers cut prices up to 40 percent—in May to excite summer wedding shoppers and in November to spark the holiday gift-giving rush.

BUY FOR EIGHT. The more place settings you buy in the same pattern, the less you'll spend. Item for item, costs drop about 20 percent when you buy service for eight compared to four or six.

COLLECT ECLECTIC. If you have an artistic eye and an independent bent, consider assembling nonmatching place settings. After all, there's no law against placing a Baroque-style fork beside a plain-handled spoon. Taste, balance and creativity are what matters—not just uniformity.

Put your collection together piece by piece by haunting estate sales, secondhand shops and other cheap sources. You'll need plenty of patience and silver polish, but the reward is a one-of-a-kind table setting in which every piece tells a story and the whole reflects your unique taste and style—for a fraction of retail.

SKI EQUIPMENT

Skiing just may be the priciest sport around. There's the cost of getting to and up the mountain, lift tickets, accommodations and various après-ski indulgences. And then there's the big budget-cruncher—the hundreds spent for skis, boots, clothing, poles and bindings. All together, even budget equipment can cost over $400, while top-of-the-line stuff retails for over $1,000. Still, more than ten million Americans manage to go skiing at least once a year. If you're among them, here's how to do it for less.

GET CARDED. Several ski associations offer membership cards that give discounts on everything for your ski trip—transportation, accommodations, dining, lift tickets and yes, even the purchase or rental of equipment. The cost of these cards is anywhere from $15 to $60 for a one-year membership, and they include savings of as much as 40 percent off regular prices. In many cases, these programs benefit various U.S. ski teams and ski programs for children and the disabled.

Even these cards can be purchased for less than their regular retail price—if you buy them during the off-season, which is from March to October in most areas of the country. For more information on these cards, contact the World Ski Association at 1-800-525-SNOW (their cheapest card is $15 a year), Ski Card International (1-800-333-2SKI), U.S. Ski Team Passport (1-800-SKI-TEAM) or the U.S. Recreational Ski Association (1-800-318-7772 outside of southern California; 714-634-1050 in southern California).

SPRING INTO BUYING. You can save up to 50 percent on most new ski equipment if you buy it during the spring and summer, when the only things that go downhill are the prices of the previous year's inventory. Spring closeouts give way to autumn preseason clearance sales, when costs could fall even more as shops get desperate to unload their unsold, usually older-model skis.

PACKAGE YOUR SAVINGS. Whenever you shop, buy your skis, boots, poles and bindings at the same time—and insist on a package price. You'll save about 25 percent compared to buying the same items individually.

SEEK OUT THE OLD MODELS. Skis and other equipment change from year to year, but usually the only real difference is a new paint job. That difference in color can save you 15 percent, so all things considered, ask to see last year's models when shopping for new ski equipment.

If you don't mind used stuff, head to a ski rental business—preferably one that's near a ski resort but not associated with it (they tend to be more expensive). After their equipment has been used for a couple of years, most rental shops sell off their inventory to make room for new stuff. Prices vary, but you can usually outfit yourself for anywhere from 35 to 70 percent below retail.

TAKE IN A SHOW. Ski and travel shows are held in most big cities from September through November to showcase ski resorts and brand-new products. These shows are also a great place to find a bargain on first-quality closeouts or used equipment. Local ski shops often sell their previous year's inventory at discounts of up to 80 percent, and ski clubs organize ski swaps. The Los Angeles Council of Ski Clubs runs the biggest, at the annual Los Angeles Ski Dazzle. You'll also walk away with free samples of everything from ski wax to hand warmers. Admission averages about $7, but nobody pays that, since you can find discount admission coupons in the newspaper's calendar listings or sports section.

For information on the Anaheim and Los Angeles Ski Dazzle events, call (714) 252-1412, and for Boston's Ski and Travel Show, call (617) 890-3234. The number for information about the Chicago ski show is (312) 622-4905, and it's 1-800-831-EXPO for the Dallas and Houston event. There's also one in Minneapolis; call (612) 943-2002.

Small Appliances

The price tags on small appliances—blenders, bread makers, toasters and the like—aren't always so small. While you can buy some for under $20 at mass-merchandise stores, other models cost several hundred dollars at department stores and specialty shops.

All told, Americans spend some big money on small appliances: over $103 million each year on blenders, $584 million on bread makers, $447 million on coffee makers and $235 million on toasters. Whatever the item, markups tend to be between 25 and 33 percent. Frills such as stainless steel, automatic on/off switches, programmable timers and designer colors can boost the cost and markup even

Outstanding Outlets

Amid the clothing and shoe stores at outlet malls, you'll often find one store where you don't have to try on the merchandise: Black & Decker. There are over 30 Black & Decker outlets around the country that carry some of the same toasters, coffee makers and other small appliances you'll find in retail stores—at savings of anywhere from 20 to 70 percent off retail prices.

While some question the durability of their power tools, Black & Decker makes fine small appliances that can stand up to the toughest use. Some items at the outlets are discontinued models, but they carry the same warranties as other new purchases. For information on a Black & Decker outlet near you, call 1-800-231-9786.

GREAT MAIL-ORDER BUYS

The best catalog for small appliances may be the Best catalog. The book features 500-plus pages of everything from jewelry to appliances, and it's from the mail-order division of Best showrooms, which number more than 160 around the country.

What makes the catalog so nice is that it's a handy reference for toaster ovens, blenders and other products that you may be thinking of purchasing. What's more, the catalog offers below-retail prices, typically 10 to 20 percent less than department store prices. You can either buy through mail order or visit one of the showrooms (where in-store markdowns can bring prices even lower). For a catalog, call 1-800-950-2378.

more. But here's how to trim costs when buying small appliances.

DELAY UNTIL MAY. Maybe they're not politically correct, but appliance manufacturers and retailers do know their market—women, who either buy the appliances or receive them as gifts.

That's one reason you'll find the best deals on small appliances around Mother's Day. During May, you'll find savings of 20 to 35 percent off regular retail prices on a wide range of small appliances—the first two weeks in an effort to get Mom the gift she "wants," the latter two for the busy wedding season. And while these discounts wane slightly during June and July, early summer is still an excellent time to buy some small appliances like toasters.

Other good times to buy small appliances include the Christmas season and "mall holidays" like Presidents' Day, Memorial Day and Columbus Day. Markdowns won't be as drastic—generally in the 10 to 20 percent range—but you can still pay less than retail.

CHARGE IT. Most department stores offer 10 to 25 percent off all purchases for one day if you open a store account. That means you could swoop in on that deluxe blender or bread-making machine and save—as long as you pay off that credit card bill when it comes. Otherwise, interest payments quickly eat up any savings.

FORGO THE FRILLS. You can buy a basic coffee maker for under $20 or spend over $100 for one that grinds beans and has all kinds of automatic controls and fancy features.

What's the difference? In terms of coffee quality, none at all—and the same goes for toast, blended drinks or homemade bread. In general, you can save up 60 percent or more on most small appliances simply by sticking with the basic unit: a blender that has three or four speeds as opposed to ten or a coffee maker that makes coffee without the fancy add-ons.

BE A SATURDAY SHOPPER. If you want top-of-the-line brands like Oster and Mr. Loaf that you won't find at warehouse clubs, spend your weekends in the housewares department—known as The Cellar—at Macy's stores. These stores have more-than-occasional "Super Saturday" sales, when prices on select small appliances are discounted between 10 and 50 percent. Keep your eye on store circulars for notice of these sales or get a store charge card so you'll get advance notice of sale dates.

CHECK OUT A COMPUTER STORE. You may not expect to find small appliances at a computer store, but some of the larger chains do carry one or two models of coffee makers and other appliances, often for 10 to 25 percent less than department stores. Warehouse clubs like The Price Club and Sam's Club also stock them for less than retail prices. The reason: These stores, while they don't specialize in kitchen products, get great buying opportunities from manufacturers because they deal in such large volumes.

CALL THE REPAIRMAN. Some factory-authorized service centers that repair small appliances also sell them after they've been refurbished, usually at prices up to 50 percent off the cost of buying new. What's more, these stores are more willing to deal than traditional retailers. So check in the yellow pages under "Appliances—Household—Small—Service and Repair."

SOCKS AND STOCKINGS

In the last few years, socks and stockings have made big steps in the fashion industry, gaining a toehold on designers and consumers alike with fancy colors and high-tech fibers. These have pushed the price higher, with a typical retail markup of about 100 percent.

Americans spend more than $5 billion on socks and stockings each year and another $500 million on tights. But the higher prices don't mean you're any less likely to find a run in your stockings or wear out the toe or heel of your socks. Sales offered by manufacturers and retailers are frequent and can offer savings in the 25 to 35 percent range. But whether you want to expand your hosiery wardrobe or just replace it, here's how to do it for less.

PLAY THE SEASONS. Like most fashion accessories, socks and stockings are part of seasonal sales. Wool and other winter-weather socks

GREAT MAIL-ORDER BUYS

If you need to stock up on stockings—or at least socks—two good places to find bargains are the One Hanes Place outlet catalog and National Wholesale Company catalog.

One Hanes Place offers a wide variety of styles, sizes and colors of popular, slightly imperfect hosiery and socks for up to 55 percent off department store prices; call 1-800-522-1151 for a catalog. And National Wholesale sells its own brand of first-quality sheers, shapers and socks at about 35 percent off suggested retail prices. You can get a catalog by calling (704) 249-4202.

THE BEST FOR LESS: DONNA KARAN

Fashion insiders say that one of the most popular—and best—styles of women's hosiery to come along in a long time is Donna Karan's Opaque Satins. You might pay $12 or more per pair in a department store, but at the Donna Karan Company Stores around the country, you can save 25 to 50 percent off retail on the stockings.

They're sold both as individual pairs and in boxes of three at the outlets, and during various times of the year they might be marked down another 25 percent. There are more than two dozen Donna Karan Company Stores in outlets across the country—in California, Colorado, Florida, Hawaii, Indiana, Maine, Massachusetts, Michigan, Missouri, New Hampshire, New Jersey, New Mexico, New York, Ohio, Pennsylvania, South Carolina, Texas, Vermont and Wisconsin.

are discounted as much as 50 percent during post-Christmas sales, while lighter spring- and summer-weight socks and stockings can be had at similar savings during July.

DON'T BUY AT SUPERMARKETS. You'll pay dearly for the convenience of getting hosiery where you buy milk and eggs. Instead look for popular brands of hosiery such as L'eggs at discount stores like Wal-Mart. You can save 50 cents to $1 compared to getting the same pair at the supermarket.

Probably the best places to buy hosiery are off-price stores like Marshalls, Ross Dress for Less and T.J. Maxx. While some of the styles may be last season's, prices tend to be as much as 60 percent off.

BUY A BUNCH. Retailers often cut prices if you buy multiple pairs. Even during a sale, you can typically save an additional 20 percent by buying three or more pairs at a time. You can reap bigger savings by buying athletic socks in special six-packs.

REMEMBER TO BE A CLUB MEMBER. Some department stores have hosiery clubs, offering a free pair of panty hose or stockings for every 12 you buy. Membership in these clubs, like the one offered at JCPenney, is free, and you're entitled to the extra pair even when you buy on sale.

STICK TO THE BASICS. Among the price-boosting innovations in hosiery are materials such as microfibers and other new ways in which the fibers are woven together. They may provide a little more comfort, but they run just as easily. And fancy designs, waistbands and control tops can also add as much as 30 percent to the price. You'll save if you don't let yourself be charmed by the extras.

SPORTING GOODS

If you think those $50 football tickets warrant more Hail Marys than a last-second, end-zone pass, note what it costs to be a weekend warrior. Americans spend $13 billion a year on sporting goods—nearly three times the national budget of Morocco. That's a lot of money for basketballs, footballs, baseballs and other sports equipment, especially when you consider that the typical retail markup is 40 percent. But there are plenty of ways to trim what you pay in order to play.

BE A JOINER—EVEN IF YOU'RE NOT. Even if you're not part of a bona fide league, you can sometimes get the same savings they enjoy. For instance, the local Little League gets a discount for buying its sporting goods in bulk—they sometimes pay as little as a few dollars above wholesale. Generally, the more items ordered, the better the savings. So if you're looking for a couple of boxes of balls or some bats, talk to the director of your local Little League.

The same is true for other sports. In fact, a good place to start when you're in the market for basketballs, volleyballs, footballs, soccer balls, tennis racquets and balls, hockey equipment and other sports equipment is at your local Y or sports youth group. Some agencies restrict this—they buy only for their own programs—but others welcome the extra orders to help get a better deal.

BUY LAST YEAR'S MODEL. Any time you see a company promoting a new line of goods, look for the "displaced" line to drop in price by up to 50 percent or even more. Since features rarely change from year to year on items like baseballs, basketballs and footballs, expect savings to be slight—maybe 10 or 15 percent. But you can really score on items like tennis racquets and other goods that depend on so-called state-of-the-art technology. When Prince introduced a new series of racquets, for instance, the price of the previous year's model plummeted from $250 to $99.

THE BEST FOR LESS: COLUMBIA BOWLING BALLS

Bowlers know that the ball of choice for pros is often Columbia, but its popular White Dot series retails for about $55. You can get Columbia quality, however, by buying its "sister" line of bowling balls: Bonanza.

These balls, which are actually Columbia balls renamed for sale in discount stores like Kmart, sell for anywhere from 20 to 60 percent less than their big-name counterparts. The best time to buy either name is in early September, when league bowling is getting into full gear.

Savings will differ, because it's up to the individual stores to cut the price on discontinued items. But large retailers typically buy these items in bulk at drastic savings, so they're able to sell them at a big discount. You'll know you're buying last year's style because it's the item that's not being fawned over by the salesclerk or featured in a fancy display.

PASS ON THE BIG NAMES. If you're shopping for balls, forget Wilson and Spalding, perhaps the best-known names. You're better off buying Baden and Mikasa, top-quality gear that's become the new choice for high school, college and other amateur athletics.

There's a good reason for this newfound status. Baden and Mikasa cost at least 20 percent less, and many say the quality of their equipment for a wide variety of sports is just as good or even better than that of the better-known brands. These brands are available in most sporting goods stores.

BUY AT AN OUTLET. The biggest name in baseball equipment—Rawlings—operates five outlets across the country that offer top-quality gloves, mitts, balls, bats and uniforms for about 30 percent off regular retail prices. These outlets also sell equipment for golf and other sports, but their prices usually don't beat sale prices at regular retail stores. To find the Rawlings outlet nearest you, call (314) 349-3500.

SHOP SMALL FOR BIGGER SEASON-END SAVINGS. Item for item, you'll usu-

GREAT MAIL-ORDER BUYS

There are various mail-order companies that offer top-quality athletic equipment for as much as 40 percent less than you'd pay for the same items in a sporting goods store. Most of these companies specialize in a particular sport, and you'll find them listed in specialty magazines for that activity, such as *Tennis*.

One of the best mail-order houses for tennis equipment is Holabird Sports in Baltimore, which sells racquets, balls, bags and other equipment for 25 to 40 percent less than even sale prices at retail stores. Holabird carries most major brands and will send you a brochure of its inventory if you call (410) 687-6400.

For volleyball equipment, Spike Nashbar, based in Youngstown, Ohio, sells all types of volleyball equipment at prices 20 percent below retail. Its catalog is available by calling 1-800-SPIKE-IT.

Soccer International in Arlington, Virginia, offers prices up to 30 percent less than retail and carries a wide selection of soccer balls, uniforms, goals and other equipment. Call (703) 524-4333.

And for "bar sports" like billiards and darts, check out Mueller Sporting Goods in Lincoln, Nebraska, which carries a wide selection of hard-to-find equipment and novelties for about 20 percent below retail. Call 1-800-627-8888 for a catalog.

ally pay less at large sporting goods chains like Sports Authority than at privately owned Mom-and-Pop sporting goods shops. But you're in a better position to wheel and deal at these smaller stores—especially after a season ends and these small businessmen need to move their inventory.

Of course, these retailers aren't about to *offer* a discount. But if you're looking for tennis or baseball equipment in the fall or a football after the Super Bowl, you can usually get discounts of between 10 and 20 percent (and sometimes more) by holding firm.

BUY USED. Common sense says that the classified section of the local newspaper will offer great deals. But other places to look for used sporting goods include the bulletin boards of local bowling alleys, ice skating rinks and even playgrounds. Also, you can save up to 70 percent off regular retail prices by looking for quality used items that are still in good shape at Play It Again, Sports, a national chain that sells previously owned sporting goods.

Stationery Items

In our hyper-paced world of faxes, e-mail and portable telephones, you might think of written correspondence as a dying art.

Guess again. From birthday cards to personal letters, more Americans than ever are reaching out and touching someone the old-fashioned way. Americans send an estimated 7½ billion greeting cards a year, at an average price of $1 per card. In the course of a year, the average person receives 30 cards—most of them with birthday wishes. Even social stationery is making a comeback.

Unfortunately, all this activity hasn't done much to lower prices. It doesn't take too many greeting cards to put a dent in your wallet, and a box of good-quality printed stationery with matching envelopes can run you in the neighborhood of $50. But still, there are several ways to save on your stationery and greeting card needs.

Writing Paper

Shop in the winter. Most people know that the best time to buy holiday cards is, unfortunately, immediately after that holiday—such as December 26, when Christmas card prices typically drop 50 percent or more. Less well known, however, is the best time to buy personalized stationery.

During January and February, many retailers tend to offer discounts on engraved and other fine stationery—including high-end brand names. For those who are planning a wedding or other special event, this is the best time to snag 50 percent off the engraving plate (which translates to an overall savings of about 20 percent). Less elaborate stationery is also discounted in the 15 to 30 percent range during these two months, both in retail shops and mail-order catalogs.

Buy more to save more. The more you write, the less you'll pay. By ordering an extra 50 sheets of personalized stationery, you can cut

GREAT MAIL-ORDER BUYS

American Stationery Company in Peru, Indiana, offers some of the best deals on personalized stationery. It's among the oldest stationery printing firms in the United States, and its catalog features a complete line of printed and embossed stationery, invitations, note cards, personal memos, envelopes, postcards and even calligraphy items for about 25 percent below retail. For your free copy of the general catalog, call 1-800-822-2577, or for the wedding catalog, call 1-800-428-0379.

Another good bet is the Write Touch in Indianapolis (1-800-288-6824), which offers printed stationery at prices 25 percent or more below retail. And for more unique styles at lower-than-retail cost, contact Kristin Elliott in Newburyport, Massachusetts, at 1-800-922-1899 (Massachusetts residents call 508-465-1899) or Current in Colorado Springs, Colorado, at 1-800-525-7170.

your per-sheet cost by 25 percent or more. That's because it's more cost-effective for stationery companies to do a lot of printing or engraving at one time. Just be sure you know the quality of the product before ordering to make sure your savings are worth it.

ASK ABOUT THE NEW TECHNOLOGY. Using engraved stationery may be the most elegant way to personalize your letters or notes, but it can also be the most expensive. Luckily, new advances in laser printing and a technique known as thermography—which, like engraving, produces raised lettering—can now provide printed sheets that look just as attractive to the untrained eye as engraved paper for 15 to 30 percent less. So if you're planning a wedding or other occasion that needs the look of engraving, ask your printer about these new printing processes.

But beware: Some printers try to pass off thermography as engraving by calling it engravo-printing or thermograving. It's usually simple to tell the difference: Engraving typically leaves indentation marks on the back of the paper, while paper printed with thermography is raised only on the front.

OUTSTANDING OUTLETS

Warehouse clubs like Sam's Club, B.J.'s Wholesale Club and the Price Club offer some of the best prices on "generic" stationery—anywhere up to 50 percent less than traditional retail outlets. But if you're not a member of a club, you can snag similar savings at a chain of outlets throughout the United States, variously called the Paper Factory, the Paper Outlet, the Paper Chase or Paper Galore, that sell cards, invitations and other paper supplies. Call (414) 738-3600 for the location of an outlet near you.

If you think engraving is worth the extra money, understand that the real cost is for the copper plate that makes the imprint. Once that plate has been produced, all you should be charged for is the paper. Some printers readily offer discounts for future supplies of engraved stationery, but others don't 'fess up to this fact. Be sure your printer doesn't charge you full price if you reorder engraved stationery.

PUT ON YOUR OWN MARK. Another way to reduce the cost of stationery is to order plain sheets of high-quality paper and then add your personal touch by purchasing an embosser for $20 to $30. If you write a lot, this can cut the cost of ordering personalized stationery by about 30 percent. If you're going to emboss the paper yourself, your best bet is to opt for paper with the highest cotton count—100 percent is the finest. You can usually tell quality by the thickness: The heftier the paper, the better it is. By ordering quality paper in bulk, you can reap additional savings.

Another item that identifies high-quality paper is the watermark, which is essentially the stamp of the maker or seller (like Crane's) and can be found anywhere on the paper. It should be visible when you hold the paper up to a light source. If there's no watermark, it's not the real McCoy.

BE A CATALOG WATCHER. Stationery companies sometimes run promotions in some unlikely places to attract new business. The L.L. Bean and Spiegel catalogs, for example, often sell embossed stationery for 20 percent less than you'd pay at a stationery store. That's so manufacturers can reach people who normally don't shop for stationery through traditional venues. Deals from these sources are periodic, but by keeping your eyes peeled, you may unearth a surprising discount.

GREETING CARDS

GO WHERE YOU GET TOOTHPASTE. A greeting card store may not be the best place to buy greeting cards. In fact, larger drugstores like CVS, Phar-Mor and other chains tend to discount their greeting cards more than places like Hallmark. Figure you'll pay anywhere from 10 to 25 percent less for greeting cards at these stores, which can offer such savings because they buy in such large quantities.

Storage Items

Even if you're not among the ever-growing masses who work at home, you probably have to work plenty hard to keep your home clutter-free—or at least not completely overrun by everything from old tax forms to tennis racquets and overwhelmed by closets so messy you'd need a guide to get through them.

Well, you're in good company, since Americans spend about $3 billion each year on storage items—everything from cardboard and plastic containers for stowing gear to closet organizers for arranging their wardrobe. Most storage items have a retail markup of anywhere from 75 to 100 percent. But no matter what you buy, here's how to get it for less.

The Best for Less: Rubbermaid

For home-organizing needs, Rubbermaid makes a complete line of storage items for every purpose. These products are innovative and durable, made of tough plastic that will last indefinitely and serve various needs. And although Rubbermaid goods are available at nearly 100,000 different retail stores across the country, your best bet is to buy them at large discount chains like Kmart and Wal-Mart, where they tend to be as much as 25 percent less during frequent sales.

Look for sales at these stores, as well as at smaller chains like Target Stores, every two months or so.

GREAT MAIL-ORDER BUYS

The catalog from Lillian Vernon in Virginia Beach, Virginia, offers a wide array of home organizers and other storage items—everything from common shoe bags and jewelry trays to the offbeat, including a copper magazine holder that looks like a tote bag and lazy Susan–type holders for jars and plants. But the best savings come with the private-sale catalog, published three times a year. Prices fall as much as 65 percent on a wide assortment of goods. Call 1-800-285-5555 to order a catalog.

Hold Everything, a San Francisco company, publishes its catalog four to five times each year. While the prices aren't great—you'll pay regular prices—its selection is top-notch, offering a wide array of storage items and organizers not available in most stores. To order yours, call 1-800-421-2264.

SPRING INTO ACTION ON CLOSET ORGANIZERS. When the weather turns warmer, do-it-yourselfers start thinking about outdoor projects—gardening, building decks, repairing the roof and so on. So home centers tend to discount their closet organizer kits to move them out and make room for seasonal merchandise. While you'll start to see some price markdowns in late February or early March, prices fall about 20 percent below retail in April or May.

KEEP IT SIMPLE. There are elaborate storage items and then there are simple substitutions that serve that same purpose for as much as 90 percent less. For real savings, bypass the specialty under-the-bed containers for some kitty litter pails; at $2.50 each, they'll hold shoes, art supplies and toys for a fraction of the cost of a "real" storage item. Meanwhile, a pegboard and some hooks will hold all the family's sporting goods just as well as one of those $30 ready-made sports organizers—for less than one-third the price. And for less than $15, a closet-size shoe bag with clear plastic compartments can hold all your winter hats, mittens and other gear—for a lot less than more elaborate containers.

The same is true for traditional storage items: Those cardboard boxes used to store files tend to be twice as much with faux woodgrain finishes as with the more modest plain brown look. And personal organizers with little extras like calculators cost at least 15 percent more than identical items without them.

BUY THE OFF-BRANDS. Buy a Rubbermaid storage item and you'll pay 10 to 20 percent more than you would for a similar product manufactured under a lesser-known name, like Oxford—although the items are nearly identical.

THINK BIG. The bigger the store—and its buying power—the less you'll pay. For most storage items, the superstore office supply houses like Staples and OfficeMax and warehouse clubs like Sam's Club and B.J.'s Wholesale Club tend to be up to 30 percent cheaper than smaller retailers. That's because these big stores buy in such large volumes, they're able to underprice the little guys and pass the savings on to you.

For shelving, few can beat Ikea, a chain of stores known for its sleek and inexpensive Scandinavian furniture. The items are available in a wide range of materials, including lacquered or veneered particleboard and finished or unfinished wood. The selection is vast, and prices are lower than for similar items at other retailers. Ikea also has dozens of wonderful smaller storage items and filing systems. Stores are located in the New York, Philadelphia, Washington/Baltimore regions and other metropolitan areas nationwide.

SWEATERS

One of the few articles of clothing that cross gender lines and age barriers, sweaters are making a fashion comeback after sluggish sales in the early 1990s. And why not? Sweaters can be as diverse in style as in material, which runs the gamut from the finest cashmere to tough-as-nails synthetics.

Whatever your taste or bank account allows, figure you'll usually pay a 50 percent markup on children's sweaters and between 100 and 200 percent on larger sizes. But here's how to buy sweaters for less.

BE A SAMPLE SEEKER. If you live in or near the Big Apple, you could

GREAT MAIL-ORDER BUYS

If you're looking for a sweater that will last a lifetime, send for the French Creek Sheep & Wool Company catalog. Established in 1970, the company features greasewool sweaters hand-loomed from wool sheared from the company's flock of Corriedale sheep, which are known for their long-fibered wool. The wool produces strong yarn that results in a rugged outdoor sweater that will withstand a lifetime of washing—and even look better with age.

Prices range from $125 to $225, but you can save 20 to 70 percent on discontinued styles and seconds by shopping in the company's showroom adjacent to the factory in Elverson, Pennsylvania. Look for showroom sales around Presidents' Day, Father's Day and throughout the spring and summer. For a free catalog, call 1-800-977-4337.

THE BEST FOR LESS: PHYLLIS O'MEARA

Sweaters with the Lainey designer label from Ireland, available at only 50 boutiques in the world (of which 15 are in the United States) are considered the finest hand-knit wool sweaters in the world, which may explain their $1,400 to $1,600 price tags.

You can find quality 100 percent wool, cotton and chenille sweaters manufactured by Phyllis O'Meara for a fraction of the cost. An Irish sweater by Phyllis O'Meara retails for $250 to $300 at specialty stores and fine department stores, but you can get one for less by shopping the midwinter sales in January and February, when these sweaters are commonly marked down by 25 to 40 percent.

take a major bite out of the cost of your sweater purchases by going to the sample sales that are held in a six-block area of the Garment District. Clothing designers, including those that manufacture sweaters, produce samples to show to store buyers. After the buyers place their orders, the samples wind up being sold for about half their retail cost along Seventh Avenue, between 34th and 40th streets. These sales, however, happen only a few days each year, and announcements are made on very short notice—usually by flyers given out in the district on the day before or the day of the sale—so keep your eyes peeled. Another great locale for these sample sales is along Orchard Street in the Lower East Side.

Don't live near New York? Fret not, since manufacturers all across the country have their own sample sales, although they're less frequent than those in New York. Look in the yellow pages under "Designers—Apparel" to find local sweater makers and call for the dates and locations of sample sales in your area.

SHOP AT YEAR'S END. The retail sweater season starts in late August and wraps up by Christmas, when prices drop by as much as 40 percent at some department stores. Wait another few weeks—for the after-Christmas sales—and you may find savings of up to 60 percent.

But be careful of preseason markdowns. Although prices may drop 25 to 30 percent when sweaters first come to the stores, industry insiders reveal that some of this early inventory is cheaply made goods that are sold to retailers for a song. And because of the early rush, the retail markup tends to be higher than usual—as much as 200 percent. If you can't wait until season's end, buy well into the middle of the sweater-wearing season.

BYPASS DEPARTMENT STORES. The stock is usually one season old and may have minor and often unnoticeable imperfections in the dye or stitching, but you can save up to 60 percent off retail prices by buying sweaters in outlets. Most sweater manufacturers or retailers operate their own-brand outlets, often in designated outlet malls, but some carry merchandise from other manufacturers as well.

Or for savings ranging from 20 to 75 percent, head to off-price stores like Filene's Basement or Marshalls. These stores carry the same merchandise as full-price department stores.

KNOW YOUR IMPORTS. Since about 75 percent of the sweaters sold in this country are imports, it pays to know the goings-on in some of the countries that manufacture sweaters.

The economic liberalization of China, for instance, has resulted in quality cashmere sweaters from that country selling here for as little as $50, a steal for cashmere lovers. Sweaters from Scotland are highly regarded for their quality and long wear yet tend to be significantly cheaper than Irish-made sweaters; look for the brands Pringle of Scotland, Ballantyne and Braemar, all manufactured by one company and retailing for about $300. And from Peru come quality wool sweaters for as low as $50. But avoid sweaters from Uruguay, which are priced right at $25 to $80 but may not fit well.

Swimwear

When it comes to swimwear, "fit" usually means finding one of umpteen bathing suits that hugs your body fabulously—or at least less badly than the rest. But then comes the other fit—the one you have when you check the price tag.

Americans spend more than $1 billion each year on swimwear, often in hopes of giving themselves a model-like look. With some women's swimsuits, achieving that look can cost as much as $200. Often you're paying for special fabric, which can run as high as $50 a yard, and details such as underwires. Since it usually lacks these body-complementing features, men's swimwear tends to be a fraction of the cost of women's.

The retail markup for both men's and women's swimwear is about 100 percent. Still, with some smart shopping, you can find a good deal on a suit with the qualities you want—well-sewn elastic and part-cotton/part-Lycra fabric to maintain stretch. Here's how.

For color, let your tan do the talking. The lighter the shade, the lighter

Outstanding Outlets

Who knows better about great deals on swimwear than those who use it the most—the folks living in sunny southern California. And they recommend buying names like Catalina and Cole of California for 40 to 80 percent below retail at a chain of stores called, appropriately enough, The Outlet. There are eight of these stores in California and one in Oklahoma. Check the phone book for locations.

GREAT MAIL-ORDER BUYS

Buying a swimsuit by mail can be tough, since fit is the most important aspect of finding the right suit. But using a catalog can reduce the anguish and time spent in a dressing room, struggling into suit after suit. Besides, if you know which brands fit well, buying by mail order can save you as much as 50 percent off retail.

Among the best catalog choices are the Sport Europa catalog, which offers some of the best prices in swimwear—up to half off full price. You can order yours by calling 1-800-695-7000. There's also Overton's, whose catalog offers brand names like Jag and Speedo. It's available by calling 1-800-334-6541. And Victoria's Secret, best known for its lingerie, also carries some swimwear for women. Your best bet: Don't order your favorite swimsuit until a sale catalog arrives (which is every few months). To get on the mailing list, call 1-800-888-8200.

the price. Suits in deeper colors cost more to make because of dyeing procedures, so expect to pay up to 20 percent more for deep colors and black—the most popular color for women's bathing suits. The same is true for print fabrics, since they require more workmanship.

COVER UP AND SAVE MONEY. It seems hard to believe, but two-piece suits often cost more than one-piece suits. True, a one-piece uses more fabric, but more workmanship is needed for a bikini—more elastic around the top and bottom, for instance. That can add at least 10 percent to the price.

SKIP THE FRILLS. Who really needs fringe and sequins for playing in the waves? If you opt for a plain suit, you'll save between 10 and 20 percent compared to one with these frilly extras. Underwires and other supports run the price up, too.

BUY IN MAY. For most articles of clothing, the best sales tend to be *after* the season, but with swimwear some of the best markdowns are offered just as the swimming season is starting to get under way—in late May. That's because swimwear starts arriving in retail stores in early March, so by May, men's and women's swimsuits that haven't moved are usually discounted around 25 percent.

Of course, the biggest markdowns are during clearance sales, which usually begin in July. You'll find 50 percent markdowns on leftover inventory in both department stores and specialty shops.

Shop off-price stores. For everyday savings that are less dependent on the calendar, hit the racks at stores like Marshalls, T.J. Maxx and Ross Dress for Less, where you can save up to 50 percent off department store prices. Some swimsuits sold in off-price stores might be leftover inventory from the previous season, but who can tell? Swimwear styles tend to vary very little from year to year.

TELEPHONES AND ANSWERING MACHINES

Conflicting claims by long-distance carriers may leave you wondering whether you're really getting the savings they claim or if the "deal" you get for talking on the phone is just talk. But this much is true: Deregulation has definitely lowered the prices of telephones and answering machines.

It's only a vague memory, but once consumers had to choose from three or four standard designs of telephones, which they were forced to rent from the telephone company. Now there are hundreds of different phone models for sale, many with dozens of sophisticated features. Whatever your needs, here's how to buy for less.

AVOID THE SPECIALISTS. You'll always pay more at the local telephone store, which may be run by the local phone company and may sell only the company's own wares, usually at list price. Instead, head to an electronics store like Circuit City or an office supply store like OfficeMax or Staples. Model for model, you'll pay anywhere from 15 to 30 percent off the list price for both new telephones and answering machines.

That's because these stores buy in such large volume that the telephone manufacturers give them a better deal than they do the smaller stores that sell nothing but telephones and answering machines.

OR CALL FOR A QUOTE. After you let your fingers do the walking through the Sunday advertising supplements for what's on sale at electronics or office supply stores, call LVT Price Quote Hotline in Commack, New York, at (516) 234-8884 for a quote on the item you like.

LVT sells phones and answering machines, along with other appliances, for up to 30 percent below retail. And LVT participates in most

GREAT MAIL-ORDER BUYS

Although Source, based in Dallas, sells primarily to business clients, you can purchase from a $12 million inventory of new and used telephones and other products—at savings of up to 60 percent below retail. The company mails out *Sourceline*, a bimonthly publication that lists the sale merchandise it stocks; call (214) 450-2600 to get a copy and a price quote.

manufacturer's rebates, so ask if you're entitled to one. The deals are great, but LVT won't accept credit cards—you must pay by postal money order or cashier's check.

BUY A "REBUILT." You can save up to 55 percent by buying an older model that's been rebuilt or refurbished. One of the best companies that specializes in rebuilts is Rhyne Communications in New Jersey, which sells telephones refurbished by AT&T with new parts on the inside, new plastic shells on the outside and a one-year warranty from AT&T that promises a new phone delivered overnight if anything goes wrong.

Rhyne sells primarily to businesses and carries one- and two-line business phones for home offices. The company will also repair your current phone or circuit pack and guarantee the work for one year, saving you the cost of buying a new model. Rhyne also accepts AT&T systems in trade as companies outgrow their current systems. Call 1-800-634-6770 for more information.

DO DOUBLE DUTY. Buy a combination telephone/answering machine unit and you can save up to 40 percent compared to buying a comparable telephone and a separate answering machine. (Besides, these units take up less space.) But keep in mind that if either part breaks down, you'll lose both to the repair shop.

DON'T BE CLUELESS WHEN BUYING CORDLESS. Nearly $1.5 billion worth of cordless phones are sold each year, and they're now in the majority of American homes. Because of their popularity, suppliers have been lowering their prices and enhancing features in the battle for a share of this market.

Cordless telephones are actually two-way radios that convert the signal from your phone line into radio waves and send them from the base to the receiver. Most operate on a ten-channel frequency between 46 and 49 megahertz—the same as baby monitors—but more expensive models use the 900-megahertz band with 25 channels, allowing for less static and a longer range. If you live in an apartment building, though, the range will be less no matter how much you spend, so save your money—the 25-channel model won't improve sound quality.

But no matter where you live, opt for a model with a battery that you can replace yourself instead of having to take the unit back for service. Also, buy a phone with a replaceable antenna—preferably made of rubber, which lasts much longer.

USE YOUR COMPUTER AS YOUR SECRETARY. Many personal computers now have built-in answering machines that can be connected to your phone line with a modem, so if you're shopping for new hardware, ask about this feature. Even if you already own a computer, you'll spend much less on software that will allow your computer to act as an answering machine than you would on a machine itself.

The only drawback is that you'll have to leave your computer on while you're away, but computer makers say this won't do any harm. In fact, they say you put more wear and tear on your computer when you turn it off and on.

LET YOUR PHONE COMPANY DO THE WORK. An even cheaper alternative comes from your local phone company. For a monthly fee—generally $3 for the basic service—the company will record your calls on a digital voice mail system. Of course, you can probably buy a decent answering machine for what it would cost for a year's worth of this service, but it is a cheaper alternative for those who want to record their messages only on a short-term basis. Call the customer service number listed in your local phone book to learn more.

Televisions and Videocassette Recorders

There are more television sets and videocassette recorders in the United States than there are people who buy them. Nearly all American homes—a whopping 98 percent—have at least one TV. That's more households than have telephones or cars. And eight in ten homes also have at least one VCR, up from a mere 5 percent of households just a decade ago.

And if you think we're videophiles now, just wait a few years: Digital and high-definition TV are changing the quality of the television picture almost as quickly as cable did, while fiber-optic and satellite services are changing the way it's delivered to your home.

Because of this, manufacturers continue to experiment with their prices, and luckily for you, the trend has been downward. The cost of popular 25-inch models has fallen 15 percent in recent years—just one factor that contributes to the fact that 23 million color TV sets are sold each year. Meanwhile, TV's cousin—the videocassette recorder—is no slouch at the cash register either, with more than 13 million units sold annually. But here's how you can enjoy all that the video age offers for less money.

Spring into action. If you're the type who likes to haggle, try your negotiation skills around April. TV and VCR sales tend to slump in early spring as the weather improves and people divert their disposable income to recreational products. You can count on seeing discounts of at least 15 percent below regular prices on many units.

Besides being a time to find more discounts blooming along with the flowers, early spring is the best season to save another 10 percent or more just by negotiating, since salespeople are more anxious to move out their slow-moving inventory. But if you're shopping for a large-screen TV—31 inches or more—do your shopping in January.

GREAT MAIL-ORDER BUYS

There's no reason not to order a TV or VCR by phone, fax or mail—long gone are the glass tubes and fragile parts that once made such products too sensitive to ship. And among the best places to buy is Dial-a-Brand, based in Freeport, New York.

Dial-a-Brand is part of a 200-member buying cooperative that allows the company to sell TVs and VCRs for up to 35 percent below retail prices. Besides the buying power of the co-op, Dial-a-Brand saves money by working in a low-rent district and having the customer do most of the work: You'll have to provide the make and model number of the merchandise you want. The company takes all major credit cards and ships by UPS—you'll receive your order in four days. For more information, call (516) 378-9694; residents of New York, New Jersey and Connecticut should call 1-800-237-3220.

It's no coincidence that new TVs and VCRs are brought into the market during football season, and discounts on these increasingly popular big-screen models tend to be pegged to the Super Bowl.

HEAD TO A WAREHOUSE CLUB. While every retailer discounts TVs and VCRs occasionally—or in some cases nearly every week—don't think all sales are alike. A department store or smaller Mom-and-Pop electronics store is the worst place to buy: Selection tends to be scarce at department stores, and even sale prices tend to be at least 15 percent higher than you'll find every day at warehouse clubs like Sam's Club or the Price Club. Even sale prices at electronics giants like Circuit City tend to be higher than what you'll pay at warehouse clubs. Because of their lower overhead and huge buying power, warehouse clubs sell their merchandise at close to wholesale costs.

ASK FOR AN OPEN BOX. Larger electronics chains like Circuit City and Best Buy sell open-box merchandise at deep discounts—sometimes even below the wholesale price. These are items that have been returned by customers or have cosmetic damage that was suffered in shipment; otherwise they work perfectly. Warranties and delivery policies almost always apply. By asking for an open-box unit, you can usually save 20 to 40 percent off the retail price of an identical item in a sealed box.

But keep in mind that open-box merchandise moves out of the store very fast, and it's likely that you'll have to make regular visits to find just the item you've been pining for. Your best bet: Let the salesperson know that you're determined not to buy the product at full price and leave your phone number so you can be called.

DISPLAY AN INTEREST IN DISPLAYS. You can get similar discounts on display models—the TVs and VCRs that are used to show customers the unit's performance quality and features. A 45,000-square-foot electronics store will eventually have about 200 TVs and VCRs to unload as new models arrive—usually over a three-month period between the end of the summer and a few weeks before Christmas.

These are also good models on which to negotiate further discounts, since they occupy valuable floor space once they're removed from the display shelf (often becoming open-box items). And if a part such as a hinge or knob is damaged or missing, the store will usually replace it—or call the manufacturer, who will replace it at no charge.

DON'T BE A BRAND LOYALIST. Since all TVs and VCRs use the same technology, industry insiders say that the picture quality of one brand-name television is virtually indistinguishable from that of another with the same size screen—unless you get into the models with more expensive dark picture-tube faces, like Sony's Trinitron, which give better contrast. (The same is true, to some extent, of VCR quality.) Yet price differences among similar models are huge—up to 35 percent.

So to save, stick with cheaper or lesser-known brands like Samsung, which, despite its lower price, is consistently rated high by consumer magazines. And don't let the display models fool you: Some are purposely made to look bad in an effort to get you interested in a more expensive model.

GO DOUBLE DUTY. Looking for a TV and a VCR? Buy one of the increasingly popular combination models—a TV with a VCR built in. These so-called TVCRs cost anywhere from 20 to 30 percent—up to $100—less than a similar TV and VCR bought separately, depending on the model. They're also considerably easier to move around.

There are some drawbacks, however. Because the TV and the VCR are connected, you can't watch one program while taping an-

THE BEST FOR LESS: SONY TRINITRON

It ain't cheap, but if you're looking for the top-quality TV, look to Sony. Its Trinitron dark-picture tube is legendary in the business for its sharp detail and contrast, and these TVs have a relatively low breakdown record. For VCRs, Sony is also the name many believe is tops.

The suggested retail prices for Sony TVs start at around $350 for a 20-inch set and about $500 for a 27-inch model. Hi-fi stereo VCRs retail for about $400, and super-deluxe models can be as high as $1,500. One place to buy Sony TVs and VCRs for less is at Circuit City, the nation's largest retailer of brand-name consumer electronics, with $5.5 billion in yearly sales. Its buying power allows it to purchase large quantities of products at lower prices and pass those savings on to the consumer.

other. Also, VCRs are less reliable than TVs, so if the VCR portion of your TVCR goes bust, the whole thing ends up out of commission and in the repair shop. Keep in mind that fewer than 10 percent of television sets will need repairs during their lifetime, which averages eight years for most households. On the other hand, more than 12 percent of VCRs break down within five years of the date of purchase.

USE YOUR HEAD REGARDING VCR HEADS. If you're like most folks who use a VCR mainly to play prerecorded tapes from a video store or tape your favorite TV shows, stick with a two-head unit. The fancier four-head models can cost up to 50 percent more, mostly because of special features like super slow motion that most people rarely use.

INSIST ON THE SALE PRICE. If you're buying at a large electronics chain, you may notice that certain TVs seem to go on sale nearly every week. Miss the sale on a model you like and you're out of luck, right?

No. If the salespeople work on commission, they know that if you walk out the door without buying, chances are you won't come back. So politely insist on the sale price: "I noticed this model was on sale a few weeks ago. Any chance I could get it for that price now?" Most salesmen will balk initially, but remind him gently that "if I have to wait, the odds are good that when I return in a few weeks when it's on sale again, I'll get another salesman, and you won't get the commission. So why not do both of us a favor?" If the salesman still won't budge, ask for the department manager.

Of course, this strategy is best used by those who keep tabs on newspaper advertisements. Keep in mind that the savings may not be great—usually no more than $20—but negotiating takes only a minute of your time.

TIRES

Few consumer products have held their own against inflation as well as tires: The list price of most tires hasn't changed much this decade, and they're actually a better buy today than they were 60 years ago.

Back then, a motorist might lay out $145 to replace four tires, but over their life, they cost about 3 cents per mile. Today tires last ten times longer, and even with an average price of $360 per set, the actual cost per mile is about 1 cent. But here's how you can save even more the next time you're shopping for tires.

LOWER THE FLAG. There are only two major U.S.-owned tire manufacturers—Goodyear and Cooper—and about a dozen foreign-owned makers. But there are dozens of private-label brands sold in the United States, all manufactured by the big guys but with different names on the sidewalls and often with modified tread patterns. The "flag brands" like Michelin, Goodyear and Bridgestone/Firestone get a lot of attention, but buying private-label tires can save you about 30 percent compared to similar (if not identical) tires from the same dealer.

BE WISE—OVERSIZE. The general rule of thumb is that the narrower the tire, the lower the cost. But beware: A smaller tire isn't necessarily the best value for your vehicle. A P185/70R14 size, for example, might cost $53 per tire, but by going to the next highest diameter recommended by the vehicle manufacturer—P195/70R14—you'll spend only another $5 per tire but gain the advantages of increased fuel mileage, longer wear and a smoother ride.

It's important to stay within the manufacturer's "fitment" recommendations to avoid compatibility problems and stress on the engine and powertrain, so check your owner's manual before oversizing.

GO FOR DOUBLE DUTY. If you live in a northern climate, you can save the $200 or so for snow tires by buying all-season radials. Although specifically designed to give better traction in the rain, all-seasons are good enough for most Americans to use in the snow. So unless you live in an extremely snowy area—where chains are required or snow blankets the roads for months on end—one set of all-season radials will do the job.

MAKE THE MOST OF YOUR MONEY—READ THE SMALL PRINT. Nearly everything you need to know about a tire—except its price—is imprinted in the rubber on the sidewall, although most people ignore three of the most important details: the tread-wear, traction and temperature ratings, officially known as Uniform Tire Quality Grading Standards. These numbers tend to be printed in smaller letters than the size and maximum load numbers (those you look at to select the correct size).

A tread-wear rating of 100 is the baseline or standard, and theoretically, the higher that number, the longer the tire should last: A tread-wear rating of 300 means the tire should last three times longer than one that is rated 100. Currently, a tread-wear index of 160 is low, and an index of 500 is quite high.

THE BEST FOR LESS: GOODYEAR EAGLE AQUATRED

From consumer magazines to automotive authorities to the man on the street, when it comes to getting a top-flight tire, an enthusiastic thumbs-up is the norm for the Goodyear Eagle Aquatred. It tends to outperform other tires on braking, cornering and handling and is especially effective in rainy weather.

But with a list price of about $150 per tire for some sizes, it's pricier than most other tires. For discounts up to 30 percent or more, however, try to buy right before or after the big summer holidays—Memorial Day, the Fourth of July and Labor Day. Folks do a lot of driving over these holiday weekends, and they buy a lot of tires—so that's when Goodyear retailers tend to offer their best savings of the year on the Aquatred and other tires.

GREAT MAIL-ORDER BUYS

Want the best tire prices in town? You'll probably have to look out of town to get them. Buying tires by mail order may sound like a bother, but you can save up to 60 percent off retail price. And shipping costs are only $4 to $7 per tire.

Of course, you'll have to pay for mounting and balancing and any applicable taxes, but total savings are still noteworthy. And most mail-order tire houses accept major credit card orders and deliver to your home, your favorite service station (notify your mechanic beforehand that you are having tires shipped to him) or a company-recommended installer, if you prefer.

Among the best mail-order companies are Tire Rack in South Bend, Indiana (1-800-428-8355) and Discount Tire Direct in Scottsdale, Arizona (1-800-790-6444).

Traction is graded as A, B and C, indicating the tire's ability to stop on wet pavement. An A is the best, a C the worst. Temperature ratings are also given as A-to-C grades. An A means a tire is best equipped to resist the heat generated by high speeds, air temperature and heavy loads, while a tire with a C rating meets all safety standards, but performance is purely basic.

By avoiding the low end of each of these scales, you can buy tires that will last much longer than expected. Sometimes a tire with a shorter warranty can be a better buy—as long as it's rated well in these often overlooked "three Ts."

DON'T OVERBUY. There's little point in paying for a premium tire to put on a run-of-the-mill car. The average age of domestic cars on the road today is nine years, the highest since 1946. Even driving the average of 12,500 miles a year, a cost-conscious motorist should realize that a set of top-of-the-line 60,000-mile tires may well outlast his car. So stick with cheaper tires for an older car—those with a 25,000- to 40,000-mile warranty—and you'll save up to 40 percent wherever you buy.

BE A SPORTS-PAGE FAN. Most tire retailers advertise in the newspaper's sports section, since tires tend to be purchased by men. And many newspapers have "popular tire days," when there are more tire ads; although it varies from town to town, more ads often appear on Wednesdays and Saturdays.

HEAD TO A WAREHOUSE CLUB. Some of the best tire deals await you at warehouse clubs like Sam's Club and B.J.'s Warehouse Club. For one thing, prices tend to be lower—up to 20 percent on some tires. But the real savings come in the extras the warehouse clubs provide: free or reduced-cost mounting and balancing and low-cost road-hazard policies that provide free repairs for flats or leaks over the life of your tire. All told, these extras can amount to $50 or more when you have to pay for them at a tire retailer.

Toys

Americans shell out big bucks to keep their small ones entertained. Over $17 billion is spent each year on toys—two-thirds of it during the four weeks that comprise the Christmas shopping season.

There are several reasons that we don't spend less. Retail markups tend to be low—only between 25 and 33 percent—so there's little incentive for sellers to offer truly great deals on their merchandise. Unlike other retail items, toys don't follow a regular sale season; even after Christmas, prices don't drop significantly. And since manufacturer-direct outlets don't exist and toy liquidators are few, there is only a handful of places across the country to pick up real steals. Anyone who's ever looked for the hottest toys during the Christmas rush knows that they're hard enough to *find*, let alone find on sale.

So with all this in mind, don't expect to find rock-bottom prices on toys—at least those your child wants. Cheaper imitations and knock-offs are a waste of money, since they usually wind up collecting more dust than ol' Aunt Martha's furniture. But there are still some ways to get the most from your toy-spending dollar.

READ THE MOVIE REVIEWS. These days many Hollywood studios realize that the biggest bucks from a movie come not from the film itself but from its merchandise—toys included. And when a new movie comes out, especially from the Disney studios, you can bet that a host of sought-after toys will soon follow.

You can make this work for you by keeping an eye on the entertainment pages and movie reviews. Within weeks of a movie's release—and sometimes a month or so beforehand—the toys inspired by it are usually offered at discounts ranging from 10 to 25 percent and sometimes even more. Often they're sold right in the movie theater lobby. As soon as the movie hits solid ground, however—a month or two after its release—these discounts are nowhere to be found; in fact, once it's a hot film and your children are hooked, the prices may actually increase. Start keeping a watchful eye for new

THE BEST FOR LESS: BARBIE DOLLS

America's foot-tall sweetheart has gained quite a foothold: The average girl owns eight Barbies, and there are enough of these dolls in the United States to circle the globe three times. Such popularity comes at a price—namely *her* price: Anywhere from $10 for a basic, no-frills Babs to as much as $300 for certain collector models, and that doesn't include her glamour house, sports car or other champagne-taste frills.

Because of her popularity, which has remained consistent if not increased since her introduction three decades ago, finding this prized plastic on sale may seem as unlikely as her dumping Ken for GI Joe. While sales on Barbies are anything but common, they do occur: The nation's biggest toy retailers—Toys "R" Us, Kay-Bee Toy and discount chains like Kmart and Target Stores—occasionally put Barbie and her accessories on sale for 10 to 25 percent off regular retail prices, but you'll have to keep a close watch for these sales. Or if you are in love with the latest Barbie, just wait a year, and you may be able to save a bundle by buying last year's model.

If money isn't an object, head to F.A.O. Schwarz, which has perhaps the most interesting collection of Barbie paraphernalia available. Besides a doll-size wardrobe selection that would make Cher jealous, four Schwarz stores—in Boston, Chicago, New York City and San Francisco—each have "Barbie Boutiques" offering child-size Barbie cars your kids can drive and look-alike Barbie clothes your child can wear. For more on Barbie selections, contact the manufacturer, Mattel, at 1-800-524-TOYS.

films and their toys during late May and early October, since studios tend to release their big children's movies just as the school year ends and as the Christmas holiday season begins.

BUY A MONTH EARLIER THAN USUAL. Although the official Christmas shopping season starts the day after Thanksgiving, and many people think that's when the best deals are offered, you can get the biggest discounts on toys a month earlier—in October. That's when larger chains—Toys "R" Us included—tend to publish multipage supplements in the Sunday newspaper offering dozens of coupons with discounts in the 30 percent range for early shoppers. The coupons are usually for those items that toy distributors predict will be the big sellers—and they're usually correct. Discount chains like Wal-Mart, Kmart and Target Stores offer similar in-store savings on the same items at the same time but usually without the fanfare of newspaper-offered coupons.

That's not to say that you won't find deals later on. But don't wait until Black Friday, the official opening day of the Christmas shopping season. A week or two earlier, there usually are "quiet" discounts of between 15 and 30 percent as retailers prep for the Yule

OUTSTANDING OUTLETS

No major toy manufacturer offers a direct outlet program that sells its wares to the public at a discount. But there are a few toy liquidators—companies that buy closeouts, overruns and the like at rock-bottom prices and then pass the savings on to the consumer. Unfortunately, many of these operations are small Mom-and-Pop stores or schlock shops that offer little in the way of selection. Even the prices aren't that much better than those at a decent sale at the local toy store.

The exception: Toy Liquidators, which has 82 stores across the country, most of them located in outlet malls. While its selection doesn't rival that of a Toys "R" Us (remember, liquidators purchase what's available, not necessarily what the public wants), the company's buying power is strong enough to ensure a sufficient inventory to satisfy children of varying interests and age groups—at discounts averaging 70 percent below retail. Check the yellow pages or call directory assistance for the location of a store near you.

GREAT MAIL-ORDER BUYS

For toys that won't wind up in the garbage—due to either boredom or breakage—check out the selections from Constructive Playthings in Grandview, Missouri, which has been manufacturing washable, durable toys for younger children for over 40 years. Its catalog offers these diehard playthings for about 30 percent below retail. You can order a copy by calling 1-800-448-1412.

Childcraft, based in Peoria, Illinois, is another company known for quality at reasonable prices that also sells by mail order. You can get its tougher-than-nails toys (mostly for toddlers and preschoolers) at discounted prices by calling 1-800-367-3255.

Some of the most interesting offerings, although certainly not the least expensive, are those in the catalog for The American Girls Collection, which features books of historical fiction and finely detailed dolls and accessories based on five fictional characters from the past. The collection appeals to school-age girls, and although it's not a discount house, the company's catalog is well worth a peek. Call 1-800-845-0005 to order yours.

tide of shoppers. The next week, the sales may be more ballyhooed, but they won't be as substantial. Of course, you'll get similar savings during the so-called after-Christmas sales—but you'll need lots of luck to find what you want.

BUY SIX MONTHS IN ADVANCE. People rarely buy summer toys like water guns, bats and balls and swim toys during the Christmas rush, but it's a great time of year to buy these items for 50 percent off seasonal prices. The same is true for buying winter toys like board games and hockey gear in the summer. Retailers offer these deals when they need the room used by summer toys for their Christmas inventory and again when they want to unload their winter gear as school is about to end.

LOOK AT THE END CAPS. The displays that line the ends of aisles rarely translate to any real savings in supermarkets or clothing stores. Instead, their prominence and bold signs are designed to make you think you're saving money on items the store owners want to unload—except when it comes to buying toys. Stores like Kmart and Wal-Mart occasionally display popular toys on the ends of aisles at drastically reduced prices. It's the old loss-leader idea—they lose profit on those particular items, but they hope to lure you into the aisles, where you might spend more on other items. You'll need to pay attention to prices, though, because not all of these end-cap displays offer substantial discounts. When they do—and that's usually between early November and January—they're usually in the 25 to 33 percent range, a super markdown for toys.

New store in town? Shop at the old one. When a new Wal-Mart opens in town, go to the existing Kmart or Target for lower-than-usual savings. In an effort to keep your business, competing stores within a several-mile radius will meet, and usually beat, the "opening sale" prices at the new store. That means toy discounts of up to 40 percent on many items—practically unheard of in the retail toy business. Of course, this is a one-time offer, and prices tend to go back to normal a month or two after the new store opens.

Try to be a toy tester. If you live in Rhode Island or the southeast Massachusetts area, you may be lucky enough to get some toys for free. Hasbro enlists the help of area children to be "toy testers": They get new playthings at no charge in exchange for giving opinions on their "playability." You can get more information on becoming a toy tester by calling the Hasbro Funlab at (401) 727-5918. Sorry, but other leading toy manufacturers don't use this once-popular concept.

Vacuum Cleaners

A good vacuum is supposed to suck up bits of dirt and dust—not dollars from your bank account. But if you've priced vacuums lately, you know that you can spend more than $1,000 on some professional-style models. Even more modest styles of popular brands can run several hundred dollars.

All told, Americans spend about $1.5 billion on vacuums every year. And no wonder: Retailers typically mark up vacuums anywhere from 30 to 100 percent. But here's how you can suck up savings and still clean your carpets.

Spring forward in the winter. Many manufacturers debut their new models in early spring, so watch for discounts on current models starting in late November and continuing through February. Discounts vary depending on the unit, but prices could be as much as 40 to 50 percent lower than in other months.

Outstanding Outlets

You won't find outlets for vacuum cleaners the way you do for clothing or other items, but there are some factory-owned stores where vacuum manufacturers sell their products for anywhere from 30 to 60 percent less than retail prices.

The Hoover Company operates several of these stores, specializing in selling leftovers, discontinued models and even factory-reconditioned vacuums. Call 1-800-944-9200 to locate a store near you.

THE BEST FOR LESS: SANITAIRE

The best names in vacuums are probably those you've never heard of, since they tend to be used only by professional cleaners. Probably the best-known among these pro units are Oreck vacuums, but insiders say that Sanitaire, a professional brand made by Eureka, is the best in the business.

What's more, it costs hundreds less than the more popular Oreck—with prices ranging from just under $200 to about $450. You can buy these units for less at Mr. Sweeper, which has three stores in the Atlanta area; for more information, call (770) 973-0774.

SHOP THE SMALL GUYS. A salesclerk or cashier at a discount store isn't likely to cut you a break on a vacuums, but you can usually get 10 to 25 percent off at a smaller specialty shop simply by asking. Vacuum dealers are in a very competitive market and know that their full prices usually can't compete with what's available at large discount stores. By bargaining at a smaller Mom-and-Pop vacuum store, you can get the same or even better prices than what's available at a

GREAT MAIL-ORDER BUYS

ABC Vacuum Cleaner Warehouse in Austin, Texas, sells vacuums by Kirby, Bissell and Eureka for as much as 50 percent below the manufacturer's suggested retail price and will ship for only $10 for most models. For a price list and even model brochures, call (512) 459-7643.

larger discounter. Besides, selection tends to be better at these smaller stores.

BUY USED. One of the best ways to save when buying vacuums is to buy a rebuilt unit at an appliance repair shop. Generally, you'll pay anywhere from 50 to 80 percent less than you would for a similar new model. Many service centers also attach warranties to the vacuums they've rebuilt, so if anything goes wrong, you can take it back. Look for these stores under "Vacuum Repairs" in the yellow pages.

Watches

You can spend less than $20 for a fake Rolex from a New York City hustler selling from a suitcase on Times Square or over 1,000 times more for the real McCoy encrusted with diamonds at a swanky jewelry counter. Either way, the watch's movement—the part that tells time—costs about $6.

So what are we paying for? The status of certain names, the watch's ability to go underwater or log our jogging times and, of course, the gold and jewels that may grace the face and band. These days the average person owns at least three watches, and timepieces have become a powerful fashion statement.

Because of this, watch retailers are in an incredibly competitive market. With the average watch carrying a 40 percent retail markup, there's some room for smart shoppers to snag a deal. Here's how to make sure you're getting the most for your money.

Haggle. When it comes to watches, there's plenty of room to negotiate for a better deal. Insiders say that while it's unlikely that you'll get a discount on a $20 Timex at a discount store counter, most jewelers will gladly sell their better wares for 15 to 20 percent below the asking price—but many consumers never ask and simply pay full price.

Most fine jewelers carry the same watches, so the odds are that if one jeweler won't sell for less, another will. Since many jewelers are often located on the same street or area of larger shopping districts, you won't have far to go to comparison-shop.

Shop the discount chains. If you're looking for an everyday watch, forget about jewelry stores and head to a discount chain. Stores like Kmart and Best and even warehouse clubs like Sam's Club and the Price Club carry complete lines of Timex, Seiko, Pulsar and other reputable brands for about 25 percent less than traditional watch retailers.

Besides, these stores tend to put their watches on sale more fre-

THE BEST FOR LESS: PATEK PHILIPPE

Rolex gets the press, but insiders say the best watch for the money is the lesser-known Patek Philippe. For one thing, there aren't as many Pateks around, which makes them more exclusive. In the company's 156-year history, it's produced fewer watches than Rolex makes in a single year.

Besides, Patek Philippe watches have more craftsmanship and hand-finishing than almost any other brand. The company's watchmakers train for nine years—the equivalent of the time it takes to become a brain surgeon—before they even begin putting watches together.

One of the best places to find these watches is in New York City, along Fifth and Madison avenues. Or call the company's U.S. distributor at (212) 581-0870 to find out where you can buy one. The classic model is the Patek Calatrava, which sells for about $8,850, but you can often save by buying a used one. Tourneau, which has stores in New York, California and Florida, has a good selection of reconditioned Patek Philippe watches; call 1-800-348-3332 for more information. Generally, you'll save about 30 percent over the price of new models, but these watches appreciate extremely well.

quently—about every two months or so. Sale prices can save you up to an additional 30 percent.

REMEMBER YOUR JS. Christmas and graduation are big times for watch-giving, so whatever watch you're looking for, try to shop after these busy times. Although there isn't an official watch "season," you may notice discounts of 10 percent or more during January and then again in July.

BUY SECONDHAND. For the best deals in top-of-the-line watches, try to buy a reconditioned watch. Secondhand timepieces by Patek Philippe, Rolex and Audemars Piguet often sell for about 50 percent less than new watches. (Pawn shops also offer good deals on more practical models.) To make sure the watch is authentic, get an appraisal. Some jewelry stores and watch repair shops charge a fee of 1 percent of the watch's value.

Keep in mind that secondhand watches fall into two categories. Used or previously owned watches (as they're called in the business) usually have all their original parts. A better find is a reconditioned watch, which has been revamped and may include new parts; they're usually sold by jewelers. Whenever you're buying secondhand, it pays to ask which parts have been replaced. Bypass models that include new, upgraded bands, since their markup tends to be very high. You're looking for new parts in the "guts" of the watch.

GET IT IN WRITING. The real cost of quality watches is for making repairs: Replacing a 25-cent battery on some watches can cost $250.

GREAT MAIL-ORDER BUYS

If you know watches and you're willing to do your homework, you can get some of the best deals by mail. Alan Marcus & Company, based in Washington, D.C., offers discounts from 25 to 50 percent on famous names like Rolex, Patek Philippe, Audemars Piguet, Baume Mercier and Cartier. Call 1-800-654-7184 for more information. Authorized Rolex dealers, on the other hand, are no longer allowed to offer discounts.

You can call 1-800-348-3332 to get a catalog from Tourneau, which has one of the largest watch selections around at its stores in New York, Florida and California. Tourneau carries 45 brands of new Swiss watches, as well as reconditioned (and guaranteed) preowned Rolex, Patek Philippe, Piaget and other fine timepieces.

And Capetown Diamond Corporation offers discounts of 30 to 60 percent on both new and preowned fine watches, including Rolex, Patek Philippe and Piaget. The Atlanta-based company has showrooms in Georgia, California and New York and offers mail-order selections; call 1-800-442-7866.

And unfortunately, the first thing that usually goes on a watch is its warranty, which offers these repairs for nothing.

If you buy a watch from an authorized dealer—one that the manufacturer knows is selling the watch—you will typically get a full warranty; top-of-the-line timepieces usually offer a lifetime warranty. But if you buy from an unauthorized dealer, the warranty is automatically voided. Most dealers have written proof of their authorization. If not, find another dealer.

DON'T ALWAYS TRUST AUCTIONS. There's a common belief that you can get top-of-the-line watches for a song at private and government-sponsored auctions. (The latter usually result when the Drug Enforcement Administration or the FBI confiscates a cache of Rolexes from drug dealers.) While auctions can provide some good deals, you'll probably fare better buying everyday watches there.

Insiders say that Rolexes, Cartiers and other top watches sold at auctions are sometimes fakes; it seems drug dealers fall for the same tricks as regular folks. Besides, the auctioneer often gets a cut—usually 10 percent or more—so the starting bid tends to be inflated. When bidding at auctions, never bid on the first "offer." Usually the auctioneer will drop it to about half the starting point unless someone accepts the first bid.

CHECK THE BAND FIRST. Whatever you're buying, one of the first things you should look at is the band. It's usually the first part of the watch to go, so you want something that is solid, preferably sewn as opposed to glued together. That's not to say you shouldn't get a watch with a cheap band, but you shouldn't pay a lot for it. New bands can cost as much as the watch itself. For sports watches, opt for plastic bands: They tend to last longer.

WATER SPORTS EQUIPMENT

Traveling across the water can set you back plenty. A pair of water skis usually costs at least $200, a surfboard averages $400, and sailboards can reach four figures. Meanwhile, jet skis, the newest way to skim the waves, go for as much as some compact cars—nearly $8,000. And heading underwater can also soak you in more ways than one: Outfitting yourself in complete scuba gear generally costs $1,000 or more.

While industry insiders guard the retail markup as though it were the combination to Davy Jones's locker, common sense tells you it's got to be hefty, since discounts on water sports equipment can be 50 percent or more. So before paying retail, try these ways to save on equipment for your favorite aquatic activity.

BE A CLUBBER. Joining a club of local enthusiasts is a great way to get equipment for less. Clubs frequently get a group discount from local retailers or directly from the manufacturer—usually in the 10 to 35 percent range.

It's also a great way to buy used equipment from other water sports enthusiasts, often for half the retail price of new goods. While the skis or boards may have a few scratches, the savings are worth it, especially if you're just starting out in the sport. To find out about these clubs, check specialty magazines like *Water Ski* or *Rodale's Scuba Diving*. Or contact professional organizations like the American Water Ski Association (1-800-533-AWSA) or the U.S. Surfing Federation (310-596-7785); you'll find a complete list in the *Encyclopedia of Associations*, which is available at most public libraries.

FALL BACK TO FALL SAVINGS. Most water sports equipment is discounted between 10 and 30 percent at the end of the season, which usually means late August through September. That's when retailers want to clear out their inventory, especially in northern climates.

POUNCE ON PROMO EQUIPMENT. As with gear for other sports, manufacturers of water sports equipment supply promotional equipment for

GREAT MAIL-ORDER BUYS

You can order skis, vests, kneeboards, wetsuits and a wide range of accessories for water skiing and other water sports at prices 10 to 50 percent off retail from Overton's, a discount boating accessory company.

The company, based in Greenville, North Carolina, began selling water skis by mail 20 years ago because of the difficulty in finding reasonably priced, good-quality water sports equipment. Overton's currently serves about two million customers, and through its price protection policy, the company guarantees that it will not be undersold: If you order an item from Overton's and then see it for less in another catalog, Overton's will refund the difference in price plus pay you an additional 10 percent of the price difference in cash.

Orders are shipped by the next business day, and shipping and handling charges range from $4.95 to $14.95 for regular delivery. UPS two-day service costs an additional $3.95; overnight service is $7.95. Call 1-800-334-6541 for a free catalog.

tournaments. But when the professional or amateur water skiers, surfers, jet skiers and sailboarders are finished competing, the equipment is often sold to spectators. It's barely used, and it's usually top-of-the-line merchandise that sells for anywhere from 15 to 35 percent less than full retail prices.

You must attend these tournaments to buy the equipment (ask the tournament director or equipment manager about how to get it); you can learn of these events by reading specialty magazines like *Water Ski*.

ASK FOR THE OLD STUFF. Retailers anxious to move merchandise will reduce the price on equipment that has been cluttering their shelves and storeroom for a year. Most changes to water sports equipment from year to year are cosmetic: new accent colors or a different design. Ask retailers for last year's goods and you could save 30 percent or more.

Women's Dresses

Hemlines may rise and fall depending on the whims of designers, but one thing remains constant in the $8-billion-a-year dress industry: The retail markup. No matter what the style or season, figure that you'll pay twice as much for a dress as the retailer pays a wholesaler or manufacturer. Designer labels, lots of tailoring and fabrics such as silk, tweed or knits drive up the price even more.

To counter this, retailers hold sales every few weeks; sometimes they offer bona fide discounts, but more often they're just trying to lure you into the store. Here's how to know the real deals from the mere claims so you can make the most of your dress-spending dollar.

Plan your shopping around the calendar. Certain months mean big-

Outstanding Outlets

For classic investment clothing with a little zing to the styling, you can't do better than St. John Knits. And with savings of as much as 50 percent off their average retail price of $700, you can't do better than shopping at a St. John Knits outlet.

You'll find these discounts on first-quality and slightly irregular garments at the five outlets—in San Jose, California, at the Great Mall of the Bay Area; Woodbury Common in Central Valley, New York; the Franklin Mills Mall in Philadelphia; the Chesapeake Village in Queenstown, Maryland; and Sawgrass Mills in Fort Lauderdale, Florida. Stock is held back from these outlets for nine months, but the timeless styling of St. John Knits guarantees that the wait is well worth it.

GREAT MAIL-ORDER BUYS

If you like shopping the off-price stores, there's an off-price catalog that slashes 25 to 50 percent from retail prices: Chadwick's of Boston.

Here you'll find inexpensive dresses by Granite, Ellen Ashley and J.G. Hook. And several times a year, the company mails a sale catalog offering even better savings. One added bonus: Unless your order is shipped to New York state, you don't have to pay sales tax. To order your Chadwick's catalog, call 1-800-525-6650.

ger-than-average discounts for certain types of dresses. During these "special" times, you'll find markdowns of anywhere from 25 to 50 percent instead of the more typical 10 to 25 percent.

Holiday dresses are usually marked down in January (although in recent years, some stores have marked them down before Christmas), while resort dresses and formal wear go on sale in February. Spring dresses move to the sale racks in May, with clearances in the range of 50 percent off in June and July. Summer dresses are discounted in August, and fall dresses have the biggest markdowns in October.

SHOP IN THE PRESEASON. These days more larger department stores are holding preseason sales, in which new merchandise for fall and spring is discounted between 10 and 25 percent during the first few weeks after it hits the sales floor. These sales usually occur in March for spring clothing and in July for fall clothing.

OR GET INTO IN-STORE FASHION SHOWS. Another way to save on the new inventory is to keep an eye out for in-store fashion shows, usually held just as the new merchandise begins to arrive. Sometimes retailers want to promote a certain designer's line, and in doing so, they offer discounts in the 25 percent range when that inventory reaches the store.

OPEN A STORE CHARGE ACCOUNT. One of the best promotions going these days is the store credit card: Most department stores and many boutiques will slash up to 25 percent off purchases the day you open the account—even for items that are already on sale. Just be sure to pay the bill when it comes, or you'll accrue heavy interest charges that will wipe out any savings.

HEAD TO AN OFF-PRICE STORE. For designer dresses, the best deals are at off-price stores. By buying overstocks, closeouts and last year's inventory, most off-price stores can sell brand-name designer dresses for up to 40 percent below retail prices. The problem is, it's usually hit or miss—sometimes you'll find a gold mine of selection and savings; other times it's drier than a well in the Sahara.

But Loehmann's tends to have both great savings and selection. Because there are 68 stores across the country, women executives tend to check the local yellow pages for the nearest Loehmann's as soon as they arrive in a city on a business trip. Typically, you can save 35 to 60 percent off department store prices.

WOMEN'S SHOES

Cinderella got a bargain. Not only did she get a great pair of ballroom slippers, she got a prince, too. But considering what some women's shoes cost these days, it seems a prince should be included.

About $14 billion is spent each year on women's shoes. They can be bought just about anywhere—at discount stores, shoe boutiques and department stores—and markups can run as high as 100 percent. Add the little extras such as a designer's name and imported leathers, and the cost soars.

THE BEST FOR LESS: JOAN & DAVID

It's a judgment call, of course, since there are many makers of fine women's shoes, but few argue over the quality of Joan & David footwear. These shoes are legendary for their style and quality—and unfortunately, also for their price.

With a typical retail price of $200 to $250, and some going as high as $350 (sandals and other casual styles are in the $140 range), these shoes are out of the reach of most women. But there's good news: Besides the retail "boutiques" in department stores like Macy's, Joan & David also operates 19 outlets in 11 states, where these shoes usually sell for 40 percent below retail—with greater discounts on some styles. In addition, these outlets have special sales, where some shoes are as low as $49 and boots go for $79. Check the yellow pages for a store near you.

OUTSTANDING OUTLETS

Nordstrom's department store began as a shoe store known for its wide range of sizes in women's shoes. And the company still operates 19 outlet stores that offer a great selection at good prices. When shoes no longer sell at the main Nordstrom stores, they're sent to these outlets—called Nordstrom Rack—and discounted 25 percent or more off the original Nordstrom price. Rack stores, which operate in California, Illinois, Maryland, Oregon, Pennsylvania, Utah and Virginia, also have sales from time to time, when even better savings can be found. For the location of the nearest Rack store, call a local Nordstrom department store.

Meanwhile, if you have petite feet, head to Cinderella of Boston, located in Chatsworth, California. This company has been a leader in women's shoes in sizes 1½ to 5 for over 50 years and sells its top-quality, stylish footwear for up to 50 percent below retail (assuming you can even find those sizes in retail stores).

Yet no other piece of apparel takes such a pounding, so it's worth it to look for shoes that are comfortable, made of quality materials and the right heel-height for the hoofing you have in mind. And here's how to get that quality for less.

KNOW THE NAME BEHIND THE LABEL. It's fairly common for a big shoe manufacturer to make shoes under several labels. If you're a fan of designer shoes but not their prices, ask clerks to give you some inside information. They may tell you that Ann Taylor stores, for instance, carry top-quality Joan & David shoes under the Ann Taylor label. Or better yet, call the manufacturer of your favorite brand of footwear and ask what private labels they also produce. You can get the number by calling 800 directory assistance (1-800-555-1212). Buying these private labels can save you as much as 40 percent off the price of name brands, and often you get the same—or similar—quality.

BUY PRESEASON AND POSTSEASON. The best times to get discounts on most women's shoes in department stores occur twice a year—just as new shipments arrive and after the "season" ends, when the stores reduce prices to clear out the inventory. Many department stores offer preseason sales in July as fall merchandise arrives on the floor: Count on discounts of 20 to 25 percent off what you'll pay a month later. For spring fashions, look for similar savings in early February.

Clearance sales are usually also held in February, when you can save anywhere from 50 to 75 percent off winter styles, and you'll find similar deals on spring footwear in July.

ASK ABOUT OFF-PRICE PROMOTIONS. You'll typically pay 20 to 60 percent less for women's shoes at off-price stores like Marshalls and Loehmann's on a day-to-day basis. But during certain times of the year—usually the postseason—these stores also have special promotions, such as two-for-one sales or one-day sales, where you can cut an additional 10 to 25 percent off your purchases. Again, look for these sales in midsummer and midwinter.

BUY YOURSELF SHOES FOR YOUR BIRTHDAY. Some off-price stores, like Loehmann's, offer special incentives for members of their store clubs. At Loehmann's, for instance, membership in its Insiders' Club entitles you to save 15 percent off the price of new shoes on your birthday. As a member, you also receive mailings throughout the year entitling you to special savings.

Women's Sportswear

Women spend about $30 billion a year on casual clothes—everything from sweaters and T-shirts to slacks, shorts and tights. And much of the time they're paying markups of 100 percent, which are typical in the apparel industry.

Consignment shops and thrift stores are good places to find women's sportswear, but there are other ways to cut your spending on new brand-name sportswear without sacrificing the features you want, such as solid stitching, fabrics that withstand many washings and well-finished seams and hems.

Shop in the boys' department. Chances are you can find sportswear and comparable casual clothing for yourself in the boys' department of your favorite department store—for about half the cost of what

Outstanding Outlets

Women's sportswear is the foundation for many outlets, and most offer savings averaging 25 percent below retail. But one outlet consistently comes through with value and selection: Esprit.

These warehouse-style stores offer discounts from 20 percent to as much as 75 percent off retail prices for a full line of Esprit junior clothing—jeans, sportswear and shoes—and its own contemporary line in women's sizes, Susie Tompkins.

One of the largest Esprit outlets is in San Francisco, where the company is based, but call (415) 957-2540 for an outlet location near you.

GREAT MAIL-ORDER BUYS

Pages and pages of glossy catalog offerings fill your mailbox regularly, many with tempting items but not always tempting prices. One women's catalog that stands out is Tweeds. This mail-order house, based in Roanoke, Virginia, offers a great selection of its private-label sportswear in the latest styles and most popular colors.

Prices are about 25 percent below retail, but Tweeds usually features a section of markdowns with savings of up to 50 percent off regular catalog prices. Call 1-800-999-7997 to receive a copy.

you'd pay in the women's department. Among the best items are T-shirts, sweaters, sweatshirts and denim shirts you can wear over a tank top.

OR BUY IN BULK IN THE MEN'S DEPARTMENT. One of today's most popular items in women's casual wear—the oversize T-shirt—can be found just about everywhere, including on the expensive designer racks. But often a T-shirt is just a T-shirt, and if you're using it to layer, rethink your approach: Pick up a three-pack of men's T-shirts in your size instead of that pricey T-shirt from the women's department and you can slash up to 70 percent on a per-shirt basis. Only the label will give your secret away.

ASK ABOUT THE "SALE" STORE. If you're shopping a favorite chain store, such as the Gap, ask a store clerk or manager which store in the area is considered the "sale" store. These aren't bona fide outlets but rather retail stores where many of the markdowns are sent—and where most sale items are consolidated. Be prepared for a longer drive, since these stores may be off the beaten path. The trip can be worth it, however, since off-sizes tend to be more available—at savings that average about 25 percent below retail and can be as much as 75 percent off.

GET A STORE CREDIT CARD—FOR THE DAY. If you're shopping for mass quantities of sportswear, it helps to open a store charge account. Many stores, from Express to JCPenney, tempt you with a one-time, across-the-board discount of 10 to 25 percent if you open an account. Insiders say this is a great way to cut your expenses, as long as you pay off the bill promptly. Otherwise, the interest rates—typically about 20 percent—can quickly wipe out any savings.

SHOP OFF-PRICE. You can find a great selection of sportswear at off-price chains such as Marshalls, T.J. Maxx and Ross Dress for Less for anywhere from 20 to 60 percent below department store prices. But be prepared to cruise the racks, since some off-price stores tend to get the best selections whenever they can. Sometimes it's a virtual gold mine; at other times there's little in the way of quality selection.

Industry insiders say the best way to save is to tour these stores often, maybe on a lunch hour. During special sales and promotions—often in April and May for spring clothing and September and October for winter clothes—your savings might reach 70 percent and more over full retail.

Women's Suits

Nothing makes a statement like a suit. Unfortunately, an even stronger statement is usually made by its price tag. And no wonder. The typical retail markup on women's suits is about 100 percent or more. A certain name on the label, special tailoring or fancy fabrics boost the price even more. All told, women spend more than $2 billion each year on suits. Some consignment shops carry used quality women's suits, but here's how you can buy new and spend less.

Cross over to the bridge lines. The full-price ticket of a designer suit can make you faint. But before you break out the smelling salts, keep in mind that most designers also sell a less expensive label called the bridge line. Ann Klein has Ann Klein II, and Donna Karan has DKNY. But whatever they're called, these bridge lines typically sell for 40 percent less than the fancier "name" lines yet tend to have a similar fit and features.

To find out about the bridge lines of your favorite designer, ask the salesclerk or call the manufacturer directly; you can get the number by calling 800 directory assistance (1-800-555-1212).

Make a markdown calendar. If you buy suits regularly, become a regular sale shopper by knowing when markdowns occur. Generally, the longer a suit stays on the sales floor, the lower the price. A good rule of thumb: Most unsold suits are discounted 20 to 25 percent within 60 days of arriving at the store. After three months, look for savings of up to 50 percent off. At the end of the season, savings can reach as much as 65 to 70 percent off the original price. Just keep in mind that sizes and colors will be limited.

Get a store credit card. Most department stores and some specialty stores have long offered their own charge cards. What's new is that some stores offer a one-time, across-the-board discount of 10 to 25 percent to customers who open a new charge account. If you're buying a top-quality suit, the savings could be $100 or more. Just remember to pay the bill right away, or you'll pay interest.

THE BEST FOR LESS: CHANEL

You're about as likely to find a Chanel suit hanging from the rack at an outlet mall or discounter as you are to find the ghost of CoCo Chanel browsing at such an establishment. That's because Chanel clothing is sold exclusively at a handful of boutiques and department stores in major cities across the country. Merchandise that doesn't sell after being marked down 50 percent is returned to company headquarters and destroyed.

So what's a woman to do if she doesn't have $3,000 to spare for a hand-stitched, made-in-Paris, better-than-the-rest genuine article? She could make her first piece a Chanel jacket, priced at $2,300, and pair it with the skirt or jeans of her choice.

Or she could wait for a sale. Spring/summer Chanel clothing is often marked down by as much as 30 percent in June; prices on winter clothes are trimmed in January. What remains after those markdowns is then further reduced a few months later to 50 percent off. She could also search consignment shops in glitzy towns where Chanel suits are most likely to be worn—like Palm Beach or Beverly Hills—where a label-in suit can be had for half the price. For more information on the Chanel retailer near you, call 1-800-550-0005.

BE HIP TO THE NAME GAME. Certain manufacturers are well-known for their women's suits—and one of the best is Jones New York. The company runs about 30 outlets across the country, mostly in larger outlet malls.

The trouble is, you may not find them in the yellow pages or outlet directories unless you look under "Executive Suite," a manufacturer-run outlet that offers men's and women's suits, mostly with the Jones New York label, for a minimum of 25 percent below retail. Call 1-800-258-5663 to find one near you. And if the name game is too confusing, J H Collectibles has about 30 outlets around the country, under its own name, that offer similar savings on quality women's suits.

Wood-Burning Stoves

A wood-burning stove is a great way to heat up your home—as well as the mood of hopeless romantics. But it can also burn your finances if you don't know how to buy. Woodstoves are generally sold in one of two ways—either through specialty stove shops or mass-marketed through large discount home centers such as Home Depot and Lowe's. While the discount chains sell them for as little as $300, this is one item for which it pays to spend more and go to a specialty store.

Cheaper, mass-marketed woodstoves tend to be constructed from thinner metal and have fewer features than their more expensive cousins. These "builder's-grade" stoves may not burn as efficiently, either, and some may be exempt from Environmental Protection Agency (EPA) emissions regulations.

Although deals may seem good at the neighborhood home center, you're better off spending at least $600 for a quality model at a specialty store. (Some woodstoves can go as high as $2,000.) Woodstove dealers have the latest information about their product, whereas a home center probably won't. And a specialist can also refer you to a certified installer, which is important since industry experts estimate that up to 95 percent of the problems they see with heating appliances are due to improper installation.

Wood heaters manufactured since 1988 must meet EPA emissions standards, but low-efficiency stoves are exempt; some areas require that they meet local restrictions, however. (You can get the EPA's latest list of certified wood heaters by writing the Wood Heater Program, U.S. Environmental Protection Agency, 401 M Street SW, Washington, DC 20460. In addition to level of emissions, the list includes the efficiency rating and heat output range for about 200 stoves, plus their brand names and model numbers and the manufacturers' phone numbers.)

When choosing a woodstove, there are other factors to consider

HOW TO BUY USED

Buying a used woodstove is probably the best way to save money, but it can be the riskiest. When buying new, you can rely on the dealer's expertise to guide you in selecting an efficient stove that's the right size for your needs. Buying used can save you 40 percent or more off the retail price, but you must rely on your own know-how—not only in finding the right stove but also in making sure that the stove functions properly.

The best deals on used woodstoves tend to be in the classified section of your newspaper or through auctions or estate sales. But don't buy *too* used: The fuel crisis of the 1970s produced a proliferation of woodstove manufacturers, many of which went out of business in the mid-1980s when the Environmental Protection Agency (EPA) instituted regulations on woodstove emissions and efficiency. So getting replacement parts for these stoves could be impossible. Here are some other factors to note.

- Inspect the stove for the Underwriters' Laboratory (UL) label that verifies the stove's safety certification. In addition, every wood heater manufactured since 1988 must meet EPA emissions standards and is required to have a permanently affixed label. If there's no UL label or EPA certification, pass on it.
- Look for cracks. Using a flashlight, inspect the interior and exterior of the stove. If possible, place the light inside the stove and close all the doors and vents while in a dark room. If any light is visible, it indicates that the stove is cracked or not sealed properly.
- Do a smoke test when possible. Build a smoky fire in the stove—paper will work fine—then close up all of the openings to see if any smoke leaks out. If it does, don't buy the stove.
- Make sure doors seal firmly and handles are easy to use. Avoid stoves with pits or flaking paint. And be wary of cast-iron construction with surface bumps and chips that might signal weak plates and future problems. Steel stoves should have smooth welds (not spotty ones) and safe rounded corners that signal quality construction.

besides price: While cast-iron stoves can literally last for centuries, will never warp and offer more distinctive design options, steel stoves heat more quickly. Whatever you buy, the retail markup on woodstoves tends to be about 35 percent. But here's how to save money.

BUY IN THE OFF-SEASON. The best deals on woodstoves occur between March and June, when retailers are trying to unload the previous year's models or are holding preseason sales. Either way, prices tend to drop between 5 and 20 percent. This is an ideal time to shop, since retailers' cash flow is at its lowest and they need the money: The national Hearth and Home Expo is held each year in March, when dealers shop for the new season's inventory.

BE HOT FOR A "BURN" MODEL. To save about 20 percent, ask dealers to

THE BEST FOR LESS: DOVRE

While there are varying opinions on which woodstove manufacturer is the best, those in the know agree that few woodstoves deliver more value than a Dovre. The Dovre Aurora, a 50,000-Btu (British thermal unit) cast-iron unit capable of heating a 1,500-square-foot area, sells for about $1,000—while comparable stoves from competitors like Vermont Castings or Waterford sell for up to $500 more.

While Dovre's design is plainer, industry insiders say it's a top-notch unit that, aesthetics aside, is every bit as good as its more expensive and better-known competitors. With a ten-year warranty, Dovre offers the best consumer protection in the business.

The best deals on a Dovre can be found at stove specialty stores in the spring; plan to shop between April and June to find the best price. For the nearest Dovre dealer, you can write Heatilator, Inc., Arrow/Dovre Division, 1915 West Saunders Street, Mount Pleasant, IA 52641, or call 1-800-843-2848.

show you the "burn" models—showroom stoves that have displayed the glow of a crackling fire for prospective buyers for one or two seasons. As with a demo car that's been driven a couple of thousand miles, you'll get a used price on basically a new product—and usually the factory warranty, which generally ranges from three to ten years from most manufacturers.

SAVE A C-NOTE WITH A SCRATCH-AND-DENT. There isn't a dealer who hasn't at one time or another damaged a stove with a forklift. These scratches and dents are usually cosmetic and don't affect the functioning of the stove, but they can result in discounts ranging from 10 to 25 percent—or generally between $100 and $200—on most models. On the downside, the manufacturer's warranty may be void on damaged goods, so be sure to check with your dealer.

AVOID THE MIDDLEMAN. You can usually save up to 35 percent by buying woodstoves from manufacturers, some of whom sell directly to the consumer. While you can save several hundred dollars this way, there are fewer choices, and you must find your own service, installation and sometimes transportation from the factory to your home.

For information on woodstove manufacturers who sell directly to the public, call the Hearth Products Association at (703) 522-0086 or write to them at 1601 Kent Street, Suite 1001, Arlington, VA 22209.

INDEX

Note: Underscored page references indicate boxed text.